NATIVE STUDIES

American and Canadian Indians

NATIVE STUDIES

American and Canadian Indians

Professor John A. Price
Department of Anthropology
York University

McGRAW-HILL RYERSON LIMITED

Toronto Montreal New York St. Louis
San Francisco Auckland Bogotà Düsseldorf
Johannesburg London Madrid Mexico New Delhi
Panama Paris São Paulo Singapore Sydney Tokyo

NATIVE STUDIES: AMERICAN AND CANADIAN INDIANS

ISBN: 0-07-082695-1

3 4 5 6 7 8 9 10 HR 7 6 5 4 3 2 10 9

Printed and bound in Canada

Canadian Cataloguing in Publication Data

Price, John A., 1933-
Native studies

Bibliography: p.
Includes index.
ISBN 0-07-082695-1

1. Indians of North America. 2. Indians of North America—Canada. I. Title.

E77.P75 970'.004'97 C77-001708-8

Contents

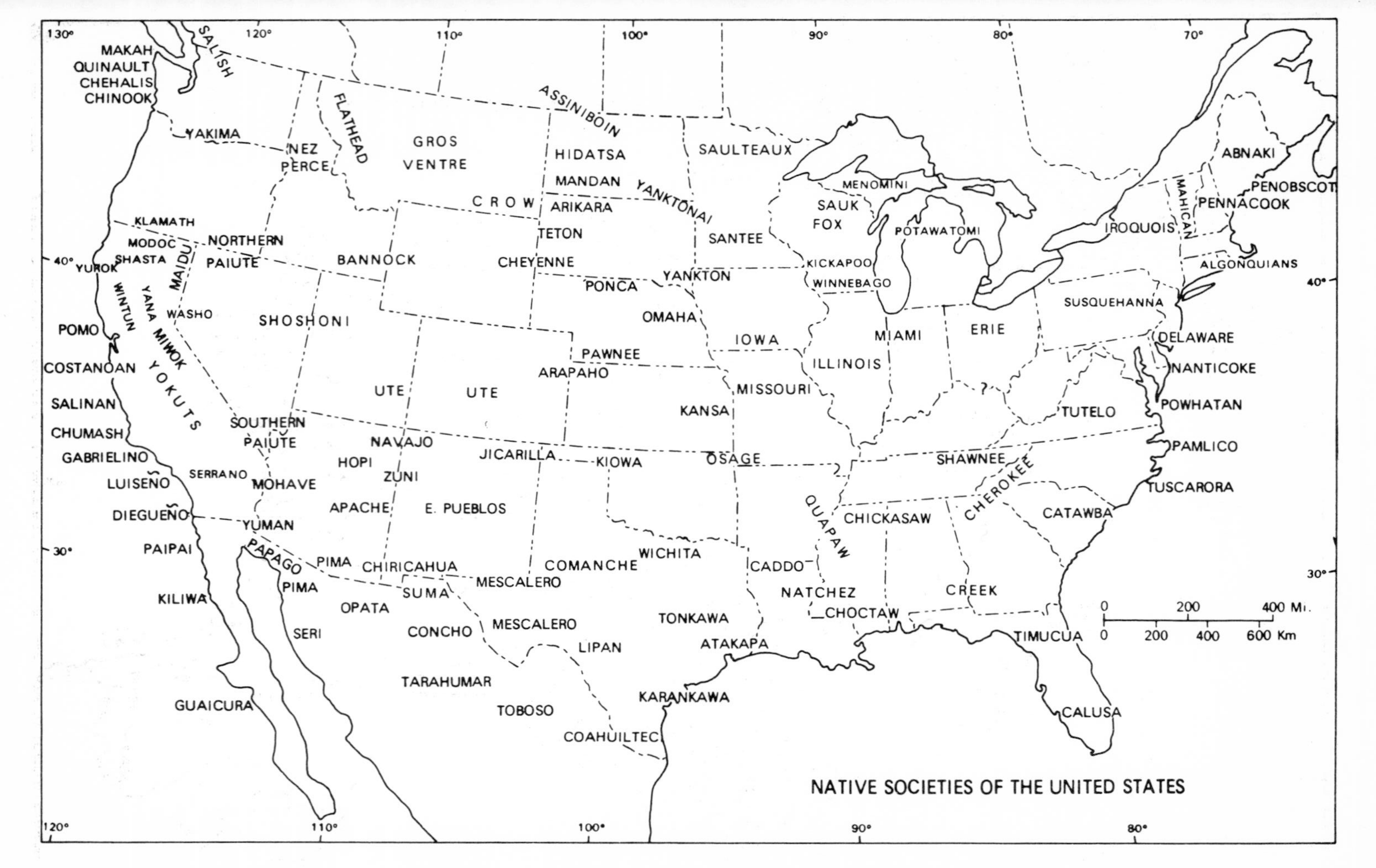

NATIVE SOCIETIES OF THE UNITED STATES

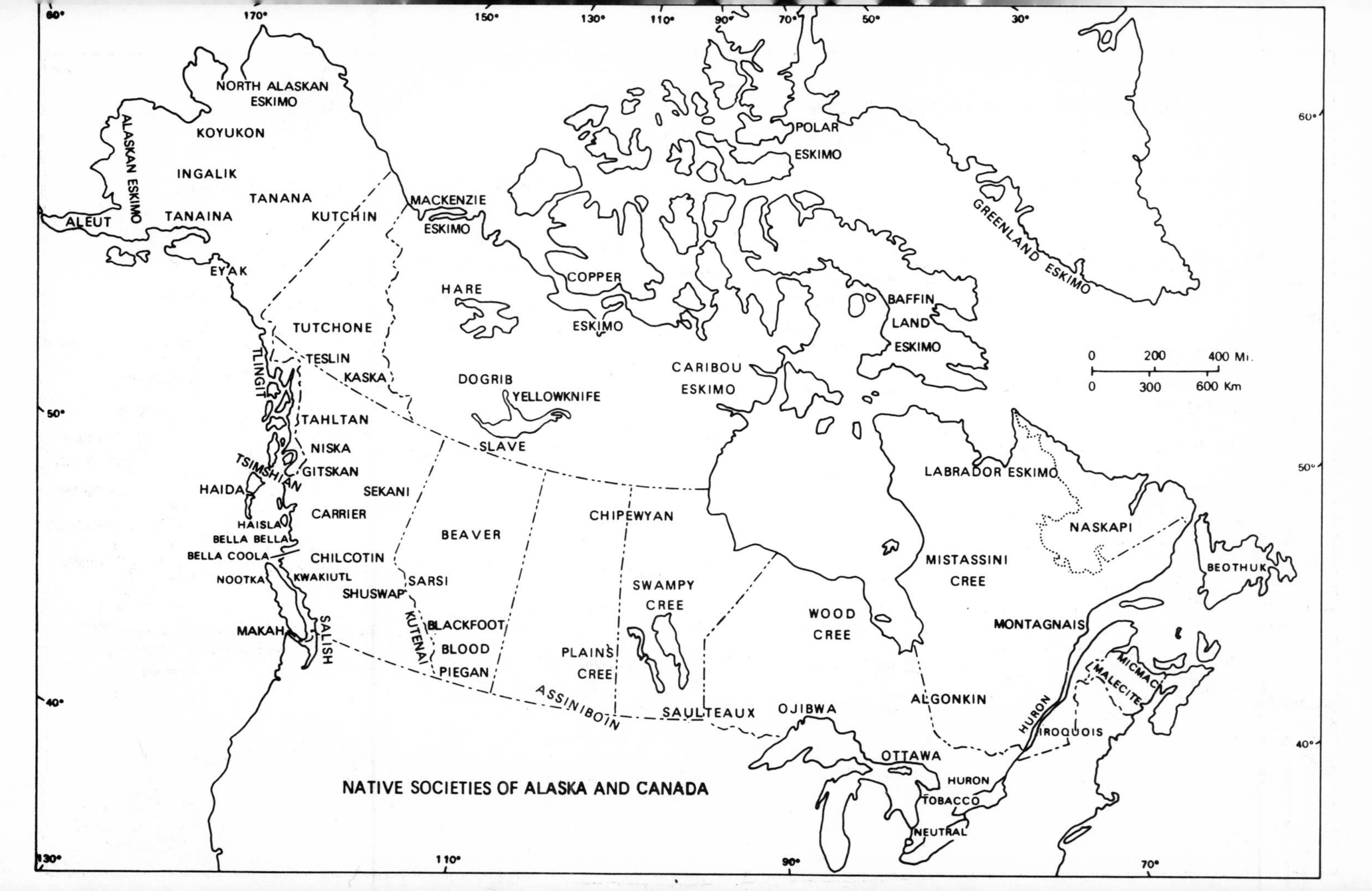
NORTH ALASKAN ESKIMO
ALASKAN ESKIMO
KOYUKON
INGALIK
TANANA
TANAINA
ALEUT
KUTCHIN
EYAK
MACKENZIE ESKIMO
POLAR ESKIMO
GREENLAND ESKIMO
COPPER ESKIMO
HARE
TUTCHONE
TESLIN
KASKA
TLINGIT
DOGRIB
YELLOWKNIFE
CARIBOU ESKIMO
BAFFIN LAND ESKIMO
0 200 400 Mi.
0 300 600 Km
TAHLTAN
NISKA
GITSKAN
TSIMSHIAN
HAIDA
SEKANI
CARRIER
HAISLA
BELLA BELLA
BELLA COOLA
CHILCOTIN
NOOTKA
KWAKIUTL
SHUSWAP
SARSI
KUTENAI
MAKAH
SALISH
SLAVE
BEAVER
BLACKFOOT
BLOOD
PIEGAN
CHIPEWYAN
SWAMPY CREE
PLAINS CREE
ASSINIBOIN
SAULTEAUX
OJIBWA
WOOD CREE
LABRADOR ESKIMO
NASKAPI
MISTASSINI CREE
BEOTHUK
MONTAGNAIS
MICMAC
MALECITE
ALGONKIN
HURON
IROQUOIS
OTTAWA
HURON
TOBACCO
NEUTRAL
60°
50°
40°
30°
70°
90°
110°
130°
150°
170°
NATIVE SOCIETIES OF ALASKA AND CANADA

Foreword

Anthropologists usually have been alone in studying Indian life while other disciplines were focused on the Old World cultures, especially Europe. What would our university curriculum look like if the Natives of the New World had discovered, conquered, and colonized Europe? Our philosophy, mathematics, history, literature and so forth would be New Worldian in orientation. We would point out how civilization started with the Olmecs and Mayas, rather than the Sumerians and Egyptians. We would have a vigesimal (20) base in mathematics, rather than the decimal base. We would study the origin of written literature in Mesoamerican sacred calendars. Instead, the conquest was the reverse so we have filled the curricula with European content.

Native studies is a new field that is branching out beyond the scientific studies of anthropology. It seems to have emerged as a result of increasing academic specialization, the shift toward social relevance in universities, and political pressures from Native people to have a place in academia for their civilizations alongside those of the Europeans. The academics are discovering the New World, at last.

While reaching for the multidisciplinary ideal of Native studies, the "views" presented here are still influenced by anthropological theory, particularly cultural evolution. Their "newness" lies in demonstrating that this originally disinterested science can be used for socially relevant ends. One dilemma of the scientist is that the development of science requires disinterested objectivity while society cries out for personal involvement in humane solutions. The answer seems to be that we must try to do both simultaneously; we must try to create a humanistic science.

The geographical scope of this book is the U.S. and Canada because I find that this is essentially the sphere of "the Native movement;" the area within which a new distinct ethnic culture is being born. In this sense Native studies is an ethnography of a new culture. Centuries of principally a common British American cultural environment have been producing deculturations, cultural convergences, and new cultural adaptations among the 375 aboriginal societies of this area, resulting in a collectivity of peoples with many ethnic commonalities and a sense of common and exclusive heritage.

In long-term relationships with Native peoples, the significant contrasts are between the British, French, Spanish, and Danish (Greenland) North American cultural traditions. The cultural environment of the U.S. and British Canada has been basically similar for Native peoples and contrasts with the cultural environments of the Latin American countries. The Inuit (Eskimo) who live in the U.S.S.R. and Greenland contrast with the Inuit of Alaska and Canada. The Yaqui who moved into Arizona from their ancestral home in Mexico are like other U.S. Indians, but those Yaqui who stayed in Mexico resemble other northern Mexican Indians. On the other hand, the Sioux and Iroquois who escaped harassment in the U.S. by migrating into Canada are today like the Sioux and Iroquois who remained there, through parallel developments.

These migrants to Canada have unique problems that arise from their migration. They have no (Sioux) or only marginal (Iroquois) "aboriginal rights" in Canadian land and they do not have treaties in the usual sense. They have compensated through active political pressure. The Dakota Organization of Canada was formed in 1969 to claim a share in the land claim settlement of the Minnesota Santee (a band of Dakota Sioux). The Iroquois who came to Canada did so primarily because of their allegiance with the British against the Americans during the American Revolutionary War, but they now fight for their rights to freely cross the international border.

There are many other situations in which tests could be made of this effect on development of national cultural environments. A band of Kickapoo were moved from Illinois to Oklahoma and then fled the U.S., seeking sanctuary in Mexico where they have continued a rather traditional Kickapoo culture. Indian and Métis fugitives of the Riel Rebellion fled Canada after 1885 and settled in with U.S. tribes. There is a wider scattering of Iroquois communities outside of their aboriginal homelands, as far as Wisconsin and Alberta. People such as the Coast Salish and Blackfoot live on both sides of an international border. Thousands of Micmacs from the Maritimes go down to live and work in New England's industrial cities, especially Boston, where they are eligible for many of the Indian programs. The Tsimshian migrated to New Metlakatla in Alaska from Canada in 1887, were given a reservation and later shared in the modern Alaskan land settlement.

One exception in Canada that fits this theory is the contrasting development of Indians in French-speaking Quebec. In one index after another (low arrest rates, low conviction rates, high prohibition of alcohol from reserves, low suicide rates, low level of Indian political activity, high rates of intermarriage with Whites, and highest average income), Quebec Indians are consistently different from and generally better off than Indians in the rest of Canada. Although the cut is hard to make in the statistics, this seems to be particularly true after the culturally cohesive Iroquois are withdrawn from both the French-Canadian and British-Canadian samples. Thus, Algonquian-speaking peoples appear to have developed in significantly different ways in English and French Canada because of differences in White relationships to Indians. The French have been more humane toward Indians than the British in the past century, perhaps because the French and the Indians developed a common bond against the British majority. Another extreme contrast exists between the French-Canadian Huron Indians who live in a community on the outskirts of Quebec City, and their Wyandot relatives who live in Oklahoma.

The twenty-one chapters here are organized in a sequence for use as an introduction to U.S. and Canadian Indians. The first chapter discusses the rise of Native studies as a new, interdisciplinary, academic subject. The body of the text has three clusters of chapters: (1) chapters 2-8 on genesis and traditional heritage, (2) chapters 9-13 on Indian urbanization and institutionalization, and (3) chapters 14-20 on modern problems and their solutions. The last chapter examines the need to bring science and humanism together in Native studies of the future. Native studies is the understanding and appreciation of the aboriginal New World peoples, their civilizations, their history, their philosophies, their heroes, and their social problems. This represents only a preliminary survey of some of the material from that whole field of study, where the current state of knowledge is weak, uneven, and open to improvements. At this stage in the development of the field it is useful to question everything, including, of course, everything in this text.

Chapter 1

Native Studies in the U.S. and Canada

The study of Indians, Métis, and Inuit (Eskimos) has been broadening in the last decade or so beyond the confines of traditional anthropology. This has been spurred on by an increasing awareness on the part of Native people that academic methods can be used to foster an ethnic cultural renaissance. Native studies can be one channel of power in the Native movement for self-respect and self-determination. It can be a positive means of adjustment to today's world. It is an expression of ethnicity that parallels and is related to militant takeovers for demonstration purposes, the forcing of courts to uphold Native legal rights, political organization and lobbying, and religious revitalization.

Academic institutions, however, have their own internal organization and purposes, primarily educating young people in the dominant culture. U.S. and Canadian colleges and universities are rather parochial when we view them in terms of the worldwide diversity of cultures. The literature that is taught (particularly English literature) is usually that of the West. Philosophy tends to be European and Anglo-North American, ignoring Asia, Africa, and the aboriginal New World. Euro-American art, history, economics, political science, sociology, etc., dominate almost to the exclusion of the rest of the world. This historically insular nature of the disciplines makes it difficult even to recruit someone to teach Native studies because few people have ever had a chance to study aboriginal New World culture.

Anthropology, of course, has not been parochial but has regularly worked with a worldwide sample of societies. However, it has been rather narrowly interested in the social science analysis of data from those societies. It has done little to write and to teach about those societies in the way that art, history, literature, and philosophy have of Western civilization. Nor has anthropology adequately worked on the applied and policy related problems. Native studies necessarily began in colleges and universities largely within anthropology, but the process of its maturation required that it separate and the process of separation has been somewhat traumatic to anthropology.

Native studies is successfully forcing a broad spectrum of changes to occur in all studies of Indians, Métis, and Inuit. For anthropologists, the shift has been toward more humanistic concerns, particularly more socially useful research and teaching and more sensitive field work ethics. However, more importantly, the birth of the new academic discipline of Native studies has meant that Native people themselves are increasingly involved in academics and that a few individuals from more of the disciplines of the humanities and social sciences are being drawn out of their Western culture preoccupations into Native studies. After anthropology, I judge the order of interest in Native studies to be strongest in art, history, and sociology and then some mild interest in geography, political science, and psychology.

Native studies programs tend to be the most developed in public universities in areas where there are large numbers of Indians: Oklahoma, North and South Dakota, Minnesota, Utah, New Mexico, Arizona, California, and in every province in Canada, except in the Maritimes. In the U.S. the term "American Indian Studies" is popular, while in Canada the broader label of "Native Studies" is preferred because it must cover Métis and Inuit. The Native studies program at the University of California at Davis had a similar problem, since it includes both North American Indians and Chicanos or Mexican Americans. Their solution was to include both an Iroquois and an Aztec creator god in their name: Deganawida-Quetzlcoatl University. Another Canadian problem is that the term "American" in Canada usually implies just the U.S.A. In Canada if I say "I'm studying American Indians," people reply "Well, why don't you study *Canadian* Indians?" Then I have to explain that in this sense the term "American" means the aboriginal people of the New World who lived here prior to the arrival of the Europeans. The term "Native" avoids the confusion with East Indians of India or the West Indians of the Caribbean and emphasizes the unique heritage of the aboriginal peoples.

The approximately 603,000 Indians, Métis, and Inuit of Canada constitute a much higher proportion of the total population (about 2.7%) than the 880,000 Natives of the U.S. (about 0.4%), so Natives in Canada have more of an impact on the national society. Americans can get a sense of the population impact of Indians on Canada by projecting the significance of Indians in the "Indian states," such as Alaska, Oklahoma, Arizona, and New Mexico, on the nation as a whole.

Viewed in terms of the institutional evolution of an ethnic group, academic activities are signs of ethnic maturation. That is, Indians have gone through periods of extreme aboriginal diversity, various forms of coalescence in historic times, and are emerging as a unified ethnic culture in modern society. Their entry into the academic world as full participants and not just as objects of study is crucial to the revolutionary effect that Native studies is having on both the academic world and on the ethnic group itself.

Native studies tends to expand in response to social and political pressure on the academic institutions and the changing interests of students (particularly Native students), rather than arising out of the isolated, ivory tower developments of academic disciplines. The general pattern is that Native studies programs develop out of dialogues between anthropologists, who represent the traditional study of Indians; university administrators, representing the social and political pressures of the general society to do something to solve Indian problems; and Indian students in universities.

Native studies is much broader than university institutions, touching many aspects of Native primary education, advanced scholarship, Native politics, and the ethical procedures of disciplines. In one dimension of academically related developments, some 255 periodicals are now published for Native readership in the U.S. (188) and Canada (67), mostly local newsletters by Indian clubs, centers, and other ethnic associations. My current list of these more than doubled from the 112 compiled in 1971 (Price 1972). The increases in the list are marked for those coming from new organizations in the national capitals of Ottawa and Washington, D.C.; from the Canadian north and from Inuit; from Indian Women's groups; from prisons; and from boarding schools, high schools, and colleges.

In this chapter, I first present historical notes on the Native movement and Native studies. Case studies are given of the first academic departments in the U.S. (University of Minnesota) and Canada (Trent University). This is followed by discussions of the initial and nation-wide meetings of Native scholars in the U.S. and Canada, and cross-nationally in the Arctic, and the messages that Native politicians have for White academics. There is a brief description of Navajo Community College. Then the chapter ends with a note on U.S.-Canada differences.

HISTORICAL NOTES

Hertzberg (1971) discussed the pan-Indian movements of the Eastern and Plains Indians of the U.S. in the early 1900s, particularly the activities of an organization called The Society of American Indians that was formed in 1911. They stressed racial unity, virtues of the traditional cultures, and the necessity for Natives to make contributions in the future to the general society. Their proposed techniques were those of acculturated middle class Indians, such as acquiring formal White education, de-emphasizing tribalism and traditional culture as a solution to modern problems, and the Protestant values of hard work and self-help. Different attitudes toward such things as the Indian

Bureau, Peyotism, and tribalism divided the Society, but it was still a valuable forum with annual conferences and *The American Indian Magazine.* They fought for equality before the law, education, citizenship, and community centers on reservations. A competing journal of the time, *Wassaja*, by an Apache who had been raised in White culture, Carlos Montezuma, stressed racial pride, hostility toward Whites, abolition of the Indian Bureau and the Reservations, and citizenship and White education for Indians.

There was a wave of new Indian organizations in the 1920s. Anthropologists such as Clark Wissler, Stewart Culin, Ralph Linton, and John Collier joined the movement, opposed the melting pot ideal, and promoted the ideal of treating tribes as separately valid cultures.

John Collier organized the American Indian Defense Association in 1923, which accomplished such things as protecting Pueblo rights to land, holding ceremonies, and fighting for citizenship (given in the U.S. in 1924 largely for the valiant role of Indians as soldiers in World War I), and the values of tribal cultures. Arthur C. Parker became chairman of the Committee of One Hundred to advise the Secretary of the Interior on Indian policy. Activities of the Committee led to the Meriam Report in 1928, which led to a broad range of improvements in Indian administration, especially in the Indian Reorganization Act of 1934.

The National Council of American Indians was formed in 1926 to take advantage of the fact that Indians acquired the right to vote after they became citizens. The National Council was involved in several election campaigns in Oklahoma and South Dakota.

Collier was made the Commissioner of Indian Affairs to implement the Indian Reorganization Act. This was an attempt by an anthropologist to apply what anthropologists had learned about the social health of Indian societies. They felt that the traditional social group was important and must be allowed to continue. To achieve this it was necessary to reverse the process of liquidating Indian lands through allotment. They encouraged Native social controls through tribal self-government, home-rule constitutions, and treatment of tribes as corporate bodies. Changes were necessary, but these must not destroy the security and continuity of group life. Indians must be allowed to participate in modern life at their own rate and in their own ways. Indians should participate more in the administration of the Bureau of Indian Affairs and they should be given more opportunities for advanced and professional education, but at the same time there should be an encouragement of traditional arts, crafts, and religious practices.

All later Indian movements have drawn from these ideals. In 1944 the National Congress of American Indians was formed in Denver and it continued to support the reforms of the 1930s. In 1961 the anthropologist Sol Tax organized the Chicago Indian Conference. These meetings became a general review of Indian policy to make recommendations for the administration of President John F. Kennedy. The official recommendations were important at one level, but a number of young Indian college students and graduates attended, were dissatisfied with the conservative methods of the older Indian leaders, and formed the more militant National Indian Youth Council. This organization developed a campaign to fight for tribalism and for solutions to local problems on a tribe-by-tribe basis, by using the tactics of the current civil rights movement. Thus, for example, they staged several "fish-ins" to secure Indian fishing rights.

In Canada in the 1940s the anthropologist Diamond Jenness pushed the New Zealand handling of the Maori as one ideal model and the Danish handling of the Greenland Eskimo as another positive case. He argued that because the Natives were relatively few in number and without political influence, Parliament voted barely enough money to fulfill treaty obligations. He also criticized Indian Affairs as being too involved with its administrative routines and forgetful of its clientele. Reverend Peter Kelly, a Haida chief and leader in the Native Brotherhood of British Columbia, also pressed for the Maori system of communal representation in government.

Parallel movements in the U.S. and Canada in the 1950s and 1960s led the federal governments to push for a decrease and eventual end to special federal services for Indians. The governments talked of this in very positive and even liberating terms. A U.S. House of Representatives Resolution in 1953 said that it is the policy of Congress to end the Indian status as "wards of the United States and to grant them all the rights and prerogatives pertaining to American citizenship." The resolution called for the termination of special federal relations with Indians in California, Florida, New York, and Texas and specific termination for several tribes: the Montana Flathead, the Oregon Klamath, the Wisconsin Menomini, the Kansas and Nebraska Potawatomi, and the Turtle Mountain Chippewa in North Dakota. This kind of movement was opposed by an increasingly well-organized Native opposition, wanting to continue and even to expand federal services and to allow for much greater Native influence on the design and staffing of programs.

In 1969, in both the U.S. and Canada, literate, young Native politicians published scathing attacks on Whites that became best sellers: Vine Deloria's *Custer Died For Your Sins: An Indian Manifesto* and Harold Cardinal's *The Unjust Society: The Tragedy of Canada's Indians*. Both of these titles reflect the cynical humor of young Indian politicians. The first was among the bumper sticker slogans, which also included such lines as "Custer Had It Coming."

Canada's Pierre Trudeau had just won his political campaign with the slogan of a "Just Society" when *The Unjust Society* came out. Trudeau had said that "it is inconceivable that one section of the society should have a treaty with another section of a society. The Indians should become Canadians as have all other Canadians." This idea goes over well with English Canada generally and with the pro-federalist faction of French Canadians, but it is anathema to most Indians. Trudeau has not been sympathetic to the nationalistic separation of Indians; it is seen as similar to the French-English split in Canada and is treated in a similar way.

A French Canadian, Jean Chretien, was appointed Minister of Indian

Affairs and Northern Development and given a free hand in developing policy. The massive social science survey on Indian policy of the Hawthorn Report (1966) and extensive consultations across the country were virtually ignored as Chretien laid out an Indian policy that was ideologically derived from French-Canadian paternalism and strong provincial government. French-speaking Quebec had been pushing for greater provincial control over Indian affairs and this became Chretien's policy.

The policy was completely rejected by almost all Native leaders, except for some of the older assimilation-oriented leaders such as Frank Calder and William Wuttunee. Wuttunee, a Calgary lawyer, even wrote a book called *Ruffled Feathers* (1971) to attack Cardinal's book. After a poor showing in the 1972 election, the Liberal policy increasingly reflected the views of Native people.

Government budgets for programs for Native people have been dramatically increasing in the last decade or so, now over $600 million dollars per year in Canada (and over $1.1 billion in the U.S.). Native people have been rapidly improving their political organizations and several kinds of programs have been running successfully, such as urban Indian centers. The great expansion of programs in Canada has probably prevented the violent type of confrontations in the late 1960s and early 1970s, such as those in the U.S. at Alcatraz and Wounded Knee. However, Canada has also had militant highway blockades; demonstration marches; and occupations of schools, Indian Affairs offices, and a park.

THE DIVERSE SETTINGS OF NATIVE STUDIES IN CANADA

There are many places now where Native studies has affected both the formal education system and other institutions with educational functions. This can be illustrated on the Canadian scene by citing several different kinds of institutions: Manitou Community College, Old Sun College, 'Ksan, Nishnawbe Institute, York University, the Heritage Stoney Wilderness Programme, and Wasse-Abin Community College.

Manitou Community College is a school with some 300 Indian students, and a predominantly Indian staff in La Macaza, Quebec. The land and buildings were donated by the government at a de-activated Bomarc missile base north of Montreal. A student at the University of Minnesota who had helped to organize the Department of Native Studies moved to Montreal to become the director of Quebec's Native North American Studies Institute, which in turn sponsored Manitou Community College, along with the Indians of Quebec Association. One step led to the next: education of Natives generally and the public about Natives was in a sad shape, text books generally were in need of more Native content, the Institute gradually got into the book publishing business to fill the needs of Native content in textbooks, and its Native Studies college became the publishing plant and focussed on teaching printing as vocational training. By the end of 1973 the Institute had written and published over twenty textbooks for reservation grade schools. Following some three years of troubles in establishing the college, the former Minnesota student and founder abruptly left the college, under a cloud of suspicion that "he was actually a White posing as an Indian. In Minnesota he claimed to be Chippewa and in Quebec he claimed to be Iroquois." By 1975-76 the school had 29 faculty and staff, 128 full-time students, and 180 summer students in a broad program of social sciences and fine arts, ranging from philosophy to photography.

Old Sun College is located on the Blackfoot Reserve near Gleichen, Alberta and is affiliated with Mount Royal College in Calgary. It is bilingual, English and Blackfoot; there are no grades or admission standards, and it has over one hundred students. The College was started in 1971 in an abandoned missionary school on the reserve, with support from Mount Royal and Indian Affairs. It concentrates on basic adult education, especially English and mathematics, and has a library and equipment for the students to explore their interests. It also has courses on such things as farm equipment maintenance, the Blackfoot language, and fine arts. Classes are in small groups under the tutorship of instructors. When the students master any subject they move into another subject of their choice. Curriculum, staff, student attendance, style of classes, etc., are much more flexible than in White colleges. The buses arrive from picking students up at about 9:00 a.m., but there's a cushion time before classes, *oomoowap*, when "people get together." Students can drop out for a week or a month when there are family problems or when farming work has to be done.

'Ksan is an authentically rebuilt Indian village that is run by the Gitskan Indians at the confluence of the Skeena and Bulkley Rivers, outside of Hazelton, British Columbia. Masks, totem poles, jewelry, and rain capes are made and sold there. Leather work by the Carrier Indians is sold. 'Ksan Indians also perform a dramatized version of a potlatch ceremony on national tours of Canada.

The Nishnawbe Institute in Toronto administers several projects: Indian Ecumenical Conference, Algonquin Project (folklore), Indian Youth Workshop, Cross-Cultural Workshop, National Indian Princess Pageant, and Native Women's Organization. The Youth Workshop brings together twenty-five to thirty young Natives from all parts of Canada for a six-week program. This grew out of the American Indian Youth Workshop in Boulder, Colorado. After being initially hosted at the University of Waterloo, it moved away from formalized instruction to a "living experiment" to strengthen identity, develop background knowledge, work with different tribes and regions in Canada, and make education relevant. The Cross-Cultural Workshop brings together Indian and White clergy, welfare workers, parole officers, school teachers, and so forth. Nishnawbe was consciously designed as an Indian revitalization program by Indian academics.

Like most North American universities, York University in Toronto offers a few courses about Native cultures, but the need is also felt for a closer liaison with Native peoples. Thus in 1972 York had a gathering of Native Canadian artists, dancers, poets, philosophers, and religious leaders. Paintings were exhibited by Norval Morrisseau, Saul Williams, and Sarain Stump. Native priests talked about their religion and philosophy. Charles Hoffman played tapes of Indian music, Verna Johnson talked about Indian cooking, and Willie Dunn sang his songs. Themes change every year, so that in 1976 York held a conference on land claims and development in the Arctic, the most relevant issue of the year.

In 1974 the Heritage Society of Canada developed a special summer camp, The Heritage Stoney Wilderness Programme, run by the Stoney Indians of Morley, Alberta, the same reserve that sponsors the Indian Ecumenical Conference. Young people from 14-18 years of age are involved in survival techniques, horseback riding, camping, tipi construction, canoeing, fishing, Native story-telling, and Native dancing. There is also an adult camp for teachers. Accordingly, Indian culture is taught to Whites by Indians on the reservation.

Wasse-Abin Community College was established on the Wikwemikong Reserve, Manitoulin Island, Ontario in 1975-76 with D.I.A.N.D. funding, academic affiliation with Cambrian College in Sudbury, and volunteer teachers from the local federal day-school. The curriculum is fairly ordinary, a mix of Native studies and White academic matters. Its importance is that it was an emergency, an almost frantic experimental creation to help stop the wave of suicides on the reserve; in 1975 this reserve had seven suicides and thirty-four attempted suicides. This is where Native studies is a last-ditch effort to give people a reason to live.

THE UNIVERSITY OF MINNESOTA

In 1964 a committee on American Indian Affairs was appointed at the university in response to "the difficult situation of American Indians in American society" (Miller 1971:315). At the time the only full-time staff members with a primary scholarly interest in Indians were anthropologists, but a multi-disciplinary committee was created anyway. No Native people could be found on the university staff and none were sought from students or the wider community for the first two years of the committee. In 1966 the committee issued a report that called for several things. In the area of improving the general education of Indians it recommended increased scholarship aid, counseling, tutorial and other supportive services, and more adult education. It called for better education of others about Indians, especially service personnel in teaching, social work, and public health. An Indian information and research center should be created as an archive, library, and center for work on languages, urban migration, and education. The university should become directly involved in such services as assisting tribal councils with various kinds of training and legal aid.

In 1967 a small Indian Affairs Center was established by the Training Center for Community Programs, under the directorship of Arthur Harkins. The Training Center then began to publish a number of monographs on urban Indians. As in several other universities at the time, an Indian Upward Bound program was held to bring Indian high school students to the university for a brief summer program.

In the fall of 1968 the American Indian Students Association began discussions with the university about American Indian studies. In early 1969 a group of Black students occupied the administration building and succeeded in getting an agreement to an acceleration in the implementation of their program. Then American Indian studies was discussed in more concrete terms with representatives from the faculty, Indian students, and the Indian community. The principal direction would be the education of non-Indians about Indians, while the Black studies program was emphasizing the needs of Black students. A bachelor's degree in American Indian studies would be offered.

The important decision was made to form a new "department," rather than just an interdisciplinary "program" because (1) it was a symbol of full acceptance within the university structure, (2) an integrated curriculum could be better offered by a core faculty with a primary commitment to that curriculum, (3) community programs would require a specially trained staff and the department would have the best means to acquire and maintain such staff, (4) community programs would make new demands that could not be met by faculty with basic appointments elsewhere, and (5) there would be greater continuity in financing. The department began operation in 1969-70. Chippewa was taught by a linguist and Native informants. Courses were also devised on Indian arts, Minnesota Indian history, contemporary Indian affairs, the American Indian in the modern world, urban Indians, and Indian industrialization and unemployment, and a seminar was formed on contemporary issues.

TRENT UNIVERSITY

In 1968 the Trent University Native Association was formed by students to organize field trips, a speakers' bureau, and assistance to Native communities. At the same time work was underway to develop a Native studies program. Several questions were considered in designing the program: How much emphasis should be placed on building a staff of Native people? How much special encouragement and leniency should be given to Native students? How should the program relate to the Native movement generally and to the need for action on current social problems in particular? How should the program relate to reserves within the region? What would be the best academic structure: an interdisciplinary program without a separate degree, a degree-granting formal "program," or an independent "department" that could foster the development of a new discipline?

Starting in 1969, Trent (Peterborough, Ontario) was the first university in Canada to have a full-time, degree-granting program in Native Studies. It began with only one year-long course and twenty-eight students, but expanding student demand, faculty support, and finally private funding and government support allowed the program to expand over the years. In 1972 it began to function as a full "Department of Native Studies." Most of the staff, as well as about one-third of the students majoring in the subject, were Native people. By 1973-74 the Department had six full-time staff members, several part-time staff, over a dozen year-long courses, and about one hundred students as majors in Native Studies. Courses included an introductory survey; politics; anthropology of Canadian Natives; Native identity, values, and personality; community development; urbanization; education; law; art; and individual research. Expansion then was developed in literature, languages, ethno-history, and applied community work in social services and education. Government and private support for the Department has poured in since its beginning. Grants have allowed the establishment of a library and archives in Native studies, including subscriptions to over 150 Native periodicals and a film library.

THE FIRST CONVOCATION OF AMERICAN INDIAN SCHOLARS

The Convocation (1970) brought together two hundred Native scholars, professional people, artists, and traditional historians. It was organized by the American Indian Historical Society and held in March, 1970, at Princeton University. In the keynote address Rupert Costo, a Cahuilla engineer, said "We must begin to teach the true history of our people, and to the American public at large . . . We should have had, long ago, practical schools for our children, to keep the languages alive, to keep the beauty of our heritage alive."

Alfonso Ortiz, a Tewa anthropologist, gave a lecture on the relation of American Indian philosophy to the modern world. "Modern America is at long last ready to listen to the 'practical wisdom' of the Indian people, as well as to share in our spiritual heritage. Indeed, modern America desperately needs to listen and to share . . . We anthropologists cannot continue year after year mindlessly reciting in the classrooms our litany of Indian exotica and assorted trivia."

Vine Deloria, Jr., the Sioux lawyer, lectured on the implications of the 1968 Civil Rights Act on tribal autonomy. He called for a positive reaffirmation of the culture, values, and common law of the tribe. "There is a real question of constitutionality here, as to whether the United States has the right to unilaterally extend its own laws over the tribes at the corporate level without the tribe's consent . . . We as Indian scholars have an opportunity to combine all these disciplines and help to develop Indian common law, tribe by tribe, eventually on a national basis."

Robert L. Bennett, an Oneida law professor and former U.S. Commissioner of Indian Affairs, said that Indians know right from wrong, accept the consequences, and tend to plead guilty, so conviction rates are high. Now Anglo legal culture is teaching them that "they are only wrong if they are proven guilty. Which is not their traditional concept."

Jeannette Henry, the Cherokee historian, said that historians have contributed to the rationalization of racist and discriminatory policies. The historian's "frontier thesis" is that the U.S. acquired its character through westward expansion and colonization of essentially "free land." This denies that the Natives had rights to their own land. "Thus, from a position in colonial, and later Gold Rush, times, that the Native had to be exterminated in order to make way for progress and civilization, was developed the more sophisticated philosophy of *nonrecognition* of Indian land rights." The history of Native-White relations shifted from early co-existence; to genocide "justified" by religion and White supremacy; to removal and occupation of "free unoccupied land," as propounded in the early historian's "frontier thesis."

George Gill, an Omaha in education, told about the Indian teacher training program that has been running for many years at Arizona State University, with practical training on reservations. The Indian education program there started in 1959 and offers sixteen kinds of courses in Indian education, culminating in an M.A. degree.

Roger Buffalohead, a Ponca historian, described the Indian Studies program at U.C.L.A. Coalitions with other minorities, such as Blacks, Chicanos, and Orientals, helped in the initial formation of the programs but then they split up, due to the competition for resources. "The proposal called for setting up a program with a director who would develop . . . curriculum, action, and research, and various ways in which the program overall could interact with the Indian people in the state of California, as well as throughout the country." Conflicts developed between the students and the local Native communities in the Los Angeles area. The local people wanted practical and remedial courses on English and mathematics while the students wanted revolutionary material on Indian nationalism and Red Power. The U.C.L.A. students joined the Alcatraz occupation and "that became part of their education."

Beatrice Medicine, the Sioux anthropologist, lectured on the "Red Power" movement. The slogan circulated among Indians in 1966 and received national prominence after its use during the 1967 meetings of the National Congress of American Indians in Denver. "One avowedly militant group has followed the 'Black' pattern with picketing, with signs, disrupting meetings and using revolutionary rhetoric complete with four-letter words. Some students of this description have not made the transition from confrontation politics to the exacting studies, which possibly are a better step to effective power. One group has organized to pressure the urban community . . . patrolling urban streets for inebriated 'brothers' and 'sisters.'" Another group favored awareness and pride of tradition plus direct social action on reservations. Medicine said that generally there had been insufficient planning of actions, too many personal struggles for the control of Indian institutions, insufficient evaluation and assessment of programs, and too much intertribal chauvinism. Well-planned action programs were needed to change the attitudes of Whites in specific towns. Indians should be included on parole boards.

The resolutions of the Convocation that have a direct bearing on Native studies included the following:

1. Support the return of wampum belts to the Iroquois Confederacy.
2. Implement prior consultation and consent for studies of tribes.
3. Endorse the Navajo Community College and the Rocky Boy Band of Chippewa-Cree in forming their own school district.

4. Involve Indians in the planning and implementation of programs on Indian leadership, higher education, and scholarship.
5. Call for a commitment to avoid "ecocatastrophe," stabilize the population explosion, and "return the environment to a more harmonious state."
6. Call a conference on Native American Studies in Canada and the U.S.
7. Support a national center for visual and performing Native arts and a national society of Indian artists.

The Second Convocation of American Indian Scholars was held at Aspen, Colorado in 1971. There were 95 participants for the panels on land use, land claims, water rights, education, health professions, and museums. There was a shift toward younger scholars and away from the general rhetoric of the Native movement toward specific issues and their solutions.

NATIVE SCHOLARS '73

In 1973 the first general conference was held for the academic and professional Natives of Canada at Harrison Hot Springs, B.C. Seventy delegates came. The majority had university degrees and were currently working for Indians in such fields as teaching, government work, social work, law, and medicine.

Melvyn Lavallee, an Indian M.D. practicing in Slave Lake, Alberta, called for "special clinics to treat the ravages brought by alcohol and drugs . . . there is an upswing in deaths through violence and suicide . . . the population of Indian reserves and Inuit settlements is increasing at a faster rate than that of any other ethnic group . . . there is a steady exodus to urban centers." He said that Indian infant mortality rates in the "post-neonatal" period were still two and one-half times greater than those of non-Indians. Overall infant mortality under one year of age accounts for from one-fourth to one-third of all Indian deaths. Dr. Lavallee said "we personally have witnessed the devastation of the imposition of the treaties and what it means to be totally conquered . . . All here today have special talents . . . and these should be used for the liberation of our Native people."

Howard Adams, a Métis professor of education, said "this is a racist, apartheid society." In a Saskatchewan survey 30% of the Natives were illiterate and 98% had dropped out before completing high school. By dropping out, Natives avoid legitimizing the White's school system, a system they do not respect. "The classroom is totally irrelevant to them . . . It is a foreign institution . . . leads Indian people from their Native world . . . It is a glorification of whiteness . . . How do you think a prairie boy ended up taking a B.A. in a British Columbia university, because I was following a blond, blue-eyed girl, that's how."

Clare Brant, an Indian M.D., described northern medical facilities. Northern communities usually have a nursing station which helps with minor ailments, sends serious cases to hospitals, and provides local convalescence for those returning from hospitals. Physicians' salaries are usually 20-30% below those of private practice in southern Canada so that, although some highly qualified people work there out of ideals and dedication, there are tendencies for the north to attract the young and inexperienced for one or two years, foreign medical people who are unable to get Canadian licenses for private practice, and others who are generally unsuited for private practice in the south.

One positive thing is that southern universities have taken over some of the public health programs. McGill University has taken over the hospital at Frobisher Bay and rotates their residents, medical students, and nursing students through service there. Queen's University supplies part of the regular staff at the hospital, especially in pediatrics. The University of Toronto has taken over many of the staffing problems of a health delivery network which includes a hospital and scattered and isolated satellite nursing stations that operate out of Sioux Lookout in northern Ontario.

ARCTIC PEOPLES' CONFERENCE

In 1973, the first Arctic Peoples' Conference was held for four days in Copenhagen, Denmark. Forty delegates came, representing the Indians and Inuit of Canada, the Inuit of Greenland, and the Lapps of Scandinavian Norway, Sweden, and Finland. James Wah-Shee, then president of the Indian Brotherhood of the Northwest Territories, was president of the Conference. Wah-Shee said that "we find that we are fortunate that the Inuit and Indian peoples have a government that is willing to respond to the rights of the Native inhabitants. Some other countries have not even recognized these rights. So I think our working relationship with our government is a better one." The final resolution of the conference declared "We are an integral part of the very lands and waters we have traditionally occupied. Our identity and culture is firmly rooted in these lands and waters . . . We request the obvious: that the government of each state from which we come recognize our rights as peoples entitled to the dignity of self-fulfillment and realization."

A Greenland delegate said "We are not interested in keeping our resources to ourselves, but we want to be in on the developing . . . We now can tell all our small communities that they are not alone, that their problems are not unique, but that there is a common fate shared by the people living along the Polar Circle." A Norwegian Lapp stated "Now we can no longer doubt that we share a common fate."

NATIVE POLITICAL MESSAGES TO WHITE ACADEMICS

In 1972 several Native political leaders participated in a symposium on "Contemporary Political Struggles of Native Peoples" at the American Anthropolical Association meeting in Toronto. The messages of several Native leaders to anthropologists are that they want them to assume less dominance in using their expertise and to employ their skills more on the behalf of and following the direction of the Native leaders and less to the ends of White society.

Tony Belcourt, a Métis leader, concluded that he did not want the help of anthropologists in making any decisions. "We will make up our own minds in our own time as to what we are going to do . . . those of you that have the access to information or records with regards to the Métis and non-status Indian land claims . . . send that information to me, and if you are willing and able to be directed we might even give you some jobs to do . . . "

Harold Cardinal, the Alberta Cree politician, stated that "Anthropologists do have a meaningful role to play, not as leaders, but as technicians who will help us analyze . . . because of their knowledge of the experiences of other peoples who have undertaken similar challenges that we have . . . There's damn few anthropologists that will come on board with us because we do not offer the security that the academic world has to offer . . . If people, Indian and non-Indian, want to participate . . . we will welcome them, but they have to come to where we are in our communities with our people rather than trying to help us from the germ-free sterilized environment of a university." Later he said, "I don't think I object to people talking about or trying to explain away Indians in universities as long as they call it by its proper label . . . it is White Studies of Indians."

Philip Awashish, a Mistassini Cree, talked about the unsuccessful attempts of the Indian people to stop the massive building of hydro-electric dams and the flooding of Indian lands on the Quebec side of James Bay. They heard of the project in May, 1971 and organized a meeting the next month with representatives from the six communities, which include 7,000 Native people. The government wrote up an environmental report on the impact of the project, with Cree translations for parts of the report, but the people still could not understand it, and they burned their copy in protest at Rupert's House.

Mike Mitchell, from the St. Regis Reserve in Ontario, said that a group of Indians are applying for a grant "to go and open up the grave sites of the early pioneers in Toronto, the White settlers . . . We are going to tell you people what your people were like, the habits, everything . . . We hope when we are finished we are going to be able to tell you why the White man likes to fight so much over things that don't belong to him in the first place, why he is so greedy, why he likes to make war on people different from him."

NAVAJO COMMUNITY COLLEGE

The Navajo have a large population on a large reservation, so they have had an excellent opportunity to develop modern tribal institutions, such as their own junior college. In 1966, Arizona State University prepared a feasibility study that recommended the establishment of a Navajo junior college teaching a regular curriculum, as well as Navajo history and culture. The Navajo Tribal Council began it in 1969 in temporary quarters at Many Farms High School. Construction on the permanent campus began in 1971 near Tsaile Lake in the Chuska Mountains in northeast Arizona.

The $11 million of buildings completed to date are laid out in terms of the circle of a traditional house (*hogan*) and ceremonial beliefs: (1) the orientation is eastward, where the entrance is related to the rising sun; (2) dormitories are in the northwest, where a person is seated when they receive a religious ceremony; and (3) classrooms are in the southwest, where the person performing the ceremony is located in a ceremony. The Native studies curriculum is 28 courses: acculturation, contemporary affairs, language, music, religion, and psychology, and crafts such as basketry, silversmithing, and weaving. Liberal arts and vocational courses include drafting, mechanics, nursing, and welding.

The enrolment in 1976 was 1,177; 432 at the Tsaile campus and the rest in 13 other reservation locations. The students were about 80% Navajo, 10% other Indians (from more than 35 tribes), and 10% non-Indian. A majority of the teaching staff so far have been non-Indian.

At the 1976 graduation ceremonies Thomas Atcitty, the College president, spoke of the College ideals. "We have tried to show you that achievement and happiness cannot be poured upon you like water on thirsty ground. They come, rather, from within yourself, welling up from your own creative being like a spring of living water . . . Education is the instruction of the intellect in the laws of nature. The art of being taught is the art of discovery. We at Navajo Community College believe that the art of teaching is the art of assisting that discovery to take place."

A NOTE ON U.S.-CANADA DIFFERENCES

It is appropriate to include Native studies in the U.S. and Canada in the same volume, but there are also many important differences between these populations so that in this book they are usually kept separate in data presentations and analysis. The historical U.S. displacement of Natives tended to be more violent than that of Canada. Canada had more of the relatively peaceful band level societies. Canada went through a longer period of cooperative trade and exploration relationships in which Indians, Métis, and Inuit played vital roles in Euro-Canadian history.

U.S. reservations sometimes began with an element of military containment, tended to be far fewer in number and much larger than Canadian reserves, and were administered by the U.S. Army before the Department of Interior took over. Indian affairs in Canada began under Mines, then moved to Immigration, and finally to the Department of Indian Affairs and Northern Development. Most importantly, Canadian Natives today are several times more populous than U.S. Natives in per capita terms, so Canadian Natives are having a much greater impact on Canadian politics and institutions of every kind. For example, special issues of Canadian postage stamps are often on an Indian subject matter. C.B.C. radio, federally sponsored and without advertising, has a nation-wide broadcast at prime time on "Our Native Land." The influence of Natives on Canadian society might be compared to that of Blacks on U.S. society, especially to Black politics and arts.

In the following chapters the reader will notice that international Native movements historically tended to start in the U.S. and then spread into Canada: Pontiac's confederacy, Tecumseh's confederacy, Peyotism, powwow dancing, etc. This Canadian lag was more marked in the sphere of government action than in Indian society as we move into the twentieth century. Thus we see that in the Indian sphere there were Indian runners competing in the Olympics for both the U.S. and Canada in 1908 and 1912. Although not officially citizens in either country at the time, Indians in both the U.S. and Canada were marked by their patriotism and volunteered to fight in World War I.

In the area of government legislation, however, there was a considerable lag. The U.S. gave Indians citizenship in 1924; Canada did not until 1960. The U.S. started its Indian Claims Commission in 1946, Canada essentially in 1969. The U.S. stopped the prohibition of alcoholic beverages to Indians in 1951 and Canada waited until forced to do so by a 1967 Supreme Court decision. The U.S. developed a termination policy in 1953; Canada considered the same in the White Paper of 1969, although both countries have now reversed themselves on this policy. A comprehensive antituberculosis program was started in Alaska in 1955 and in Canada in the early 1960s. An Indian was elected to the U.S. Senate in 1907 and he became the U.S. Vice President in 1928, but the first Indian was not appointed to the Canadian Senate until 1958.

I think we can take the nearly simultaneous occurrence of Native events in the two countries as evidence of the strong international integration of Native society in recent years. In 1968, A.I.M. started protests in Minneapolis and the Canadian Iroquois blocked the international bridge at Cornwall, Ontario. That year the Hotevilla Hopi affirmed their traditional culture and protested the installation of electrical power; Chief Smallboy established a wilderness community to maintain traditional ways in the Canadian Rocky Mountains. In 1969, protest books by Indians became best-sellers in both the U.S. (*Custer Died For Your Sins*) and Canada (*The Unjust Society*). That same year, Native studies was first offered simultaneously in three formal college level programs: Navajo Community College and the University of Minnesota in the U.S., and Trent University in Canada. Although it is difficult to trace the paths of communication, social inventions such as the Indian protests ("occupations," "caravans," and "blockades") have a distinct and international history, comparable to the "sit-ins" that the Blacks used to integrate services or economic boycotts. Today the People are struggling with land claims, ecumenical religion, the rights of Indian women, the rights of Indian prisoners, and many other concerns. Native studies research should try to explore these movements internationally, instead of the current narrow trend to limit research to the Natives of only one country.

Chapter 2

Physical Anthropology and Linguistics

Physical anthropology and linguistics have made major contributions to the understanding of Native people. This chapter reviews some of the findings of these fields, especially in unraveling the story of prehistory.

Human evolution occurred over millions of years in the Old World, with humans arriving in the New World only in the last phase of the Pleistocene Ice Age. Even after entry by humans the two hemispheres remained largely separate, because (1) a land connection between the hemispheres was available only in one place—across the Bering land bridge between Siberia and Alaska, (2) that place was difficult to cross because of the cold climate and meagre sources of food, and (3) it could be crossed only for certain periods of time, due to glacial barricades and fluctuating ocean levels that periodically submerged the land bridge (Stewart 1973).

In cold periods the moisture of the world was increasingly locked up in the form of glaciers and ice sheets. This removed enough water to lower the ocean levels over 150 feet, so that the shallow continental shelf areas of the world became dry land, particularly the Bering Straits between Siberia and Alaska, as well as the shallow lands around such places as Indonesia and Australia. The inter-hemisphere land bridge is called Beringia. It was a tundra and grassland plain on which herbivorous animals fed and early man undoubtedly hunted. Beringia was probably dry land between about 26,000 B.P. (before present) and 10,000 B.P., with the exception of two closings by submergence during warm periods around 13,500 B.P. and 12,000 B.P..

With extreme cold, however, the continental ice sheets closed off passage between the hemispheres. The Cordilleran and Laurentide ice sheets probably merged into a single ice sheet between 24,000 B.P. and 12,500 B.P., thus closing off the route, the Yukon-Mackenzie Corridor, and any possible passage between western Alaska and internal North America.

This leaves only two relatively short periods when everything was right, first around 25,000 years ago and then 12-10,000 years ago. Optimum crossing conditions declined somewhat after 10,000 years ago but, with the decline of the ice sheets, crossing was continuously possible from then on to the present. The presence of a dry land crossing at the Bering Straits is not absolutely necessary in order to cross on foot. Thus, for example, Inuit living in the area can cross in winter over the frozen ocean ice. There are Inuit villages on the Siberian side of the Straits. In fact, travel per se in this country is generally easier in winter over frozen ground than in warm weather, because the tundra turns into a terrain of lakes and soft ground. Survival on land in the Bering area during an Ice Age winter would be hampered by the scarcity of land animals for food in these extremely cold climatic conditions. The early people were land animal hunters and did not have the technology (the harpoons, kayaks, and specific hunting knowledge and skills) to hunt sea mammals, as the Inuit do.

Very little human skeletal evidence has been recovered from the early periods, but all of it is of *Homo sapiens*, or modern humans. There are indications over time of a racial change in the migrations into the New World toward more classic Mongoloid features, because the migrations drew from slightly different populations in eastern Asia. The oldest find is a fossilized jaw bone that dates back more than 20,000 years, found in the Old Crow River area in the Yukon. From scattered but good hunting areas there are several younger finds from the ancient hunting period: Browns' Valley, Minnesota; Melbourne, Florida; Natchez, Mississippi; Cochise, Arizona; Los Angeles, California; and Tepexpan, Mexico.

The difficult crossing conditions probably biologically eliminated individuals with genetic diseases or other problems that made them inferior in terms of the hard physical life of Arctic hunters. Over the tens of thousands of years there was some evolutionary selection and movement away from the broadly "Mongoloid" racial stock to form an American Indian sub-race.

Native Americans usually have (1) straight black hair, (2) very little facial or body hair, (3) brown (not red) skin, (4) a slightly broad face with some prominence of cheek bones, (5) a tendency toward the Mongoloid eyefold, (6) little colour blindness, but eye pigmentation that contributes to an identification of green with blue, (7) "dry" rather than "sticky" earwax, (8) the ability to taste the chemical PTC as bitter, (9) fingerprints with frequencies of loops and whorls similar to those of Asians, (10) a general absence of the RH-blood factor, and (11) in the ABO blood system, a very high frequency of O (up to 100% in some populations), and a very low frequency of B (less than 5% in most populations). There was some diffusion of B, apparently recent, into the Native populations of western Alaska from Siberia.

The Inuit are generally more similar to the classically defined Mongoloid type than other Native Americans and are thought to have arrived in the New World only in the last 5,000 years. The basics of Inuit culture seem to have developed in western coastal Alaska around arctic marine mammal hunting, and that allowed them to fill out an almost unoccupied ecological niche along the coasts from Siberia to Greenland. At one point they were also in Newfoundland but disappeared from there for some reason, after the brief Viking settlements in Labrador and Newfoundland around 1,000 A.D. but before the European settlements of the 1600s.

Within the Native American sub-race there are populations that vary widely in such things as pigmentation, facial features, and stature. For example, the Western Hemisphere followed the world-wide tendency to associate tallness with temperate climates. The tallest people live in central and eastern Canada and the U.S., in North America, and Argentina in South America. The shortest people live in the Arctic, and from southern Mexico through northern South America.

While racial variations are still of some interest, physical anthropology has turned much of its attention to such topics as physical deformations, diseases, and population dynamics. The aboriginal American Indians were extreme in the ancient world in the extent and diversity of the modification of their bodies for aesthetic, religious, and status reasons. In addition to such practices as tattooing and facial and body painting, which were practiced by primitive societies in all parts of the world, certain Native societies purposely shaped the soft heads of their infants.

Aesthetic head shaping probably came from appreciating the permanent flattening effect that a cradleboard has on the back of the skull. This shaping apparently has no effect on the brain or on intelligence because the soft and plastic brain can easily adjust as the infant grows. Shaping was achieved by tying small boards or bands on the infant's head. This has been reported as occasionally used in most of the agricultural areas, and in the non-agricultural Northwest Coast cultures.

In the Northwest, head shaping was used as a mark of high status that helped to distinguish the nobility from commoners and particularly from slaves. In the north, circular grooves were made around the head by such people as the Koskimo. In the central area, the Cowichan and their neighbors used front and back flattening. In the Chinook area in the south, at the mouth of the Columbia River, a squarish shape was achieved by using front, back, and side boards.

Among some of the advanced Middle and South American societies, the teeth were occasionally carved with grooves or notches by filing. A few cases are known in which circular holes were drilled into the teeth as settings for inlays of pyrite, jadeite, turquoise, or gold. Natives had very little tooth decay because they had very little sugar in their diet. However, the teeth of older people were badly ground down from grit in areas where food was processed on grinding stones.

A major biological advantage of the aboriginal American Indians over people of the Eastern Hemisphere was their relative lack of the major epidemic diseases. From the study of ancient feces in archaeological sites it is known that individuals occasionally did have intestinal parasites, such as whipworm, tapeworm, and pinworm. Indications of broken bones and arthritis are common in skeletal collections. A bone damage that is similar to arthritis also indicates that tuberculosis was probably present in pre-Columbian America.

An Old World origin and limit prior to Columbus seem "definite" for smallpox, typhus, measles, and malaria and "probable" for syphilis. These diseases did not spread into the New World with the migrations across the Bering area. Stewart (1973) postulates that a "disease filter" was formed in the migrations because of the cold climate of the area and the small groups, isolation, and slow movements of the populations that migrated. When Europeans did arrive, the Native people had not developed an immunity against these diseases. Epidemics of smallpox, typhus, and measles consistently followed the arrival of Whites into one area after another.

Warfare and famine contributed to declines, but epidemic disease became the major reason for the decline in aboriginal populations. For an extreme example, in one of the most densely populated parts of the New World it appears that about 80% of the Native population in the central part of Mexico died out within thirty years of the beginning of the Spanish conquest (Stewart 1973:36). The most infamous smallpox epidemic in the U.S. occurred in 1837 among the Mandan along the Missouri River. They were reduced to thirty-one survivors from about 1,600 in a period of a few weeks.

The aboriginal population in the Western Hemisphere prior to Columbus was probably around 20 million. The lowest points of population had come by about 1570 in the Caribbean (almost total extinction in the area), 1650 in Latin America, and 1930 in North America, a reduction to low point totals of about 4.5 million. The estimated average life expectancy of aboriginal Indians at birth, on the basis of skeletal remains, is 37 years plus or minus three years. This compares favorably with the estimated average of 35 years for White Americans in the late eighteenth century.

The Arctic has such a unique environment that a special branch of medicine has developed to work with its problems. Exposure to the cold is obvious; but the north also has unusual rhythms of light and darkness; isolation; a lack of fresh fruits and vegetables in the diet; and, among the Native people, high rates of certain medical problems such as middle ear infections and dental problems. Siberian scientists are studying what they call the "syndrome of polar tension" that they relate to a greater amount of cosmic radiation, which gives a greater ionization of the oxygen, and thus influences body chemistry (Shephard and Itoh 1976).

There is the phenomenon of cold habituation in which people who work in cold environments adapt to them over a period of years. Probably less important than habituation is racial adaptation to the cold. The Inuit have a small ratio of weight in relation to the area of their body surface able to expel heat. The Inuit also have only one-fourth to one-sixth as many active sweat glands per area of skin as Whites have at normal body temperatures, so they retain more body heat.

Native adults tend to have a deficiency in the lactase enzymes, necessary for the digestion of the complex sugar in milk called lactose. It means that individuals who are deficient in lactases have digestive problems, such as cramps and diarrhea, when they drink a significant quantity of milk. People without lactase enzymes can usually consume the equivalent of about a pint of milk a day, as a liquid or in cooked foods, without symptoms, because up to a certain level of consumption the body just uses the water, protein, calcium, and vitamins in the milk and passes the milk sugar off as a solid waste. They also have no problem eating cheese because most cheeses contain no lactose.

Adult lactase deficiency seems to have a genetic base that controls the production of three lactase enzymes. This deficiency is correlated the world over with the lack of pastoral dairy cultures and the drinking of milk. The aboriginal New World lacked pastoralism, except for the keeping of llamas and alpacas in Peru and Chile—and even this was for transportation, meat, wool, and hides, rather than milk. This lactase deficiency in adults seems to vary somewhat individually and by populations but is very common among Native Americans—ranging from 63% to 100% in about one dozen studies from the Greenland Inuit to South American samples (McCracken 1971, Harrison 1975). This condition means that Native communities should be advised to use milk in moderation and individuals should be tested and notified if they are deficient in lactase enzymes.

Tuberculosis was extremely widespread among Native people between the late 1800s and the 1930s. Around the turn of the century the entire student body of some Indian boarding schools was infected with tuberculosis. The situation then progressively improved, so that today the disease has disappeared from most Indian communities. Indian diets have become better and modern drugs, vaccinations, and improved medical care have contributed to a marked increase in life expectancy, now in the 60s (64.9 in 1974 in the U.S.). This figure is still six years less than the non-Indian populations (70.9 in the U.S., in 1974).

Pulmonary problems such as colds, influenza, and pneumonia are attributed as the final cause of about 30% of Indian deaths. A healthier diet, home environment, and medical services could greatly reduce the number of these kinds of deaths. About 25% of Indian deaths are due to accidents, especially automobile accidents, house fires, and drownings. Again, these too could be greatly reduced. Finally, in 1971 the U.S. Indian infant death rate was 1.2 times higher than the general rate, a difference that could be largely eliminated by improved pre-natal and infant care.

Poor families often eat more of the basic nutritious foods than those with slightly better incomes, who buy luxury foods with low nutritional content. However, in studies of Navajo malnutrition those who lived in remote areas more frequently had vitamin and mineral deficiencies than did the urban Navajo. The Canadian Inuit today tend to have deficiencies of the vitamins C and D and the mineral calcium. Over half of Inuit adults have occasional problems of bleeding gums because of their poor diet. Aboriginally the Inuit ate almost nothing but *raw* meat so they got all the vitamins and minerals, as well as fats and proteins, that they needed. Now cooking destroys some of the vitamins. They did not have dental caries because they did not have any sugar in their diet. They now commonly have dental caries.

The Bureau of Nutritional Sciences (1975) surveyed the nutrition of Canadian Natives. They found that Natives were more often "at risk" than the national averages because of obesity and deficiencies of vitamins A, C, D, calcium, and folacin. Intake of protein, thiamin (B_1), riboflavin (B_2), and niacin were generally found to be above or equal to the standards of adequacy. The deficiencies were more marked for women than men, more for the young and old than for those in the 20 to 60 age range, and more for pregnant women. Vitamin and mineral deficiencies occurred most frequently in isolated reserves and among the Inuit.

Many special patterns were noted. Caloric deficiencies were noted for the Inuit elderly and women. Indians in remote areas and Inuit are not receiving enough ascorbic acid (vitamin C), contained in fresh fruits (particular citrus), vegetables (such as tomatoes), and liver. Thus clinical problems show up, such as bleeding gums. A deficiency in dietary vitamin D (liver, milk, eggs, meat, etc.) can be offset by a small amount of daily exposure to sunlight, but certain people *do not get outside enough*, such as infants, Inuit children, invalids, and pregnant women. Teenage and pregnant females had inadequate intakes of calcium, which comes from meat, fish, dairy products, and eggs. The use of daily multi-vitamin and mineral pills would help these people with deficiency problems.

Health care facilities specifically for Indians in the U.S. generally equal those for rural people, with 51 hospitals, 87 health centers, and 300 health stations and clinics (Guyon 1973). The Indian Health Service has an annual budget of over $300 million. Over half of the employees of the U.S. Indian Health Service are Indians. However, there are still few Natives in the U.S. in the top ranks of the medical profession. In 1974 there were 53 physicians, two veterinarians, two optometrists, one dentist, and five pharmacists. There is an Association of American Indian Physicians based in Oklahoma City. In 1976 Canada had 10 physicians and 221 nurses of Native ancestry. The National Indian Brotherhood has been campaigning for the training of paramedics selected by Native communities, similar to the "barefoot doctors" program in China.

LANGUAGE PHYLA

One dimension of extreme diversity in aboriginal North America is that of languages. However, the work of linguistic historians has already made great progress in unraveling the connections, groupings, and history of these languages. The youngest families of languages to spread over sizable parts of North America are those that now dominate the north, Eskimo-Aleut and Na-Dene.

Eskimo-Aleut is related to such northeastern Asian languages as Kamchadal and Chukchi; it stretched rapidly across the marine Arctic as these peoples filled a previously unoccupied ecological niche with their new kit of specialized marine Arctic tools: igloo, kayak, mukluks-snowpants-parka, sealing harpoons and floats, and dog sleds. Some Na-Dene (Athabascan) peoples left their Alaskan and northwest Canadian heartland and scattered out to the south some time after about 1,000 A.D., going to the Pacific Coast in a few places and into the arid southwest, where they split into Navajo (who adopted agriculture early) and Apache (who continued hunting well into the historic period) divisions.

In other historically curious connections, the Penutians of Oregon and California are related to the Maya of southern Mexico and Guatemala. We can only speculate about the migrations that produced this distribution, but certainly the ancestors of both, in terms of linguistic heritage, were together several thousand years ago. In a similar case, there are Hokan-speaking people scattered around in California, northwest Mexico, southern Mexico, and Belize in Central America. By its distributions, Aztec-Tanoan diffusion *appears* to involve (1) an early heartland in northwest Mexico and the Southwest, (2) some early migrations deeper into Mexico and to coastal California, and (3) finally, some late migrations and expansions of people like the Aztecs (speaking Nahuatl) and Shoshoneans (Northern Paiute, Bannock, Gosiute, Shoshoni, Comanche, etc.).

Seneca, Cayuga, and Onondaga are considered to be dialects of the same language. This implies that the Seneca, Cayuga, and Onondaga tribes have something of a common history. On a higher level of abstraction, implying a deeper time depth in history, this language is related to Mohawk, Oneida, Huron, Tuscarora, and Cherokee. All of these belong to the Iroquian family of languages. Perhaps there was a single Iroquian language more than 1,000 years ago and these languages diverged from the parent language, first as dialects and then as completely separate languages. On examining history, that is, more distant relationships, more closely, we see that the Iroquian family is related to other families we call Siouan, Catawba, Caddoan, and Yuchi. All of these language families belong to what is called the Macro-Siouan phylum of languages. There are, of course, differences of opinion among linguistic historians about these relationships.

It is possible to estimate time depth for a language classification in a very sketchy way. Significant dialectical differences within a single speech community evolve after a few hundred years of moderate separation. People speaking different *dialects* of the same language can understand each other most of the time, but they typically have a number of different words for the same things and they can recognize differences ("accents") in each other's speech. In the following classification, the names of speech communities that are given in a line after an Arabic numeral are dialects of a single language (for example, Choctaw-Chickasaw).

When two speech communities with a common origin are separated for over several hundred years the differences become so great that people generally cannot understand each other and we say that they have different *languages*. As this process of the splitting and resplitting of language communities continues for thousands of years, separate *language families* are formed. The *phylum* level of classification implies a time depth of several thousand years.

The following classification and map is from C. F. and F. M. Voegelin's "Map of North American Indian Languages" (1966). The Voegelins derived their classification from a consensus reached by the First Conference on American Indian Languages. There is now a significant amount of literature written in eight of the languages: Cherokee, Cree, Creek, Crow, Dakota, Eskimo, Navajo, and Ojibwa. One estimate is that only 45 U.S. Indian languages are still spoken (Washburn 1975:261).

NORTH AMERICAN NATIVE LANGUAGES

AMERICAN ARCTIC-PALEOSIBERIAN PHYLUM

I. Eskimo-Aleut Family (four languages in Alaska, Canada, and Greenland)
II. Chukchi-Kamachatkan Family (in Siberia)

NA-DENE PHYLUM

I. Athapascan Family
  1. Dogrib-Bear Lake-Hare
  2. Chipewyan-Slave-Yellowknife
  3. Kutchin
  4. Tanana-Koyokon-Han-Tutchone
  5. Sekani-Beaver-Sarsi
  6. Carrier-Chilcotin
  7. Tahltan-Kaska
  8. Tanaina-Ingalik
  9. Eyak
  10. Chasta Costa-Galice-Tututni
  11. Hupa
  12. Kato-Wailaki
  13. Mattole
  14. Tolowa
  15. Navajo

16. San Carlos Apache
17. Chiricahua-Mescalero
18. Jicarilla
19. Lipan
20. Kiowa Apache

II. Tlingit Language Isolate
III. Haida Language Isolate

MACRO-ALGONQUIAN PHYLUM

I. Algonquian Family
    1. Cree-Montagnais-Naskapi
    2. Menomini
    3. Fox-Sauk-Kickapoo
    4. Shawnee
    5. Potawatomi
    6. Ojibwa-Ottawa-Algonquin
    7. Delaware
    8. Penobscot-Abnaki
    9. Malecite-Passamaquoddy
    10. Micmac
    11. Blackfoot-Piegan-Blood
    12. Cheyenne
    13. Arapahoe-Atsina
II. Yurok Language Isolate
III. Wiyot Language Isolate
IV. Muskogean Family
    1. Chocktaw-Chickasaw
    2. Alabama-Koasati
    3. Mikasuki-Hitchiti
    4. Muskogee (Creek)-Seminole
V. Natchez Language Isolate
VI-IX. Language Isolates: Atakapa, Chitimacha, Tunica, Tonkawa.

MACRO-SIOUAN PHYLUM

I. Siouan Family
    1. Crow
    2. Hidatsa
    3. Winnebago
    4. Mandan
    5. Iowa-Oto
    6. Omaha-Osage-Ponca-Quapaw
    7. Dakota (Teton, Yankton, Santee, Assiniboin)

II. Catawba Language Isolate
III. Iroquoian Family
   1. Seneca-Cayuga-Onondaga
   2. Mohawk
   3. Oneida
   4. Wyandot (Huron)
   5. Tuscarora
   6. Cherokee
IV. Caddoan Family
   1. Caddo
   2. Wichita
   3. Pawnee-Arikara
V. Yuchi Language Isolate

HOKAN PHYLUM

I. Yuman Family
   1. Walapai-Havasupai-Yavapai
   2. Mohave-Maricopa-Yuma
   3. Cocopa-Kohuana-Halyikwamai
   4. Diegueño-Kamia-Akwa'ala-Kiliwa-Nyakipa
II. Seri Language Isolate
III. Pomo Family (four languages)
IV. Palaihnihan Family
   1. Achumawi
   2. Atsugewi
V-XVII. Thirteen scattered language families and language isolates: Shastan, Yanan, Chimariko, Washo, Salinan, Karok, Chumashan, Comecrudan, Coahuiltecan, Esselen, Jicaque, Tlapanecan, Tequistlatecan.

PENUTIAN PHYLUM

I. Yokuts Family (3 languages)
II. Maidu Family (4 languages)
III. Wintun Family
   1. Patwin
   2. Wintun
IV. Miwok-Costanoan Family (3 languages)
V. Klamath-Modoc Language Isolate
VI. Sahaptin-Nez Perce Family (2 languages)

VII. Cayuse Language Isolate
VIII. Molale Language Isolate
IX. Coos Family
X. Yakonan
  1. Alsea
  2. Siuslaw-Lower Umpqua
XI. Takelma Language Isolate
XII. Kalapuya Family
  1. Santian-Mackenzie
  2. Yonkalla
XIII. Chinookan Family
XIV. Tsimshian Language Isolate
XV. Zuni Language Isolate
XVI. Mixe-Zoque Family (6 languages)
XVII. Mayan Family (31 languages)
XVIII. Chipaya-Uru Family (in Bolivia)
XIX. Totonacan Family
XX. Huave Language Isolate

AZTEC-TANOAN PHYLUM

I. Kiowa-Tanoan Family
  1. Tiwa (Taos-Picuris)-(Isleta-Sandia)
  2. Tewa (San Juan-Santa Clara-San Ildefonso-Tesuque-Nambe-Hano)
  3. Towa (Jemez)
  4. Kiowa
II. Uto-Aztecan Family
  1. Mono
  2. Northern Paiute-Bannock-Snake
  3. Shoshone-Gosiute-Wind River-Panamint-Comanche
  4. Southern Paiute-Ute-Chemehuevi-Kawaiisu
  5. Hopi
  6. Tubatulabal
  7. Luiseño
  8. Cahuilla
  9. Cupeño
  10. Serrano
  11. Pima-Papago
  12. Pima-Bajo
  13. Yaqui-Mayo
  14. Tarahumara

15. Cora
16. Huichol
17. Tepehuan
18. Nahuatl (Aztec)
19. Nahuat
20. Mecayapan
21. Pipil
22. Pochutla
23. Tamaulipeco

UNDETERMINED PHYLUM AFFILIATIONS

I. Keres Language Isolate
II. Yuki Family
   1. Yuki
   2. Wappo
III. Beothuk Language Isolate
IV. Kutenai Language Isolate
V. Karankawa Language Isolate
VI. Chimakuan Family
   1. Quileute
   2. Chimakum
VII. Salish Family
   1. Lillooet
   2. Shuswap
   3. Thompson
   4. Okanagon-Sanpoil-Colville-Lake
   5. Flathead-Pend d'Oreille-Kalispel-Spokan
   6. Coeur d'Alene
   7. Middle Columbia-Wenachi
   8. Tillamook
   9. Twana
   10. Upper Chehalis-Cowlitz-Lower Chehalis-Quinault
   11. Snoqualmi-Duamish-Nisqualli
   12. Lummi-Songish-Clallam
   13. Halkomelem
   14. Squamish
   15. Comox-Sishiatl
   16. Bella Coola
VIII. Wakashan Family
   1. Nootka
   2. Nitinat
   3. Makah

4. Kwakiutl
5. Bella Bella-Heiltsuk
6. Kitamat-Haisla

IX. Timucua Language Isolate
X. Tarascan Language Isolate

OTO-MANGUEAN PHYLUM
(six language families)

MACRO-CHIBCHAN PHYLUM
(five language families or
language isolates)

Eskimo - Aleut
Eskimo - Aleut
Eskimo - Aleut
Eskimo - Aleut
Na - Dene
Penutian
Macro - Algonquian
Beothuk
Macro - Algonquian
Salish
Macro - Siouan
Penutian
Na - Dene
H
H
Aztec - Tanoan
Macro - Algonquian
Macro - Siouan
Macro - Algonquian
Penutian
H
Macro - Siouan
Aztec - Tanoan
Z K A
0 300 600 MI.
Hokan
Na - Dene
Timucua
Karankawa
H
Aztec - Tanoan
Hokan
Guaicuran
?
Aztec - Tanoan
Arawakan
LANGUAGE PHYLA
A Aztec - Tanoan
H Hokan
K Keres
O Oto - Manguean
Z Zuni
Penutian
Penutian
Tarascan
A
H
O
A
Penutian
H
Macro - Chibchan
H
O

GLOTTOCHRONOLOGY

It is possible to estimate roughly the time of separation of two historically related languages by counting the extent of vocabulary they still retain in common. It is judged from the history of written languages in the Old World that the "basic vocabulary" of all languages has a common rate of "decay," usually substitution of new words for the same concept. In glottochronology, this decay formula is applied to historically related unwritten languages to increase understandings about early connections, migrations, and separations.

Basic vocabulary words are ones that refer to fairly universal concepts, such as mother, father, sun, moon, one, two, and three. Languages generally have words for these concepts. They are words that would not be affected by migrations into new environments. They are words that are learned early in life by children. They are words that are basic in any language, so they change slowly, steadily, and more predictably than specialized or environmentally sensitive words.

The calculation is made on common "cognates," words in different but related languages, words that historically were the same but gradually may have become pronounced differently in the various languages over the centuries. Knowledge of the systematic phonetic changes that occur in languages enables linguistics to determine whether or not two words that are pronounced differently in separate languages came historically from the same root word.

The general rule is that over a period of 1,000 years, a language retains about 80% of its basic vocabulary. Theoretically then, when a language divides into two, each new language retains 80% of the original basic vocabulary, so 64% cognates would remain in common. The formula can be applied to historically related languages to calculate their closeness.

The following are the glottochronology relationships between ten of the Aztec-Tanoan languages in centuries (Swadesh 1964:551). Shoshoni and Comanche are very closely related to each other. By this kind of data we would say that two hundred years ago they were essentially one language, one mutually intelligible speech community. These are in turn next related to Northern Paiute and Southern Paiute, then in turn to Hopi, Pima, Luiseño, Tarahumar, Taos, and Aztec (Nahuatl). With the exception of Taos, there is an expected close correlation between the estimated time of separation from Shoshoni-Comanche and the geographical distance between the languages. Still, the historical relationships are much more complex than simple migration and distance, involving such possibilities as recontact and word borrowings off and on through history.

AZTEC-TANOAN DIVERGENCES IN CENTURIES

	Shoshoni	Comanche	Northern Paiute	Southern Paiute	Hopi	Pima	Luiseño	Tarahumar	Taos
Shoshoni									
Comanche	2								
Northern Paiute	11	10							
Southern Paiute	14	13	12						
Hopi	35	30	31	30					
Pima	36	38	39	36	32				
Luiseño	39	37	36	34	31	41			
Tarahumar	40	40	39	37	29	30	31		
Taos	45	45	50	45	76	76	50	64	
Aztec	52	51	51	47	33	39	32	32	51

The theoretical homeland of this language phyla is somewhere in the greater Southwest, beginning several thousand years ago. Early migrations then are indicated south in Mexico (Tarahumar, etc.) and west to coastal California (Luiseño, etc.). Finally, recent migrations account for the historic positions of the Aztecs and Shoshoneans (Shoshoni, Comanche, Northern Paiute, Southern Paiute-Ute, etc.). Peoples such as the Taos, Pima, and Hopi have been linguistically separated from each other for thousands of years, but they are all probably still close to their ancestral homelands.

Chapter 3

Evolution, Ecology, and Innovation

In order to understand the historical development of Native American cultures, it is necessary to work with a vast amount of information from archaeology, ethnology, and history. Two theoretical perspectives that help to organize that data are *evolution*, the idea that cultures make similar changes over time, and *ecology*, that cultures make similar adjustments to similar environments. This chapter reviews the evolution and ecology of North American Natives and then adds, judging by today's values, a negative and a positive case in the story of New World history. The negative case, the Pleistocene overkill, is that the Natives did contribute to the destruction of elements of their physical environments. The positive case is the story of the inventions the Natives have given the world.

In waves of migration, the American Indians apparently walked into the New World across the Bering Land bridge 30,000 years ago. Fleshing tools and other artifacts made from caribou bone that were found near the Old Crow River in the Yukon have been dated by the radioactive carbon technique to be between 25,000 and 29,000 years old. This was a time in the Late Palaeolithic when people were spreading into areas where they could continue to hunt, presumably because of the overpopulation of big game hunters in more favorable hunting areas in the Old World. As the large game were brought to extinction people shifted their orientation to the extensive exploitation of a wide variety of resources in a smaller ecological niche. This is the Palaeolithic to Mesolithic shift that began about 10,000 years ago, bringing on the creation of a wide range of new tools designed in these fresh and diverse adaptations. In some niches this meant a reliance on fishing, in others it meant shellfish gathering, in others a mixture of hunting small game and plant collecting, etc. Those societies that were still engaged in this "Mesolithic" style of life when the Europeans arrived are called "band organized."

There was a transition from this "food gathering" way of life to one of "food producing" in places in the world where the foods were primarily plants, particularly in the arid parts of West Asia and Western North America. People in these areas acquired a great amount of knowledge about plants, their cycles of growth, their need for water, and their dependence on growing from seeds. This led to domestications with purposeful planting and eventually the selection of seeds to produce the most desirable qualities in the plants. The earliest cultivated plants in the New World were plants with obvious utility and large seeds. The avocado was probably first, and following that the gourd, beans, certain squashes, corn, and finally a variety of tropical plants, such as peanuts, tomatoes, pineapple, and manioc (tapioca).

Food production brought on a greater abundance of food, a more sedentary way of life, population expansion, more leisure time and florescence of arts, crafts, politics, religion, trade, and other features of advanced civilization. This Neolithic or food-producing revolution took place over a period of about 2,000 years in West Asia, between about 10,000 and 8,000 years ago.

For unknown reasons, the food-producing revolution started later and took about twice as long in its New World center in Mexico, from about 8,500 to 3,500 years ago. This late start by some 4,500 years for developed agricultural civilizations in the New World was apparently crucial in their relative backwardness to those of the Old World at the time of Columbus. Civilizational developments take time and the New World simply had less time laying the crucial foundation of agriculture, compared to elaborate civilizations.

Band society has hunting and gathering, a sharing kind of economics, and a style of leadership that is based on common residence and divisions of labor by sex, age, and ability. It is the women who specialize in handling plants in band societies, so we have them to thank for the Neolithic Revolution through the domestication of plants, and probably also for the invention of a broad range of domestic equipment such as basketry, pottery, and the mortar and pestle. The men were responsible for our heritage of hunting, warfare, religion and politics. Bands were predominant in the Arctic, sub-Arctic, Plains (before the Spanish introduced the horse), Plateau, Great Basin, and Baja California.

After about 3,500 years ago, agriculture diffused in all directions, from southern Mexico, into the Caribbean, into the Southwest, and up the Mississippi Valley. The Northern expansion of agricultural civilization moved roughly as far north as was ecologically feasible for the kind of corn agriculture practiced at the time. One exception is California, presumably because the large population there already had rich food sources, particularly from acorns and shellfish. The resulting northern limit of agriculture cut a diagonal line from the Yumans in the delta of the Colorado River, through the Southwest, to the Mississippi Valley, and then northeast to the valley of the St. Lawrence River in Canada. North of that line the societies were generally "bands," and south of it they were usually "tribes."

Tribes develop economic, social, and political ties that are broader in scope than those of bands. Sharing continues to prevail in the intimate sectors of life, such as the household, but the calculations of reciprocity are developed as a basis of economic distribution beyond such spheres. Impersonal trade develops. Lineal kinship groups and other "pan-tribal sodalities" create social ties beyond the residential communities and give political cohesion to the society as a whole. Most tribal societies of the world are horticulturalists, engaging in simple hand gardening, but the tribal level was achieved by hunters in the Plains after the Spanish introduced the horse; and it was very effectively used to harvest the wealth of buffalo that roamed in herds of millions in the early 1800s. Instead of simple hunters, they became horse pastoralists, until the over-kill brought the buffalo close to extinction.

At even richer levels of production, a central integration of economic, social, political, and religious factors develops. This is referred to as a "chiefdom," usually consisting of a chief and some kind of microbureaucracy that serves as an integrating center to tax and redistribute goods and services and to organize feasts, warfare, major religious ceremonies, and long distance trade. Chiefdoms typically have elaborate social ranking and a class system, often with some slavery; well-developed arts, in part because some people are allowed to specialize as artists; spectacular pageantry; etc.

Several societies of the Southeast (Natchez, Creek, etc.) moved beyond the tribal level to become chiefdoms on a rich horticultural base, while in the Northwest Coast chiefdomship was achieved by several societies (Haida, Kwakiutl, etc.) on the base of a rich fishing economy. Beyond the chiefdom, the "state" level was achieved in southern Mexico and neighboring Central America, and in the Andean region of South America. There were also some small city states in the Mississippean archaeological tradition, such as at Cahokia, Illinois. States have intensive agriculture, a centrally administered economy with markets, a legal structure with a large scale bureaucracy, and priestly religions.

Figure 1 shows some of the general traits of each evolutionary level or stage that we use to build our theoretical model. We have to keep in mind that reality, in fact, does not come so neatly packaged and this kind of model is only a conceptual tool that we find useful.

FIGURE 1
A MODEL OF THE EVOLUTION OF CULTURE

Stage	Economic Production	Economic Distribution	Political	Religious
State	Agriculture	Administration and markets	Laws and bureaucracy	Priesthoods
Chiefdom	Horticulture, Pastoralism, or Fishing	Redistribution	Chieftainship	Public dramas
Tribe	"	Reciprocity	Pan-tribal sodalities	Religious societies
Band	Hunting and gathering	Sharing	Residential and task leaders	Curing Food increase

The state is the result of an extension of some processes that are present in the chiefdom, such as the centralization of government and the development of an administrative bureaucracy, the specialization of labor, and the separation of society into ranked social classes. One traditional idea on the nature of the state is that it develops a legal monopoly on the use of force and thus intervenes in private and group disputes. However, a study of legal evolution shows that legal processes can be separated into different parts that appear at different stages in cultural evolution.

Schwartz and Miller (1964) isolated *mediation*, "regular use of non-kin third party intervention in dispute settlement;" *police*, "specialized armed forces used partially or wholly for norm enforcement;" and *counsel*, "regular use of specialized non-kin advocates in the settlement of disputes." The authors use the data from fifty-one societies to show an additive evolution from none of the legal characteristics; to mediation; to mediation and police; and finally to mediation, police, and counsel. There are a few exceptions, but generally the societies with none are bands or tribes; those with mediation alone are tribes or chiefdoms; those with mediation and police are tribes, chiefdoms, and states; and those with mediation, police, and counsel are states. These stages are illustrated in Figure 2, along with the classification of legal activities carried out by the ten North American societies used in their study.

Carneiro (1968) developed a scalogram on the presence or absence of 50 traits in 100 societies around the world in order to study the sequence in the evolution of certain traits. In Figure 3, I present those traits that were present in 15 U.S. and Canadian Indian societies from his sample, showing them in a sequence based on number of traits present in each society. The data on these traits are sometimes questioned by the ethnographic specialists on these societies and a slightly different sequence of societies would result if we used different traits. For example, on other bases I would rank the Kwakiutl between the

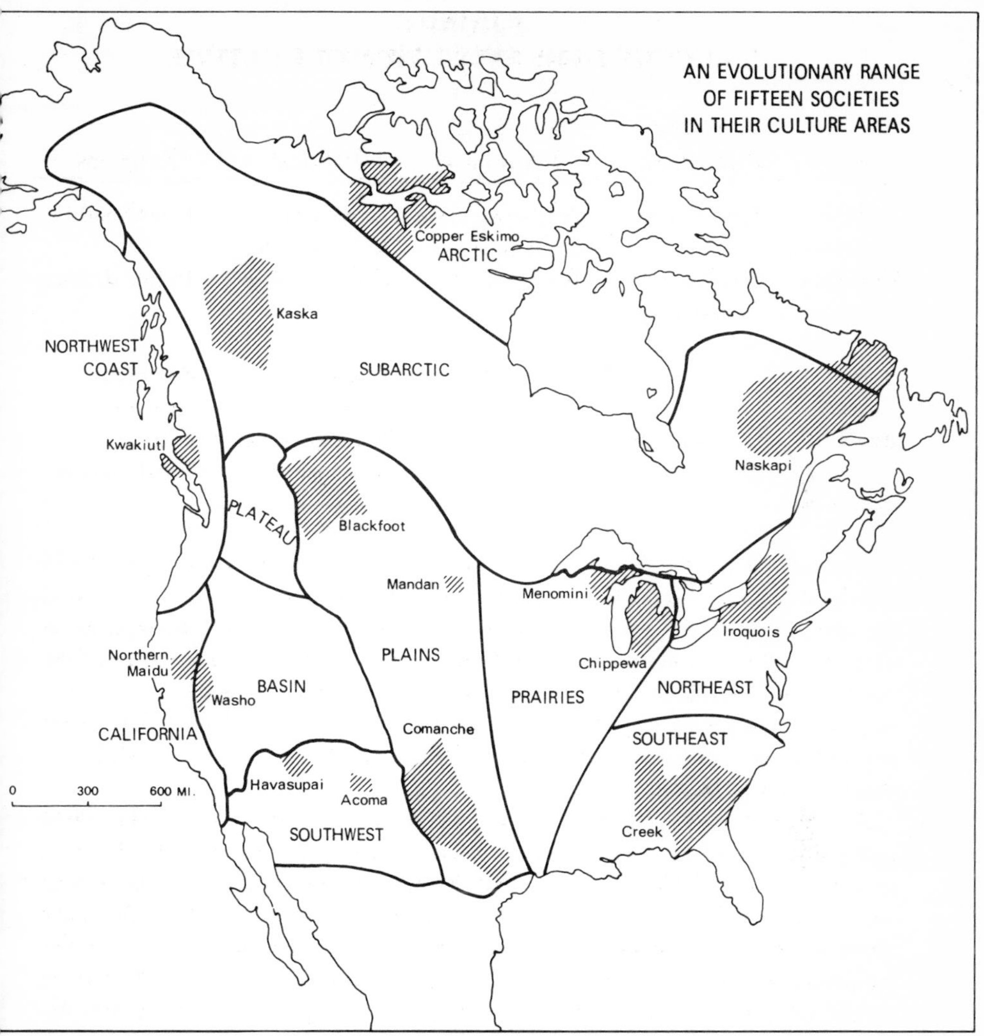

Iroquois and the Creek. However, this scalogram is useful in presenting the idea of systematically different levels of cultural complexity in aboriginal North America. I think of Naskapi, Washo, Kaska, and Eskimo as band societies; Chippewa and Maidu as band-tribe transitional societies; and the rest as tribal, except Kwakiutl and Iroquois at the tribe-chiefdom transitional level, and Creek as a full chiefdom. Then the locations of these societies are indicated on Map 1 in their conventional "cultural areas," zones of similar cultures.

FIGURE 2
THE EVOLUTION OF LEGAL SYSTEMS

	None	Mediation	Mediation & Police	Mediation, Police, & Counsel
States			X	X
Chiefdoms		X	X	
Tribes	X	X	X	
Bands	X			
		North American Examples		
Creek			X	
Hopi			X	
Cuna			X	
Cheyenne			X	
Crow (Police without mediation)				
Navajo		X		
Menomini		X		
Yurok	X			
Comanche	X			
Eskimo	X			

THE SIGNIFICANCE OF EVOLUTIONARY LEVELS ON INDIAN-WHITE RELATIONSHIPS

An adequate analysis of Indian-White relationships would have to include a study of the kinds of Indian and White societies in terms of their relative evolutionary positions. The Spanish tried to impose their feudal-state type of society on the Native people wherever they colonized, but they were much more successful when the aboriginal societies were already agricultural state systems. In state societies men tend to do the bulk of the agricultural work, while in simple societies the women predominate. Here were people who were accustomed to obeying laws, paying taxes, serving in a standing army, worshipping in the religion of the state church, and participating in other activities that are normal to state societies. In Native states the Spanish could replace the Native leadership and remold it into a feudal hacienda society. Chiefdoms could also be co-opted into working on haciendas, particularly by continuing to use the Native leaders, although they were more difficult to handle than people from state societies. People from tribal societies were the most difficult, often giving significant armed resistance for centuries, as did the Huichol and the Yaqui. Band-organized societies were incapable of warfare or any significant resistance, but they were also extremely difficult to change into stable agricultural laborers.

Very few Spanish women were brought to the New World because Spanish

FIGURE 3
SCALOGRAM OF 18 TRAITS IN 15 SOCIETIES (CARNEIRO 1968)

Traits / Society / Level	1 Naskapi Band	1 Washo Band	2 Kaska Band	2 C. Eskimo Band	4 Chippewa Band-Tribe	5 No. Maidu Band-Tribe	6 Comanche Tribe	7 Blackfoot Tribe	7 Havasupai Tribe	8 Kwakiutl Tribe-Chiefdom	9 Mandan Tribe	10 Menomini Tribe	11 Acoma Tribe	12 Iroquois Tribe-Chiefdom	13 Creek Chiefdom
Political leader appoints officials													X		
Special deference to political leader															X
Administrative hierarchy															X
Supra-provincial organization														X	X
Full-time retainers for political leader										X					
Death penalty decreed												X		X	X
Full-time political leader										X			X		
Craft production for exchange													X		
Judicial process												X	X	X	X
Domesticated food sources predominant									X		X		X	X	X
Craft specialization								X	X	X	X	X	X	X	
Significant social status differences							X	X		X	X	X		X	X
Communities of 100 or more					X	X		X	X	X	X	X	X	X	X
Peace-keeping machinery							X	X	X		X	X	X	X	X
Social segments above family			X		X	X	X	X		X	X	X	X	X	X
Formal political leadership						X	X	X	X	X	X	X	X	X	X
Trade between communities				X	X	X	X		X	X	X	X		X	X
Special religious practitioners	X	X	X	X	X	X	X	X	X	X	X	X	X	X	X

objectives were simply colonial. However, this practice led to a great amount of intermarriage between Whites and Natives which means that, with the large size of the Native population in most Latin American countries, the general population of a country often has a significant genetic Native heritage. This is particularly true in Mexico, Peru, and Chile, where the aboriginal populations were very large. However, there are exceptions such as Brazil and Argentina where the aboriginal societies were tribally organized, gave some resistance to Whites, and have been largely eliminated by genocide. In the other countries the factor of racial mixture and the historical heritage, in which Indians were the main population and the workers of the society, has led to a modern position in which the Native heritage has a respected place both racially and culturally.

The British of New England came as settlers with their wives and children and settled down to do the farming themselves. Even if they had tried, they would have had a hard time making the tribal agriculturalists of the area (Massachuset, Mahican, Iroquois, Delaware, etc.) work for them in a feudal system. In addition to their difference of evolutionary level, agriculture was considered by the tribes of the area to be women's work. In the slightly later settlement of the Southeast, a feudal-type plantation system failed in attempts to use Indians and successfully used Negro slaves from the more advanced state societies in Africa. In both of these cases, and generally in British and French North America, the Natives were usually driven from their lands if they were valuable, and then given minor reservations. In the more hostile environments that Whites tended to avoid, such as the Arctic, deserts, and the wet tropics, Native cultures have survived more fully. The most genocidal geographical setting the world over has been that of islands or peninsulas because the Native people cannot escape. Total genocide has been carried out by Whites in Newfoundland; hundreds of Caribbean Islands; the Channel Islands near Santa Barbara, California; the southern part of the peninsula of Baja California; and in such Old World places as Tasmania.

The genocide of the Guaicura appears to have been inevitable, even though the Spanish motives primarily were to Christianize and civilize the Natives through missionary settlements in Baja California. The Guaicura had one of the most primitive cultures ever described. They made no shelters, except for an occasional boulder wind break for sleeping and a tiny brush hut for sick people. They wore no clothing, except for sandals and an occasional headdress. They made no pottery, almost no basketry, and for containers used bowls of palm bark, turtle shell, and sea shell and bags of animal skins and bladders. They were still using the spear thrower and lacked the harpoon or hook and line for fishing. They did not use the hot stone technique for boiling, only earth ovens, parching seeds in shell dishes, and roasting meat by placing it directly on the fire. Fish was eaten raw. The shamans wore a cape of human hair. Thin flat boards were made of mesquite wood with holes in them, through which the shaman would speak and wag his tongue, as if the tablet were speaking.

The Guaicura killed a few Europeans in various feuds from time to time, but they themselves died in large numbers due to new diseases, social and economic disruption, and European guns. The major conditions that determined the Native demise were (1) their insular location at the tip of Baja California that removed the possibility of withdrawal or other flexible responses to destruction by the Spaniards, (2) the extremely primitive nature of Guaicura society so they did not have the population or the cultural resources to defend themselves, and (3) the virulence of European diseases among the Indians.

Inevitable conflicts between people from band and state societies also come from their different concepts of property: sharing property versus private ownership. The Beothuk freely shared their goods with Whites, but when they borrowed from Whites without asking, the Whites killed the Beothuks. Racism flourishes when the cultural differences are as extreme as the band-state contrast. Thus, the hunting of people from band level societies as a sport was developed by Whites in Tasmania, Australia, South Africa, Utah-Nevada, and Newfoundland. Beothuk bows and arrows were no match for European guns, but the Beothuk genocide was complete only because the Europeans systematically shot every man, woman, and child.

There was almost no resistance from bands, extreme resistance from tribes, and moderate resistance from chiefdoms. Both bands (Beothuk of Newfoundland) and chiefdoms (Natchez of Mississippi) have been destroyed by systematic genocide. Except for that great destructiveness of the Atlantic seaboard tribes in the early centuries of the European occupation of North America, it is generally true that the more culturally advanced a Native society was aboriginally, the more sophisticated its historical relations have been with White society. Thus, despite the tragedy of the forced removal of the Five Civilized Tribes (Cherokee, Choctaw, Chickasaw, Creek, and Seminole) from their homelands in the Southeast to Oklahoma, people from these former chiefdoms, along with the Iroquois, have been playing particularly important roles in the general (as well as Indian) history of the U.S. and Canada for some two hundred years.

Plains Indians have historically been more important in pan-Indian movements, such as Peyotism, the Ghost Dance, and the Sun Dance, than in institutions that relate more directly to White society. The communication and social exchange between Indian societies was particularly good in the Plains and a kind of common front opposition to Whites carried over from the time of organized Indian military resistance in the late 1800s.

The other area of early sophisticated work by Natives in the terms of White society is along the British Columbia coast, the ancestors of the most highly evolved aboriginal cultures in Canada. These people also had no history of common military resistance to White society and were more prone to assimilation. In the last few decades this aboriginal background has become generally less important and there has even been a kind of systematic reversal with many of the young educated leaders today coming from societies such as the Washo or Cree, that were band organized in aboriginal times.

Evolutionary differences come out in the way White individuals were treated by the various Native societies. Assimilation of quite young White children into Indian societies went well everywhere, especially if the children were younger than twelve (Heard 1973). For example, Geronimo's raiding band at the height of its harassment by the U.S. Cavalry included two assimilated non-Indian boys, a Negro and a White. Many individuals of all ages became highly Indianized and resisted returning to a White way of life in less than five years. Adoption and assimilation, however, were quicker and easier among the sedentary farming tribes of the East. West of the Mississippi the lives of captive children were harder. Captives were often the last to be fed and the first to be blamed for accidents and problems.

Neither bands nor chiefdoms assimilated many Whites so that most of the "captivity narratives" are about life in tribal level societies. Bands were not oriented toward warfare and did not have the social structure to hold people against their will or even to set people apart, so that foreigners of long residence were quickly adopted and married into the society. Chiefdoms had the elaboration of social structure to hold captives in a separate social category, often as slaves, but they also had the regular economic and political mechanisms to sell off or negotiate the release of White captives. Whites then had very different experiences depending on whether they were captured by a band, a tribe, or a chiefdom.

MILITANCE UNDER STATE CONQUEST AND NEOCOLONIALISM ACCORDING TO EVOLUTIONARY LEVEL

Band societies had extremely low population densities, more than one square mile per person; small, semi-nomadic communities; very little of anything that could be called political or economic linkages between communities; and an orientation toward physical survival. They did not carry out warfare among themselves, militance was limited to some inter-personal feuding, and they were fairly easily destroyed, displaced from desirable territories, or placed in reservation zones by people from state societies. People from band societies were generally passive as their territories were taken from them, their social practices were outlawed, and the ideologies that guided their lives were systematically destroyed by missionaries and other agents from the conquering state.

Their heritage of extreme freedom and individualism, however, made them poor subjects in a state society. That is, it was hard to get them to work steadily for others, either for pay or to avoid punishment. They simply escaped and retreated to where they could continue self-sufficient survival. Band societies were extemely egalitarian, resisting the imposition of a social hierarchy or any political rule. They opposed obedience to abstract state practices, such as rule by laws, the payment of taxes, free market bargaining, and the ownership of land or resources beyond individual immediate and practical uses.

The historical reservation period has fundamentally changed Indian societies, acculturating them to a low position in a heavily bureaucratic niche of state societies with a European heritage. They have also been forced by White discrimination and government bureaucracies into forming a somewhat homogeneous ethnic group out of hundreds of distinct and autonomous societies, that is called "Indian." Beyond these forces of acculturation and homogenization, however, there is some significant cultural continuity from aboriginal through historical to present times. To that extent of continuity we can still see some continuing evolutionary patterning.

People from band societies tended to be the last to enter the homogeneous

Native ethnic culture because of their individualism; their small, scattered, and often isolated residence; and their fairly passive but also intractable acceptance of the neocolonial culture. Philip Turnor of the early Hudson's Bay Company said "the farther north, the more peaceable the Indian." They tended to be outside of or only lightly touched by the pan-Indian movements of the nineteenth century and the first half of the twentieth century. Even the early phase of the Red Power movement in the 1960s almost passed them by and we see them now entering the Native movement enthusiastically in the 1970s.

Tribal level societies were much more difficult to conquer and to colonize than bands. The population densities of tribal societies were such that they are read off in terms of persons per square mile, not square miles per person. The communities tended to be fairly stable villages, moderate in size. Political and economic linkages between communities integrated the society, making it capable of coordinated, society-wide reactions to society-wide problems. Tribes tended to develop small-scale raiding patterns of warfare, emphasizing individual male heroism and the taking of war trophies, including women to be married and children to be adopted into the tribe.

Tribal warfare was primarily a masculine game to demonstrate a warrior's bravery. Young warriors in the East often wore their hair with just a high central ridge as a "scalp lock," a challenge to enemy warriors to try to come and take their scalp. The Plains tribes developed elaborate means to count, symbolize (such as feathers in a war bonnet), and recite individual acts of bravery (called *coups* today after the French word for a brilliant "stroke" or act) much like the modern wearing of war medals. The Yuman societies along the Colorado River had rather ritualistic warfare, in which only young men who were members of warrior societies met on a field of battle with clubs. The individualistic raiding tactics and organization of tribal societies was in sharp contrast to the regimented, chain-of-command campaign tactics of state armies. When the two met in warfare, they were playing different war games, each by their own rules.

Like people from band societies, tribal peoples made poor subjects for state laws, taxes, etc. Even when they were aboriginally agricultural, that kind of work was largely carried out by women so it was difficult to get them to carry out the male agriculture of state societies. In the case of the horse-riding, buffalo-hunting tribes of the Plains, the military resistance to state conquest was particularly effective and attempts to settle down the Indians as farmers were difficult because they were militarily mobile.

People with a tribal heritage have always been in the forefront of the militant resistance to state conquest; they have been the major source of the more separatist, nationalistic, and culturally revitalistic pan-Indian movements. The Iroquois of New York, Ontario, and Quebec, for example, formed a military confederation or "league" in early historical times, pan-tribal ethical systems in the Code of Handsome Lake and the White Roots of Peace, and a religious movement in the Longhouse Society. *Akwesasne Notes* is a monthly Native newspaper that tends to be sympathetic to the use of militance and is published by a

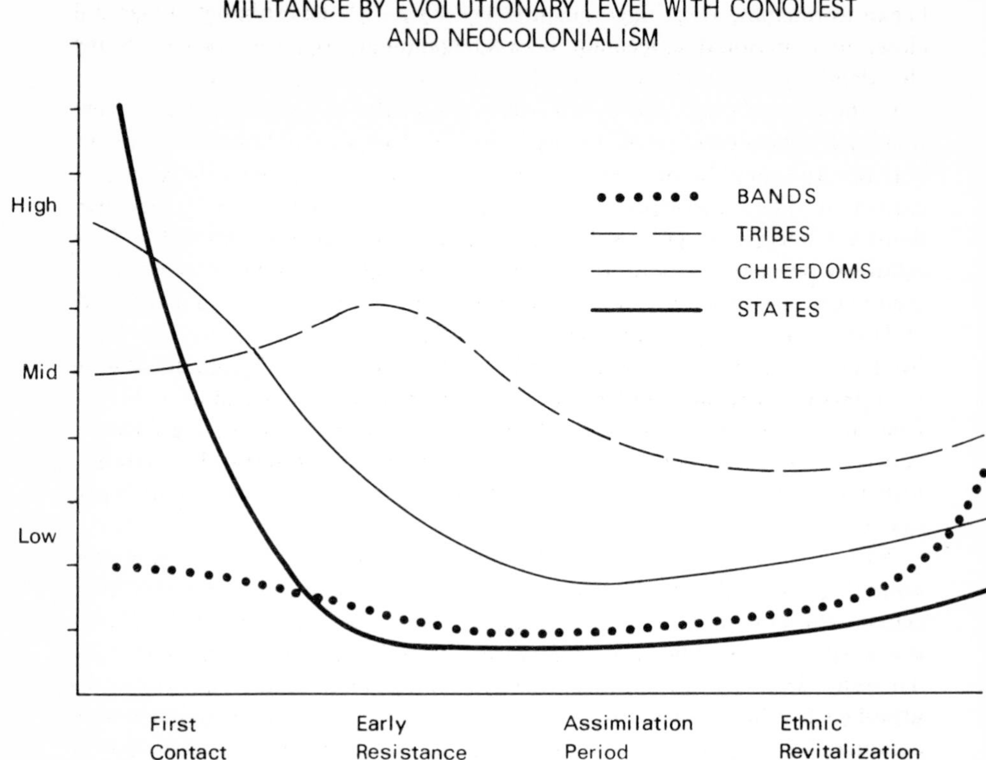

group of Iroquois for an international readership. The Mohawk Warriors' Society is an affiliate of the American Indian Movement which recently forced White tenants to move off the Caughnawaga Iroquois Reserve in Quebec.

Chiefdoms were even richer, more densely populated, more centrally organized, and more militarily effective than tribes, thus making them quite capable of giving strong resistance to state conquest. Their warfare, for example, was usually well organized and they often kept captives as slaves. However, they were also more amenable to conquest and colonialism by peaceful means through co-option of their leadership by leaders from state societies. Chiefdom societies invariably had some internal social ranking, often including named and hierarchical social classes. The usual state-chiefdom relationship therefore was one of military restraint and negotiation with the chiefdom leadership on the part of the state society, leading to a slower, more peaceful achievement of the goals of the dominant state.

The British indiscriminately signed treaties with U.S. and Canadian Indian societies regardless of the evolutionary level of those societies, apparently on a model of their state-to-state relationships in the Old World. These were meaningless to band societies and usually meant something similar to a military and trade alliance to tribes, although the intent of the state was usually to acquire sovereignty permanently over Indian land. With chiefdoms, however, treaties began to resemble what they meant to the state societies, although it was still closer to a personal agreement between genuinely powerful people in the chiefdom's view than the impersonal legal contract of the state's view.

In the case of trade and the displacement of the southeast chiefdoms from their rich agricultural lands, the early French had a period of peace with the Natchez and then, because of some stupid mistakes, an outright bloody war of extinction. The Americans achieved the removal of such southeastern chiefdoms as Choctaws and Chickasaws and most of the Creeks and Cherokees by a relatively peaceful "relocation," into lands in Oklahoma that everyone considered to be fairly worthless. There was amazingly little resistance to that "Trail of Tears" relocation, considering the facts of what was done to the "Five Civilized Tribes" and the Creeks who fled from U.S. Army attacks into the Florida Everglades to become the Seminoles. State-chiefdom relationships in British Columbia were even more peaceful because there was less need to displace the Natives from their lands. Since the Indians there did not farm, they required little land, but instead lived in large villages and drew their food resources primarily from stream and coastal fishing.

Native states in the New World were even more easily conquered and administered by the Spaniards than were the chiefdoms—by stepping in to replace the Native elite and gradually replacing the diversity of the Native states with a fairly uniform European-style system of haciendas and other rule. To some degree, however, the Spaniards were also racially and culturally absorbed by the Natives. In the current states where aboriginal states were conquered, such as Chile, Peru, and Mexico, there are still very large populations of people who speak Native languages and have other dimensions of Indian culture as well, where the national culture itself has been profoundly influenced by the Native cultures, and where *indigenismo* is an important ideological force.

CULTURAL ECOLOGY

Since the cultural development of the Western Hemisphere is so historically separate from that of the Eastern Hemisphere, the diffusion of culture between the two can be largely ruled out as *the cause* of similar developments in similar environments in the hemispheres. Thus the role of ecology can be studied by comparing the cultural developments in similar environments in the different hemispheres. The greatest exception to this "separate development" rule is in diffusions across the Arctic or boreal zone, the area of communication between the hemispheres because of the Siberia-Alaska link. We think, for example, of circum-boreal traits such as shamanism, bear ceremonialism, the flat drum, the compound bow, sleds, snowshoes, braided hair worn in pigtails, tailored skin clothing, and semi-subterranean houses. In fishing technology, gill and seine nets, the harpoon, the leister, and ice fishing in a dark hut with a decoy and leister probably came to North America from Asia, but several other things were invented in North America: trawling with large nets between canoes, the A-shape dip net, and the herring rake.

Even in the Arctic the Inuit culture is distinctive in its development of such things as parkas, kayaks, and igloos, while not developing the reindeer herding of the Eastern Hemisphere arctic. The caribou would not be much more difficult to domesticate than the original stocks of their reindeer were, since the Western Hemisphere caribou are closely related to the Eastern Hemisphere reindeer. The divergence appears to be for a primarily "historical" or "diffusionist" reason in the Old World and an "ecological" reason in the New World. That is, reindeer hunters in the Eastern Hemisphere learned and adapted pastoral techniques from their southern neighbors in the Asian steppes, while the Inuit (and Aleuts) adapted to and filled out an almost unpopulated ecological niche by sea mammal hunting in the marine arctic.

The temperate environments were rich enough to support an even higher level of cultural evolution. In the Eastern Woodlands they became farmers and in the historic Plains they became horse pastoralists. The spread of Spanish horses in the Plains was so ecologically advantageous, and thus a rapid spread, that we have virtually no ethnographic data on the pre-horse Plains. In the East, archaeology is turning up some rich Mesolithic ("Archaic") cultures with local ecological specializations, such as shellfish gathering and fishing in the Ohio Valley and the Tennessee River Valley. The Old Copper Culture around Lake Superior could be considered as having a local adaptation in mining and making tools such as projectile points, knives, and axes from veins of copper in the area.

The Mesolithic Desert Culture of the west did persist so well among Western Shoshoni, Paiute, Washo and in Baja California that we do have ethnographic reports on that way of life with its subsistence based largely on gathering wild seeds. Archaeology helps us to understand how a local specialization of this desert culture in Mexico domesticated the plants they gathered. The northward diffusion of domestication then brought about the radical ecological shift toward Neolithic farming in the Eastern Woodlands and in the Pueblo cultures of the Southwest.

The development of the Northwest Coast cultures around fishing has been something of a mystery because it does not have a great time depth. It seems to have developed only in the last 3,000 years or so and began primarily by diffusion from fishing cultures in the Plateau of the Columbia River Valley and Fraser Canyon. This development, however, apparently included some late northern imports from Asia, such as slat armor, compound bow, and tambourine drum, by way of the Inuit.

There have been many ecologically parallel developments in the two hemispheres. The climatic, vegetational, and faunal changes during the European Paleolithic were similar to those in North America, and similar cultural changes occurred in the European Mesolithic. There is a persistence of hunting as in America's Eastern Woodlands, with local specialization around shellfish gathering and fishing, particularly in the northwest part of Europe, such as the

French river valleys. North Africa and the Near East seem to have been a general zone of a Mesolithic desert culture that subsisted in large part on wild seeds. Within that area, cultures in an upland zone (that runs from Israel to southern Turkey and then along northern Iraq and western Iran) domesticated wheat and barley, comparable to Mexico's role as the center of domestication within the American desert culture.

The rapid and radiating spread of Neolithic agriculture out of West Asia then followed a pattern that is parallel to that of the New World. In both hemispheres agriculture spread to ecological limits set by coldness and dryness. In both cases the initial Neolithic wave stimulated new centers of domestication at the fringe of its initial ecological limits, such as the Sudan in Africa, Southeast Asia, tropical America, and the Andean highlands of Peru. Both hemispheres developed irrigation systems, but this was much more important in the Old World; the early centers of civilization there are based in river valleys: Tigris-Euphrates, then Indus and Nile, and then the Yellow River in China. Moving north into Europe, the Danube Valley became the diffusion route of agriculture, but the rainfall was sufficient for a rich agriculture there without extensive irrigation. Thus the Danube functioned more simply as a communication route into Europe, comparable to the Mississippi River system in the spread of agriculture in North America, or the Orinoco and Amazon River systems in South America.

For purposes of teaching and rough analysis, we group the cultures of a continent into "culture areas," geographical regions of somewhat similar cultures. Another related concept that was invented was the "ethnographic present," the nature of a society at the time that it was first described in writing. The ideal behind this concept is to try to group and compare societies prior to their influence by literate cultures. The ethnographic present is unique for each society in terms of real time, but it is the same in terms of relative time. In terms of real time we have data from the sixteenth into the twentieth century, but we can put all the "ethnographic present" descriptions together. The result is a composite of descriptions that covers the continent, relative in terms of time and space but the best picture we can reconstruct of the Native world prior to European influences.

The most common culture area classification for the ethnographic present of the U.S. and Canada is Arctic, Subarctic, Northwest Coast, Plateau, Plains, Prairies, Northeast, Southeast, California, Great Basin, and Southwest. These areas can be analyzed as large ecological niches, each with a distinct pattern of topography, climate, flora, and fauna that have contributed to the determination of the cultures that developed within them. Cultural evolution, however, is to a large extent an increase in the capacity to use physical environments for human ends. Thus the ecology that has the greatest patterning on human life gradually shifts with the evolution of culture from the inorganic-organic or the so-called "natural" environment to the superorganic or cultural environment. The city is the end product of that process so far, an environment of exclusively human construction. If we tried to draw culture area lines today according to similarities in contemporary Indian cultures, the heaviest line would be between those Indians who live in cities and those who live in rural areas. That is, the great differences in the ecological settings of Indians today are not in terms of temperature, or precipitation, or altitude, but the environments invented by mankind.

THE PLEISTOCENE OVERKILL

One popular idea that Indians are now promoting is that their ancestors had nondestructive ecological relationships with their environments. This seems to be generally true because of their low population level and their lack of ecologically destructive modern manufacturing and machines. Certainly aboriginal ideologies involved a close relationship between man and his environment that we could learn from today. It does not necessarily mean that if Indian cultures had evolved into high-population, heavily industrial societies they would have avoided the same problems. Also, there is evidence that their ancestors contributed to the extinction of over one hundred species of mammals through wasteful techniques of hunting. They may also have radically changed many environments by using fire to drive or to kill game.

Thirty-three genera of mammals were extinct at the end of the Wisconsin glaciation in North America; 31 of them were the herbivorous type of animals that were hunted by man at the time (the other two were carnivores), and there are direct archaeological associations between most of these genera and hunting cultures (Martin and Wright 1967). Most of the extinctions seem to have occurred between 11,000 and 8,000 years ago. Mammoth, mastodon, giant ground sloth, saber-toothed tiger, and certain extinct types of buffalos, camels, and horses might still be around if it were not for the "Pleistocene overkill." In certain parts of the world large animals evolved away from the presence of man and thus never developed defenses against this dangerous predatory animal.Thus, human migrations into North America, Australia, New Zealand, Madagascar, and other previously isolated areas brought on many extinctions. It may even be that some awareness of these extinctions contributed to the aboriginal sensitivity to man's symbiotic relationships with animals.

The evidence from Upper Palaeolithic kill sites indicates that very early hunting people tended to concentrate their predation on a limited number of species, locally acquiring specific skills in killing them. This would put great pressure for extinction on these few species. The caribou and buffalo managed to survive through having an extremely wide range and large numbers. The North American buffalo had the largest animal herds of record, about 20 million in total.

Corresponding with the rapid extinction of one species after another, there came the Mesolithic broadening of kinds of food resources used, including more fish, shellfish, plant foods, and finally the sea mammal specialization of the Inuit as they spread along the shores of the Arctic. Totemism and other supernatural relationships between people and animals may have some conservation effects and may have arisen at this time as species were dying out. Totemism is strong in aboriginal North America and Australia, two areas where the greatest number of species became extinct after man entered the area in the Upper Palaeolithic. Totemism usually involves a taboo against eating the animals one has a totemic relationship with, thus distributing the predation across different species, since different social groups have different totems.

NEW WORLD INNOVATIONS

Certain traits were absent in the aboriginal New World. Technologically important absences were iron smelting, the use of the wheel (although a few toy dogs have been found with wheels), the plow, and the keystone arch in architecture (although the dome roof of the Eskimo igloo involves a similar principle of construction). Stringed musical instruments were generally absent, although certain Southeast Indians plucked the bow from a bow and arrow set and placed one end by the side of the player's mouth to use changes in the mouth's shape as a changing resonating chamber, the "mouth bow." Riddles, in the strict sense of a conundrum or puzzle with a specific answer, were absent. Also absent were alchemy, alphabetic writing, castration and eunuchism, coins, compass, divination from body organs of animals, falconry, gunpowder, tanning hides with plant tanning, and wind and water wheels.

The plants and animals of the Old World were generally missing, unless similar species were domesticated in the New World. Thus the New World had no barley, wheat, or millet, and did not plant the wild rice of the New World, although the gathering of the wild rice crop was fairly systematic among people like the Menomini and Chippewa-Ojibwa. Both areas raised cotton and the American long staple type, called Pima cotton (and "Egyptian" after being introduced there), is preferred. Gourds were raised very early in both areas, largely for containers, although they are edible. Sweet potatoes were probably domesticated in South America and may have actually been carried westward across the Pacific by men travelling a few hundred years before the coming of the Europeans.

The New World was very poor in domestic animals, lacking cattle, sheep, goats, swine, horses, asses, camels, and elephants. If advanced cultures had been in contact with buffalo and caribou they would probably have domesticated them. Neither of these would have been more difficult to domesticate than the ancestors of beef cattle or the reindeer.

The Old World domesticated many animals and few plants while the New World domesticated many plants and few animals. Domesticated dogs probably evolved in the New World around 11,000 years ago and eventually a wide variety of New World dogs were bred. The world's oldest known bones of domestic dogs came from Jaguar Cave in Idaho, dated 8,400 B.C. Some of the highly agricultural societies, such as the Aztecs, bred a special type of barkless, short-legged dog that could be easily penned and raised for eating, similar to the Chinese practice. The cameloids of South America, llama, alpaca, and vicuna, were domesticated. The llama is large enough to serve as a pack animal with about a forty- to fifty-pound pack, but is too small to carry an adult on its back. The alpaca and vicuna were raised for their wool and meat. The guinea pig, turkey, certain ducks, and honey bees were also raised on a limited scale in some agricultural societies.

Corn was raised in some 150 varieties from Chile to southeastern Canada and was the major agricultural staple, except in the wet tropics, where manioc (tapioca) was more important. Beans (common, lima, summer, tepary, jack, etc.) were next in importance, and provided protein in the diet. The third major crop was the squashes and pumpkins. These three, corn, beans, and squash, formed a sacred trilogy in many agricultural societies. Sacred fertility dances were performed in the East with women in costumes portraying corn, beans, and squash. Indian corn preparations we still use include such things as succotash (boiled corn and beans), hominy (corn with the covering of the grain removed by soaking in lye water), tortillas (thin fried corn bread made from hominy dough), popcorn, roast corn-on-the-cob, and tamale (baked corn cake with meat in the middle). The Pueblos still make a paper-thin tortilla called *piki*, often out of purple corn, for festive occasions. Chili beans, "Boston baked" beans, roast turkey, roast pumpkin, and clambakes are all Indian preparations.

Tobacco was raised in all agricultural societies and gathered wild in most of the rest, except the Arctic where not much of anything will grow. Thus, the use of tobacco, although its context tended to be much more religious than today, was one of the most widespread cultural traits of the New World. The Inuit first received tobacco by way of trade from the Russians.

Certain cultigens had limited, more ecologically bound distributions. White potatoes were used in the Andean highlands. They came into North America only in historic times by way of Europe, so there is at least some truth in calling them the "Irish potato." Sweet potatoes were a tropical American cultigen. Sunflowers were probably domesticated in the Mississippi Valley and diffused from there. There is a very long list of plants that came from the tropics, most of which are still limited to tropical or sub-tropical varieties: tomato, pineapple, guava, papaya, peanuts, chocolate, vanilla, chili, rubber, and so forth.

Collectively, the Indian societies north of Mexico used an estimated 1,112 different species of plants for food. Of these, 86 were cultivated: 58 imports from Mexico and the tropics; 19 indigenous to the Southwest; and 9 indigenous to the East. Then there are the semi-cultivated curiosities, such as the Kwakiutl tending beds of clover because they liked to nibble the protein-rich roots.

Certain ecological adaptations produced important new technologies. The Inuit are the first people to ever adapt to the marine Arctic and in so doing they gave the world the (1) *igloo*, a domed snow house; (2) *parka*, a tailored sealskin jacket with a hood; (3) *mukluk*, sealskin boots; (4) *kayak*, a small, skin-covered hunting canoe; (5) *umiak*, a large, skin-covered open "women's boat" for family travel; and (6) improved *harpoons*, sea mammal spears with a line to a detachable head. Although of Old World origin, the Inuit developed fine *sleds* with runners that were pulled by dog teams, for crossing ice and hard snow. The flat *toboggan* for crossing soft snow and at least certain types of *snowshoes* are from the sub-Arctic.

The significant developments of technology in the Plains were (1) the portable *tipi*, a conical tent of skins, bark, or mats covering a frame of poles; (2) the *travois*, a two-pole drag to carry the tipi and other goods on the back of a dog or horse; (3) the *parfleche*, a large rawhide envelope carrier; (4) the *bull boat*, a small skin-covered, cup-shaped boat to cross rivers; and (5) the *calumet*, a long ceremonial pipe, often made of a soapstone called "catlinite" after the artist George Catlin, who made paintings of Indians working a pipestone quarry.

One of the world's great basketry traditions was in the Desert Culture of western North America. They made crudely plaited bedding and wicker carrying baskets, as well as finely twined, twilled, and coiled baskets for winnowing, storage, and eating. Weak in animal products, they even wove plant materials into a wide variety of tools, including rope, water-tight canteens and cooking bowls (covered with pine pitch to make them watertight), and a woven reed raft. This tradition gave us the world's earliest sandals, woven from sagebrush bark, from Fort Rock Cave and dating back several thousand years ago. This tradition gave the world the first seed-grinding or milling tools, from Danger Cave, Utah and dating back to some ten thousand years ago. We still use the Aztec word *metate* for the basal part of the milling tool, and the Spanish word *mano* for the hand-held part of the tool.

Tropical America gave the world the hammock, the poncho, and rubber. The world's earliest mining and metal working tradition is the Old Copper Culture of the Great Lakes area, and the metallurgical skills of the high cultures of southern Mexico and the Andes in some ways surpassed those of the Old World at the same time. The high cultures produced many specialized inventions and did very high quality work in architecture, engineering (such as the great roads and bridges of the Inca), ceramics (such as Mimbres, Sikyatki, and Mochica), weaving, and so forth. All agricultural peoples in North America had pottery, and its use also spread somewhat beyond agriculture, particularly into the Plains. Beyond the pottery area, cooking was primarily by stone boiling, earth ovens, roasting, and smoking over fires.

In addition to the *igloo* and *tipi* already mentioned, many kinds of houses were invented that were appropriate to the various environments, degrees of sedentariness, and kinds of social structures across North America. Semi-subterranean *earth lodges*, with a log frame and an earth covering, were used at wintering sites from the Arctic to the Southwest. The sub-Arctic peoples used small, temporary bark-covered conical (*tipi*) and dome-shaped (*wigwam*) structures. A small, quickly built wigwam form called a *wickiup* was often used in the Great Basin. The Northwest Coast built permanent villages of huge *plank houses* with either single or double ridge-poles, as well as small mat-covered houses at their temporary fishing camps in the summer. The *longhouses* of the East were arched, bark-covered, and used by several families of the same lineage. Southeast houses were usually grass or palm-thatched, in both rectangular and circular forms. The Seminole *chickee* was open-sided and palm-thatched. The Southwest *pueblos* were compact villages of apartment-like structures that often went two or three stories high and were made of heavy timbers, stones, and mud or clay bricks. The Navajo *hogan* is a circular log house with a cribbed roof covered with earth.

The Mayan scholars are noted for their mathematics, calendrics, and astronomy. For example, they invented a place-numeral system of mathematics like the East Indian "Arabic" numeral system, rather than the crude "Roman" numeral system. The Mayans had a true zero, but the base unit in Mesoamerican mathematics was twenty instead of ten, it was a "vigesimal" rather than a "decimal" system, with symbols for 1s, 5s, 20s, and 400s. Their calendrics were also extremely accurate for the time, giving them a solar year calendar of 365¼ days.

There have been countless important influences on White cultures. The semaphore system using flags in each hand was invented by a U.S. Army officer, James Myer, after he watched a Comanche chief signal his warriors with his lance. In 1912 Clarence Birdseye was engaged in fur farming in Labrador when he observed that the local Inuit perfectly preserved their fish for indefinite periods of time by allowing them to freeze. Later he went on to initiate the frozen food industry. Benjamin Franklin apparently borrowed some of the organizational ideas that he used in his Albany Plan of Union of 1754 from the league of Iroquois, which in turn influenced the design of the U.S. Constitution. While Europeans had individualistic competitions in tournaments, they apparently learned team sports such as lacrosse from the Native Americans, and then went on to develop such games as hockey and football.

Chapter 4

A Chronology

A chronology is given here as an historical time frame for the events that will be discussed in later chapters. Sources used are primarily such historical syntheses as Crowe (1974), Leacock and Lurie (1971), Patterson (1972), and Washburn (1975). The emphasis is on historical events that significantly affected Indian cultures or are symbolic of the broader inter-cultural relationships that were occurring at the time.

PREHISTORY (ALL DATES APPROXIMATE)

26-24,000 B.P. (before present) Probable first major wave of migration across Beringia into the New World.

12-10,000 B.P. Second major wave of migration across Beringia into the New World.

11-9,000 B.P. Folsom, a hunting culture, flourished in the Plains.

11-8,000 B.P. Period of frequent mammalian extinctions.

10,400 B.P. First domestic dogs, Idaho. Bones at the Koster Site in Illinois show the spread of dogs by 7,100 B.P..

9,800 B.P. First milling stones, cordage, and basketry at Danger Cave, Utah indicate beginning of a plant-collecting Desert Culture.

9,000 B.P. First woven sandals at Fort Rock Cave, Oregon.

8,500 B.P. Domestication of plants began in Mexico.

6-3,000 B.P. Old Copper Culture in the Great Lakes made copper projectile points and knives.

5,500 B.P. Primitive domestic corn was used in Bat Cave, New Mexico.

5-4,000 B.P. Aleut-Inuit migration into the New World.

4,500 B.P. The Boylston Street Fishweir in Boston, a two-acre fish trap, indicates a rich marine-oriented culture in the area.

3,500 B.P. Major agricultural diffusions northward from Mexico into the Southwest and the Mississippi River Basin.

3,000 B.P. A marine-oriented Northwest Coast culture began to develop from an earlier Plateau river fishing base.
—Adena (or Burial Mound I), an agricultural tradition, flourished in the Ohio Valley and surrounding areas.

2,300 B.P. Hopewell (or Burial Mound II), an agricultural tradition, began to spread throughout the upper Mississippi River Basin and the Northeast Woodlands.

700 A.D. The Temple Mound Period began in the East with indications of towns, such as Cahokia, and chiefdom societies in the central Mississippi Valley.
—Pueblo I of the agricultural Anasazi tradition began in Arizona, New Mexico, Utah, and Colorado. The Anasazi reached its Classic Period and maximum area between 11-1300 A.D.

EUROPEAN CONTACTS

1000-1024 A.D. Vikings explored and settled in Greenland, Newfoundland, and Labrador.

1497-8 *John Cabot*, a Venetian navigator employed by the English, explored the Maritimes and contacted the Micmac.

1500-1 The Portuguese *Gaspar Corte-Real* captured 57 Indians in Labrador to be sold as slaves.

1504 Breton fishermen began working the Grand Banks of Newfoundland.

1528 The Karankawa of Texas cared for survivors of a Spanish shipwreck.

1534-5 *Jacques Cartier* contacted Micmac in New Brunswick and found Iroquois in summer fishing camps along the St. Lawrence River. He found Iroquois living in a palisaded village at Hochelaga (Montreal), where later explorers found Algonquins. He wintered at Stadaconna (Quebec City) where, after the death of 25 of his men from scurvy, the Indians saved the rest of his crew with a vitamin-C tea made from evergreen tree needles.

1539-42 *Francisco de Coronado* invaded the Zuni, Hopi, Acoma, and other Pueblo societies.

1541 Choctaws resisted *Fernando de Soto*'s invasion.

—*Cartier* sent two French youths to study under Iroquois teachers, to learn their language and culture. *Champlain* later repeated the practice of sending young men to learn to be interpreters and learn how to live in the forest as *coureurs-de-bois*.

1565 The Spanish destroyed an Indian village in Florida and established St. Augustine.

1570 League of the Iroquois was formed. Similar political confederacies or alliances were later formed by Blackfoot, Huron, Ojibwa, Delaware, Dakota, Powhatan, Creek, Caddo, and Pueblos.

1584-7 *Walter Raleigh*'s two expeditions to North Carolina, *Richard Grenville*'s to Virgina, and *John White*'s to North Carolina brought in English settlers.

1589 About 400 Spaniards settled in the Puebloan Southwest. In 1599 Acoma was conquered by the forces of *Juan de Onate*, and hundreds of Indians were killed in the battle. Missions were established and by 1630 they claimed to have built 90 chapels and baptized 60,000 Indians.

1600s: WHITES SETTLED IN THE EAST AND SOUTHWEST

1605 Port Royal established by the French to trade furs with the Micmac in Acadia. In 1606 Marc Lescarbot started the first school in Canada, teaching the Micmac.

1607 The English settled Jamestown.

1609 *Samuel de Champlain* established a trading post at Quebec and began the French opposition to the Iroquois. In the same year, the French killed some Mohawks. In 1615 they attacked Oneida and Onondaga villages.

—The Spanish settled Santa Fe. Horses apparently spread into the Plains from here. They diffused south to the Texas gulf coast by 1690, north to Wyoming by 1700, and to the Canadian Prairies by 1730. Horses were also introduced into New France and New England in the early 17th century. The Iroquois were raising them prior to 1736, but they were never widely used in the East.

1609-10 *Henry Hudson* explored the Hudson River and then Hudson's Bay. He exchanged manufactured goods for furs in both areas, which stimulated later trade.

1613 The first treaty was made between the Iroquois and Dutch traders near Albany, New York.

1614 *John Rolfe* married *Pocahontas*.

1620 The Plymouth Colony established in Massachusetts. The next year a treaty was made between *Massasoit* (chief of the Wampanoags) and the Pilgrims that was kept by both sides for over fifty years.

1622 The Powhatan attacked Jamestown, Virginia, killing 347 of the 1,240 population.

1626 The Shinnecock negotiated the "$24 sale" treaty with the Dutch in Manhattan Island.

1632-3 The Hopi and Zuni expelled the Christian missionaries.

1633 Massachusetts Colony General Court began providing land allotments to Indians.

1637 The Dutch and English attacked a Pequot village, killing about 500 and selling the rest into slavery.

1638-40 Smallpox epidemic killed several thousand Hurons.

1641 The Dutch started the practice of paying bounties for Indian scalps.

1642 The Shinnecock were massacred by the New York Dutch, killing 120 men, women, and children in a night attack.

1645 Sillery became the first Christianized community of Natives under French control. Attempts had been made by the Jesuits since 1637 to establish them on the model of Mexican and Paraguayan *reducciones*. Several of these mission "reserves" struggled to convert, settle, and educate Indians to French ways.

1649 With British guns and superior organization, the Iroquois of Upper New York, composed of over 1,000 warriors, defeated the Hurons of Ontario in a war over trapping lands and control of the fur trade. The Hurons had largely depleted the beaver in their territory by 1635 and the Iroquois had done the same in their territory by 1641. The French outpost, St. Marie-Among-the-Hurons, was destroyed and the Hurons retreated to Christian Island and later to Quebec City, where about 1,200 live today in the suburb of Loretteville. Some Hurons also escaped by migrating into the U.S., where they are called Wyandots.

1656 Indian reservations were established in Virginia.

1660 The first Christian Indian church in New England was founded in Natick, Massachusetts. The next year a 130-page abridgement and translation of the Bible was published in the Massachusetts Indian language. In 1670 *Hiacoomes*, a Massachusetts, was ordained as a Christian missionary and began preaching at Martha's Vineyard, Massachusetts.

1661 Pequot attacked the English and their allies, the Naraganset and the Mohegan.

—Franciscan priests raided the Pueblo churches (*kivas*) and destroyed religious articles. This kind of religious repression, combined with whippings, imprisonment, and hangings for practicing the traditional religions, eventually led to a Pueblo Revolt.

1668 Christian Iroquois allied with the French settled in mission villages, eventually to Caughnawaga near Montreal in 1680. In the next century (about 1755), a group of Mohawks from Caughnawaga moved up the St. Lawrence to Akwesasne or St. Regis. Refugee Iroquois who had fought for the British also came to St. Regis after the Revolutionary War but the reserve was later divided, with the creation of the international boundary and by provincial boundaries. Thus parts of this reserve are in New York, Ontario, and Quebec. Another group from this migration

went all the way to the Gibson Reserve on Georgian Bay in Ontario.
1670 Hudson's Bay Company was established and granted its charter.
1675-6 *King Philip*'s War.
1680 Pueblo Revolt.
1686 The Delaware made a long-lasting treaty with *William Penn.*
1688 The Miami saved the French garrison at Niagara by providing them with food during an epidemic.
1688-9 Iroquois attacked the French in Montreal and Lachine.
1691 The College of William and Mary was chartered in Virginia, in part as a school for Indians.
1692-3 Spanish reconquered the Rio Grande Pueblos. A new rebellion in 1694 was defeated by 1696.
—Virginia Whites who married Indians were banished.
1696 Onondaga and Oneida lost a major battle to the French.

1700s: WHITES PUSHED BEYOND THE APPALACHIAN MOUNTAINS

1700 The Ottawa made a long-lasting treaty with the French in Montreal.
1703 Bounties on Indian scalps were set in Massachusetts at $60 each.
1703-4 The Apalachee of Florida were killed or captured and sold into slavery, becoming extinct as a society.
1706 The Hopi and Navajo defeated Spanish slave raiders.
1706-12 Slave raids against the Yamasee.
1711-12 Tuscarora War on the southern frontier. The survivors moved to the north and joined the League of the Iroquois in 1722.
1713 Treaty of Utrecht divided much of North America between England and France. France got the interior of the continent with the drainages of the St. Lawrence, the Great Lakes, and the Mississippi River. England got essentially the East Coast and the Hudson's Bay area.
1714-15 *Slave Woman*, a Chipewyan, escaped from her Cree captors, went to York Factory at the mouth of the Nelson River on Hudson Bay to complain to the post governor about the Cree, and then went to arrange the peace between the Cree and the Chipewyan. She alone is credited with resolving the Cree-Chipewyan disagreements in the face of such difficulties as eight days of starvation and the killing of some Chipewyan by Cree. Today the Cree of the Northwest Territories, although not in the Dene linguistic family, are included in the Dene Declaration and its political organization.
1720 The first permanent Indian school was created in Williamsburg, Virginia.
1721 Permanent settlement by the Danish in Greenland.
1722 The Abnaki allied with the French were defeated by the English. English attacks since the 1670s had driven the Abnaki and later the Penobscot into an alliance with the French.

1729 The French warred against the Natchez.

1738 Smallpox epidemic in South Carolina and Georgia.

1741 Russians began to explore and settle in Alaska, although they did not explore the interior of Alaska until 1833.

1751 The Pima rebelled against the Spanish.

1754 The Albany Congress of English Colonies met to develop a united colonial policy toward Indians. In this indirect way Indians stimulated the unity among the colonies that led to their amalgamation into the U.S.A.

1756-63 "The French and Indian Wars" with the British. *Pontiac*'s forces joined the French and took Detroit and several English forts in the Great Lakes, but the French rule still ended in Canada and French holdings in Canada were ceded to Britain. The British commander, *Jeffrey Amherst*, became an arch-villain to Indians because of his policy of killing all prisoners and particularly his recommendations to distribute smallpox-infested blankets freely to Indians.

1758 The Lenape and Unami were assigned a reservation in New Jersey until it was sold in about 1801.

1763 The Royal Proclamation set official British policy toward the Indians, such as the need for treaties, the control of trade, and the necessity for the Appalachian watershed to separate the European-settled country from Indian country. Except that the cession of land legally could be only to the crown or federal government, these provisions were largely ignored as trade and White migration continued to be wide open. In 1768 the British changed a significant element in this by returning the control of Indian affairs to the North American colonies.

1767 Secularization of the missions in New Mexico ended that Spanish mission program.

1769 Spaniards began to colonize California, especially in the south and along the coasts.

1771 The Moravian Mission began to establish stations with trading posts to the Inuit along the Labrador coast.

1775-83 American Revolution.

1778 *James Cook* came to Nootka Sound, some of his men gathered sea-otter pelts, and these became items of great demand in China. This stimulated a fur trade along the British Columbia coast, until the sea-otter was depleted by about 1830.

—*Peter Pond* established a trading post south of Lake Athabasca. It was abandoned the next year, reestablished in 1783, and then replaced by Fort Chipewyan in 1788.

—The first *U.S.* treaty was made with the Delaware, promising them statehood and a seat in Congress.

1780s and 1790s Eastern Indians were under widespread military attack and many groups migrated westward, often coming in conflict with other Indian groups.

1781 First British treaty in Canada ceded the island of Michilimakinak between Lakes Huron and Michigan.

1782 *L.V. Sabatannen*, a Huron, became the first Canadian Indian to receive a college degree, at Dartmouth College, New Hampshire.

1781-4 Smallpox epidemics among the Plains Cree and Chipewyan.

1782 Massacre of the Christian Delaware of Gnanenhutten, Ohio. Indian-hating Whites, under *Col. David Williamson*, killed 35 men, 27 women, and 34 children who were caught harvesting agricultural crops.

1783 Cree warred against the Beaver Indians over the fur trade.

1784 The Iroquois who sided with the British in the Revolutionary War were granted nearly 70,000 acres in Canada.

—Thomas Jefferson carried out the first field archaeology in the New World, excavating a mound in Virginia.

1787 The U.S. Congress developed an explicit "divide and conquer" strategy in response to signs of an opposing confederation of Iroquois, Wyandot, Delaware, Chippewa, and Ottawa tribes. The governor of the Northwest Territories was ordered "to defeat all confederations and combinations among the tribes."

1791 Wea villages were destroyed by U.S. troops.

—*Little Turtle*'s Miami and other forces defeated those of the U.S. Northwest Territory on the Wabash River, killing 630.

1793 Muncey Delawares were driven out of Ohio and settled in Ontario on the Thames River.

1794 The Jay Treaty gave border Indians the right to freely cross the U.S.-Canada border.

1799 *Handsome Lake* began to preach.

1800-1849: EASTERN REMOVAL AND WESTERN EXPLORATION

1802 The Osage moved from Missouri to Oklahoma.

1804-5 Lewis and Clark expedition to explore the Louisiana Purchase.

1808 *The Indian Princess*, an operatic melodrama, was performed in Philadelphia.

1811 *Tecumseh*'s brother, *Tenskwatawa*, led the forces that were defeated by the Americans at the Battle of Tippecanoe.

1812 War of 1812 and *Tecumseh*'s Confederacy with the British against the Americans.

1812-14 Creek War.

1821 *Sequoyah*'s writing system was adopted by the Cherokee.

—Secularization of the California missions followed the Mexican Revolution and led to widespread starvation for Indians.

—North West Company was incorporated into the Hudson's Bay Company. This monopoly brought some peace to the conflicts between Indian groups based on different alliances, but it also reduced the number of posts, brought down the prices paid for furs, and caused the northern Indian people to become more dependent, settling into small territories that were centered on a trading post.

1822-4 U.S. Bureau of Indian Affairs was established after a variety of bureaucratic forms were attempted that involved Congressional committees, the War Department, and an Office of Indian Trade.

1828 *The Cherokee Phoenix* was published in Cherokee until 1835, when it was forcibly closed down by the state militia under order of the Governor of Georgia.

1829 *Shanadithit*, the last Beothuk, died in Newfoundland.
—The Delaware were forced to go to Oklahoma.

1830 The Indian Removal Act was passed to move Eastern Indians west of the Mississippi River, especially to Oklahoma. White settlement was also supposed to be restricted in the west. In effect, the Royal Proclamation line of the Appalachians was moved 1,000 miles west to the Mississippi and reestablished.

1830-6 *George Catlin* made a pictorial record of life in the Plains.

1831 Choctaw removed to Oklahoma.

1832 Black Hawk War.
—U.S. state laws declared invalid on tribal lands.

1834 U.S. Indian Trade and Intercourse Act forbade the sale of firearms and alcoholic beverages to the Indians.
—Bounties on Apache scalps were set at $100 each.

1835-42 Seminole War.

1836 Creek forced march to Oklahoma in which thousands died.
—Smallpox epidemic among the Assiniboin in Canada killed about 4,000.

1837 Smallpox epidemic among the Mandan, Hidatsa, Arikara, Blackfoot, Sioux, and Pawnee killed about 14,000 people.

1838 About 18,000 Cherokee began a forced march to Oklahoma called "The Trail of Tears," and about 25% died.

1840 *James Evans*, a Methodist missionary at Norway House, Manitoba, developed a syllabic alphabet for Cree.

1841 The Potawatomi were removed by military force from Indiana and settled in Ontario on Walpole Island.

1843 The Russian Orthodox Church established the first mission school to the Inuit in Nushagak, Alaska.

1845-8 *Paul Kane*, after meeting Catlin in London, recorded Native life in drawings and paintings from Ontario to British Columbia and Washington.

1846 49th parallel set as western boundary of U.S. and Canada.

1848 U.S. acquired the Southwest and California from Mexico.

1849 California gold rush displaced Indians there. Massacres were carried out on the Wintu of Yosemite in 1850; the Indians of Weaverville, California in 1852; and the Indians of Eureka, California in 1860.
—An Oneida band entered Canada and settled on the Thames River in Ontario.

1850-1899: WESTERN WARS

1852 Fort Rae established where the Dogribs brought in 8-10,000 caribou each year. The meat was dried for trail provisions for the York boat crews, who transported goods in and out of the North in the summer.

1853-57 52 treaties ceded 157 million acres to the U.S.

1854 Near the Smoky Hill River in Kansas, a loose alliance of about 1,500 Kiowa, Kiowa Apache, Comanche, Arapaho, Osage, and Crow set out to exterminate a party of 80 displaced "Eastern" Indians (Sauk, Fox, and Potawatomi), who had recently come into the Plains to hunt buffalo. The Eastern Indians were surrounded and attacked but, due to their superior ability with rifles, they drove off their attackers, killing twenty, wounding about one hundred, and losing only six of their own men.

1859 First Arizona reservations created.

1860 Hudson's Bay Company discontinued the trading of "spirits."

1861 First Inuit language newspaper in Greenland.

1861-65 U.S. Civil War. Indians fought on both sides. Those in Oklahoma fought primarily for the Confederate side. *Stand Watie*, a Cherokee, became a Confederate Brigadier General and commanded two Cherokee regiments in the Southwest. Many Creek and Seminole fought against White Confederate forces, but Indians generally refused to fight against other Indians. However, an allied force of Shawnee, Creek, and Delaware killed over one hundred Tonkawa on the Wichita Reservation in 1862, apparently because of the Tonkawa allegiance to the South.

1860s and 1870s *Ipilkvik* and his wife *Tukkolerktuk* trained, guided, and repeatedly saved the lives of a generation of Arctic explorers.

1862 Many Indian lands opened up to Whites through the U.S. Homestead Act.

—Sioux refugees entered Manitoba following a battle in Minnesota.

1863-4 Most of the Navajo and Apache were defeated by the scorched-earth strategy of the U.S. forces under *Kit Carson*'s commission. They took the "Long Walk" to concentration camps, the 9,000 Navajo to Fort Sumner, New Mexico. The Navajo were allowed to return to Arizona in 1868. Today the Navajo are the largest tribe in the U.S., with a population of about 125,000.

1866 A force of several hundred Indian Scouts was established within the U.S. Cavalry as paid mercenaries for wars against Indians. Their last military campaign was as an Apache Scout detachment to the 11th Cavalry in a battle against forces of the Mexican Revolutionary *Pancho Villa* in 1916.

1867 U.S. bought Alaska from Russia and many Christian missions were established in Native communities over the next twenty years.

—Canadian Confederation. British North American Act, especially in its amendments in the next few years, established Native policies in Canada: treaties, land use, road maintenance, prohibition of liquor, etc.

1868 U.S. Indians were explicitly denied the right to vote, when it was granted to Blacks in the "Emancipation Amendment."

1870 U.S. policy was developed to eliminate Native religions. Also first federal funds were specifically granted for Indian education and the practice of giving reservation Indians food and clothing rations was started.

—*Riel* led the approximately 9,000 Métis in a provisional Manitoba government. The first "Riel Rebellion."

—Grand General Indian Council of Ontario and Quebec formed. This lasted until 1919.

1870s and 1880s Massive destruction of millions of buffalo, brought them close to extinction. The last great herd was exterminated in 1885.

1871 U.S. formally ended treaty making with the Indians, but they were still occasionally made until 1889. This was brought about when the House of Representatives refused to provide funds called for in eleven treaties made in 1867-8 with Sioux, Cheyenne, Arapaho, Crow, and Assiniboin. Even the 1971 Alaskan Settlement was basically a treaty, exactly one hundred years later.

—Spirit dancing was outlawed in Washington territory.

1872-3 Modoc War.

1873 North West Mounted Police established. Northwest Council was established at Fort Garry (Winnipeg), and their first act was to prohibit the sale of alcoholic beverages in the Northwest Territories. The ban, however, was not applied to Whites.

1874 Red River War in Manitoba.

1875-6 U.S. developed the policy that off-reservation Indians are to be considered as hostile and returned to their reservations.

—The Comanche ended their resistance in Texas, but war continued with the Sioux and Apache.

1876 First Canadian Indian Act. This was largely a consolidation of previous laws.

—Battle of the Little Big Horn, "*Custer*'s Last Stand," in which over two hundred U.S. cavalrymen were killed. Sioux refugees settled in southern Manitoba.

1877 The Nez Perce resistance under *Chief Joseph.*

1878-9 Cheyenne "broke out" of Oklahoma and returned to their homeland, but were hunted down by the U.S. Army and most were imprisoned. A few made it to Montana, where they were eventually given a reservation.

1879 National Indian Association formed, the first modern association not based on tribal affinity.

1880 Indian police forces formed by BIA for on-reservation control. By 1884 they had been established on 48 of the 60 U.S. agencies.

1881 The Sun Dance was banned in the U.S. Medicine men were arrested.

—*John Slocum* founded the Indian Shaker religion in the Puget Sound area.

1882 Hopi reservation was established, "to protect them from the railroads and the Mormons."

—Indian Rights Association founded.

—*Piapot*'s band camped on the right-of-way of the Canadian Pacific Railway as a demonstration of protest.

1883 Indian-operated courts were established on U.S. Indian reservations.

1884 Canada outlawed certain Indian cultural and religious practices, including the potlatch, until 1951. In fact, the potlatches continued under some harassment.

—Kiowa and Comanche developed the modern rites of peyotism at about this time.

—*Helen Hunt Jackson* published *A Century of Dishonor* on Indian mistreatment.

1886 Final surrender of *Geronimo*'s band of Chiricahua Apaches.

1887 U.S. General Allotment Act was passed to allow the division of Indian lands to individuals and the sale of "surplus" Indian lands to Whites. Indian lands controlled in common by tribes dropped from 138 million acres in 1887 to 39 million in 1968.

1889 *Wovoka* began the Ghost Dance in Nevada.

—Whites were allowed to settle in Oklahoma.

1890 Massacre of Ghost Dancers at Wounded Knee in South Dakota.

1895 *Anton Dvorak* used Omaha music in *The New World Symphony*.

1896 BIA carried out the policy of forcefully cutting the long hair of Indian men.

1896-1927 *Edward Curtis* photographed the western Indians. About 1,500 of his photographs were published in twenty volumes.

1898 Yukon gold rush brought thousands of Whites into the North. Yukon Territory was established as separate from the Northwest Territories. In Dawson City only one pool hall was open to the Indians; one dance hall had a white painted line on the floor to keep the Indians on one side; and Indians had to travel below decks on the steamboats. However, this gold rush had a much more benign impact on the Indians than did the one in California. Indians sold meat, fish, and firewood, or worked as packers and deckhands, and in time as carpenters, cooks, river pilots, and mechanics. Three Tagish Indians (*Kate, Skookum Jim,* and *Tagish Charlie*), and Kate's White husband became millionaires when they found the main seam of gold and staked claims to what became known as Bonanza Creek off the Klondike River.

1900-1949: BUREAUCRACY AND ETHNIC CONSOLIDATION

1907 *Charles Curtis*, a Kaw from Kansas, was elected to the U.S. Senate. In 1928 he became the U.S. Vice President. Mexico had two full-blooded Indian presidents, *Benito Juarez*, a Zapotec, and *Lazaro Cardenas*, a Tarascan, as well as several others with significant Indian ancestry.

—All-American Indian Days founded in Sheridan, Wyoming.

—*Tom Longboat* (Onondaga) won the Boston Marathon in record time.

1910 BIA re-enforced the 1881 ban on the Sun Dance, until 1934.

1912 Osage of Oklahoma sold millions of dollars of oil leases.

—The Alaska Native Brotherhood was formed by the Tlingit and Tsimshian at Sikta. This was formed on the model of an earlier White fraternal organization, the Arctic Brotherhood, and in turn became one model for the Canadian provincial Indian Brotherhoods.

—*James Thorpe* (Sauk-Fox), *Louis Tewanima (Hopi)*, and *Joseph Keeper* (Cree) competed in the Stockholm Olympics.

—The Nishga Land Claim Petition was first presented to Ottawa.

1916 *Ishi*, the last Yana Indian, died in San Francisco.

1916-18 *Crescencio Martinez* of San Ildefonso started the modern school of Southwestern painting.

1917-18 More than 8,000 U.S. Indians served in World War I.

1921 Hudson's Bay Company started a herd of Norway reindeer with Lapp herders on Baffin Island. This experiment failed but was repeated on a larger scale in 1931-35, when 2,370 animals were driven over 2,000 miles from Alaska to the Mackenzie Delta, where there is still a small herd.

—An Indian treaty was made in the Northwest Territories after oil was discovered there at Norman Wells in 1920.

1922 Inter-Tribal Indian Ceremonials began in Gallup, New Mexico. This annual exposition of dancing, sports, and arts contributed to making Gallup the "Indian Capital of the World."

—*Robert Flaherty*'s *Nanook of the North* was released, the first feature-length documentary motion picture.

—The All-Pueblo Council was formed at Santo Domingo, originally to remove 3,000 non-Pueblo families living on Pueblo land.

1923 Last Canadian Indian Treaty, in southern Ontario to settle Ojibwa claims.

1924 U.S. Indians were given citizenship because of their valiant role in World War I, although they were not subject to the military draft at the time. The right to vote in state elections was withheld in most states where there were significant numbers of Indians until 1938. Indians were excluded from state elections until 1948 in Arizona and New Mexico, 1954 in Maine, and 1960 in Utah. Western states also outlawed inter-racial marriage between Whites and Indians.

1926 National Council of American Indians was formed in the U.S. and organized the Indian vote.

—All Arctic Islands were established as a game preserve for Inuit in Canada.

1927 Canada outlawed Indian political fund raising for the development of claims in response to the Nishga Land Petition.

1931 The Native Brotherhood of British Columbia was formed.

1934 U.S. Indian Reorganization Act stopped the individual allotment system, promoted reservation industries, and allowed tribes more self-government.

1939 *Kateri Tekawitha* (1656-1680), "the Lily of the Mohawks," was beatified by Pope Pius XII. She had become the the first Indian nun in 1679.

1941 The Alaskan Highway was built through British Columbia and the Yukon to Alaska.

1941-45 More than 25,000 U.S. Indians served in World War II.

1944 The National Congress of American Indians was founded in Denver to expand the reforms of the 1930s. It became an important forum for the analysis of Native problems, the education of Native leaders, and the unification of a common political front.

—*William Stigler*, a Choctaw from Tallequah, Oklahoma was elected to U.S. Congress.

1946 U.S. Indian Claims Commission was established to compensate for lost lands. By the final date for filing in 1951, 370 cases were filed, involving 611 claims.

1950-PRESENT: MODERN STRUGGLES

1950 The pro-Indian film *Broken Arrow* became a commercial success.

1951 New Canadian Indian Act. The closest to this in the U.S. is the *Handbook of Federal Indian Law*, first compiled in 1940 and involving an analysis of about 4,000 statutes.

—Arizona State University began developing a special Indian education program.

—Urban employment assistance program started for U.S. Indians.

1953 U.S. stopped the prohibition of liquor to Indians.

—Termination and urban relocation became the official policy in the U.S. Indians in California, Florida, New York, and Texas were to be terminated, as well as Flathead, Klamath, Menomini, Potawatomi, and Chippewa. Between 1954 and 1960, 61 Native social units were terminated from federal trusteeship and jurisdiction.

—The annual Miss Indian American contest was started at the All American Indian Days in Sheridan, Wyoming.

1955 Beginning of the North American Radar Network. The Distant Early Warning Line and the Mid-Canada Line scattered small military bases across the Arctic and sub-Arctic, influencing many communities of northern Natives.

1957 Reservation industries program started in the U.S. Hundreds of enterprises were established over the years: electronics, missile parts, carpets, motels, etc.

1958 *James Gladstone*, a Blood, was appointed to the Canadian Senate.

—Building of a museum by Indians at Hazelton, B.C. started the 'Ksan program.

1959 First commercial sale of Inuit block prints.
—First urban Indian center in Canada established in Winnipeg.

1960 Canadian "status" Indians given citizenship under the Bill of Rights.
—The Indian-Eskimo Association of Canada formed.

1961 The American Indian Chicago Conference was held with 90 tribal groups sending 460 representatives. In reaction to the traditional approaches, the activist National Indian Youth Council was formed at the Conference and had its first meeting later in Gallup, New Mexico.
—The U.S. Employment Assistance Program shifted emphasis to vocational training, thus sending large numbers of reservation Indians for vocational training in the cities.

1963 The Institute of American Indian Arts was started in Santa Fe.

1964 A fish-in in Washington was the first large-scale, intertribal, modern expression of civil disobedience. The fishing rights to the Quinault, Lummi, Nisqually, Puyallup, and other Washington tribes were upheld in the U.S. District Court finally in 1975.

1965 *Abraham Okpik* became the first Inuit appointed to the Council of the Northwest Territories.

1966 Rough Rock Demonstration School was started by the Navajo.

1967 The Supreme Court of Canada decided that the prohibition of drinking for *Joseph Drybones*, a Dogrib, and by extension all other Natives, was unlawful under the Canadian Bill of Rights.

1968 American Indian Movement was started in Minneapolis.
—National Indian Brotherhood of Canada was formed by the status Indians after years of failing attempts to create a national organization that combined status and non-status Indians.
—*Len Marchand* (Kamloops-Cariboo riding) became the first Indian to be elected to the Canadian House of Commons.
—*Chief Robert Smallboy* led 143 Indians from the Hobbema Reserve in Alberta back into the Rocky Mountain wilderness east of Jasper to return to the traditional way of life. In 1977 the community size was about 75 and had a school, health clinic, and log cabins.
—*Kahn-Tineta Horn* led a blockade of the Cornwall Bridge to force customs officials to recognize that Indians do not have to pay customs duties. They also protested the government's failure to enforce a 1933 agreement by which the Indian's sale of land for the bridge included the perpetual right to cross the bridge without the payment of tolls.

1969 *Louis R. Bruce* (Mohawk-Dakota) became the third Indian to be the U.S. Commissioner of Indian Affairs. *General Ely S. Parker* (Seneca) held the post historically (1869-71), and *Robert L. Bennett* (Oneida) immediately preceded Bruce. All three were raised in Iroquois communities.
—University of Minnesota started its Department of American Indian Studies, Trent University in Ontario started its formal degree program in Native Studies, and Navajo Community College began full operation.
—*N. Scott Momaday*, a Kiowa, won the Pulitzer Prize for *House Made of Dawn*.

—Two protest books by Indians became best sellers: *Custer Died for Your Sins* in the U.S. and *The Unjust Society* in Canada.
—Alcatraz Island in San Francisco Bay was occupied.

1970 First Convocation of American Indian Scholars, at Princeton University.
—The first Indian Ecumenical Conference was held on the Crow Reservation in Montana. Subsequent conferences have been held on the Stoney Reserve in Alberta.
—Blue Lake, with 48,000 acres, was returned to Taos Pueblo.
—Inuit Tapirisat of Canada formed.

1971 Four new Indian community colleges started up: Lawrence, Kansas; Pine Ridge and Rosebud Reservations in South Dakota; and Blackfoot Reserve in Alberta.

1971 —A Chipewyan group from Churchill, Manitoba on James Bay tried to reject the urban way of life and return to Tadoule Lake to live.
—The Alaska Native Claims Settlement Act was signed.

1972 Muck-a-Muck House, the first Indian foods restaurant in Canada, was started by Haida in Vancouver. There was an earlier Cherokee restaurant in Oklahoma. Mexican tortillas and beans are also widely served foods.
—Mount Adams, comprising 21,000 acres of land, was returned to the Yakima of Washington.
—Trail of Broken Treaties caravan protested in Washington, D.C. and occupied BIA headquarters the weekend before the U.S. presidential elections.
—Ban on commercial fishing because of mercury pollution in the English and Wabigoon Rivers in northern Ontario. The Reed Paper Company in Dryden had dumped about 20,000 pounds of mercury into the river system between 1962 and 1970. This became a residual poison in the fish, even though no additional mercury was introduced. By 1973 it was realized that the subsistence fishing of local Indians also had to be stopped.

1973 Wounded Knee, South Dakota was occupied.
—*Morris Thompson*, an Athabascan, was appointed U.S. Commissioner of Indian Affairs.
—The first Arctic Peoples Conference was held in Copenhagen, Denmark.

1974 Anicinabe Park in Kenora, Ontario was occupied.
—A Native caravan that started in Vancouver culminated in a protest at the opening of Parliament in Ottawa.
—U.S. Indian Land Claims Commission in March had dismissed 182 cases and completed 237 with judgments of $486 million. The average claim has taken 15 years to process.

1975 185,000 acres of land on the rim of the Grand Canyon was returned to the Havasupai.
—The Dene Declaration was made at the second General Assembly of the Indian Brotherhood of the N.W.T. and the Métis Association in Port

Simpson, N.W.T.

—The James Bay Agreement was signed.

—A Federation of Survival Schools and Indian-Oriented Alternate Schools was formed. This movement for Native-operated elementary schools borrows from earlier developments, but is more urban based. They began in Minneapolis in 1971 and in 1975 there were five schools in Minnesota; one in Rapid City, South Dakota; one in Denver, Colorado, and three more planned, including ones for Manitoba and Wisconsin.

—Indian prisoners in Lincoln, Nebraska won a U.S. District Court decision to "permit the wearing of traditional Indian hairstyles, allow access to Indian medicine men and spiritual leaders, and pay clergy expenses just as with other religious faiths." The prison was also ordered to initiate "accredited courses in Indian studies."

—Menomini tribal land was returned to federal trusteeship.

—The United Bank of Alaska in Juneau was established as a Native-owned and operated bank. There is also an American Indian National Bank in Washington, D.C. that was established in 1973.

1975-76 There was an inquiry, held across Canada, into the proposed Mackenzie Delta natural gas pipeline.

1976 Coal gasification plants to generate electricity proposed for the eastern side of the Navajo Reservation near Burnham, New Mexico. Navajo coal in five scattered plants already produce power for Phoenix, Tucson, Albuquerque, and Los Angeles. Coal is also strip-mined on the Blackfoot Reserve in Alberta.

1977 The U.S. government backed large Penobscot and Passamaquoddy land claims in Maine.

—American Indian Policy Review Commission recommended that tribal governments have full legal powers to levy taxes, try all local offenders (including non-Indians) in tribal courts, control all fishing and hunting on reservations, etc.

Chapter 5

The Heritage of Heroes

The discipline of history includes both the scientific calculations of cultural processes and the human interests of a culture's legendary heritage. It has a place in both the social sciences and the humanities. Several chapters illustrate history as a social science by referring to causative elements in an historical analysis. That is, the data is presented according to a theoretical model which can be abstracted out, compared with other similar models, and used in the construction of general theories of cultural dynamics.

Legendary histories also include some assumptions of cause and effect, but they are implicit, untested, and not scientific. Most commonly, these theories assume simply that the heroic people of the heritage caused the history to occur the way it did. History in this sense is presented as great people causing great events. Legendary histories are simplified into a story form that the listener or reader can enjoy through his own psychological projection and identification. Thus biographies are a basic form of history. This kind of humanities history is an important element in a culture's ideology. It is essential to the common identity of an ethnic group.

To present something of the Native heritage of heroes, I give short biographies of twenty-five people in both the U.S. and Canada, each in their historical sequence. The Canadian list is the official Canadian Indian Hall of Fame. In 1967 the Indian-Eskimo Association started to select Indians for a Hall of Fame. The pictures and biographies of these individuals are exhibited each year in the Canadian National Exhibition in Toronto. Chosen for this honor are "Those Indians of the past and present who have, in some field of endeavor, excelled and contributed substantially to the present situation of Indians in Canada." The Canadian list seems biased toward central Canada, especially Ontario. It does not include any people from the Maritimes or northern territories and has few in the west. For example, it should at least include such major western figures as *Peter Kelly*, a Haida, and *Andrew Paull*, a Salish, who were two of Canada's most influential advocates of civil rights for Indians in the early twentieth century. There is no official Indian honor roll in the U.S., but there is a large biographical literature by and about Native people. I have selected the names of Indians who would be widely accepted as historically prominent.

A U.S. INDIAN HONOR ROLL

1. *Powhatan* (ca. 1550-1618) Chief of the Powhatan Confederacy who led some 200 villages of Virginia Algonquians in the early years of English settlement in their territory. He provided food to the Europeans, maintained trade with them, and kept generally peaceful relations between the Europeans and the Indians. In 1622, four years after Powhatan's death, the Indians revolted against English expansions. They destroyed many of the English settlements and killed about 350 colonists. The English then mounted a massive campaign of Indian genocide, with about three punitive expeditions a year for the next fourteen years. They usually burned the fields and villages, killed the adult males, sold the boys into slavery in the West Indies, and kept the females as domestic slaves.

2. *Pocahontas* ("Frisky") (1595-1617) She was the daughter of Powhatan. When she was seventeen, the English Governor of Virginia kidnapped and held her as a hostage to control her father. She charmed many of the English colonists who were holding her. The next year she married *John Rolfe*, an English planter. Rolfe was then taught tobacco cultivation by the Indians, which contributed to the development of tobacco as the basic cash crop of Virginia. Rolfe and Pocahontas moved to London in 1616, where she became a social success, had a son, and later died of smallpox, at the age of 22.

3. *Massasoit* (-1662) Chief of the Wampanoag in eastern Massachusetts, who helped the early Plymouth Colony, traded with them, and then resisted the displacement of his people and their loss of territory by later European settlers. *Tasquantum* also helped the Plymouth plantation by teaching them the Indian techniques of farming, fishing, and hunting from 1620 until his death in 1622.

4. *Philip* or *Metacomet* (-1676) He was the son of Massasoit who led the Wampanoag, the Naraganset, the Pequot, and other New England Indians in

a resistance against the Whites in 1675-6. This general New England war developed only after repeated shocks to Native societies of European massacres: against the Pequot in 1636-7, the Delaware in 1643-4, and the Esopus in 1660-3. In 1637 the colonists managed to get the Naraganset to attack the Pequot, killing 600 adult males and enslaving their families. A Pequot band called Mohegan, under their chief *Uncas* (-1682) sided with the Whites and killed the Naraganset chief *Miantonomo* in 1643 when he began organizing a pan-tribal resistance to the Whites. Philip was forced to pay a yearly tribute to the Plymouth Colony to avoid their military attacks.

In 1675 the Naraganset joined the Pequot and other tribes under Philip against the 50,000 Europeans in New England, the 500 well-armed Mohegan warriors, and the communities of about 4,000 Christianized Indians. Under their chief *Ninigret*, the Rhode Island Naraganset stayed out of the war. Philip's forces killed about 600 men and the Puritans retaliated with a campaign of genocide and slavery. Philip was killed and his wife and grandson were among the 500 who were sold as slaves to the West Indies from the town of Plymouth alone.

5. *Popé* (1625-1692) He was a San Juan priest who, in 1675, was imprisoned by the Spaniards in Santa Fe, along with 47 other Indian priests, for practicing the Indian religion. Upon his release he hid at Taos and organized a unified Pueblo rebellion. In 1680 the Indians killed about one-fifth of the Spanish population of 2,400 in the Southwest and drove the rest southward to El Paso. In time, the Pueblos divided again, warred with each other, and after eight years of almost kingship powers, Popé was deposed. The Spaniards then made a concerted effort to reconquer the Rio Grande Pueblos, and, in 1692, after four years of fighting achieved the conquest.

6. *Tomochichi* (ca. 1665-1739) Many of the chiefs of the Southeast chiefdoms visited England in the 1700s to arrange peace treaties, land settlements, and trade. Tomochichi was the Creek town chief who helped the White settlers of Georgia, arranged a peace treaty between the Whites and the Lower Creeks, and visited England in 1734. His visit to London helped to set a pattern for visits by later chiefs, such as the Cherokee chiefs *Austenaco* and *Stalking Turkey*, in 1762.

7. *Pontiac* (1720-1769) He was an Ottawa from the Maumee River area in Ohio who sought to unite all the tribes in the Ohio-Illinois area against the British in the French and Indian War. In 1763-5 his people captured eight of the ten British forts in the Great Lakes area, but they were eventually defeated, largely by Indian bands that sided with the British. This forced the development of the Royal Proclamation of 1763 that defined the rights of Indians to their lands: (1) Indians had full ownership west of the Appalachian watershed, (2) Whites must leave Indian lands, and (3) all land purchases must be in a public meeting between agents of the crown and the interested Indians.

8. *Cornplanter* (ca. 1740-1836) He was a Seneca chief who fought with the British against the Americans and then was effective in supporting Indian interests in the establishment of U.S. reservations for the Iroquois. He traveled

to England and negotiated with George Washington in Philadelphia in the pursuit of Iroquoian interests.

9. *Handsome Lake* (1735-1815) He was a Seneca who rose as a prophet of the Iroquois in 1799, preaching the morality of the traditional Indian life and setting down guidelines of proper behavior that are still important today, the Code of Handsome Lake.

10. *Sacajawea* ("Birdwoman") (ca. 1786-1884) She was an Eastern Shoshoni who guided the Lewis and Clark Expedition in 1804-5 from a Hidatsa town on the Missouri River over the Rocky Mountains to the Northwest. She acted as their interpreter. She arranged for their horses when the expedition reached the Shoshoni. Her presence, and that of the infant she carried, was a silent declaration of peaceful intent that is also attributed as a major factor in the peaceful passage of the expedition through the territories of so many societies. Another woman, *Maria Dorion*, an Iowa, helped her Métis husband guide a party from St. Louis to Oregon in 1811-12. She took her two children with her and gave birth on the way to a third, which died.

11. *Black Hawk* (1767-1838) He was a Sauk chief who signed the Treaty of 1804 but, feeling deceived, fought against the Americans in the War of 1812 and later led a brief resistance movement in 1832 against the Whites by Sauk, Fox, Potawatomi, Shawnee, and Kickapoo. They were all being forced off their lands in a White drive to move all Indians west of the Mississippi River. *Keokuk* (ca. 1790-1848), another Sauk chief, kept his people out of the Black Hawk War and was made head chief in 1833.

12. *Osceola* (ca. 1803-1838) After the Revolutionary War, the Southeast chiefs traveled to Washington to settle their affairs with the Whites, until the crushing oppression and eventual removal of the Indians between 1832-1839. *William McIntosh*, the head chief of the Lower Creeks, was executed by his own people in 1825 for signing a treaty that ceded Creek lands to the U.S. Several other chiefs were similarly executed. In forcing their removal from their homeland, the U.S. Army burned villages and fields and killed several thousand Creek men, women, and children.

Some Cherokees successfully avoided the "Trail of Tears" to Oklahoma by hiding out in the mountains in North Carolina, where their ancestors still are today. Some Choctaws scattered out in Mississippi. A large band of Creeks and the remnant of other tribes eluded removal by going into the Florida swamps, becoming known as the Seminole. In a protracted campaign, the U.S. Army and Navy attempted to kill all free Seminoles, but eventually gave up because of the skill of the Indians at guerilla warfare in the swamps. The Seminole War cost the U.S. an estimated 1,500 men and $50 million. The Seminole are technically the only Indians in the U.S. who have never surrendered to the U.S.A. Osceola was the head chief in the wars of resistance. While holding a peace conference under a flag of truce, Osceola was seized and put in prison, where he died.

13. *Sequoyah* (ca. 1770-1843) He was born in Taskigi, Tennessee and first became a hunter, trapper, and trader. He was crippled in a hunting accident

and then became a silversmith and mechanic. By 1821 he had invented and spread a Cherokee writing system. After 1822 he promoted the settlement of Cherokees into Arkansas to escape the destruction going on in their homelands. He died while pursuing historical and linguistic research in Tamaulipas, Mexico.

14. *Seattle* (1786-1866) This Squamish and Dwamish chief signed the Treaty of Port Elliott in 1855 through which the Puget Sound tribes submitted to U.S. administration. He led and defended his people through difficult times. He gave his name as a potlatch gift to the town of Seattle.

15. *Quanah Parker* (1845-1911) He was the son of a Comanche chief and a captured White woman, *Cynthia Ann Parker*. After a series of battles with Texans and the U.S. Army, most of the Comanche, Kiowa, and Cheyenne agreed to settle on reserves in 1867. However, Whites came in and squatted on the Indian reserves, sparking new fights in 1874 in which Parker lead a confederation of 700 Plains Indian warriors against White buffalo hunters and a U.S. Army unit. After a peaceful settlement he became the most prominent Indian leader in a confederation of Comanche, Cheyenne, and Kiowa in Oklahoma for over 30 years. He became a prominent practitioner of Peyotism.

16. *Joseph* (1840-1904) In 1855, a large area of the Plateau where Washington, Oregon, and Idaho meet was reserved for the Nez Perce. However, gold was discovered there in 1860 and miners came into their territory. Through bribery and coercion the U.S. government pushed through a new treaty in 1863 that designated a much smaller reserve for the Nez Perce. For fourteen years Joseph's Wallawa band resisted leaving their homeland in northeast Oregon and moving onto the new reservation. When the band of about 500 people did begin moving in 1877, Whites stole several hundred of their horses. A group of young warriors of Joseph's band then got into a fight with White settlers in Idaho and killed 18 of them. U.S. troops were immediately sent to punish the band, but were defeated by the Indians.

A series of military units were then sent to destroy Joseph's band, but the band fought a long defensive retreat for over 1,000 miles through Idaho, Wyoming, and Montana in an attempt to escape to Canada. In one battle 89 Nez Perce were killed, including 50 women and children. *White Bird*'s unit of about one hundred followers did make it to the safety of Canada, but the main unit was stopped just short of the line and forced to surrender. The band was sent to Oklahoma, but Joseph pleaded their cause with the government in 1879 to allow his people to return to their homeland. They were eventually placed on the Colville Reservation in Washington.

17. *Captain Jack* (1837-1873) Troops came in 1872 to force his Modoc band of about 250 men, women, and children on the Lost River to move to the Klamath Reservation. Jack and his band fought back and killed several soldiers and settlers. They defended themselves in the lava beds south of Tule Lake, California for several months, against increasingly larger numbers of armed forces, vigilantes, and paid Indian mercenaries. At the height of the campaign there were more than 1,000 soldiers in action in a fixed battle against about 75

Indian warriors. Army casualties ran over 100 killed or wounded. A peace attempt was then aborted when Jack killed the Army commander and a Methodist minister. The Army then brought in artillery guns and blasted the Modocs out of the lava beds. Jack and his lieutenants were hanged and the rest of the band were shipped to Oklahoma.

18. *Sitting Bull* (1834-1890) He was a religious and political leader of the Hunkpapa band, Teton Dakota tribe, Sioux nation. As a result of the successful defense of their territory led by *Red Cloud* (1822-1909), the Sioux were recognized as sovereign over the Black Hills in the Treaty of 1868. However, White miners squatted in the Black Hills in 1874 looking for gold, which led to Indian-White conflicts, and the U.S. declared that the Indians were to be moved to reservations. In March, 1876, a U.S. Cavalry was sent out to round up the Sioux. A band of Cheyenne on its way to surrender to the agency was attacked by the Cavalry. Some Oglala Sioux, under *Crazy Horse* (1849-1877), joined in to successfully defend the Cheyenne. The Cheyenne then abandoned its attempt to surrender and joined the Oglala. In June, 1878, the Oglala stopped one unit of the cavalry in a battle in southern Montana. Then a unit of 600 troopers of the Seventh Cavalry, led by *George Custer*, attacked a mixed Indian encampment organized by Sitting Bull on the Little Big Horn River. The U.S. Cavalry was again defeated and about 225 soldiers were killed. The U.S. Army further expanded its forces, leading some Indians to surrender and Sitting Bull and his band to retreat to Canada. Crazy Horse surrendered in 1877 and was murdered in prison by the guards. Sitting Bull returned to the U.S. in 1881 and was murdered in 1890, as a part of the over-reaction by Whites to the Ghost Dance.

19. *Wovoka* (1856-1932) He was a Northern Paiute shaman who began having visions of being an incarnation of the Messiah in 1888. Like the earlier prophets, *Smohalla* (1815-1907), a Nez Perce, and his uncle (or father), *Tavibo*, he preached that there would be a revitalization of Indian life. He taught that if Native people would dance and chant a Great Basin style round dance, a millenium would come through the help of the ghosts of their ancestors and Native people would again control a rich world. *Kicking Bear* (1853-1904) was a Dakota Sioux who became the most outstanding disciple of Wovoka. He traveled to Nevada, participated in the Dances, and then spread the Ghost Dance to the Plains.

20. *Geronimo* ("One who yawns") (1829-1909) After White settlement of Texas and the Southwest, the semi-nomadic Apaches were militarily forced to settle on reservations. Following a period of resistance, in 1872 *Cochise* (-1874) made peace with the Whites. *Mangas Coloradas* was lured into a peace talk and then shot. The Apaches were then bureaucratically moved around, starved, and cheated. This led to new fights and the development of raiding bands by such chiefs as *Victorio, Nana*, and *Geronimo*.

Geronimo took his Chiricahua band of about 130 into the mountains of Mexico to raid border ranches occasionally and carry out a guerilla resistance for fourteen years. He was captured and escaped a few times. The band, which had been reduced to 36 men, women, and children, for 18 months eluded capture by an army of about 5,000 military troops, vigilantes, and Indian mercenaries. In 1886 Geronimo was finally talked into surrendering by other Apaches and spent a number of years as a military prisoner in Florida, then Alabama, and then Fort Sill, Oklahoma. His fame was so great that he was virtually exhibited as a tourist attraction by the U.S. Army. In his later years he became a farmer and joined the Dutch Reformed Church.

21. *Washakie* (1804-1900) This is the chief of the Eastern Shoshoni in Wyoming who kept the peace and consistently helped thousands of immigrant settlers. He fought for, and began to regularly receive, in 1859, transit payments from the U.S. government for maintaining a safe wagon road through Shoshoni territory, the Overland Trail. In 1863 he signed a treaty that established the Wind River Shoshoni boundaries over a huge territory and granted $10,000 a year in goods, in exchange for peace, safe passage on the Overland Trail, mining on their land, and future railroad passage. Unfortunately, treaties made the same year by the same government agent established boundaries for the *Western* Shoshoni in Idaho that overlapped so much that they included most of the *Eastern* Shoshoni territory in Wyoming; the Western Shoshoni were just included in the annuity fund promised to the Eastern Shoshoni.

The annuities were not given as promised, White miners and settlers flooded in, and the railroad was to be pushed through. The government then proceeded to make a new treaty in 1868, reducing the Wind River Shoshoni from about 7 to 2.8 million acres, but promising education and other facilities. Washakie agreed as long as his people were free to hunt beyond the mountains surrounding the established territory. In 1872 a further agreement reduced their land again by 600,000 acres in exchange for a supply of cattle and food for five years. In 1878 the government denied them the rights they had been promised in the treaties of 1863, 1868, and 1872, and moved 938 starving Arapahoes (a traditional enemy) in order to eventually take over two-thirds of their best land and to share in their provisions. Washakie continually appealed to the government about these injustices, as well as day-to-day issues such as White theft of their cattle and Whites hunting on their lands.

22.*Sarah Winnemucca Hopkins* (1844-1891) Granddaughter of a prominent Northern Paiute leader, *Captain Truckee*, she became an important leader in a fight for Indian civil rights. She was ordered off her reservation when she complained about the dishonesty of the Indian agent. She served as a scout and interpreter in the Bannock War of 1878. She wrote an autobiographical history, *Life Among the Piutes: Their Wrongs and Claims* (1883), that is a classic essay of protest and one of the first books ever written by an Indian in English.

23. *Henry Chee Dodge* (1861-1947) This is the Navajo who became the most influential chief after *Manuelito*. He learned English at Fort Sumner and became an interpreter. He became a rancher, a businessman, and the tribal chairman. His son, *Tom Dodge*, became the first Navajo lawyer and his daughter, *Annie Dodge Wauneka* (1910-), in addition to having eight children, became a member of the tribal council and successfully campaigned for improved med-

ical practices. *Raymond Nakai* became the most well-known Navajo politician after Dodge.

24. *James F. Thorpe* (1888-1953) In 1912 this Sauk-Fox from Oklahoma won both the decathlon and pentathlon at the Olympics. The King of Sweden told him, "Sir, you are the greatest athlete in the world." He played major league baseball, amateur football for Carlisle Indian School, and then professional football. In 1953 he was voted the greatest athlete of the first half of the century. A Hopi, *Louis Tewanima*, won three medals in long distance races in both the 1908 and 1912 Olympics. A Chippewa, *Charles Bender*, became one of the great baseball pitchers, starting in 1903 with the Philadelphia Athletics.

25. *Maria Martinez* (1887-) This San Ildefonso woman reinvented the ancient form of black-on-black pottery and established Pueblo pottery as a modern medium of art. By involving her husband, *Julian*, and her son, *Popovi Da*, Indian men were drawn into the ceramic arts.

THE CANADIAN INDIAN HALL OF FAME

1. *Joseph Brant* or *Thayendanegea* ("He holds the bets") (1742-1807) Education for him was the stern training of the Mohawk warrior and a mission school at Fort Hunter, New York. He went to the school that became Dartmouth College and translated religious works into the Mohawk language. His first battle came when he was thirteen, with the British against the French at Lake George. Later he secured help from the British in his fight against the American colonists. He followed the northern migration to Canada of people loyal to the British side after the American Revolutionary War, where he was granted outright a large part of southern Ontario (not a "reserve"), the watershed of the Grand River, for the use of Six Nations Iroquois. Although he sold much of this land to White settlers to buy equipment and supplies, Six Nations is still a large and prominent community.

2. *Tecumseh* (1768-1813) He was born in the Shawnee village of Piqua, Ohio. He was a genius who, without formal schooling, learned English and several Native languages, plant medicines, history, legends, and the tribal treaties. Statesman, orator, warchief, he tried to organize all the tribes into a strong political confederacy. He traveled widely among Indian societies making speeches in the war effort against the Americans. He argued that Indian land belonged in common to the Native people, so that the U.S. could not buy land from a single isolated tribe. He was commissioned a Brigadier General in the British Army and became a Canadian leader in the War of 1812, until he was killed in the Battle of Moraviantown in Ontario in 1813. He was considered to be a very effective military strategist.

3. *Pequis* (ca 1774-1864) This is the chief of the Red River Saulteaux who aided the settlers along the Red River in Manitoba with food, shelter, and protection after the Battle of Seven Oaks in 1817. This battle was essentially the killing of Métis affiliated with the North West Company by forces of the Hudson's Bay Company, two corporations competing for the fur trade. The

Bay settled in Scottish immigrants to displace the Native people and employed a regiment of Swiss troops to give them military backing. The two companies were finally unified in 1821 to complete the monopoly, decrease the number of forts, and reduce prices paid for furs.

4. *Big Bear* (1828-1888) He was a Plains Cree and chief in the Fort Pitt-Frog Lake area of Saskatchewan. Big Bear tried to unite the Indians in a common front to attain better treaty terms. He opposed settling down on reserves based on agriculture and thus attracted many young people to his band who opposed reserve life. At Frog Lake in April 1885, after exploitations and humiliations, his people killed several Whites, including a corrupt government agent, a farm instructor, and two priests. This was triggered by the Métis defeat of the Canadians at Duck Lake on March 26 and Fish Creek on April 24. By the end of April the Natives had captured three forts (Pitt, Carlton, and North Battleford) and defeated the Canadian Army and the Northwest Mounted Police in major battles. On May 28, Big Bear's warriors beat nearly two hundred Canadian troops at Frenchman's Butte, forcing them to retreat. The Canadians, however, had stopped the Métis rebellion by laying seige to the town of Batoche and defeating the forces of Riel and Dumont on May 12th. They then concentrated on the Indian forces of Big Bear and Poundmaker. Big Bear finally surrendered on July 21 and was sentenced to two years in prison.

5. *Crowfoot* (1821-1890) Chief of the Blackfoot and head of the Blackfoot Confederacy who signed the treaty in 1877. He was a philosopher, an eloquent speaker, and a powerful politician in his pursuit of Blackfoot interests with both Whites and other Indians.

6. *Poundmaker* (1841-1886) His father was an Assiniboin and his mother was of the Red Pheasant Crees. When Crowfoot lost his own son he adopted Poundmaker, although there was a political purpose involved in the maintenance of peace between the Blackfoot and the Cree. Poundmaker tried to end intertribal warfare and, together with Crowfoot, tried to create an alliance of Prairie tribes for the treaty making of that day. Poundmaker even tried to encourage his people in agriculture. Individual acts of violence, however, involved his people in the Northwest Rebellion. Poundmaker then led the forces that defeated the Canadians at Cut Knife Hill on May 2, 1885, but then he was arrested on May 16. He was convicted as an insurrectionist and served one year in Stony Mountain Penitentiary. Native casualties in the Northwest Rebellion were 9 executed, 49 killed in action, and hundreds wounded.

7. *Louis Riel* (1844-1885) He was a Métis born in St. Boniface, Manitoba and educated in Montreal. He played a central role in the multicultural government in the Prairies during the transitional period between rule by the Hudson's Bay Company and the establishment of direct British colonial rule by military force. He claimed that the Métis people owned their land by aboriginal title, by a history of military defense, and by cultivation and inhabitation. Although he never carried a gun, he was one of the political organizers behind both the civil war in the Prairies in 1870, and the Native resistance of 1885. In 1874 he was elected by the people of Manitoba to the Canadian Par-

liament, but the members of Parliament refused to let him take office. When a warrant for his arrest was issued in 1875, he moved to Montana. *Gabriel Dumont* (1838-1906) and other leaders of Batoche, Saskatchewan went there in 1884 and employed him to help them with their problems with the Canadian government. As Adjutant-General in the provisional government, Gabriel Dumont was probably more important than Riel in the 1885 battles. However, Riel was held responsible for the rebellion and he was hanged in Regina, Saskatchewan in Canada's most famous political execution. Rarely heard about are the eight Indians who were hanged for the same rebellion.

8. *Oronyatekha* ("Burning Cloud") or *Peter Martin* (1841-1907) He was a Mohawk from the Grand River community in Ontario who studied medicine at Oxford University, became a medical doctor, and was an authority on fraternal organizations. He was influential within both Iroquoian associations and the Independent Order of Foresters, a life-insurance cooperative.

9. *Thunderchild* (1857-1931) A Cree who was made a chief when he was only 25. He signed the treaty and took no part in the Northwest Rebellion. He was thus able to be a part of the settlement of the dispute. His reservation was named after him and the best Indian school in the west was erected there by the Cree during his lifetime.

10. *Oozawekwun* ("Yellow Quill") Chief of the Saulteaux at Portage la Prairie, who after 1871 fought for reasonable land assignments, insisting that they be given the land at Hamilton's Crossing. They finally were in 1919.

11. *Emily Pauline Johnson* (1862-1913) This Mohawk of the Six Nations Reserve became a well-known poet, reading her works to audiences in Canada, the U.S., and England.

12. *Thomas Longboat* (1887-1949) The Onondaga became a famous long-distance runner, setting new records at the Boston Marathon and many other races. He competed in the 1908 Olympics.

13. *Joseph B. Keeper* A Cree who won over fifty trophies as a middle-distance runner, competing in the Stockholm Olympics in 1912. He was also honored for his service in Canada's Armed Forces in World War I.

14. *Cameron Dee Brant* (1888-1915) This Mohawk of the Six Nations Reserve became a Lieutenant and died in battle in France.

15. *Francis Pegamagabow* A Parry Sound Ojibwa who became a corporal in World War I and was honored for his skill as a sniper.

16. *Oliver M. Martin* (1893-1957) Mohawk of the Six Nations Reserve who became a Lieutenant in World War I, a Brigadier in World War II, and then a Magistrate for the County of York.

17. *Gilbert C. Monture* (1896-1973) This Iroquois became a Lieutenant in World War I, the officer in charge of the disposition of mineral resources in Canada in World War II, and a recognized authority on mining economics.

18. *Dr. Elmer Jamieson* (1891-1972) A Cayuga from the Six Nations Reservation, Jamieson served in France in World War I, became a Doctor of Pedagogy, and taught in North Toronto Collegiate as head of the Department of Chemistry and Biology.

19. *James Gladstone* (1887-1971) This Blood was a president of the Indian Association of Alberta, a cattle rancher, and an appointed member of the Senate of Canada, beginning in 1958.

20. *Dan George* (1899-) A Squamish Salish from Vancouver who has been a longshoreman, a logger, a chief of his people for twelve years, and an actor in many plays and movies. His most famous portrayal was in *Little Big Man.*

21. *George Clutesi* (1905-) This Nootka from Port Alberni records the life and legends of his people, writing such books as *Son of Raven, Son of Deer* and *Potlatch.*

22. *George Armstrong* (1930-) After his early years in Skeed, Ontario, Armstrong, an Ojibwa, became a professional hockey player for the Toronto Maple Leafs, then turned to coaching after 21 years.

23. *Ethel Brant Monture* (1894-) A prominent Mohawk teacher, historian, and author.

24. Andrew T. Delisle (1933-) A Caughnawaga Mohawk who founded the Mohawk Recreation Association, assisted in the establishment of the Indians of Quebec Association, and served as director of the Indians of Canada pavilions at *Expo '67* and *Man and His World.*

25. *Frank Calder* (1915-) This Nishga of the Nass River has been president of the Nishga Tribal Council, the North American Indian Brotherhood, and the B.C. Indian Art and Welfare Society. He is an MPP to the B.C. legislature, the first Indian to hold such an elected office in Canada.

Chapter 6

Family Life Acculturation and Ethnicity

This chapter reviews the forms of Native families and then examines the historical impact on family life of relationships with the Europeans. The concept of acculturation is used for this process of cultural change. The concept of ethnic group is used for the Indian societies in later historical times, after they were incorporated as minorities in the modern states.

Almost all of the world's major variants of marriage, incest prohibitions, post-marriage residence customs, and in-law relations were practiced by one Native North American society or another. This wide variation represents great historical depth and diverse adaptations to natural and cultural environments. In comparison, the Europeans who came to North America had almost uniform marriage and family practices.

Indian marriages were invariably public and customary, while European marriages could be private, even secret, and were legal and in the nature of a contract between individuals. Indian marriages were more in the nature of a contract between kin groups. Indian cultures tended to be far more tolerant of variant forms of marriage. Thus, for example, monogamy, polygyny, and polyandry were all acceptable forms of marriage in most societies. Polyandry was in practice very rare, fraternal when it did occur, and usually brought on by special circumstances, such as the crippling of an older married brother with the subsequent additional marriage of the younger brother to the older brother's wife.

Polygyny was "common," occurring in more than 20% of the marriages in most of the Plains and along the Northwest Coast, while monogamy was almost the exclusive form among certain northeastern agriculturalists, such as the Iroquois and Huron. Matrilocal post-marital residence and matrilineal descent were common among agriculturalists in the Eastern and Southwestern U.S., where women played a major role in food production. With the intensification of agriculture, such as in Mexico, men became the predominant food producers, and post-marital residence and rules of descent shifted to patrilocal and patrilineal, as in Europe.

Puberty reckoning, particularly related to a girl's first menstruation, was universal among Indian societies and usually associated with some ceremony. At the time of initial menstruation the girl was held to be in a potentially dangerous state of close contact with supernaturals and therefore must behave properly. The girl's conduct at puberty was believed to predetermine her behavior for the rest of her life. Typically she was secluded, where she fasted and learned the duties of a wife and mother from an older sponsor, worked for other women, and finally ended her taboo period by bathing and dressing in new clothing.

Premarital sexual relations were less of a problem to Indian societies than to European societies. Indians married young, usually between fifteen and twenty years of age. Most Indian societies were also more permissive toward premarital relations, except where it violated rules of incest, endogamy, or adultery. Premarital pregnancies were accepted and the child was usually reared by the mother's kinfolk.

Such customs as bride price and bride service were common in the Plains and Northwest Coast. Inter-familial exchange marriage, when two families exchange daughters to marry a son in the other family, existed in areas where there were few marriage formalities, such as the Great Basin and Sub-Arctic. Among families without sons, adopting a son to marry a duaghter, inherit the family property, and carry a line of descent existed in several patrilineal areas. First cross-cousin marriages were permitted or even preferred in some strongly lineal societies where the father's brother's daughter or mother's sister's daughter were in a different descent line than the groom. This was common, for example, among such wealthy fishing matrilineal societies as the Tlingit, Tsimshian, and Haida of coastal British Columbia and the Alaskan panhandle.

EUROPEAN IMPACT

With the seventeenth and eighteenth century spread of the horse into the Plains from Spanish settlements in New Mexico, many tribes of Indians migrated there to take up the highly productive hunting of buffalo. This ecological shift brought on an initial convergence of their social structures. Highly integrated societies that had previously been horticultural "regressed" to more flexible hunting bands and emphasized "generational" kinship, while formerly simple gathering societies tended to build up their structures with more decisive military and political organization. Finally, the Plains Indians were defeated by Whites and the demise of the buffalo herds, relocated on reservations, and began to acculturate to European forms of social structure.

Missionaries, teachers, and government agents to the Choctaw of Mississippi were concerned that Indian women worked in the fields, the usual practice in horticultural societies, and that fathers failed to materially provide for their own children, in accordance with the matrilineal system of inheritance. "New regulations regarding land were introduced that emphasized the position of the man as head of the family. Marriage was regulated by law, widows were entitled to dower rights, and children could inherit their father's estate. The leaders no longer came from the clans but were elected by the adult male members of the district, and the old town rituals were largely replaced by the church and its activities" (Eggan 1966:29). These changes broke down the clan and kinship structures, emphasized nuclear families and territorial ties, and shifted kinship from a matrilineal system to a patrilineally biased bilateral system. Similar historic shifts occurred among other Southeast societies, such as the Creek and Cherokee.

Indians were forcibly removed from most of the U.S. lands east of the Mississippi River, except in isolated spots: Cherokees in the North Carolina mountains, the Seminoles of the Florida everglades, some Iroquois in northern New York (and Canada), and some Algonquians in the northern woods. There are small communities of Wapanoag, Nipmuc, Shinnecock, Pequot, and Mohegan in the northeast. Removal was later and not as complete west of the Mississippi River so this is where most of the U.S. Indians live today, particularly in Oklahoma, the Dakotas, Montana, New Mexico, Arizona, and along the West Coast. The pattern of displacement was similar in Canada except that the European population was much smaller, making the extent of displacement and deculturation less. Also, in the long period of fur trapping and northern exploration there was more use and respect for Native skills than in the U.S. However, the Beothuk were brought to extinction by the French and Scottish fishermen of Newfoundland, wars between Indians were actively promoted by competing French and British interests in the Canadian fur trade, and Indians were generally displaced and enclaved in "reserves" in the east-to-west sweep of European immigrant agriculturalists across Canada.

Differences between the Europeans who arrived in the New World played an important role in determining the nature of Indian-European relations. For example, the French, Spanish, and Portuguese were more tolerant than northern Europeans of intermarriage with the Natives. Thus, since early historical times there have been significant populations of Spanish-Indian "Mestizos" and French-Indian "Métis," but few British-Indian "half-breeds," considering the size of the British population in North America. A major reason for this seems to be that in the sixteenth and seventeenth centuries the French, Spanish, and Portuguese came largely as single men, while the British tended to come as whole families. It also appears that southern European discrimination has been largely based on differences of culture and social class while northern European discrimination has been more simply racial.

Europeans imposed their concepts of proper marriage and family relations on the Indians, especially through the preaching of Christian missionaries and through laws which were applied to Indians. For example, I once attempted unsuccessfully to help a Washo retain some land that he had inherited from a polyandrous marriage. The court did not comprehend how a woman could have two husbands at the same time and how her property could be inherited equally by both husbands (also brothers) upon her death. In countless ways the Europeans impressed their particular social system on Indians. Christian missionaries usually tried to eliminate plural marriages and matrilineal customs, without understanding the crucial roles these practices had in the normal functioning of Native societies. In Canada the potlatch ceremonies of the Pacific Coast that were so crucial in validating titles and bringing order to the kinship systems were outlawed because of Protestant concerns about wasteful feasts.

The Indian Act of Canada was written by Euro-Canadians who applied their assumptions that household heads should be male and wives should be dependent on them, that inheritance should be patrilineal, and that families should be nuclear. This Act has been destructive of the social structure of matrilineal and bilateral Indian societies and supportive of patrilineal Indian societies. "Indian status" is essential to inclusion in rights to Indian-band lands and to programs of the Indian Affairs Branch, but an Indian woman can lose this status if her husband loses his or if she ever marries a person without Indian status. A man with Indian status does not lose his status if he marries a non-status woman, instead, his wife acquires Indian status. If a status woman marries a non-status person and thus loses her status, then later divorces that person, she still cannot reacquire status, except by marrying a status Indian. The law supports patrilocal postmarital residence because at marriage a woman becomes a member of her husband's band. Women who have lost status in their natal band are not usually buried there.

The family statistics on status Indians in Canada are presented for 1974 below (D.I.A.N.D. 1975).

1. 276,436 individuals registered
2. 2,015 marriages
3. 585 or 29% of these were of females to persons who were not status Indians, so the 585 females lost their Indian status
4. 121 divorces
5. 8,248 births and 2,217 deaths for a net gain of 6,031
6. 365 adoptions of Indian children, 104 by Indians and 261 by others

This Canadian system was designed to bolster the position of men and stabilize family life, but it does exactly the opposite when inter-racial sexual relations become frequent. This is because Indian women tend not to marry their

White lovers so that they will not lose their Indian status. Thus the males are displaced, families become matri-centered, and the children are classified as illegitimate. Stanbury and Siegel (1975) reported a high, increasing level of common law marriages and matricentered families among Indians in British Columbia: 40% of all "single" Indian women in B.C. in 1971 had one or more children, 57% of status and 38% of non-status Indian births in B.C. in 1972 were "illegitimate." They also found high rates of children being deserted, placed on provincial care, and adopted out. Many of the fathers of these children were Indians, of course, but an increasing number are also Whites.

The Indians of British Columbia are consistently at the creative edge of solving their problems with the majority society. They typically develop the legal and organizational models that become used throughout Canadian Native society. The following example of this creativity is in the form of a selection from the recommendations made by the B.C. Commission on Native Families and the Law.

5. When native children are apprehended in urban areas, their band should be notified and given first option for planning.
9. Native children requiring foster care should be placed in native foster homes whenever possible.
12. The Department of Human Resources should notify Indian foster children of their band of origin, where this is requested.
17. If a mother with Indian status wishes confidentiality and her newborn infant can be placed for adoption with status parents belonging to another band, the mother's own band should not be advised of the birth.
19. Non-Indian parents adopting Indian children, whether status or non-status, should sign an agreement at the time of placement confirming their willingness to familiarize the child with his Indian heritage.
21. The Superintendent of Child Welfare should be required to notify the adopting parents of the fact that the child is a status Indian and of his band membership.
24. An Indian custom adoption should be recognized as a legal adoption under new adoption legislation.
36. The qualifications for some social work positions, as set out by the Public Service Commission, should be re-examined with a view to recognizing the importance of "Indian expertise," aptitude and life experience, in lieu of academic education.

A case on the status of adopted Indian children that was started in British Columbia went to the Supreme Court of Canada. It was decided in 1975 that Native children with status rights who become adopted continue to retain those rights, regardless of who adopts them.

In 1973 two of the women who had lost their status through marriage appealed to the Supreme Court of Canada. The Attorney General and a coalition of Indian organizations through the National Indian Brotherhood opposed them, claiming that the egalitarian provisions of the Canadian Bill of Rights should not apply to the special rights and procedures of the Indian Act.

The two women, in spite of the backing they received from women's liberation organizations, lost the case.

ACCULTURATION AND ETHNIC GROUP FORMATION

Several acculturation hypotheses are used to analyse historical Indian culture continuity and change. Isolation on reservations is seen as a factor supporting their cultural continuity. Some cases of forced acculturation may have led to resistance towards change and the development of effective institutions that have helped to preserve cultural continuity, such as techniques to ward off religious and government agents of social change. This seems to have occurred especially when the Native community has had a strongly bonded "corporate" structure, as among the Hopi. Also racist attitudes by Europeans against Indians set up a barrier against Indian assimilation, even to the extent of making Indian-European marriages illegal in the early state legislation of several western states. One hypothesis holds that material aspects have changed more readily than social and ideological aspects, so that Indians are still able to revitalize some social and ideological dimensions of their cultures.

The individual wage employment and entrepreneurship of industrial society are inclined to disrupt the cooperative, communalistic, pooling kind of economic arrangements that are an integral part of tribal kinship economics. In fact, these mutual ties of rights and obligations are seen as deterrents to economic advancement in an industrial society, that kinfolk claims reduce the individual incentives that bring healthy competition into a capitalist society.

The modern law of state societies is universalistic. It applies to every sociocultural unit within the geographical jurisdictions of the law and thus reduces their diversity to common practices. Not only is the society-by-society diversity that existed among the hundreds of Indian tribes reduced to conform with national and state laws, but the tolerant diversity that existed within single Indian societies must conform as well. Polygyny was almost universally allowed by Indian societies and is eliminated through the law. Indian children must, by law, attend school, undermining traditional education. Marriages must now be legally registered. Marital differences that were once handled by kinship councils may now come before the courts. However, it is very hard for even the post-industrial state society to control the non-empirical or ideological world of its internal sub-cultures, and it has no reason to control the ineffectual façades of cultural difference. Thus we are allowed the myth of a legimately plural society. The customs that survive are usually those innocuous ones that escape the conforming crush of law, such as religious practices, music, and tastes in food. These, then, become the hallmarks of ethnic difference, remnants of once truly different cultures.

The basic pattern of cultural retention is that as separate socio-cultural entities are integrated into expanding nation states, they are converted into ethnic sub-cultures. Assuming some continuity, rather than outright destruction, the first significant changes tend to include material, economic, and some legal elements of integration with the dominant society. Internal adjustments, as well as direct pressures by missionaries and government agents, then usually produce a variety of social and political changes. Finally, there is typically not only a survival but a creative readjustment of ideology, identity, religion, and other materially unimportant symbols of ethnic uniqueness: ethnic costumes, music, dance, art, etc. Language acculturation takes place over the whole period of acculturation, usually takes the form of bilingualism during the phase of significant social and political changes, and is complete when all that is left of the original language for most people are the ethnic words and phrases that have been incorporated into the dominant language as used by speakers of that ethnic group.

Societies that are native to a country have many differences from those that are migrants to the country. Thus Indians identify with no other land, while all other immigrant groups have other geographical identities. Indians are more widely scattered across North America than any other ethnic minority. More Indians have a rural residence than any other sizable ethnic population. In line with this identification with the land, scatter, and predominantly rural residence, Indians are probably the most opposed to assimilation and integration into majority society and culture of any sizable ethnic population.

THREE CASE STUDIES

Cultural continuity has been greater where European influences came later, as in the Tropics and the Arctic, or were less destructive, as in Mexico and Peru. Certain reservation enclaves have also provided sufficient isolation from European influences to adapt family structures gradually and with continuing social integration. I have sketched three brief case studies of family life to illustrate the changes occurring in different settings of European contact and ecology: (1) *Inuit* of North Alaska, (2) *Hopi* of northern Arizona, and (3) *Menomini* of Wisconsin. These are presented in an order based on the extent of change from aboriginal life styles. The Inuit are used here as a relatively traditional people, but the Inuit now seem to be acculturating more rapidly and completely than the neighboring Na-Dene and Algonquian Indians of the sub-Arctic. It is only in reference to the more acculturated Indians, such as the Menomini and urban Indians, that we can accurately speak of an active membership in an "American Indian ethnic group," comparable to the European ethnic minorities in North America. That is, the Inuit and Hopi are inclined to be still so involved with their own cultures that they do not actively participate in a self-conscious, integrated, Indian ethnic minority, even though they may be racially and culturally defined as members by the majority society. In fact, specific tribal identities are almost universally much stronger and more important than the identity as a Native American.

THE INUIT OF NORTH ALASKA

Chance's (1966) study of the Inuit of North Alaska showed that large families are welcomed, that children enjoy much love and affection, and that adoption between kin is easy and widespread. Children are often named after a deceased person and some of the qualities or even the spirit of the original person continues in the namesake. Children are packed or carried in the back of a parka a great deal until about two years old. Weaning may not be completed until the third or even fourth year while toilet training begins before the first birthday. There is generally no shame or secrecy about excretory functions.

Childhood training emphasizes egalitarian social cooperation and skills of survival. Boys may begin to shoot a rifle as young as seven years of age, while girls learn the techniques of butchering. The sexual division of labor, however, is not rigid; boys may occasionally cook and girls may go fishing or bird hunting. Storytelling, wrestling, and hand games now combine with such Western games as volleyball, Monopoly, and Scrabble. Children from six to sixteen are required to attend the local B.I.A. school. Adolescents become more peer-centered in social groups and in many ways emulate Euro-American teenagers in dress (denims and leather jackets), slang ("Man, I don't go for parkas."), music, and dance steps.

Whale, seal, and caribou are still the main sources of food, while they are now usually served on the Western three-meals-a-day plan. Government control has removed the need for mutual protection of kin during feuds. Individual wage labor has decreased the economic interdependence that operated in the traditional bilaterally extended family. Sharing is now more in such secondary economic activities as baby-sitting, butchering meat, and the distribution of household items. Young people today are more free from parental restrictions on selecting marriage partners, but the tradition of first-cousin marriage is still common in some communities. Formal wife exchanges between friends is no longer practiced, but sexual mores are still relatively free. There is very little display of emotions between husband and wife, although the mutual bond may in fact be close, affectionate, and satisfying. Couples rarely go visiting together or entertain friends together and non-kin adult social gatherings are not usually mixed by sex. However, very casual visiting between friends of the same sex is a feature of daily family life. The friend may come in, watch the activities of the household for some time, and leave again without anything more being said between the host and visitor than a brief exchange of greetings.

Chance (1966: 85-87) wrote that in Kaktovik and other new small Eskimo villages, relatively smooth adjustments to modern culture have occurred because of such things as (1) their intensive interaction and communication, (2) the kinship system remaining stable enough to support individuals in stressful situations, (3) most of the newly defined goals, particularly for material goods, being successfully realized, and (4) maintenance of traditional leadership and pride. In larger communities, such as Barrow with a population over 1200, there have been more problems related to the residential and social separation of Euro-Americans and Eskimo, the marked lower status of Eskimos, and discrimination against Eskimos.

A Point Hope study (VanStone 1962) indicated that women prefer only three or four children, but contraceptives are practically unknown and never used. Many traditional beliefs surround childbirth; e.g., windstorms are associated with movements of the fetus. Several elderly women act as midwives and attend each birth in the village. Women who have had a few children apparently acquire a rather casual attitude toward childbirth. "One older woman, far advanced in pregnancy, was travelling by skin boat from Jabbertown to Point Hope. She asked to be put ashore 'to go to the toilet' and gave birth after the boat had moved on without her. She cut the cord and scraped sand over the afterbirth, put the baby in her parka and ran up the beach to catch up with the boat." (VanStone 1962: 79).

Cloth diapers are used, but the infant is still carried on the back inside the mother's parka. The mother stays near the baby, giving the breast as soon and as often as they desire, but breast-feeding is relatively undemonstrative and without much emotion. "There appears to be no stress placed on rapid toilet training . . . . A two-year-old boy was heard to say 'toilet' and then went toward the can normally used for the purpose but urinated on the floor. The parents were amused by this 'near miss' and the child, obviously partially trained, was given credit for taking a step in the right direction." The importance of naming, the widespread practice of adoption, and a socialization toward cooperation with mild discipline seem to be general Eskimo traits. Premarital sex relations are not uncommon, but it is difficult to find secluded places for love meetings in a small Arctic village.

THE HOPI OF NORTHERN ARIZONA

Pueblo cultures have had more continuity and homogeneity in their histories than most Indian cultures in the U.S. The western Pueblos (Hopi, Zuni, Acoma, and Laguna) tend to have matrilineal exogamous clans and extended matrilocal households, while the eastern Pueblos of the Rio Grande are primarily bilateral with moieties. The isolation of the Hopi has shielded them from some of the pressures of change, although they have periodically been threatened with extinction through drought, disease, and warfare. Each Hopi village tends to be endogamous and independent, except for intermarriage with nearby "colony villages." The history of the matrilineal clans in the village according to their order of arrival, occupation of the clan house, ceremonial possessions, and clan lands is important in determining village social relations.

Marriage is monogamous. Men join their wives' households and economically support them but retain ritual, leadership, and disciplinary roles in their natal households. Thus, they discipline their sisters' children and play a passive role in their wife's household. The tension in these contrasting roles contributes to a high divorce rate among the Hopi (Eggan 1966: 126). Another tension exists in the conflicts between the basically theocratic organization of the Hopi and the modern demands for decisive political action that have been imposed upon them. While community welfare is highly valued, there is competition between clans and villages in terms of such things as ceremonial performances.

Pueblo socialization is permissive, with gradual weaning and toilet training and little explicit discipline of children until they are over two years of age (Dozier 1970). Admonitions then center on such things as hard work, enduring discomforts, and not wasting food. Masked disciplinarians with whips are used to threaten disobedient children. Initiation of girls and boys into a Kiva or religious society occurs between the ages of six and nine, with rigid physical and dietary restrictions. There is little opportunity for privacy, particularly in those villages which are still constructed as compact, adobe, apartment-like pueblos. Gossip, ridicule, and the discipline of Kiva societies keep down social deviancy, maintaining a kind of Taoist or quietistic solution to social relations. In the past, Hopis executed witches and evicted other deviants, but today the rebellious individuals usually move to the freer life of cities and just visit their villages to renew kinship and ceremonial ties. One example of a semi-urban adaptation is that about 600 Hopi live a suburban type of life at Moenkopi with such appliances as refrigerators, gas ranges, and running water and automobiles.

Religious ceremonialism, with its rich traditions of costuming, dance, music, and theology, is still at the center of Hopi life and is more attractive to the Hopi than the Christian alternatives. Developing within a context of Spanish and then Euro-American curiosity and pressures to change, the Hopi religious societies developed defensive secrecy and theological adjustments that rationalized Hopi religion in relation to Christianity and American culture. Hopi is an Indian society that has had sufficient autonomy from Euro-American pressures to evolve a modern culture with a consistently high level of internal integration. Wage work, Western education, automobiles, electrical appliances, Western dress, weekend supermarket shopping, etc., are now accepted practices, but the aboriginal language is being retained as a second language to English and the Hopi religion has never been replaced by Christianity.

The Hopi and their ancestors have lived where they are now for at least several hundred years. Old Oraibi was initially built around 1100 A.D. and is the oldest continuously occupied village in the U.S. The Hopi have had to create cultural mechanisms to defend their traditional way of life against U.S. and state laws concerning such things as taxes, the military draft, compilation of the U.S. census, compulsory education for children in U.S. schools, and so forth; they have had to change culturally in order to retain as much of their traditional culture as possible. In the 1920s missionaries and Indian agency officials tried to prohibit Hopi religious ceremonies and dances because they were pagan practices. This persecution was stopped by John Collier's administration of the Bureau of Indian Affairs. However, even the most well-intentioned moves to reorganize Hopi political administration from their traditional kinship and religious forms to those of voting, written constitutions, representative government, tribal councils, etc. have been resisted. The U.S. government needed a legal representative of the Hopi people so that rapid bureaucratic decisions could be made. Thus they pressured the Hopi into designating such a representative by a means that would legally satisfy the U.S. government.

Clemmer (1974) did a study of the movement to resist White culture at Hotevilla, perhaps the most traditional of the twelve Hopi villages. Hotevilla does not allow a census in its village. Hotevilla does not recognize the validity of the Hopi Tribal Council and they refuse to appoint representatives to it. They claim that the Hopi are an independent nation and thus should not pay taxes, be drafted, or have to accept government programs to develop their village. They rejected the Land Claims Commission. "We will not ask a white man, who came to us recently, for a piece of land that is already ours." They rejected the drilling for oil on Hopi land because the soil is sacred and must not be disturbed. They tried, unsuccessfully, to reject a new school building, a water tower and water line, and a sewer system. The agencies of White society simply demand that the Hopi accept these "modern advantages."

In 1968 the heredity village chief organized a successful protest to stop the installation of electrical power in the village.The B.I.A. agency-acting superintendent was installing utility poles on the strength of a petition of ninety names from one Hotevilla faction. The anti-utility Hotevillans then gathered a petition with 130 names (Clemmer 1974: 238-9).

> *Anti-utility Hotevillans also pulled down several utility poles, and the chief sent telegrams of protest . . . . A few days later, the acting superintendent returned with his men and equipment, reinforced with several members of the Hopi police force from the agency and a number of county sheriff's deputies . . . . Anti-utility Hotevillans . . . jumped into post holes to prevent poles from being placed. Police dragged them out, and anti-utility Hotevillans scuffled with police and pro-utility Hotevillans. In the midst of the sit-ins and struggling, however, the utility poles were installed by sunset . . . resisters, aided by pressure exerted as a result of publicity, prevailed. Within a week the poles had been removed . . .*

THE MENOMINI OF WISCONSIN

Spindler and Spindler (1971) found five social segments along the continuum of socio-cultural adaptation among the Menomini living in a Wisconsin reservation: (1) Native-oriented, (2) Peyotists, (3) transitionals, (4) lower-status acculturated, and (5) elite acculturated. The Native-oriented group receives a definition and identity through maintaining the Dream Dance and other formalized dances and rituals. The Peyotists are involved in the pan-Indian "Native American Church," a religion that serves to resolve some of the ideological conflicts between the Christian and Indian traditions. The transitionals lack a firm identity and religious affiliation, but individuals in this large category are moving to either Native-oriented or "Whiteman" identity and religion. The more acculturated people tend to have a significantly higher economic status and no affiliation with either the aboriginal religious practices or the historical Peyotist movement. The acculturated, especially the elite, are usually Catholic in religion.

The Native-oriented group tend to have the personal qualities of equanimity under duress, control of overt emotionality and aggression, autonomy, a sense of humor, and hospitality. They believe in having supernatural power, from a guardian spirit through a vision while fasting, or simply through displaying quiescent receptivity to power; that dreams can be used to predict the future.

Children in the Native-oriented group are received as reincarnated elders and, like old people, are close to the supernatural power that pervades all things. Naming is ceremonious and very important. Children are treated with tolerance and permissiveness, with gradual weaning, casual toilet training, and mild discipline. When a boy kills his first game he is given a feast and praises are sung to him. When a girl fills her pail with wild berries she is commended. Children participate in the important social happenings, such as the dances. They are told stories by the elders, including formalized "preachings" about proper behavior. The group is child-oriented because the transmission of traditional culture is a central purpose of the group. This results in a quite different kind of family life than that found among the "acculturated" Menomini. The Spindlers see the Native-oriented cultural system as a conscious attempt to maintain a way of life that is dying, a reaffirmation of the traditional way while attempting to exclude the foreign way. In this they are similar to the Hopi Kiva societies or the Long House Society people among the Iroquois, who follow the Code of Handsome Lake.

The elite acculturated tend to live in a different community than the traditionals, in homes like business and professional people in nearby Euro-American communities. They are active in the Catholic Church; often play golf, or bowl, or go snowmobiling; do not speak Menomini; and are consciously oriented toward Euro-American culture, but still derive some pride and identity from their Menomini heritage.

In 1961 the U.S. Bureau of Indian Affairs terminated its relations with the tribe, the reservation became a county of Wisconsin, and Menominee Enterprises, Inc. became the tribal management. The U.S. government had decided that the Menomini were sufficiently acculturated to entirely operate their own affairs. Still the determination to keep Menomini identity and lands intact is strong. Determination of Rights and Unity for Menominee Stockholders (DRUMS) was organized to protest the tribal management policies, particularly the sale of land, and to argue for a repeal of the termination proceedings (Lurie 1972). Termination proceedings were stopped.

THE FUTURE OF NATIVE ETHNIC GROUPS

A number of simultaneous processes are at work among Native peoples: (1) a high population increase, (2) government programs to bring Indians out of their poverty life style, (3) convergent social adaptations to the dominant society, (4) urbanization, and (5) an ethnic renaissance that involves (a) the creation of a general pan-Indian ethnicity, (b) several special political and religious pan-Indian movements, such as Peyotism and the Sun Dance, (c) the cultural revitalization of certain tribal and regional customs, and (d) a renewed interest in Native history, literature, crafts, art, dance, foods, etc.

The future of Native peoples is first of all one of *population expansion*. They are probably the fastest growing ethnic or racial population (3.2% annual increase rate in Canada and 3.0% in the U.S.). The U.S. Indian birth rate is estimated to be 37.4 per 1,000 per year, over twice the national average (Levitan and Hetrick 1971). Around 1980 the American Indian population of the U.S. and Canada will again reach the estimated two million mark that they had when they were first contacted by Europeans.

Indian life is generally one of *poverty*. Some cultures define a life of poverty as valuable in that it is non-materialistic, spiritual, non-competitive, and in tune with the natural environment, but in North America it is defined as stupid and without value. Indian life does look poor in terms of such majority society criteria as employment, income, housing, education, and health standards. The average family income of Indians on reservations is only about 45% of that of White families.

One should not, however, project too much misery into conceptions of the day-to-day life of Indians. Where the non-Indian visitor might suffer cultural shock in perceptions of reservation uncleanliness, drinking, and fighting, the person raised there usually looks back with loving warmth to his childhood in a close-knit community. Indian societies have values which, if used as criteria of evaluation of the majority society, could in turn make the style of life of the majority look "poverty stricken." These values differ somewhat from one Indian society to the next, so that Inuit, Hopi, and Menomini would all judge the pathologies in our styles of life in different ways. The majority North American society in the past received mostly material, rather than social or ideological, elements of culture from Native societies. Today, however, there is some evidence that Indian social and ideological culture is influencing the majority society. Vine Deloria claims that "American society is unconsciously going Indian" in its search for individual freedom within a socially tolerant community that is in ecological harmony with its environment.

We have already examined the process of convergent *social adaptation* through acculturation. In family life we have seen this in the increasingly predominant pattern of the monogamous, bilateral, patrilineal biased, nuclear family. However, there appear to be some residual differences in family life between even urbanized Indians and the majority society. Indian families seem to be less child-centered and have less emphasis on such things as toilet training, cleanliness, punctuality, competition, and worldly achievement. Another social feature is that, compared with non-Indians, modern Indian political processes tend to work more slowly and less aggressively, have more consensus, and involve more personal rapport between leaders and their constituency. When we examine Indian politics we first see that it is extremely complicated by factionalisms, but gradually we also see extensive gossip about politics and signs of genuine and personal involvement. Staying away from a political meeting is usually a sign of apathy in urban society, but it is often an active political protest of individuals or factions in Indian communities. Then, by having those most opposed away, the rest can continue with their working consensus politics.

We can expect to see many of the small tribes become assimilated while other larger, or more isolated, or more well-defended tribes survive as distinct socio-cultural units. That is, the Hopi should survive indefinitely because they have a relatively large population, they have some physical and social isolation from the majority society, and they have created defenses against assimilation. The Menomini, even though they have a large population and a large territory, have been strongly pressured toward termination by federal Indian Affairs and do not have well-developed defenses against assimilation.

The *ethnic renaissance* of Indians has had about a century of significant pan-Indian developments, but became a major movement only about fifteen years ago, at the Chicago Indian Conference in 1961. Since then, in addition to existing reservation and band administrations, about two hundred Indian political organizations developed in the U.S. and Canada. In Canada alone, 74 Native political associations were formed between 1960 and 1973 (Whiteside 1973: 38). Indian organizations have pressed all levels of government for action on their behalf, bringing changes in everything from the handling of Indians in history books to support for the economic development of reservations.

Chapter 7

The Evolution of Religion

Indian religious beliefs and rituals have changed so extensively in historic times that they make an excellent subject for the study of the evolution of religion. We see in this evolution systematic changes in supernatural beliefs and rituals to increase understanding and to control events that are beyond the realistic or naturalistic capacities of these cultures. Religion is defined here as a supernatural means to understand and to control events that are important to a society. It is a cultural means to cope with the unknown. An important part of what is unknown in an absolute sense is what one *should* do. Religion helps to define what is good, the problem of social values.

One evolutionary aspect of this religious support of social values is in terms of the way that society uses religion for what can be broadly classified as "political" ends: social pride, commitment to social goals, obedience within the existing social order, etc. Thus there is a correlation between the evolution of politics and religion, a correlation that is particularly apparent in conditions of rapid change. This pride, commitment, and involvement of individuals is seen here as essential for the health of both individuals and societies, and in this way religion contributes to humanistic ends. Religious activities are pronounced in social forms under conditions of rapid cultural change because of the society's attempts to reformulate its ideological system, and to develop supernatural means to cope with the new kinds of unknowns that precipitate the rapid cultural change.

This chapter begins with a brief description of the differences between the religions of Indian societies according to their aboriginal evolutionary levels. Then there is a description of religious reactions during the period of conquest by Whites. This illustrates that religious reactions are somewhat predictable according to the aboriginal evolutionary level of the society when it comes into contact with a state society. The Ghost Dance is selected as a case study which supports the above point.

The Luiseño-Cupeño case study is used to illustrate the introduction of Christianity in one cluster of reservations.

Sun Dance, Peyotism, and the Guardian Spirit Ceremonial, three nativistic pan-Indian religious complexes, are described as illustrations of the contemporary construction of social values, ethics, and social commitments through religion. Finally, I conclude with the most recent development in pan-Indian religious activity, the Indian Ecumenical Conference.

ABORIGINAL PERIOD

Aboriginally there were some 275 "societies" north of Mexico. The type of religion pursued in each society was correlated with the evolutionary level of society, as well as the specific environmental patterning in the tasks of the society. Band religion was primarily focussed on curing illnesses through shamanism and on the successful passage of life crises: birth, puberty, and death. They had increase rites for the major subsistence foods and a wide variety of very personal magical rituals, especially to ensure a continuing positive equilibrium with the forces and spirits of the supernatural world.

Among the Washo Indians, one might give an offering upon leaving a trail one had just used, by snapping a small twig. One might give a pinch of pinenut meal at every meal to feed the ghosts or other spirits. One would avoid walking near a certain cave where a cannibalistic monster lived, or going near a specific place along a particular stream where small, mischievous supernaturals were known to live under the water. People lived out their lives within a few connected valleys, but this small world was filled with history and supernaturals, as well as hot springs for ritual bathing, good food-gathering and hunting places, and traditional camping places.

Tribally organized societies have well-organized lineal kinship groups and often other "pan-tribal sodalities," such as warrior societies and curing societies, that go beyond the residential clusters of "bands" and tie the entire tribe together. While religion generally permeates tribal life, these sodalities invariably become social foci in the cultural expression of religion. They sponsor and perform rituals that are simultaneously social (in that they may be held in public and are presentations for the public), religious (in that they relate to and often are designed to influence the supernatural world), political (in that the gathering encourages political integration and political messages are conveyed), and economic (in that the sharing of food and trade occurs along with the rituals).

Tribal rituals that are well described in the ethnographic literature are things like the Pueblo calendar of Kiva society dances and the Huron-Iroquois "Feast of the Dead," mass reburials every several years. Explorers such as Samuel de Champlain and Gabriel Sagard described the Huron burial ceremonies of the early 1600s in this way:

Soon after death, the body was placed on a mat in a flexed position, wrapped in a robe, and set on a raised platform or interred in a below-ground grave in a small cemetery near the deceased's village. There was a small feast ceremony for relatives and close friends with lengthy orations at this time. However, every several years (reports range from eight to twelve years), a tribal-wide reburial was held. The timing may correlate with the planned abandonment of a sponsoring village which has exhausted the fertility of its surrounding agricultural soils. A tribal council of village representatives would try to decide which village would be honored by sponsoring the "Feast."

Prior to the "Feast," the bodies in the local temporary cemeteries would be disinterred, their bones stripped of flesh and tied up in bundles ready for transport to the new tribal grave site. Up to two weeks of feasting, dancing, and speeches then ensued as the villagers gradually converged, stopped at other villages along the way, celebrated the mass reburial, and then returned again to their home villages. "The final mass grave was usually a round pit, varying in size with the number of bodies and grave goods to be placed in it. The one at *Ossossane*, for example, was some 30 feet in diameter and five feet deep . . . containing about 1,000 skeletons. When the ceremony was finished the pit was covered with skins, logs, tree bark, and finally earth. The grave was then marked with a solid wooden fence." (Heidenreich, 1971:150). These burial mounds are found in most of the eastern agricultural areas from Southern Ontario through the Mississippi Valley.

Compared to "tribes," "chiefdoms" had still higher population densities; a more efficient food-producing technology; more specialization of labor; more ramification of social ranking and classes; and more centrally integrated economic, political, and religious systems around such "chiefs" as the heads of lineal kinship systems, village headmen, and the heads of powerful voluntary associations. In religion we find that the general shamanistic traditions of North America were modified into forms that were still more professional, more often performed at social gatherings in concert with political ends, and more standardized through the internal traditions of religious sodalities.

The integration of politics and religion was so great among a Southeastern chiefdom such as the Natchez that a certain ruler, called "Great Sun," had dictatorial powers through a theocracy with a priesthood bureaucracy, a temple on top of a large earthen mound, and a complex system of ranked social classes. The temple mound probably evolved in part at least from the earlier burial mounds, like those discussed for the Hurons, and the temple on top of the mound even contained the bones of former rulers.

Like North American tribally organized societies, the chiefdoms of coastal British Columbia aboriginally had (1) a cosmology, world view, and value system with both naturalistic and supernaturalistic dimensions; (2) curing by shaman specialists; (3) the vision quest or guardian spirit tradition, which was an individuation of the shamanistic spirit helper concept; (4) life-crisis observances; and (5) increase rites, especially through the placation of the spirits of the fish and game that was caught. The chiefdom quality of religious practice in these societies was expressed in the specific forms of the above features of religion, but it was especially revealed in the religious support of the elaborated status and political system and in the public, religious dramas performed by secret societies. These costumed dramas were largely reenactments of the adventures of the lineage or clan ancestors with supernaturals during the age of creation. They reiterated the sanction of political authority by supernatural powers, often telling about or displaying the gifts bestowed on an ancestor by the spirit powers. These were often held in conjunction with the "potlatch" feast that validated titles and the relative positions of social-political status. They are also completely integrated with the elaborate totemic system of the area.

RELIGIOUS REACTIONS TO CONQUEST

In religion, bands are rather individualistic, instead of having religion linked to a tribal political structure. Thus, although they reworked their religions throughout early historic times, they did so rather passively and without the formation of militant reactive church movements. There were almost no religious revitalization movements among the Inuit, northern Athabascans, northern Algonquins, Great Basin, or Baja California band societies. Tribally organized societies were generally the most difficult to control,often giving significant armed resistance, and it is primarily the tribes who formed revitalistic religious movements. They were also the most common kind of society in North America so the tribal patterns of reaction to conquest were the most widespread.

Religious reorganization is a universal process under cultural change, but the form that it takes depends very much upon the kind of society undergoing the changes, as well as the context of pressures for change. Thus religious reorganization in band societies does not usually take on a political character, while it does in tribal societies. It is these politically related religious changes which have attracted the most attention from researchers who ignore the quiet adaptations.

Popé, a Tewa priest, led the Pueblo Revolt of 1680 against the Spanish, but this did not emerge from or cause a religious revitalization. Other famous prophets who did lead religious revitalization movements were the Delaware Prophet in the 1700s; Tenskwatawa, the Shawnee and brother of Tecumseh, in the early 1800s; Handsome Lake, a Seneca, between 1799 and 1815; the Drum or Dream Dance of the Sault Sioux and other northern Plains tribes in the 1870s; John Slocum, who founded the Indian Shaker religion in the Puget Sound area in 1881; Smohalla, a Sahaptin of the Columbia River, 1864; Wodziwah, the Northern Paiute, who founded the first Ghost Dance in 1869; and Wovoka, the son of one of the older prophet's disciples, who started the second Ghost Dance in 1889. Famous revitalization movements were also started in California by the Chumash and in Northern Mexico by such groups as the Tepehuanes, the Tarahumaras, and the Mayos. There were literally hundreds of religious revitalization movements in the 1700s and the 1800s. Crowe (1974:150-1) mentions several prophet movements that appeared in northern Canada in the 1900s.

Wallace (1972:354) found no less than fifteen separate new religious movements among the Delaware Indians over a period of three hundred years, averaging once every twenty years but primarily clustering in five specific decades. Both situational stress on the Delawares and the stimulus of one movement which soon set off a later movement are suggested. The movements are seen as realistically adaptive or useful in terms of the culture's problems. They were apparently correlated with but lagging behind periods of cultural deprivation.

"The five decades of new religious acceptance followed some years after the years of impact of disaster, and they were not so much adaptations to the disaster itself as to the derivative, long-term cultural distortions which the disaster revealed and induced . . . it is loss of confidence in a familiar and explicitly reliable pattern of social relations . . . that stimulates the innovation or acceptance of new religions" (Wallace 1972:361). The new religions were not aimed at the restoration of land, the issues of war, or material hardships as much as the restoration of morality, identity, and social cohesion.

Waves of Christian missionaries preaching a wide variety of Christian doctrines have swept through the hundreds of different Indian societies over a period of some four hundred years. The resulting Native reactions are extremely diverse. Some societies maintained their old religions as fully as possible, and most successful retentions have been among those societies which generally had less deculturation for one reason or another. In the U.S. one thinks of certain groups in the Southwest: Hopi, Navajo, Eastern Pueblos, and Papago. The Hopi have the most successful retention of religion through their Kiva societies and an annual calendar of elaborate public dances, with a strong preservation of religious meanings. This conservative retention requires far more effort on the part of the Hopi than those societies which have simply accepted the Christian missionaries and their doctrines, but the Hopi in return have one of the most proud, aesthetic, and theologically sophisticated cultural traditions in North America.

The Navajo elaborated ancient shamanistic curing and anti-witchcraft practices into beautiful ceremonies with sand paintings and male choral singing. The Navajo (along with the Apache) arrived into the Southwest fairly recently (about 1400 A.D.). They learned sandpainting (as well as agriculture and weaving) from the Pueblo societies, but whereas the Pueblos used religion primarily for agricultural ends, the Navajo continued their typical band society religious orientation on curing. Thus sand paintings not only have different functions in Pueblo Kiva societies and Navajo curing "sings," but those differences conform to what we would predict from the theory of cultural evolution.

The Navajo rejected the Ghost Dance, probably because of their fear of the dead, but since the spread of Peyotism among them in the early 1940s they have become the major center of the Native American Church in the Southwest, with thousands of members. The Eastern or Rio Grande Pueblos had much closer contact with the Spanish missionaries than the Hopi or Navajo, so they incorporated some Catholic forms of beliefs and rituals into their existing ceremonial system. "The Papagos accepted certain Catholic elements as alternative ways to their aboriginal religion, with a minimum of integration of the two," and "The Yaquis reworked the whole ceremonial system, integrating so many Catholic elements into it that a wholly new religion appeared to result" (Spicer 1962:506).

Very often Christian supernaturals were placed within the Indian pantheon or considered as other names for aboriginally identified supernaturals. God, Jesus, the Virgin, and the Christian prophets were incorporated into existing systems of belief, although this indigenization process modified their qualities. Spicer (1962) wrote that the major influences of the Protestant missionary program in the Southwest between 1870 and 1920 were (1) often to regenerate a community life that had been disorganized by the government reservation system, (2) to stimulate political factionalism within communities, and (3) to form new Christian sects, especially through the formation of independent churches that withdrew from their national parental organizations. Much of the latter was the result of accommodations to local Indian customs that were not sanctioned by the national organization.

Just as there were religious *revitalistic* reactions to White conquest, there have been religious *repressive* movements led by White religious leaders. By a religious repressive movement, I mean an organized and coordinated attempt to use the diverse institutions of the conquering state to destroy the aboriginal religion. This seems particularly true when Whites came in contact with advanced tribes such as the Hopi, chiefdoms such as those of the Northwest, and states such as the Aztecs. The religions of these societies could effectively resist the missionaries because they were backed up by politically supported priesthoods.

In British Columbia the Protestant missionaries had a difficult time winning converts from the aboriginal religions, so they convinced the Canadian government to outlaw the major aboriginal religious ceremony, the potlatch. The Potlatch Law was established by proclamation in 1882, by statute in 1884, and finally repealed in 1951. "Every Indian or other person who engages in celebrating the Indian festival known as the "Potlatch" or in the Indian dance known as "Tasmanawas" is guilty of a misdemeanor, and shall be liable to imprisonment for a term of not more than six nor less than two months . . ." Some White police officers and judges rebelled against the law, in part because it did not define what a potlatch was and what specifically was wrong with it. The law was extremely difficult to enforce, but it still legalized the harassment of Indian religious services.

Among many others, the Nass River Indians petitioned to repeal the law. "We see in your graveyards the white marble and granite monuments which cost money in testimony of your grief for your dead. When our people die we erect a large pole, call our people together, distribute our personal property with them in payment for their sympathy and condolence; comfort to us in the sad hours of our affliction. This is what is called a potlatch—the privilege denied us."

In the U.S. there was widespread repression of Indian religions. The most infamous was the massacre of the Ghost Dancers at Wounded Knee in 1890. There were many attempts to outlaw the Pueblo kachina dances. The Sun Dance was forbidden by the U.S. B.I.A. between 1910 and 1934. The Native American Church has had a continuous history of persecution.

THE GHOST DANCE

The Ghost Dance was one of the most widely spread religious revitalization movements of the nineteenth century and it has the unusual feature of having been started within a band-organized society, the Northern Paiutes of western Nevada. The 1849 Gold Rush in California and the 1859 (and later) silver mining in western Nevada brought many Whites into Northern Paiute territory, rapidly displacing the Indians. By 1869 the Union Pacific Railroad line was completed through their territory. In that same year a shaman by the name of Wodziwah began to prophesy that the world would end and the dead Indians would return to help rebuild a new world. He called on his followers to take the traditional ceremonial baths, dance the traditional round dance of the Great Basin, and sing certain chants with the dance. Among the Paiute the movement remained as only a slight reworking of traditional Paiute religion without stimulating a militant reaction against White culture. These band-organized people continued their relatively passive relationship to White dominance. However, these prophecies had more impact when they were spread by Indian missionaries to tribal societies in southern Oregon and northern California (Barber 1972). In California the Ghost Dance apparently stimulated the Earth Lodge Cult in 1871 among the Wintun, which predicted the end of the world through fire, wind, or flood, from which the Indians would be saved by gathering underground in traditional earth lodges. It probably also stimulated the Bole-Maru Cult of 1872 which had dances, ornamental uniforms, and a Christian-like heaven as a reward.

Wovoka, a son of one of Wodziwah's assistants, revived the Ghost Dance in 1889. He visited the spirit world in a trance and God directed him to give the Indians a message of love, peace, returning to the old ways, and dancing and singing to bring the millennium. If the Indians would do these things, the Whites would disappear, and the dead Indians would return to help build a happy new world without death or disease. Although missionaries again traveled to California, the second Ghost Dance had little success there, probably because they were now disillusioned from the earlier failure of the prophecy and, although their deprivation was still great, they were rapidly adapting to a White Christian ideology. It had no effect on the Pueblos or the Navajo. It was well received by many other tribal societies. The recently displaced Walapai practiced it for three years and the Havasupai for one year. It was enthusiastically received and modified into a more militant, political movement by such recently defeated Plains tribes as the Arapaho, Cheyenne, Comanche, and Sioux.

The Sioux version involved the return of the buffalo, bulletproof magic shirts, and the idea that the return of the Indian dead would mean that the Whites would be outnumbered in future battles. In 1890, the U.S. Army massacre of over two hundred Sioux, including women and children, at a Ghost Dance at Wounded Knee, South Dakota, crushed the movement in the Plains.

THE INTRODUCTION OF CHRISTIANITY TO THE LUISEÑO-CUPEÑO

The Luiseño and Cupeño live principally on four reservations in San Diego County, California: Pala—a fairly heavily populated Indian town centered on an old Spanish mission, Pauma and Rincon—two lightly populated agricultural communities, and La Jolla—essentially a retirement community on the flank of Mount Palomar with only old people who stayed on when the young families moved to cities for jobs. This case study illustrates that a gradual and passive conversion to Christianity was the most common experience among these Indians who had had an advanced band level society aboriginally. They have had a slow and gradual loss of aboriginal beliefs and rituals. The case shows the factionalism among Indians that can be generated by factionalism among the diverse proselytizing Christian sects. Finally, the case illustrates that conversions to Protestantism tended to follow kinship connections.

What remains of the aboriginal religion at Rincon and Pauma is organized in this way. The Indians on each reservation are divided into two clans, each of which has a ceremonially reciprocal clan in another reservation. Thus the two Rincon clans are traditionally reciprocal to two Pauma clans. The religious officials are arranged in a hierarchy down from the religious chief or *noth*. Four ceremonial officials are below the *noth*, each with specific duties. Today there are three remaining *noth*, each with no more than three assistants, and the clan system is dying out with the death of the old leaders. It is a common complaint among the Indians that the wakes and clothes-burning ceremonies (*tchoiyish*) have turned into drinking feasts attended by the young only because free food and drink are provided throughout the night.

Catholicism first came to the Luiseño in 1798, with the founding of the Mission San Luis Ray by the Franciscan Fathers. In 1816 the Indians were subjected to more intensive Catholic influence, when the Mission San Antonio de Pala was established as a subsidiary to San Luis Ray and a further link to the inland chain of missions. Because there was no resident priest in Pala until after 1903, the effectiveness of this effort was limited. Little more was taught the Indians than a summary of beliefs, emphasizing the need to at least baptize all Indian babies. Before 1908 there were no churches at Rincon or La Jolla, but itinerant Protestant priests began coming at least once every few years and Catholic mass was held in a series of schoolhouses or temporary shelters. In 1925 permanent buildings were constructed at La Jolla and Rincon, but mass was still held no more than once every two or three months by the fathers from Pala until 1948 when it became weekly.

There is only one church in Pala, the Catholic Mission San Antonio de Pala: church, rectory, two wings of class rooms, and recreation center. Although all the Indians in Pala are baptized Catholics, active participation in church activities is very low. A small group of church leaders attend church weekly and do a great deal of volunteer work, but the majority of the Indians seldom go to church. The Catholic Church allows the Indians to continue religious ceremonies such as wakes and clothes burnings, the priest even performing Catholic rites at the wakes. In addition, some Indian elements were incorporated into certain Catholic ceremonies, such as an emphasis on honoring the dead in a yearly All Saints' Day ceremony.

In 1904 a Protestant missionary group of two couples passed through La Jolla and Rincon, spending a few days at each place. During their stay in La Jolla they gained one strong convert. He began preaching to his relatives, thus easing the acceptance of Protestantism by other Indians. Today his family is central to Protestantism in La Jolla, while a branch of a related family are central to Protestantism in Rincon.

THE SUN DANCE

The Sun Dance is the most widespread, distinctly religious Native dance ceremony in North America today. It has been practiced at one time or another among almost all the tribes of the Plains. Extensive theorizing about the origin and historical spread of the dance was done in the first half of this century. Now these arguments ("diffusion," "revitalization," "supernatural power is sought when political power fails," etc.) are being reexamined in light of a whole new revitalization of the Sun Dance.

The dance is held by the tribe for several young men who make an agreement between themselves and God, and vow to take part in the dance. It is a ritual that by its performance asks for supernatural assistance, perhaps to cure oneself or a relative. The decision to dance may have initially come to the dancer in a dream or a vision. The dancers sacrifice themselves in the following ways:

1. Fast for four days, although water is allowed.
2. Behave in an ideal way with bravery, generosity, strength, and honesty.
3. Abstain from sexual intercourse before and during the dance.
4. Accept the guidance of an instructor who has gone through the dance.
5. Speak little. Pray with your instructor while preparing for the dance and each morning as the sun comes up during the four days of the dance. Pray while smoking tobacco. Pray while you dance for four days staring at a symbol on the sacred pole.

6. Avoid anger or the joking, drinking, and gambling of the hundreds of non-participants who come to the dance.
7. Ritually purify yourself by some combination of bathing, sweat bathing, smelling the incense of sweet grass smoke, rubbing sage leaves over the body, and sleeping on beds made of sage branches.
8. You may also offer parts of your flesh at the end of the dance as you tear away from skewers fastened by thongs to a pole attached to your breast or back.

Depending on the tribe, there are often minor religious or social ceremonies that accompany the dance, such as the ritual opening and recitation of events associated with sacred bundles, the recitation of "coups" or acts of distinctive bravery by the participants, the piercing of children's ears to wear earrings, social dances, and gambling. There are also variations in the way the Sun Dance itself is performed.

The Shoshoni emphasize purification and curing. The Southern Ute are said to relate it more than others to dreaming. The Crow use it for personal power while the Cheyenne believe it is a world renewal ceremony that recharges the energy of the universe. A large pole in the center of the dance ground is universally used and high on this pole, usually in a "Y" crotch of the "sacred tree," is a religious symbol that the dancers stare at. There are, however, many tribal variations on such things as the kind of tree used, its form, how the tree is designated, cut down, brought in, placed in a hole dug for it in the dance ground, and the specific symbol on the tree (buffalo head, bear head, eagle, etc.). Facial and body paints and costumes are variable and usually individualistic. Today dancers often wear only shorts or denim pants, but they may add traditional things such as rabbitskin anklets or bison hair armlets.

The Sun Dance is held in mid-summer, traditionally when the bands of a tribe were united for buffalo hunting and when the sun was the highest in the sky. A round dance lodge with a high fence made of poles and brush is constructed. This has an entrance to the east, the sacred tree in the center, a buffalo-skin altar slightly west of that, small stalls for the dancers to lie down in along the west wall of the lodge, and places for drummers and officials on the southeast and visitors on the northeast.

Facing the sacred tree, the dancers dance a short, shuffling dance from their stall on the edge of the lodge toward the tree and back again, toward the tree and back again, hour after hour. As they dance, they blow on a whistle having a high chirping note, made from the wing bone of an eagle. Some may become exhausted and lie down and sleep for an hour or two. Sometimes people who have not made a vow this year but have gone through the ceremony in earlier years will join in the dancing for awhile. Four men at a time play the big drum to accompany the dancing. Some tribes add men with rattles and mixed choral singing to accompany the dancing. The drummers will play for about two hours, stop for an hour, play for two hours, etc.

At the end of the four days, the dancers may further torture themselves by being tied by skewers through the flesh to the tree, to poles in four directions, to something such as a buffalo skull which is dragged, or to thongs that pass through the crotch of the tree,by which the person.is pulled off the ground. They then "sacrifice the flesh" by forcibly pulling the skewers through the flesh. The resulting scars are worn with the great pride of men who have publicly demonstrated their fortitude and bravery. Most dances today end simply with prayers, but this "being pierced" is still allowed in some groups for individuals who have vowed to do it.

THE NATIVE AMERICAN CHURCH

Peyote is a small, grey-green, spineless cactus that grows wild in parts of Northern Mexico and the Rio Grande Valley in Texas. The head or "button" grows about two inches in diameter and one to two inches high. The mature plant contains nine alkaloids, including mescaline, that have various strychnine-like and morphine-like reactions in people: intoxicating, pain-killing, and hallucinogenic (Stewart 1944). Since the several alkaloids have different physiological effects, the reaction of peyote in man is very complex but usually follows a pattern of initial euphoria and exhilaration followed by lassitude, the impulse to vomit, and sensory hallucinations, especially color hallucinations. It is neither physiologically addictive nor regarded by modern medicine to be of significant medical value. It has a bitter, unpleasant taste, but has been eaten for centuries by certain Native societies in order to acquire visionary experiences, as a means to cure illness, and in other Native religious contexts. In historic times peyote was incorporated into a pan-tribal religious movement that spread out of the southern Plains in the late 1800s as far north as some Canadian Ojibwa use, reported for 1936. The Kiowa and Comanche developed the modern rite in about 1885 and it had traveled as far as Taos Pueblo by the 1890s.

Scare stories of the narcotic effect of peyote (addictive, killing, sexual arousal, etc.) were widespread in the early decades of this century and led to the persecution and arrest of practitioners. The religion was then formally incorporated as the Native American Church in 1918 to more effectively fight for freedom to use peyote in services under the constitutional protection of freedom of religion. After decades of legal battles the use of peyote was legalized in the U.S. for members of the Church. The Church claims a membership of about 250,000.

The Native American Church members use the Bible and are generally close to Christianity, except that rituals have a Native origin and peyote is used. Peyote is seen as a medium through which the believer communes with God. Through peyote the essential knowledge for life is revealed as long as one is devout in the Church. It is treated with respect and sacredness, comparable in some ways to a sacramental offering such as the Eucharist. For example, one common procedure is for the peyote to be taken in the right hand, motions are made four times toward the fire, the peyote is placed in the mouth, and then the person rubs his hands over his body. Peyote is used informally as a medicinal herb, but its most powerful impact is felt to be when it is taken in the context of a religious service. I will describe my introduction to Peyotism among the Washo Indians in Woodfords, California in the summer of 1961.

One of my principal informants was the head of the local Native American Church and he often liked to change the topic of our interview sessions to that of Peyotism. Eventually he introduced me to the various local church leaders and I attended two of the all-night meetings. One of the Church leaders told about what had happened when they were persecuted for using peyote. "The Deputy took our medicine away and stamped on it in the street. Later his car rolled over. He was seriously injured and he was fired from his job. A similar thing happened when his replacement took our medicine out of our car." He told many stories of how people had been helped by the Church. "Last Saturday a woman was paralyzed on the right side. We went over and had a short service for her. She got a lot better by morning. She could move her right arm right away." These were the procedures for the regular service:

1. A tipi is constructed with the opening flap to the east and an aesthetic V-shaped style of log fire in the center.
2. An altar mound of dirt covered with clean sand is shaped into the form of a one-third moon crescent just west of the fire. The chief of the service sits behind the altar and places a large peyote button in the center of this crescent during the service.
3. The chief drummer sits on the right side of the chief of the service. The drummer prepares a water drum from an iron kettle, tuned to the right pitch by pouring off a small amount of water.
4. The cedarman sits on the left of the chief of the service and puts small branches of cedar on the fire at appropriate times to produce an incense smoke that practitioners brush on themselves or on an ill person to purify themselves.
5. Everything involving the taking of turns passes from person to person in a clockwise motion around the tipi and is usually initiated by the chief of the service.
6. Ritual is patterned in fours: four balls of peyote are taken at one time, sage-tobacco cigarettes used to accompany prayers are puffed in sets of four puffs, the rattle and feather fans are passed four times through the incense of cedar smoke, songs are sung in sets of four.
7. Services last from about 10:00 p.m. on Saturday evening until after dawn on Sunday morning and are held about once every month or two.
8. The chief gives a prayer at the entrance and then the group enters, moving clockwise around the tipi to their assigned positions. Adult males take the first row, closest to the fire, and when their wives and children come to the service they sit behind their men, close to the sides of the tent.
9. Prayers spoken to the group are made while smoking a cigarette made of crushed sage leaves and tobacco. The chief begins with invocations for help for sick members of the community, help on community problems, and help for other Peyote churches.
10. A bowl of ground-up peyote rolled into small balls is passed around;

each man takes four and swallows them. This is repeated a few times during the service, each man deciding for himself when he has had enough.

11. The chief starts off the singing. He shakes a rattle in his right hand, holds a feather fan in his left hand, and sings four of his Peyote songs while the drummer on his right accompanies him. It is usually a fast beat on the drum and the singer slips in and out of a falsetto voice, singing a chant with a fairly complex melodic line. The equipment and roles then shift clockwise, one person at a time. Although temporarily stopped by several other rituals that come up during the night, the drumming and singing continue until the end.
12. Special curing rituals are performed for ill persons who have come to the service. A prayer is made while smoke from cedar or sage-tobacco cigarettes is blown on the sick person's body, which is then brushed with a feather fan.
13. At dawn, a ritual breakfast in the tipi is served of corn, beans, and other Indian foods, such as acorn biscuits, pinenut gruel, and roast rabbit. The service ends when the peyote button is taken from the altar and water is poured from the drum. People then talk casually, such as asking the chief for interpretations of their visions.

THE SALISH GUARDIAN SPIRIT CEREMONIAL

The acquisition by individuals of some supernatural power seems to be a universal value in traditional Native American societies, although the power may be dangerous to its human vessel. Shamanism is essentially an extreme concern about and use of that power, usually aimed toward curing the illnesses of others. The most common means of acquiring such power is to induce an existing spirit to act in one's behalf, particularly in a continuing or "guardian spirit" relationship. The initial search for and contacts with a guardian spirit are normally made by putting oneself in a special state of sacredness: through removal from ordinary daily activities; through physical removal from the community; through physical stresses such as fasting, running, and bathing in cold water; and through auto-hypnosis engendered by such things as meditation and chanting. In this state, an individual spirit appears to the initiate and instructs him on how to call on the powers the spirit possesses by taking on a new name, a costume, a dance, a distinctive facial painting, a song, and perhaps other rituals. Powers come from a wide variety of spirits: Owl, "the father of all trees," "a great tall old man with long hair like a woman," Deer, etc.

In the Plateau area the guardian spirit quest was extended as a puberty ceremony for all boys, while in the Northwest Coast culture area it was used more in relationship with the social hierarchy as a mark of aristocratic rank in a dramatic secret society initiation. The Coast Salish around Vancouver and Seattle are geographically between these two areas and intermediate in their guardian spirit practices, combining the general emphasis on the guardian spirit quest and on Shamanism with the secret society initiation of the Northwest chiefdoms.

This "spirit dancing" was outlawed in 1871 in Washington Territory and was suppressed under the anti-Potlatch law in Canada from 1884 to 1951.However, White society was never able to completely eliminate the Native religion. It was revitalized as a small sect in the 1950s and then flourished as the basic Coast Salish religion, first in Washington in the 1960s and then in the Fraser River Valley in British Columbia after 1967.

Indian healing power is now seen as a divine compensation to Indians to balance the technological superiority of Whites. Women today participate in the spirit dancing. Individuals are now usually drawn into a spirit society through a "death and rebirth" initiation when they have a spirit possession they cannot handle, resulting in a "spirit illness."

The initiate is ceremonially "killed," made unconscious and rigid, and is reborn in the society. He is physically grabbed by ritualist aides with blackened faces who throw him in the air, carry him around, bite him on the chest and abdomen, "club" him with a power-filled cane or rattle, and "kill" him by such things as manhandling or throwing him in ice-cold water. He is kept quiet, blindfolded or covered with blankets and secluded in a small cubicle for at least four days, except for periods of extreme exertion such as being chased at full speed around the church, called a "longhouse" or "smokehouse." He must fast even when tempted by having food placed in his mouth, which he must spit out. He is not allowed to smoke tobacco during the initiation nor to take alcoholic beverages for one year. He is deprived of sleep by the nearby drumming and chanting of the initiating workers. Finally the vision comes.

One participant described the initiation as "brainwashing." "*Your brain is back to nil*, anything you're taught during those ten days is going to stick with you, you'll never forget it." Another compared the new power to a drug state. "I was jumping three feet high and I had such a thrill, a terrific feeling as if you were floating . . . . I've only had such a feeling once before in my life when I was on heroin mainlining, but then I went through hell afterwards." An Indian elder described his "trance." "When you are sitting there you feel a real jolt that makes you jump up and dance . . . your muscles get really strong . . . there is a shield coming down over your eyes so that you don't see anything . . . you just hear your song and the drums . . . you wouldn't run into the fire or fall down, your spirit guide will not let you do this . . . . You always turn to the left, never to the right; so in turning to the left you go right around the hall . . . you sober up . . . suddenly you are back to reality."

Novices of both sexes wear a long woolen headdress that covers the head, face, and shoulders during ceremonies. Today this headdress may include a colourful ribbon printed with the date and place of a novice's rebirth. The novices also hold a long decorated pole which is hidden in the forest at the end of the ceremonial season. Then the established dancers wear a headdress with human hair and feathers.

The church in any Salish community has a small number (a dozen or so) core members: elder ritualists, established "black-face" dancers, and novices in their first ceremonial season after their initiation. Beyond these people are the relatives, friends, and initiation sponsors of the core members who support the winter ceremonials in local churches, the "smokehouses." Patients are brought in and treated at the ceremonies. Then, an even broader circle of hundreds of Native people come occasionally as spectators of the psychodramatic ceremonials, much like the passive attendance of church services. The ceremonials are seen as a means to restore and preserve physical and emotional well-being, to overcome problems of addiction and suicidal tendencies, to promote self-actualization, and to promote the social integration and acceptance of individuals. These are a psychiatrist's comments (Jilek 1974:92):

> *At the Salish winter ceremonial, each spirit dancer . . . re-enters a trance-like state in order to feel and display the personal spirit power originally acquired in the altered state of consciousness induced by initiation procedures. Some dancers are experienced virtuosi in achieving such a state; they work themselves up with loud hyperventilation and vehement commotion, to pass into song and dance when dozens of deer-hide drums strike in. The dancer's spirit finds its dramatized expression in dance steps, tempo, movements, miens and gestures: in the sneaking pace, then flying leaps of the ferociously yelling "warrior," or in the swaying trot of the plump, sadly weeping "bear mother," in the rubber-like reptilian writhing of the "double-headed serpent" as well as in the desperate wailing and gesticulation of the "mother seeking her child."*

The church uses four objects of power in the ceremonies: two loops of cedar branches or roots wrapped with scarlet cloth, and two "power boards"—black or red, rectangular with holes with which to grasp the boards, and sometimes with a carved or painted face or skeleton. Pairs of assistants hold on to an instrument.

> *"As drums beat fast rhythms and women sacrificed food by throwing it into the fire, the two instruments seemed to swiftly drag their bearers through the hall. Pulling together with irresistible magnetic attraction, the powerful tools could only be severed again and handled by the Indian Doctor himself. Soon the instruments moved toward the persons singled out for treatment, gently stroking along the heads and bodies of the clients."*
>
> (Jilek 1974: 90).

THE INDIAN ECUMENICAL CONFERENCE

In the 1960s many Christian churches in the U.S. and Canada reexamined their relationships with Native people. As a part of that movement the Anglican Church of Canada commissioned Charles E. Hendry to survey Church policies and his final report, *Beyond Traplines*, called for consultations and programs that led to the formation of the Ecumenical Conference. In 1961 the Anglican Reverend John MacKenzie called on the Cherokee anthropologist, Robert K. Thomas, and the Odawa Ojibwa Director of Toronto's Institute of Indian Studies, Wilfred Pelletier, to start the planning of the Conference. With financial aid from the Anglican Church, planning meetings with about twelve Native religious leaders were held in Manitoba, Missouri, and Oklahoma. The first Conference was held in August 1970 at Crow Agency, on the Crow Indian Reservation, Montana.

It was decided that the Conference would be in official session for four days because four is the sacred number for most Indian tribes. Medicine men would pick out and consecrate an area of ground for the Conference site itself. They would also arrange religious ceremonies at the dawn of each of the four days. Formal sessions were held during the days and there were informal visits in the evening, including attendance at the Crow Fair, held at the same time. There was great freedom and tolerance in the discussions in spite of a wide diversity of cultural backgrounds. The strong consensus was that modern Indian religious life must be built on the Indian historic traditions, values, and philosophies. It was agreed that both traditional and Christian ceremonies must be part of that continuity and can be mutually supportive and integrated.

I have abstracted the resolutions of the first Conference as follows:

1. We oppose all interference in the natural and sacred relation between the Indian people and the animals and birds which the Creator placed on this island for our physical and spiritual sustenance. By interference we mean such things as requiring Indians to have a permit to hunt eagles, the disregarding of Indian hunting rights in Oklahoma, the encouragement of commercial hunting of caribou in the Northwest Territories, the promotion of sportsman hunting to the detriment of hunting for food by Indians, etc. . . . Conservation officers should consult Indian religious leaders about conservation practices.
2. We recommend that the governments of Arizona, New Mexico, and Utah cease harassing members of the Native American Church.
3. We express the strongest disapproval of the perversion of Indian sacred dances for commercial purposes by unauthorized groups, the taking of the Peyote sacrament by non-Indians in a secular context, and all other mockeries of our ancient traditions.
4. We petition denominational authorities to permit those who work among Indian groups the freedom to use Native languages, traditions, dances, legends, and their own ancient religions as instruments of expression of the Christian life.
5. We request that mission activity be coordinated so as not to encourage excessive competition among sects in Indian communities.
6. We point out to the governments of the United States and Canada that our treaties with them are not secular contracts to us but sacred covenants, ordained and sanctioned by God, which guarantee our existence as people and which establish a sacred reciprocity among the Indian, God, the natural world, and our recent European brothers.
7. We encourage the teaching of Indian culture and language in schools. Non-essential educational standards should be waived so that Native religionists can be utilized in such programs.
8. We recommend that it be the policy of all public health agencies to work in cooperation with Indian medicine men.
9. We call upon the national church organizations to take specific action

to ensure that all its members extend their respect and assistance to small Christian denominations, such as the Native American Church.

10. We oppose the indiscriminate desecration of our historic and religious monuments, burial grounds, and pictographs by universities, park services, the Army Corps of Engineers, Highway Department, and so forth. Indian religious leaders of the tribes involved should be consulted before any excavations of these sacred places take place. The sacred relics which are now in museums, and which were collected by quasi-legal and immoral methods, should be returned on request to the tribe involved.

Later Conferences were held in about the third week in July on the Stoney (Assiniboin) Reserve near Morley, Alberta in the foothills of the Rocky Mountains about forty miles west of Calgary. It was felt that the noise and the midway of the Crow Fair were not appropriate to the Conference so a new time and place was selected. The third (1972) Conference began with the laying of a sacred fire and the blessing of the Conference grounds with the Navajo tobacco ceremony. Highlights included dancing, the sweetgrass pipe ceremony, and an Anglican Mass by Reverend Andrew Ahenakew, held in a tipi. His mass was in Cree and he wore black vestments, a traditional religious color of the Cree. The fourth (1973) Conference had tents set out in a circle and increased the time from four to seven days to allow time for "the young men to accompany the old people into mountain retreats for religious fasting." Attendance steadily increased from 250 (93 official delegates from 47 tribes) in 1970 to about 2,000 in 1976.

The Indian Ecumenical Conference is a new religious revitalization movement, although it is occurring in a very modern form. It was initially designed by sophisticated Indians with educations in the social sciences and it took the format of a conscious attempt at pan-Indian religious integration. The call to the Conference went out to Indians all across the U.S. and Canada. When we take into account the relatively small numbers of Indians from aboriginally band-organized societies, it is clear that the response has been biased in favor of these people, particularly Cree, other northern Algonquians, and northern Athabascans. These are people from societies which have been the last to be drawn into intensive contact with Whites. They are societies which were largely beyond the sphere of diffusion of earlier religious revitalization movements such as the Sun Dance and Peyotism. Thus a combination of evolutionary and historical relationships helps to account for this difference in participation.

Official delegates tend to have a broad geographical representation, in part because they are helped with transportation costs. Still, even the delegates show this bias in favor of people from aboriginally band-organized societies. For example, the ninety-three Canadian delegates in 1972 were distributed according to region as follows: British Columbia 3, Alberta 20, Saskatchewan 17, Manitoba 2, Ontario 21, Maritimes 4, and Northwest Territories 26. Since the Conference is held on an Assiniboin reserve in Southern Alberta, we would expect, on the grounds of simple geographical proximity, a predominant attendance by the local people from such aboriginally tribal-organized societies as the Assiniboin, Blood, Blackfoot, and Sarsi. Instead we find that the Conference particularly attracts the aboriginally band-organized Cree from northern Alberta and Saskatchewan and the Athabascans from the Northwest Territories. Few people have ever come to the Conference from such aboriginally tribal societies as the Iroquois or the British Columbia chiefdom societies (Tsimshian, Kwakiutl, Haida, etc.), although they are very populous societies.

SUMMARY

The evolution of U.S. and Canadian Indian religions has been presented as systematic changes in the use of supernatural means to understand and control events that have been important to these societies. Band level hunting and gathering societies focussed on curing illnesses, the successful passage of life-crises events, increase rites for the major subsistence foods, and the maintenance of a positive, personal equilibrium with the forces of the supernatural world. The evolutionary shift in tribes toward greater food production in the horticulture of the Southwest and Eastern Woodlands, intensive fishing along the North Pacific Coast, and the late horse pastoralism of the Plains brought along higher population densities, more political coordination, *and added politically relevant, socially held religious rituals*. The individualistic and personal levels of religious belief and practice are not lost. It is just that now there is an added layer of public religion, such as the "Feast of the Dead," that helps to support and integrate the "political" system in a broad sense and build commitments to common social values. The Southeast and Northwest Coast chiefdoms evolved richer economic bases, higher population densities, social classes, more centralized politics, *and elaborate religious dramas*.

Bands, tribes, and chiefdoms had systematically different religious reactions to their conquest by the Europeans than state level societies. Bands tend to passively accept conquest without religious reactions. Their involvement with new religious movements has been late and largely in religions developed elsewhere, such as the fundamental Protestant churches among the Luiseño, Peyotism among the Washo, and now the Indian Ecumenical Conference among the Cree and other Northern Canadians. The Ghost Dance began as a passive religious movement among the band-organized Northern Paiute and was then converted into a militant religious reaction to White conquest by surrounding tribal societies.

Tribally organized societies have generally been the source of the strongest reactions to conquest, both military and religious. Both the Sun Dance, a nativistic revival, and Peyotism, an accommodation between Christianity and pan-Indian Nativism, had their origin and greatest impact among the Plains tribes. Through cooption of their leadership, the chiefdoms have had a relatively peaceful acceptance of White authority. By their pre-adaptations to a very socially and politically relevant religion, people from chiefdom societies have been generally receptive to Christian missionary efforts.

The historical perspective has been deemphasized here to concentrate on the evolutionary perspective, but it too is important for a complete understanding. For example, the specific and historically derived values of the conquering Europeans created a legal screen which contributed to selective patterns of destruction of aboriginal religions. Features of Indian cultures, with their religious support, that were in sharp conflict with European values were quickly destroyed while other features were left intact. Intertribal warfare, plural marriage, the Northwest Coast potlatch feasts, and countless other religiously supported customs were suppressed through state laws while the Indians were allowed to continue most of their "harmless" costumed dances. The use of peyote and the self-torture of the Sun Dance do flaunt an Indian difference. To some extent, however, it is that part of Indian religion that was conceived by the Europeans as harmless that has been allowed to survive as Indian religion. Thus, for example, there have been recent strong pressures on the Salish in the Fraser River Valley to soften their initiation ceremonies into spirit-dancing societies because of the death of an initiate in 1972 and another in 1973.

The difference between evolutionary and historical analysis here is that *evolutionary* theory tells us that any conquering state society would have systematically changed things. Certain kinds of things, such as intertribal warfare, would be eliminated by any conquering state. *Historical* theory helps us to understand the relationships between specific cultures and specific changes. Therefore, if another state tradition, such as the Chinese, had conquered aboriginal North America they might have allowed plural marriages and potlatch feasts, but eliminated cultural features that conflicted with their own specific values.

Chapter 8

The Arts

Art is defined here as a type of sensual and symbolic play that is characteristic of adults and in which acts or objects are created and appreciated. It is a very human extension of our primate senses and physical propensities. We find joy simply in doing what we are biologically and neurologically designed to do. Dance is an extension of our universal biological joys of physical movement, with accretions of culturally specific meanings attached to the dances: beautiful, religious, etc. Singing is an extension of our primate, sign type of oral communication or "calling." Poetry and literature are extensions of the human, symbolic type of oral communication or "language." Music draws both from the rhythms of dance and the melodies of singing. It is common, of course, to have dance, singing, poetry, and music all combined in one social presentation. Compared to the physical and auditory arts, basketry, carving, painting, potting, and weaving are tactile and visual; their products are usually more tangible and permanent; and their presentation is usually more private.

There is little evidence of cultural diffusion of artistic practices between the Eastern and Western hemispheres (such as the diffusion of the flat drum in the North) and yet there are a great many similarities because of human and other universals. Art competes for human time and energy with many other general activities, such as food production, warfare, and courtship, and particularly with other symbolic games, such as those found in religion and politics. Hunters and gatherers have little time for art over the needs of food, shelter, clothing, and travel, and since they must travel very lightly they have a poor capacity to carry objects of art. Thus, there is some correlation between general social complexity and the complexity of art. At one extreme, the Paiute produced very little graphic art and what they did produce, such as in basketry, tended to be uncrowded, symmetrical, unenclosed, and in straight lines. At the other extreme, the Kwakiutl produced a large amount of art and this tended toward an intense, involuted, graphic style: enclosed and crowded figures with predominantly curved lines. Simple cultures tend to have round houses and straight-lined visual art, while complex cultures have rectangular houses and more curvilinear art.

The evolutionary direction, of course, is not *always* toward something such as crowded figures, but toward specialization, elaboration, and artistic play within a cultural context. In Mesoamerica, for example, there seems to have been some cyclical fluctuation over time in dominant styles: to simplicity in Olmec art in the early east, then to a continuing run toward complexity in Mayan art in the south, but with a northern swing during Toltec times from complex to simple, and finally a return in the north to extreme complexity in Aztec art. In the Eastern Hemisphere, the ideal of simplicity permeates the Taoist and Zen aesthetics of East Asia, focusing on such things as an uncarved block of wood, raw silk, and fortuitous events in nature as aesthetic.

Beyond biological and neurological patterning, artistic play is also patterned by (1) the inherent "structure" of the art medium, such as the angular tendencies in basketry and weaving and the more fluid tendencies in carving and painting; (2) the specific material culture of a society, with its tools and technical skills; (3) the "functional" expression of a society through its art, as art is used in the social ends of religion, politics, and economics, and now ethnic identity; and (4) the content of the ideological symbols of each cultural tradition, what people within a society believe is the meaning of their art. Symboling is "arbitrary," creatively "open," and an inventive process within this cause-effect system.

We see more art in the acts and objects that are extraordinary in society, such as in gift exchange and sacred rites. Art appreciation is itself an ideological context within which people play, so we can in effect refer to anything and say "How artistic is this?" Art or the aesthetic is not a universal ideological construct, any more than technology or social organization are constructs; but it is an analytical category that can be applied universally. Claws, teeth, feathers, crystals, nuggets of native copper, and so forth were picked up and used by Indians as objects of scavenger art, in much the same way as we might today pick up interesting stones or pieces of driftwood.

Artistic symboling is a much more playful manipulation of the senses than language symboling. In the latter the play is eliminated because of the need to communicate exact meanings. The play in art is in its inexactness, its multiple meanings, and its use of simultaneously emotional and intellectual messages.

Skilled craftsmanship and beauty are frequent dimensions of this play, but highly valued art can still be crude in craftsmanship or even ugly. We go beyond the mastery of technique when technique becomes dull and boring. When a pottery surface can be made consistently smooth by polishing, then humans will play with it by creating a patterned surface texture, or painting it, or glazing it. We play with the ordinary to create satisfying variations. Artistic play in the visual arts concerns such dimensions as colors (hue, intensity, and value), shapes, perspectives, symmetry, size, and the relationship of a figure to its ground.

This definition of art allows us to include a wide variety of U.S. and Canadian Native arts. My comments here on Native arts are arranged in what I judge to be something of an evolutionary sequence in the arts: oral literature, music, dance, rock art, and carving, all of which have a heritage that probably goes back to the Paleolithic; basketry and weaving that began to flourish in the Mesolithic; pottery that began in the Neolithic; and contemporary Native arts.

Another organizational method would have been to present the arts area-by-area because there is some correlation between the advancement of art and the level of cultural evolution of the societies within each area. Also, there was considerable areal specialization. Oral literature, music, and dance were universally important, but beyond that there were specializations: Arctic and Northwest Coast—carving, Northwest Coast—dance costumes, sub-Arctic—engraving on bark and quillwork, Plains—painting on hide, Basin and California—basketry, Southwest—pottery (females) and dance costumes and weaving (males) in the Pueblos; weaving (females) and sandpainting (males) among the Navajo, and East—carving and pottery.

ORAL LITERATURE

Aboriginal literature was created and maintained within an oral tradition of poetry, legends, songs, speeches, jokes, and so forth. Thus, the Native literature had a social context and function comparable more to radio and television than the relatively private written literature. The skills of memorization and of dramatic oral presentation were important. The telling of stories as a dramatic and social event emphasized such things as how well the story was being told this time and how the audience was reacting to it this time, rather than the actual plot of the story. It paralleled telling the stories of the Bible over and over again.

Boas (1955:311) pointed out that rhythmic repetition is a common oral narrative device. "The tales of the Chinook Indians are often so constructed that five brothers, one after another, have the same adventure. The four elder ones perish while the youngest one emerges safe and successful. The tale is repeated verbatim for all the brothers, and its length, which to our ear and to our taste is intolerable, probably gives pleasure by the repeated form." The recitations of these traditional stories are judged and enjoyed on accuracy, rhythm, voice, etc. —on how well the story is told, not on the content of the story.

Dundas (1965) illustrated his ideas on the structural analysis of folktales by comparing the patterns of motifs in Indian and European tales. For example, both traditions have tales in which a lack is followed by a liquidation of a lack, but European tales tend to be more "cumulative," to have greater "depth" of motifs, such as an interconnected series of lacks to be liquidated. Indian folk-tales used familiar mythical characters and small story units that are used over and over in different tales, such as Trickster taking his eyes out or girls falling in love with stars. Indian tales also usually end with an explanatory motif. Something such as all the fish, water, seasons, or fire is hoarded by someone (lack) and then a heroic figure brings about a worldwide distribution (liquidation of lack). Another common Indian pattern is lack, deceit, deception, and lack liquidated.

A different pattern is interdiction, violation, and consequence, with an occasional attempted escape from the consequence. "In a Swampy Cree tale, a little boy is told by his sister not to shoot at a squirrel when it is near the water (Int). The boy shoots at a squirrel near water (Viol.) and when he seeks to retrieve his arrow which had fallen in the water, he is swallowed by a fish (Conseq.). Eventually, the fish is directed to swim to the sister, who cuts open the fish, thereby releasing her brother (AE)." (P. 209.)

A simpler form would be violation, consequence, and attempted escape, with an implicit interdiction. Trickster defecates on a rock (Viol.), the rock rolls after him (Conseq.), and he escapes with the help of animals who destroy the rock (AE). A complex form may combine patterns. In a Zuni tale, "A girl discovers a singing cricket and wants to take it home (L). The cricket goes home with her (LL), but warns her that she must not touch or tickle him (Int.). The girl in playing with the cricket tickles him (Viol.) and the cricket bursts his stomach and dies (Conseq.)." (P. 210.) This is the same structure as the European tale of Orpheus, where a man is able to bring his wife back from the dead if he will not look at her but he succumbs to temptation.

There are suggestions of how a European tale would change when it is incorporated into an Indian tradition. There is a European tale about wolves that climb on top of each other to catch someone in a tree but all fall down when the bottom wolf runs away. "In the Zuni version of this tale, Coyote wants to climb up a cliff to get some corn (L). Coyote gathers together his fellow coyotes and the group decides to ascend the cliff by holding on to another's tail or by holding on to corn cobs inserted in their anuses (LL). The coyotes are all warned not to break wind (Int). However, the last coyote does so (Viol.), causing the whole chain to tumble down. All the coyotes are killed (Conseq.)." (P. 212.)

The Hopi use an artistic chanting format to make formal announcements to the village from the roof tops (Black 1967). Work parties are called by an adult male to plant corn, to clean a spring, etc., or they may publicly voice a grievance. The message may be projected for over a mile by careful enunciation, undulating musical pitches, and vocal pulsations. The message is divided into "paragraphs" that are ended with a characteristic tone that rises, holds, and then rapidly falls. The larger structure of the message is first "Listen to the announcer, you ______ (men, boys, women)"; then the substance of the message with repetitions and summations; and finally ending with "It is like that." For example, the chants that tell of the substance of a rabbit hunt involve the following: time, men and women involved, activity, game itinerary, rendezvous, summons to dream about the hunt the evening before, and the sources of information. The chanter promotes the activity by allusions to the abundance of game, how good they taste, that girlfriends may accompany their boyfriends on the hunt, and so forth.

In poetry there is more of a fixed rhythmic form, but spoken in a fairly normal voice without "singing," by vibrating the vocal chords and lengthening the vowels. In fact some presentations moved back and forth between speaking poetry and singing songs. In certain genres, such as Inuit song duals, creative repartee was developed as a form of art and entertainment.

Speech making was a special genre of oral literature in many societies. In Kwakiutl potlatch speeches, a strongly accented *ai* syllable was added to many words for rhythm and chanting emphasis. Rich metaphors were used to tell of the greatness of a chief: a mountain, a rock which cannot be climbed, the post of heaven which supports the world, and a cliff down which overwhelming wealth rolls. "The people follow him as the young sawbill-ducks follow the mother bird." (Boas 1955:321). There is a lot of use of figures of speech, such as giving a part for the whole, as in the use of "my brother" for men of my society.

The stereotype of the stoic Indian of few words is false, except perhaps in some foreign cultural contexts with Whites. Certainly in comfortable situations Indians are talkative, vivacious, joking, and traditionally had a rather spectacular literature of oral narratives. Unfortunately, very little of this oral literature has been adequately recorded, translated, and explained. Instead, it has been trivialized into brief little stories told at a.childish level with the scatological and sexual parts edited.

The Aztecs, Mixtecs, Maya, and other state societies of Mesoamerica had writing systems, particularly emphasizing sacred histories, calendars, tribute and trade lists, and maps. However, even in these societies most of the literature was in the oral tradition. There is some written literature in the historic period in Cherokee, Cree, Creek, Crow, Dakota, Inuit, Navajo, and Ojibwa. Finally in the twentieth century there has been a florescence of Indian literature in English, particularly in the Native periodicals.

MUSIC

Aboriginal Indian music is so different from European music that it is studied and appreciated in White cultures only by a handful of musicologists. One has to learn a musical tradition in order to appreciate it and that can be as difficult as learning a language.

North American music was usually presented as accompaniment to dancing and singing, rather than being performed in its own right as a strictly instrumental composition. The musical instruments were almost all rhythm instruments, various kinds of foot drums, bass drums, tomtoms, tambourines, rattles, raspers, and tinklers. These were made in an extreme variety of forms and materials. Rattles, for example, were made of rawhide, turtleshell, pottery, gourd, bark, carved wood, cocoons; basketry, animal hoofs, horn, and split sticks. The Indians did not use drums for signaling, as in Africa. In some western societies the bow string was plucked with the end of the bow placed in the mouth as a resonating chamber. In the Southeast the conch shell was used as a trumpet, particularly to call signals in war. In California, the Southwest, the Plains, and the Eastern areas single flutes played by men provided a melody in courting music, and in some ceremonies in the Southwest. Double whistles were occasionally used along the West coast, especially in imitation of a spirit voice.

The most melodic "instrument" is the human voice itself, which in many societies was used in very beautiful group singing, such as in the mixed choirs of the Pima-Papago and the male choirs of the Navajo. Indian singing tends to have more vocal chord tension and more frequent use of a falsetto voice than Western singing. A raspy singing voice is particularly common in subsistence hunting societies, possibly because of the influence of male assertiveness on the male singing style in these societies. Harmony was apparently absent. The melody scale is usually pentatonic and the key of singing changes so that songs are not in a fixed key. Only one basic pitch is sounded, but women may sing along with men in a higher octave or provide a droning background to men singing the melody. The time construction is heterometric so that rhythmic beats and their speed can change within the song. One begins to appreciate Indian music by studying these rhythmic meters. Rhythmic complexity apparently has evolved so that there is a correlation between rhythmic complexity and cultural evolution generally. Also we find that stratified societies tend to embellish melodies more than egalitarian ones. Wilhelmine Driver (Driver 1969:196) suggests that complex, polyphonic music was absent because women were relegated mainly to a passive role in rituals.

The songs tended to be brief, from twenty seconds to three minutes, with longer forms made by repetitions or strings of short songs. There is a strong similarity between the rhythms in telling a poem or folk story and the rhythmic structure of songs. There were (1) individual to spirit songs for healing, for love magic, for war success, etc., (2) individual to individual songs, such as private lullabies and love songs or public ridicule and boasting songs; (3) songs by groups for spiritual purposes, such as the Navajo curing chants; (4) songs by groups to accompany their own dancing or working; and (5) group to group songs, such as those used to create distractions in team competitions in hand-game gambling. Indian songs usually have the qualities of magical chants and rhythmic accompaniment to other activities more than an aesthetic meaning. There are usually ritual and supernatural reasons why a song should be sung right and judgements about the quality of the singing are more in these terms than in the terms of beauty or emotional appeal.

Nettl (1967) divided the continent north of Mexico into six musical areas.

The Great Basin style is probably the most ancient form of music: simple in style, small melodic ranges, and very short forms. Simple lullabies, tale songs, gambling songs, and puberty songs that are widespread in the continent are characteristic of the Basin. In the California-Yuman area there is a characteristic rise in almost all songs with a relaxed and nonpulsating vocal technique. In the music of the Plains-Pueblo area there is extreme vocal tension and pulsation, tile-type melodic contours, relatively complex rhythms, and the incomplete repetition forms, with two large sections, the second being an incomplete rendition of the first. The Eastern area is characterized by "short phrases in iterative and reverting relationships; the use of shouts before, during, and after songs; pentatonic scales without half tones; simple rhythmic and metric organization; and . . . a great deal of antiphonal and responsorial technique."

Two area styles were probably later in development. The Eskimo-Northwest Coast traits are recitative singing with complex rhythms and a melodic prominence of major thirds and minor seconds. Eskimo melody is undulating while Northwest is pendulum-like, moving from one limit of the range to the other. One Inuit style is called "throat singing," in which two people place their mouths together and sing down each other's throat, thus vibrating the partner's vocal chords. In the Northwest there is some interplay between the voice melody and the musical instrument. The Athabascan style of the Navajo-Apache is characterized by the limited number of durational values, simple rhythms, an arc-type of melodic contour, large melodic intervals with leaps of an extra octave and "broad acrobatic maneuvers in the melody." The use of falsetto, pulsations, and a nasal sound are also characteristic of this style.

Witmer (1973) wrote about the contemporary playing of White music by Blood Indians. They work from songbooks and have a repertory of largely country and western classics, such as "Born to Lose," "Tennessee Border," "You Win Again," and "Release Me." Indian music is fairly common on the Blood Reserve and these people do not have a negative assessment of Indian music. They do question their personal ability to memorize and perform it. They are critical of the social situations (i.e., boisterous drinking) in which Indian music is usually performed. And they associate the playing of White music with the positive values of education, self-improvement, and the mastery of a difficult White activity. Bloods who play White music were found to be unusual in the extent to which they abstain from alcoholic beverages and are active in Christian churches.

DANCE

Traditional Native dancing was community oriented, not individualistic or directed toward pairing off males with females. There was nothing resembling the modern, sexually paired, coordinated "ballroom" style or the individual "twist" style of dancing. To the extent that sexual attention and stimulation did exist, it was the males who were the "sex objects." Women tended to dance in female social groups, with small steps, quietly, decorously, with their arms close to their bodies, and very little movement of hips and breasts. Men also participated in social group dances, but in most areas there were individual male dances in which men twisted, leaped, and waved their arms. All regions had some solo dancing by males.

In Inuit ceremonial dances the women swayed gracefully while the men jumped and turned. The Inuit also had improvised pantomime dances in which they impersonated animals or spirit beings. These were usually solo dances in which the dancers took turns while the others watched. These were appropriate for the small space of the Inuit house and they dispelled the monotony of the long winter with a touch of competition. There were special women's songs, such as work songs or those sung to make a game task (such as making string figures or juggling pebbles) a bit harder. The competitive song contests between Inuit men are famous because they set up a dramatic spectacle. Two men could solve an argument in a social context by taking turns at improvising and singing insulting songs at each other. The one given the greatest support by the audience was the winner.

In the Northwest Coast there were winter ceremonial dances in which individuals of both sexes took turns singing and dancing their personal guardian spirit song and dance. People usually wore a costume that symbolized the individual's guardian spirit. A person would begin the song, a group of musicians might add accompaniment, the person would enter a trancelike state, and would dance in imitation of the possessing spirit. Since these dances took place around a central fire and the dancer went into a trance, it was necessary for others to prevent the dancer from falling into the fire. The theme of spirit possession was widespread and was emphasized in dances that were done to acquire supernatural power.

The majority of dances had a strong ideological content: life cycle rituals, agricultural or hunting increase rites, war magic dances, curing dances, and so forth. People had a good time and enjoyed going to dances, but recreation was not usually the explicit purpose of the dance. The major dances of the Washo and the other Great Basin peoples were in a large social circle, with individuals interlinking fingers (not "holding hands"), facing inward, and shuffling in a clockwise direction in a left foot step-right foot drag manner. Men and women were traditionally separated into two different arcs of the same circle, although now male-female pairing is common.

The main California-Southwest dances occurred in lines of dancers, single lines and parallel lines. Usually the dancers in parallel lines faced each other and moved back and forth in a uniform step. Among the Luiseño and Diegueño the lines are now sexually paired up, but in the Southwest Pueblo dances the long lines of costumed dancers are of the same sex, usually men. The body position of single male dancers tends to be forward-bending with arms generally low or down. A rattle is often held in the right hand and another object symbolic of the specific dance in the left hand: a feather wand, a sprig of juniper, a bow, etc. In the eagle dance the dancer squats and hops and careens in turning, with his arms covered with feathers as wings. In the horsetail dance the dancers imitate horses at play in prancing, kicking, and swishing their tails. In the later dances the women often play a musical accompaniment on drums, rasps, and rattles for the male dancers. Again, there are variations. In the San Ildefonso dog dance individualistic dancers imitate dogs, snarling and scrapping for bread thrown on the ground. In the Navajo Yeibichai, lines of men dance first in place; then with small, energetic, sliding steps forward; and the line turns about face and moves slowly back.

Evans and Evans (1972:22) described several Indian dances, such as the following Apache "Devil Dance." "The position is a low squatting one, with both knees turned out. The jumps are in even rhythm and close to the ground. They are made with both feet simultaneously, and flat for the greater part. At intervals the dancer stretches out one leg and taps the top of the toe on the ground; twisting leg and foot so as to turn the sole of the foot upward . . . Meanwhile there is a simultaneous jumping movement on the other foot. These movements . . . are intentionally comic, grotesque; as are the costumes worn in the dance, which include black masks and huge head-dresses. The painted bodies of the dancers are nearly naked."

Dances of the Eastern agricultural area generally were in an open-ended circle that moved counter-clockwise with the dancers facing forward or facing an object or person in the center. Dances with lines of dancers in spirals or in snake-like lines were also performed. Agricultural dances were predominant, with women representing corn, beans, and squash. Men had dances that imitated animals, such as the buffalo and eagle.

Closed circle dances like those of the Great Basin were also traditionally widespread in the Plains, but in the nineteenth century the powwow style became the basic form and spread outward in the twentieth century in a general pan-Indian diffusion. Traditionally these seem to have been more individualistic, even privately owned, dances by men. They were men's war and hunting dances. The most widespread form of Indian dancing in the U.S. and Canada today is the powwow style, derived from the Plains. In powwow dancing usually four men beat a big drum and chant the dance songs. The dancers move clockwise around in a circle, men as individual dancers and women as individuals or side by side in small clusters of two, three, or four abreast. Women face forward and dance in a demure shuffle, wearing long dresses and shawls. Men do highly individualistic dances, whirling, dipping, stamping, waving, and so forth in bright, feathered costumes. Powwow dance competitions in hundreds of communities have produced one of the most active pan-Indian networks today, the "powwow circuit."

Modern innovations have added dances that pair off male-female couples. For example, the Navajo have what they call "squaw dances," in which a woman selects a man as a partner and he is obliged to give her a gift of a small silver coin for dancing with him. The dance step is the shoulder-to-shoulder, forward shuffle of the woman's powwow dance. This paired dance, without the Navajo gift of silver, is common today across the Plains all the way to the Canadian Dakota of Manitoba, where it is called *kahomani*. The songs that accompany the *kahomani* are romantic love songs and are occasionally sung in English or a mixture of English and an Indian language. They "are phrased in the verbal forms of women, and are presumed to express the thoughts of women, although in fact *kahomani* singers are men . . . 'Dearie, I love you. Here I am in the jail up north. Don't be broken-hearted; soon I'll have lots of friends (here)'." (Corrigan 1970:268).

ROCK ART

Rock art has been made almost everywhere where bedrock surfaces are not covered with soil. Thus the major regions of rock art are the major regions where rock surfaces are exposed at the earth's surface, in the glacial scoured landscape around the Great Lakes and in the folded mountains and eroded canyons of the west. There is very little rock art in the north or in the Eastern and Gulf Coasts. The arid country of the Plateau, Basin, and Southwest has been particuarly good for the preservation of rock art because of its relative lack of rainwater erosion.

An engraving in the rock surface by pecking, scratching, abrading, or cutting is called a *petroglyph*. A painting made by applying pigments on the rock surface is called a *pictograph*. Petroglyphs are preserved much better than pictographs, and that fact influences our available data, but it still appears that petroglyphs were much more commonly made than were pictographs. The two forms occur in the same geographical regions, sometimes on the same rocks, and occasionally a petroglyph has also been painted.

The most common kind of petroglyph technique appears to be that of striking the surface with a hard stone or chiseling with a pointed stone hit by a hammer stone. Since the minerals in the surface of the rock oxidize and turn dark, the cuts expose the lighter rock underneath, until that too darkens with oxidation. Lines were often made with strings of dots. Flat tones were then added by slight pecking all over or by scraping the surface. Paints were made from the iron oxide hematite for red, charcoal or manganese ore for black, and chalk or gypsum for white. There was also some limited use of copper ores for blue and green, the iron oxide limonite for yellow, and a baked yellow ochre for red. These pigments were usually molded and dried into cakes. The caked pigments could be applied directly as a body paint or mixed with an oil binder for more permanent applications to rock or wood surfaces.

Most of the rock art appears to be playful, abstract designs, often perhaps the result of a magical ritual. The most amusing petroglyph I have seen is a series of three deeply cut human-like footprints (each with six toes) up the side of a vertical rock face, as if someone had walked up the wall (Chaco Canyon, New Mexico).

The specific geographical location of many of the sites appears to be where men were waiting to spot animals moving along game trails. One can imagine a hunter whiling away the hours while waiting for game by pecking a magical design into the rock. When the designs are naturalistic, the scenes portrayed are of animals and the hunt, not domestic scenes, or plants, or children, things traditionally associated with women. Thus we assume that the rock art was made by men.

When the visual symbols have a consistent meaning within a culture, we refer to them as pictographic writing. There is some naturalistic content in these symbols, so that there are occasional historically independent similarities in these symbols. Thus, for example, the sun is portrayed as a circle in Egyptian, early Chinese, and Plains-Southwest Indian pictographs. Rain is portrayed as descending wavy lines in both Egyptian and Plains-Southwest writing, although the sky is a horizontal bar in Egypt and a curved arch in the Plains-Southwest. There are many suggestions of naturalistic elements in Plains-Southwest pictographs: sunrise as a circle on the top of a line; lightning is a zigzag and often pointed line; there are several types of clouds, but a common form is a series of ascending roundish lines; mountains may be a series of ascending jagged lines; and lines from the appropriate parts of a human head show human powers: speech lines from the mouth, sight lines from the eyes, and hearing lines from the ears.

The Midewiwin religious society of the Ojibwa has produced some interesting engravings on bark that visually illustrate some of their ideas and have strong similarities to the rock art of the Great Lakes area (Dewdney 1975). There appears to be some continuity from aboriginal rock art, to historic bark scrolls, and finally to contemporary Ojibwa acrylic painting on stretched canvas. One bark design shows a line drawing of a shaman in a field of several skies, represented by concentric circles, with a half moon and stars of crossed lines. Lines that circle out of the shaman's head show the power he has to enter the skies. Another simple line drawing shows a person in a state of holiness or power with lines coming out of the ears, representing knowledge of the holy beings of the skies; lines that go down represent the secrets of the earth. Incising, painting, and stamping designs into bark, particularly of curvilinear floral motifs, seem to be a general sub-Arctic trait. These floral designs were sewn into clothing in modern historic times.

PLASTIC AND GRAPHIC ARTS

Most of the visual art was produced as aesthetic elaborations on utilitarian objects, such as knives, harpoons, tent covers, and canoes, or on religious objects, such as fetishes, masks, dance costumes, and sand painting. Inuit men carved and engraved in wood, bone, horn, and ivory, including masks and small animal amulets. Inuit women did some decorative sewing, such as working different-colored pieces of fur into a garment. The historic Plains had a weak aesthetic orientation, but there was some painting of hides for tipi covers and linings and folded carrying pouches. Men painted naturalistic figures, especially of horses, men, and buffalo, usually in profile and in a flat color. Women painted geometric figures and designs and added quill embroidery. Ceremonial pipes were carved in the Plains and the East.

Carved designs in stone, shell, mica, and copper in the Southeast show strong Mesoamerican influences: eagles, snakes, and warriors. Council buildings were elaborately decorated with carved front posts (snakes, alligators, etc.) and painting on the walls. The Southeast was also noted for spectacular tattooing, body painting, and cloaks.

Northwest Coast wood carving and painting emphasized the "totems" or lineage crests of kinship groups. These were symbolic motifs of animals from which there has been human descent and a continuing supernatural rapport. The motifs were repeated in every media of art: dance, music, basketry, woven cloth, and beaten copper emblems. These designs were carved especially by men into wood in the form of totem poles, storage boxes, and food bowls. In the Northwest Coast art style, there is a tendency to fill the available space with design details, to split the portrayal of an animal into laterally symmetric halves, to wrap the parts of an animal around an object such as a box, to include "X-ray" portrayal of internal parts, and to emphasize certain conventional features of each species: (1) the short snout, large teeth, and tongue of the bear; (2) the long snout of the wolf; and (3) the protruding upper incisor teeth and wide, flat, cross-hatched tail of the beaver.

Basketry is older than pottery and was functionally replaced by pottery in most of its storing and cooking uses with the development of sedentary agricultural societies. The Aleuts and western Inuit wove grass into such objects as soft bags and socks. Soft twined bags were made along the Northwest Coast, often with added embroidery or painted decorations. California and the Great Basin are noted for their variety and quality of basketry. They wove very tight baskets with fine elements and geometric designs, occasionally adding feathers or beads to the outer surface. Plates and shallow bowls were highly decorated in the Southwest.

Pottery in the East was usually given an aesthetic texture by pressing the soft clay with a cord-wrapped paddle, a stamp, or a punch. The general evolution of Northeastern pottery decoration was dentate stamping, then cord-wrapped impressions and paddle-edge techniques, and finally incising patterns. In some Eastern areas effigies of people, animals, and plants were modeled on vessels and pipes. Compared to the Southwest, however, Eastern pottery is uniform and mundane.

The Navajo made a style that is similar to that of the Northeast, dark grey with a decorative band of lines engraved near the top. The Pueblos produced a variety of sizes, shapes, and decorations of pottery objects. Rough utilitarian bowls were made for cooking and finely painted bowls were made for some storage and ritual uses. The Hopi and Zuni painted abstract bird and feather designs on some of their pottery. The eastern Pueblos produced geometrically painted pottery in several locally distinct styles. Thus, it is easy to distinguish between the styles of Acoma-Laguna, Sandia-Isleta, Santa Domingo, San Ildefonso, and Taos.

Pottery is extremely plastic so it is amenable to stylistic variations in forms, pigments, firing in an oxidizing or reducing (blackening) atmosphere, glazes, and so forth. This malleability enabled pottery styles to become a distinctive mark of ethnic differences between Southwestern societies.

In sand painting, dry pigments are poured on a ground picture from the hand, between the thumb and first finger. Different colors of sand are used, but in the Southwest the palette was broadened to include such plant materials as corn pollen, powdered flowers, leaves, and wood charcoal. In southern California and the southern Great Basin, sand paintings were laid out during the instructions about the creation and mysteries of the universe in puberty ceremonies. Thus, symbols were used for the sun, moon, stars, and the primeval creator spirits.

The Hopi universe painting has four direction-oriented sides in a series of concentric squares, each related by a color to a direction: white—east, red—south, blue—west, and yellow—north. The directions are represented in both a concentric and true directional way in the sand painting because, it is explained, wherever you are in the world there are always four directions. On each side there is a cloud symbol, a magical charm for rain, and, on top of the cloud, an ear of corn and a stone axe. A line representing the road to the underworld runs diagonally through the picture, ending outside the picture with symbols for walking sticks.

The Navajo learned sand painting from the Pueblos, applied it to healing the sick, and today make very elaborate polychrome sand paintings. The Navajo developed a separate range of symbols, although there is some similarity between the anthropomorphic *kachina* spirits of the Pueblos and the *yei* spirits of the Navajo. The Navajo painting uses the basic North American Indian division into four: four *yei* figures, four "whirling logs," four sets of four buffalos or eagles, etc. The four elements are centrally connected by some visually dynamic means and enclosed on three sides by a border, such as another *yei* figure or a string of arrows.

CONTEMPORARY NATIVE ART

A leading Indian artist in Canada is Norval Morriseau, an Ojibwa painter from McDiarmid, Ontario. He has become an increasingly better artist by successfully struggling with the compromises that the White art-buying public has forced on him. Art buyers want something distinctively Indian from an Indian artist and that has usually emphasized the primitive, simple, and child-like in technique and the use of traditional Indian symbols and forms. An Indian artist who works with Western techniques and symbols is just another Western artist who must be judged by Western criteria, and few people—Indians or Whites—can be financially independent in the competitive field of Western art. Indians usually adjust to this and produce that which sells well to Whites, distinctively "Indian" art. The problem with this is that it tends to reduce the amount of aesthetic play and honest creativity in Indian art.

Around 1960 Morriseau began trying to peddle his paintings in Toronto, painted on brown building paper, birch bark, and even hides. He was clearly expanding on artistic traditions from the Ojibwa Midewiwin or Grand Medicine Society bark scroll: line drawings of men, animals, and supernatural beings, particularly mythic animals; themes of sacred history; and graphic portrayals of such powers as the physical senses, magical influences, and animal spirits inside humans. The Pollock Gallery was able to sell his paintings as primitive work that appeals to the upper class, art-gallery type of buyer. Jack Pollock encouraged Morriseau to use canvas and acrylic paints, to continue the primitive style, and to emphasize the Ojibwa legends. Morriseau had his first show in 1962. Since then he has gradually become more personal, using his own dreams and experiences, and sometimes including a projection of himself. In one picture he portrays himself as a 16th century warrior surrounded by his four wives and in another picture as a person "Devoured by His Own Passions."

Morriseau paints fantastic human and animal forms with solid blocks of color outlined with heavy black lines. They often have a stained glass effect. The figures frequently are filled with small, abstract forms that repeat the theme of the larger figure. Thus a large bird might be composed of many smaller birds. Another technique is to show the internal parts of the animal in some symbolic way, as in the "X-ray" of the coastal British Columbia Indians. The signature also reinforces the Indian identity of the painter because it is in Ojibwa syllabics, rather than English.

In recent years a large number of Ojibwa painters have followed the basic style set by Morriseau. Carl Ray works in the Morriseau style, but tends to be more intellectual and authentic in his depiction of Ojibwa legends and customs. Ray's subjects include adventures at the time of genesis and the shaman's power in the shaking tent ceremony. Blake Debassige is a young artist who seems to be working in the Ray tradition of fantastic stories, with little of the color or expressionism of Morriseau. Noel Ducharme modified the Morriseau style by simplifying and formalizing it. The composition is more balanced. The internal parts of animals are carefully executed blocks of color rather than little animals or diverse structural parts. Isidore Wadow seems to be basically formal in the Ducharme style, but with little twists of the bizarre, such as a formal four-footed bird-like creature, but with a beak at one end and a jaw full of sharp teeth at the other end.

Allen Sapp is a successful Cree painter from a reserve near North Battleford, Saskatchewan. His techniques are a bit crude and his subject matter is strictly in the Western tradition, but the aesthetic sense of his work, rather than its primitivism or nativeness, has made him financially successful. Sapp's work is realistic and usually sentimental about daily life in the Canadian prairies. The fact that his scenes are usually drawn from an Indian reservation is a minor element in the painting itself, except that those scenes of Indian life today, such as a lonely cabin in the snow or a horse-drawn wagon on a road through the woods, are sentimentally beautiful to Prairie Whites who left that way of life a generation or so ago.

Since 1910 the Canadian Handicrafts Guild has promoted the sale of Inuit carvings, but it was not until the Guild's 1949 exhibition in Montreal that these carvings began to sell well. The first commercial appearance of Inuit block prints was in 1959, the year of the first cooperative. Then modern commercial carvings entered the general market in 1960. In the 1960s the appearance of imitations brought out the use of a trade mark for genuine Inuit art. In 1965 a central marketing agency was created.

Although a Western artist, James Houston, had a lot to do with the introduction of printing techniques to the Inuit, they clearly took that medium off in a unique direction. Houston (1971:30) was impressed with how their view of scenes and objects differed from that of Western artists. "Their point of view may be from above, as in looking down at fish in the water, or from below, as in looking up at birds in the air. They sometimes hang bird prints on the ceiling . . . They show us how to drive the caribou and how to hold a child. They understand the patterns of fur and feathers . . . the rolling gait of the polar bear, the great weight of the walrus, the sleekness of seals . . . for these things are life's blood to them."

Lucy's stone cut print of a polar bear reflects the point of view of an Eskimo woman. She is not a hunter, but a person who knows the bear as a large piece of warm fur with hair patterns that flow in certain directions. "Her bear is strong, thin headed, well fed, well understood, with big splayed feet to carry it over the thin ice . . . The fur of the bear is indicated with precise and loving care, for Lucy thinks of the bear as a sleeping skin." (Houston 1971:74)

The art industry at Cape Dorset was stimulated by Whites to provide employment to Inuits, both in carving and print making. The carving techniques have little relation to traditional Inuit carving. The old work was (1) by men only, (2) of small hand-held objects which were appreciated in a tactile way and turned freely in visual perspectives, (3) of ivory, (4) usually considered to be capable of acquiring some supernatural power, or at least the creator's personal power, and (5) simply kept by the maker or given away to close friends. The new work is (1) done by both men and women, (2) of large objects with flat bases with a favored visual perspective to sit on shelves or mantlepieces, (3) of heavy soapstone, (4) considered to have no supernatural characteristics, and (5) produced only for sale.

Modern carving by coastal British Columbia Indians uses the traditional animal conventions, but the modern artists usually work in more than one medium. Walter Harris, Ken Mowatt, and Earl Muldoe, along with dozens of other Tsimshian of 'Ksan, carve totem poles, wood masks and bowls and engrave in silver and gold. The 'Ksan movement started in the 1950s, with the building of a museum in 1958. After 1967 the carving crafts began to be reestablished and the core of the reconstructed village was opened for tourism in 1970. Since then, additional buildings have gradually been added and a professional dance program was developed. Elsewhere, Robert Davidson, a Haida, engraves in silver and Henry Hunt, a Kwakiutl, carves in wood, everything from masks to totem poles. Ron Hamilton, a Nootka, carves masks and paints on wood panels.

The Navajo learned weaving from the Pueblos and are recognized as the finest of Indian weavers. They learned silverwork from the Mexicans and are commercially successful in producing jewelry, noted for its massive use of silver and turquoise. Hopi silverwork, by contrast, is light, sophisticated, and creative in abstract designs; Zuni jewelry is technically more proficient in stone inlay work, particularly the "needlework" inlay of turquoise by women and the symbolic mosaic stone inlay of a variety of stones by men. However, the heavy silverwork of the Navajo has a strong appeal on the art market. Finally, the Navajo have excelled in the Studio School of Indian Art: horizontal rectangle pictures; watercolors with the background left unpainted; strong perspective by size, position, overlapping, and outlines of mountains in the backgrounds but without shading or shadows; and "Southwest" subjects, such as purple horses and stylized clouds.

Crescencio Martinez was raised in the pueblo of San Ildefonso and worked decorating pottery with his wife. His wife was the sister of Maria Martinez, the woman who became famous when she discovered and reinvented the ancient black pottery for sale to tourists. Edgar Hewitt was an archaeologist who excavated near San Ildefonso and employed Crescencio. In this way Crescencio became familiar with pictographs and mural paintings in the excavated sites and told Hewitt that he too could paint. In 1917 he showed Hewitt his paintings. Seeing the ethnographic value of the work, "Hewitt furnished paper and paints and engaged Crescencio to 'produce in watercolor, pictures of all the characters that appear in the summer and winter ceremonies' of his pueblo." (Dunn 1968:199)

A teacher at San Ildefonso had encouraged the school children to paint, so that artists such as Quah Ah and Alfredo Montoya were somewhat active at the same time as Crescencio in 1916-1918. Awa Tsireh is a nephew and a contemporary of Crescencio from San Ildefonso who was encouraged in art at St. Catherine's Indian School in Santa Fe. From his pottery painting skills he developed a distinctive watercolor painting style of decorative realism that framed a central, often surrealistic, figure within a formal rainbow-cloud stage. Ma-Pe-Wi, from the pueblo of Zia, developed a warm, naturalistic style in portraying ceremonies as well as scenes of daily life. His balanced cornstalks and spruce trees and successive-arc cumulus clouds became a convention in later Southwest painting. Fred Kabotie, a Hopi, worked in a variety of styles and emphasized Hopi Kachina ceremonials in his work.

At the same time that the San Ildefonso style was being formed, a similar phenomenon was taking place on a smaller scale among the Kiowa in Anadarko, Oklahoma. Susan Peters went there in 1917 as a field matron in the U.S. Indian Service, encouraged young people in their drawing efforts, and established a studio and fine arts class. She visited the Pueblo area and studied their art movement; in the decades to follow she managed to encourage her students through their entrance into the University of Oklahoma's art classes and sales of their work. The style has a poster quality of decoration, heavy color, strong color contrasts, uniform stylization, and single central figures or small groups.

A strong backing and sponsorship of Indian artists developed among certain White artists and art buyers in the Santa Fe and Taos areas, especially after 1919. Thus, an environment that encouraged Indian artists developed over the next few decades. In that setting the Santa Fe Indian School was designated as the center for arts and crafts within the U.S. Indian school system and craft classes started there in 1931. In 1932 several prominent Indian artists and Indian art students were invited to the school to design and paint a mural in the dining hall. The Navajos drew from their sand painting tradition, the San Ildefonso painters from their traditions, and so forth, including a Hopi, a Zuni, and a Kiowa. Some panels were the joint work of several artists. These artists then formed The Mural Guild and began producing large canvas oil paintings for sale. Dorothy Dunn also came to Santa Fe in 1932 and started the art studio.

Chapter 9

Living with an Urban World

The next five chapters are on the urbanization and institutionalization of Native people. This chapter is on rural-urban relationships, showing that the distance of a reservation from cities is an important factor in the development of that reservation.

Whether Indians continue their traditions of living in rural and reservation areas or move to towns and cities, they must come to terms with the omnipresent processes of urbanization. Just the conservative retention of traditional language and culture requires elaborate defensive strategies against the penetration of White laws, religions, economics, government bureaucracies, and so forth into Native communities. Some Indians have attempted to physically remove themselves from White influences, such as Chief Robert Smallboy's Cree band in Alberta which is trying to return to the aboriginal life of hunting and fishing. Others have tried to isolate the reservations by building barriers against outside intrusions, such as Ernest Benedict of the St. Regis Iroquois, who lectures on the need for separatism and self-determination of Native societies. The most common strategy is to become involved in the development of a new, separate Native society that accepts much of what the modern world has to offer, but simultaneously builds from the traditional heritage.

The scattered reservation segments of a single U.S. or Canadian Indian tribe have often culturally diverged from each other in recent historical times. This divergence is particularly marked in more urban regions, such as California, and among tribes where some of the reservations are near cities. As tribalism has become less important and urban adaptation more important, cities have a differential impact for change according to their distance from the various Indian communities. The most distant reservations tend to be abandoned, to survive as retirement communities, or to turn to a conservative, low cost-of-living and welfare-dependent adaptation. Those reservations closest to the cities tend to develop a pattern of commuting to jobs in the city, population increase, and a new sophistication in working with modern bureaucratic politics.

Particular Indian societies were often allocated more than one reservation, rancheria, colony, or other type of land held in trust by the federal government. Those local segments of the Indian society had a relatively homogenous culture when they began reservation life. Under common federal policies, state laws, and other influences they generally evolved in the same way, until recently.

In brief visits to the Unitah-Quray, Ute Mountain, and Southern Ute reservations the differences seemed only moderate to me. Perhaps their relative wealth from a general Ute land claim case and tribal income from oil and gas discoveries on the Ute Mountain Reservation had slowed their divergence. However, some parts of these large reservations still prospered more than others. Thus, the tribal centers at Fort Duchesne and Ignacio were small modern towns while in the rural outback people lived in quite a different way.

Among the Navajo there is wide cultural divergence between such regions as Navajo Mountain and Window Rock. The latter area has a sizable town with close ties to Gallup, New Mexico. Zuni, also close to Gallup, is more urbanized than the Hopi Pueblos, a comparable society. Some of the outlying Rio Grande pueblos are being abandoned, others are continuing a somewhat traditional agrarian life, and those close to urban areas, such as Taos to the north and Sandia and Isleta to the south, are prospering as ex-urban bedroom communities.

The continued viability of many U.S. reservations is clear, reflected in terms of area and population. Indian lands held in trust by the federal government total 50.4 million acres in the lower 48 states (nearly one-half of it in Arizona), including 12 million acres allotted individually to Indians. There are also 2.1 million acres administered by the B.I.A. and 40 million more acres in Alaska. The Indian and Inuit population in the U.S. is now about 880,000 and roughly 550,000 of them live on or near reservations. The B.I.A. still has some jurisdiction over 266 separate Indian land units (reservations, pueblos, rancherias, colonies, and communities and 35 groups of scattered public-domain allotments and other off-reservation lands). These range in population from a dozen or so with zero population, where they have been abandoned, up to over 100,000 for the Navajo Reservation. The B.I.A. also has some service relationships with 216 Alaskan Native communities and Native-owned town lots in

Alaska. Additionally, there are 26 *state* reservations. These are generally newly established, in the east, and in several cases they are adjacent to older federal reservations.

Canada has 576 bands of "status" or governmentally recognized Indians living on 2,281 "reserves" and 85 "crown" (government) land settlements; 74% of the status Indians live on their reserves or on crown land. The total Native population includes approximately 322,000 status Indians, 300,000 non-status Indians and Métis, and 20,000 Inuit, for a total of 642,000. See Tables 1 and 2 for detailed population information in 1972. About 700,000 acres of the total of 6.2 million acres of reserve Indian land in Canada, or 11%, is adjacent to or within urban centers. The current per capita acreage of the reserved land of Indians in the U.S. (105.5 acres) is over ten times greater than in Canada (10.2 acres). This situation will reverse when the upcoming huge land settlements are made across northern Canada.

TABLE 1
INDIAN POPULATIONS IN CANADA AND THE U.S. BY AREA

(Status[1] Indians, 1972)

Area	Number	National Proportion	Proportion of Area Population
Maritimes	10,250	4%	.6%
Quebec	30,000	11%	.5%
Ontario	61,000	22%	.7%
Manitoba	37,000	14%	3.6%
Saskatchewan	38,600	14%	3.9%
Alberta	31,000	12%	1.8%
B.C.	54,150	19%	2.2%
Territories	10,000	4%	16.8%
TOTALS	272,000	100%	1.2%

1 "Status" Indians in Canada constitute about one-half of the Native population in Canada. Thus, as a rough guideline to total Native populations, the numbers and proportions of area populations can be approximately doubled in the provinces (and tripled in the northern territories).

U.S.[2]
(1970 Census)

State	Number	National Proportion	Proportion of Area Population
New England	10,872	1.3%	.1%
Maine	2,195		
New Hampshire	361		
Vermont	229		
Massachusetts	4,475		
Rhode Island	1,390		
Connecticut	2,222		
Middle Atlantic	38,594	4.9%	.1%
New York	28,355	3.6%	.2%
New Jersey	4,706		.2%
Pennsylvania	5,533		
South Atlantic	67,126	8.5%	
Delaware	656		
Maryland	4,239		
D.C.	956		
Virginia	4,853		
West Virginia	751		
North Carolina	44,406	5.6%	.8%
South Carolina	2,241		
Georgia	2,347		
Florida	6,677		
East North Central	57,732	7.3%	.1%
Ohio	6,654		
Indiana	3,887		
Illinois	11,413	1.4%	.1%
Michigan	16,854	2.1%	.2%
Wisconsin	18,924	2.4%	.4%
West North Central	93,555	11.8%	.6%
Minnesota	23,128	2.9%	.6%
Iowa	2,992		
Missouri	5,405		
North Dakota	14,369	1.8%	2.3%
South Dakota	32,365	4.1%	4.9%
Nebraska	6,624		
Kansas	8,672	1.1%	.4%

State	Number	National Proportion	Proportion of Area Population
East South Central	10,363	1.3%	.1%
Kentucky	1,531		
Tennessee	2,276		
Alabama	2,443		
Mississippi	4,113		
West South Central	123,733	15.6%	.6%
Arkansas	2,014		
Louisiana	5,294		
Oklahoma	98,468	12.4%	3.8%
Texas	17,957	2.3%	.2%
Mountain	235,439	29.7%	2.8%
Montana	27,130	3.4%	3.9%
Idaho	6,687		
Wyoming	4,980		
Colorado	8,836	1.1%	.4%
New Mexico	72,788	9.2%	7.2%
Arizona	95,812	12.1%	5.4%
Utah	11,273	1.4%	1.1%
Nevada	7,933	1.0%	1.6%
Pacific	155,316	19.6%	.6%
Washington	33,386	4.2%	1.0%
Oregon	13,510	1.7%	.6%
California	91,018	11.5%	.5%
Alaska	16,276	2.1%	5.4%
Hawaii	1,126		
TOTALS	792,730	100.0%	.4%

[2] *Proportions are presented for those populations that are greater than 1% of the national Indian population. North Carolina has had a recent large increase in Indian population statistics by counting the racially mixed Lumbee people as Indians. By proportion of Indian population the order of the four first-ranked states is Oklahoma, Arizona, California, and New Mexico; but by proportion of total state population the four first-ranked states are New Mexico, Arizona, Alaska, and South Dakota.*

TABLE 2
POPULATION OF LARGEST U.S. TRIBES

(1970 Census)

Tribe	Population	Proportion
Apache	22,993	3.0%
Blackfoot	9,921	1.3%
Cherokee	66,150	8.7%
Cheyenne	6,872	.9%
Chickasaw	5,616	.7%
Chippewa	41,946	5.5%
Choctaw	23,562	3.1%
Comanche	4,250	.6%
Creek	17,004	2.2%
Iroquois	21,473	2.8%
Kaw, Omaha, Osage	6,849	.9%
Kiowa	4,337	.6%
Lumbee	27,520	3.6%
Menominee	4,307	.6%
Navajo	96,743	12.7%
Papago, Pima	16,690	2.2%
Potawatomi	4,626	.6%
Hopi, Pueblo	7,236	.9%
Keresan, Pueblo	10,087	1.3%
Tanoan, Pueblo	6,342	.8%
Zuni, Pueblo	7,306	.9%
Seminole	5,055	.6%
Shoshone, Paiute	14,248	1.9%
Sioux (Dakota)	47,825	6.3%
Ute	3,815	.5%
Yakima	3,856	.5%
Yuman	7,635	1.0%
All other tribes	92,962	12.2%
Tribe not reported	161,543	21.1%
TOTALS	763,594	100.0%

A rural-urban model can account for much of the divergence, but for a complete explanation one must also consider features such as differences in economic viability and the differential impact of government and missionary programs on the various reservations. However, this chapter will focus on the relationship between cultural divergence and urban proximity. Cases of the Washo and Luiseño reservations are presented in detail because they both have communities that have been strongly influenced by urban proximity and they illustrate two slightly different forms of cultural divergence.

The closer a reservation is to a city the more it is likely to be drawn into the economic, political, religious and other affairs of that city and of national urban society generally. One crucial element of attraction to the city is the availability of much better paying jobs. This attraction draws people away from every reservation but it is currently having more impact in the highly urbanized regions, such as California. Thus, when the attraction of city jobs and city life is great, we find Indians abandoning the most rural and isolated reservations or parts of larger reservations. Urban amenities, such as electricity, piped water, and markets have become too important to live without. However, the cost of living is less on the reservation and the reservation provides an emotionally satisfying personal community usually lacking in the city. In addition to the pattern of permanent migration into the city, therefore, Indians often commute between the city and the reservation. Some of this "commuting" is just on weekends or vacations, but the pattern of visiting back and forth is extremely important. Reservations tend to expand in population when they are close enough for easy commuting to city jobs.

In small towns and cities, Indians tend to be isolated, segregated, and held in a static social and economic position. Whites rarely ever know much about Indian life, but this is true even in small towns with a nearby Indian reservation. Indians, on the other hand, are inclined to resist the visits of Whites who might be critical of their way of life. The security that the reservation provides is protected by building social barriers against the intrusion of outsiders. Social distance can have some of the same isolating effects as geographical distance. These lines of segregation that diminish the cultural influence of Whites and Indians on each other often break down in the larger cities. Indians in the large cities are much more diffused among Whites and tend to align with other Indians in kinship-friendship networks and voluntary associations, rather than in residential communities. The reservation is the setting for a personally significant, residential community. The city is a socially heterogeneous place to work. The Indian thus often "commutes" between the two and has a "dual orientation"—to the city economically and the reservation socially.

In a city in Kansas three-fourths of the 1,000 Natives are Potawatomi or Kickapoo from nearby reservations (Steele 1975). This limited ethnic diversity and the proximity between the city and the reservations promote (1) a high level of tribalism, rather than pan-Indianism, and (2) extensive commuting *to the city*, especially for work and entertainment, and *to the reservations* for religious activities, powwows, dinners, and informal socializing. Steele (1975) studied eighteen Indian-White marriages in this urban community and found a variety of patterns of assimilation, with Whites being drawn into Indian values, life styles, and social associations as frequently as the opposite direction of assimilation occurred.

Guillemin (1975) described the Micmac as a *tribal* social network in Boston. There is a low level of *pan-Indian* ethnicity because about 80% of the 3,000 or so Indians in Boston are Micmacs. Other Indians in New England were largely eliminated or assimilated, although there are several hundred people today in Boston who have such Indian identities as Malecite, Mohawk, and Penobscot. The urban Micmac network is integrated to their loved but economically poorer reserves in Nova Scotia, New Brunswick, and Prince Edward Island by regular commuting and extensive visiting between friends and relatives.

CANADIAN PATTERNS

It was a conscious design in the planning of Canadian reserves to make them small and to scatter them among the White communities, rather than to provide large separately viable territories. This was done to encourage Indian-White interaction and Indian adoption of White culture. The assumptions were that White culture was superior to that of Indian culture, that this would become obvious to the Indians, and that they would change through a natural process of emulating their White neighbors. Given the greater population and dominance through White institutions of law, police, education, and business, Whites never seem to have imagined that Indian cultures may be superior in some ways to White cultures and that the borrowing through proximity could flow the other way. However, social barriers proved to be generally stronger than geographical proximity and have tended to retard interaction and acculturation in either direction.

A Canadian survey (Hawthorn 1966: 107) examined the hypothesis that relative urban proximity influenced the various Indian bands. Economically expressed, the hypothesis is that greater proximity leads to greater culture contact, which leads to more White-influenced consumer tastes, which in turn induces Indians to seek and hold better-paying jobs and to accumulate their material resources more effectively. Urban migration or commuting is also linked to this since the better-paying and more stable jobs tend to be in the cities. They found only a low correlation between urban proximity and economic prosperity for the bands, except at the extremes. The more isolated northern bands and rural bands in the Prairies are among the least developed, while most of the economically well-developed bands are near cities. The report (p. 108) states that "modern improvements in transportation and communication have tended to reduce the importance of physical distance, or proximity, as factors determining the frequency or intensity of contact and demonstration effect . . . . The main distance facing most Indians and the main barriers that prevent them functioning effectively in the national economy are essentially social rather than physical in character."

The Canadian study included a special analysis of a representative sample of thirty-five bands classified into three types: developed, transitional, and depressed. The developed bands had a good employment situation, tended to be in or near large metropolitan areas and industrial towns and cities, and had a high level of mobility "in terms of the proportion of band members willing or able to reside away from their reserves for extended periods or permanently." Two more minor factors associated with "developed" bands were ownership of or accessibility to resources (such as logging or commercial fishing operations) and a tendency for a higher degree of social organization and participation on the reserve.

"Large metropolitan centers are cosmopolitan and multi-racial or multi-ethnic in composition and more tolerant of deviant behavior or physical or cultural differences than are small or medium-sized towns. The criteria of employability are more likely to be the objective ones of formal training and measurable efficiency rather than family or racial background. On these grounds, then, it could be argued that Indians could be absorbed into employment in larger numbers and would find the adjustment to urban living easier in large metropolitan centers than in small towns" (Hawthorn 1966:142).

The concentration of Indians and Eskimos in the Arctic into 52 permanent villages and new towns, the building of the Distant Early Warning Line radar stations, the building of the Alaskan Highway, and other events in the North have brought the Native peoples largely within the expanding urban network. Indeed, these urban ties seem to be stronger in many ways for them than for Indians living on the more isolated northern reserves. The Distant Early Warning Line of radar stations that stretches some 3,000 miles from Western Alaska to Baffin Island runs roughly along the 68th parallel, just north of the Arctic Circle. A number of communities have now formed around these defense installations, leading to intimate relations between Eskimos and Whites. Outlying Eskimo settlements that depended entirely on hunting and trapping have essentially died out. The process of settling at permanent villages or towns where a number of Whites are based was accelerated after World War II and can be said to have been essentially completed in the 1960s. The military construction, small weather stations, air fields; recent mineral prospecting and mining, oil exploration; the extension of medical facilities, missions, and trading services; and welfare, education, and other programs of the Northern Development Branch of Canada have brought the autonomous Inuit community to an end. Inuit still hunt and fish, but they range out from the administrative centers. They also often have wage work and snowmobiles.

There are important towns at Frobisher Bay on Baffin Island: Eskimo Point, Churchill, and Great Whale River on the shores of Hudson Bay; and Aklavik and Inuvik (a "new town") in the Mackenzie Delta. Frobisher Bay, with 1,300, has the largest group of Inuit in Canada. Inuvik was established in the 1950s when the government decided to improve the lot of the residents of Aklavik, a town seventy miles to the southwest. Eventually many facilities were built: a hospital, schools, hostels, a theater, a hotel, radio station, the Navy and

RCMP bases, the government administration building, and residential houses. East Inuvik is a typical suburbia, except for its "utilidor" conduit which carries in fresh water and steam for heating and carries out sewage. White officials, teachers, doctors, and Navy and RCMP personnel reside in East Inuvik. West Inuvik is where the Inuit and Indians live, separated by the commercial district and not linked to the utilidor. This segregation and the inequality of the facilities is common in the north and has been widely criticized.

Most of the northern towns have only about one hundred to three hundred people, but these concentrations have brought on many changes. For example, the population concentrations have meant more susceptibility to diseases. There has been much mixing of previously separated groups of Inuit, of Inuit with Indians, and of Inuit with Whites. With firearms, snowmobiles, and ranging out from concentration points, the caribou have been seriously depleted in many areas.

A study of Great Whale River indicates that the Inuit are more acculturated to town life than the local Cree Indians (Barger and Earl 1971). The Inuit tend to be in higher paying and higher status jobs than the Indians. The Inuit hold all the technical jobs in town, working as carpenters, mechanics, electricians, etc. The Inuit are also seen as more socially and politically sophisticated. The two ethnic groups do not work well together and there is an unofficial policy of ethnic segregation in employment. The Inuit have had better opportunities in government technical training and advanced education programs and, perhaps because of some cultural preadaptations, they seem to have grasped the technical skills more easily. Aboriginal Eskimo culture emphasized high technical abilities with the hands, displayed in such things as ivory sculpture and kayak and parka construction. These skills have been a "preadaptation" for the tasks of such things as modern mechanics.

Inuit are more satisfied with their town life than the Indians. They are concerned about increases in stealing and marital problems. Native housing in the North is usually inadequate. Still, the basic attitudinal relationship of Inuit to Whites seems to be much more favorable toward assimilation compared to the Indians in southern Canada.

The Yukon Territory was even more dramatically affected by the Alaskan Highway than the changes described above, because of the concentration effects of road transportation. A line of new towns developed along the road and many old outlying settlements and towns died out. The only city, Whitehorse, is at the major junction where the road forks to Fairbanks one way and Dawson City the other.

In the pioneer days the Whites were dependent on the Indians for survival techniques and they often worked intimately as partners in the bush. But, after the Highway, and as the Yukon developed, the Indians were increasingly ignored. In a study of Teslin ("Mopass"), King (1967) describes Indian-White relations. "Indians were fine bush partners; they were inappropriate as storekeepers, as guests at tea parties . . . The Alaska Highway literally opened the door to the world, and Indians moved. They rapidly acquired automobiles and moved from town to town: a construction job here, a friend to visit there, some wood to be cut in another place, the big town to be visited for a good time, and always the hope that enough wage credit could be earned during the summer to qualify for unemployment insurance during the winter. Sullen resentment has not decreased as Indians experience over and over again the job discrimination . . . but at least a man is no longer stuck. He can always go 'up the highway.' "

The proportion of urban residence is low everywhere for Indians. In a 1971 survey of status Indians, the national average for residence off reservations and crown land was only 26%. Non-status Indians do not have reserves. The off-reserve residence of status Indians by area was as follows: Maritimes 49%, Quebec 22%, Ontario 35%, Manitoba 20%, Saskatchewan 23%, Alberta 15%, B.C. 31%, and Northern Territories 13%, with a total of 26%. The more generally urbanized provinces (Ontario and B.C.) have a higher proportion of status Indians living off reserves, and lower population growth rates of Indians. Stanbury and Siegel (1975) found that the population increase of Indians in B.C. in 1962-72 was matched with an equal migration away from reserves, so that the population on reserves remained the same. The prairie provinces (Manitoba, Saskatchewan, and Alberta) have extremely high Indian population growth rates, but low off-reserve residence, indicating an over-population build-up of reserves that will create many problems and a major wave of new Indian migrants to the cities in the next decade or two. Indians are a highly visible racial and cultural minority in the prairies because there they constitute a relatively large proportion of the total population, about six per cent.

Davis (1965) described a survey of urban Indians in Northern Saskatchewan. The economic potential for Indians is poor in the area. Trapping and commercial fishing are dying out and mining and tourism are being taken over by Whites. Many big towns have developed in the north without any benefit to the surrounding Indians. About three-quarters of the town Indians surveyed still lived within sixty miles of where they were born. Reasons given for coming to live in the towns from the surrounding reserves were better jobs, living conditions, public services, welfare services, and kinship. They complained about the hardships of life on the reserves, in terms of such things as hauling water, chopping and hauling wood, and walking miles for groceries.

Cultural conflicts in the towns are strong between the traditional Indians or Métis and the middle-class White Canadians. The Indians are obviously lower in housing, jobs, and incomes; social status in the community; and in their lower levels of education. Particularly evident is the presence of many low-skill level unemployed youths. The middle-class Canadians disapprove of such Indian behavior as public (as opposed to private) drinking; physical (as opposed to verbal) fighting; and "conning" the institutions of government for welfare, property, and hunting and fishing rights.

Still, life goes on and it has its positive side. There is a lot of visiting, beer-drinking in the pubs, television watching, watching the local baseball or hockey games, and fishing. Some people belong to associations, such as a patriotic veteran group or a community service or religious organization. Their self-identity is usually given as "Indian" or "Breed," rather than "Cree" or a band name, or "Canadian." Some 44% commonly spoke more than one language, 38% spoke mainly English, 14% spoke mainly Cree, and 4% spoke mainly French. It was found that 62% were in the labor force but unemployed, the median school grade completed was six, and the average household size was 5.3 persons (compared to 3.8 persons for Saskatchewan generally).

WASHO URBANIZATION

The traditional communities, where there are a few old people who still speak the Washo language, are the most isolated from urban influences: Woodfords in California and Dresslerville in Nevada. The other major Washo colonies at Carson City and Reno have been surrounded by the expanding growth of those cities. They have become Indian reservations within cities. The Washo of Carson and Reno have essentially moved into the skilled trades of the city, lost most of the distinctively Washo elements of their culture, and acquired a new pan-Indian identity.

The rural Washo colonies are also involved in pan-Indianism, but it tends to be of an earlier time level. Thus, pan-Indian religious Peyotism was introduced to the Washo essentially in the 1930s, flourished briefly at both Dresslerville and Woodfords, and since then has survived only at Woodfords, the most rural colony. Reno, the most urban colony, never converted to Peyotism. The rural-urban continuum applies to the forms of pan-Indianism that are important on the various reservations, in part because rural is correlated with traditional and urban is correlated with modern activities. In the 1970s, customs introduced in the 1930s can be "traditional" in reservation life, as well as generally in North America.

Historically, the Washo were contacted very late by Whites, essentially in the California gold rush days after 1849. This late contact favored their survival as a people and a culture. However, they were a small, passive, and ignored society who never received a reservation in the usual sense. They (528 individuals) received a large allotment (62,713 acres) for pinenut collecting in the Pine Nut hills, mostly in 1899 under the General Allotment Act of 1887. About thirty Washo families also received land in California.

Under the General Allotment Act the plots are individually owned and are not technically part of a reservation. However, they are still held in trust by the B.I.A. and cannot be leased or sold without B.I.A. permission. In the early 1900s small plots of the tribal land were also allotted to individuals, making them inheritable and, with B.I.A. permission, even saleable. Without a will, all of the descending relatives are entitled to a share of the allotted or homestead land. This has led to great confusion over time and forced the B.I.A. into the monumental task of record keeping on the ownership of allotted property.

These "Indian homesteads" under the Act of 1887 were usually 160 acres to heads of families, 80 acres to single persons over 18 years of age and orphan children under 18, and 40 acres to single persons under 18. Double allotments

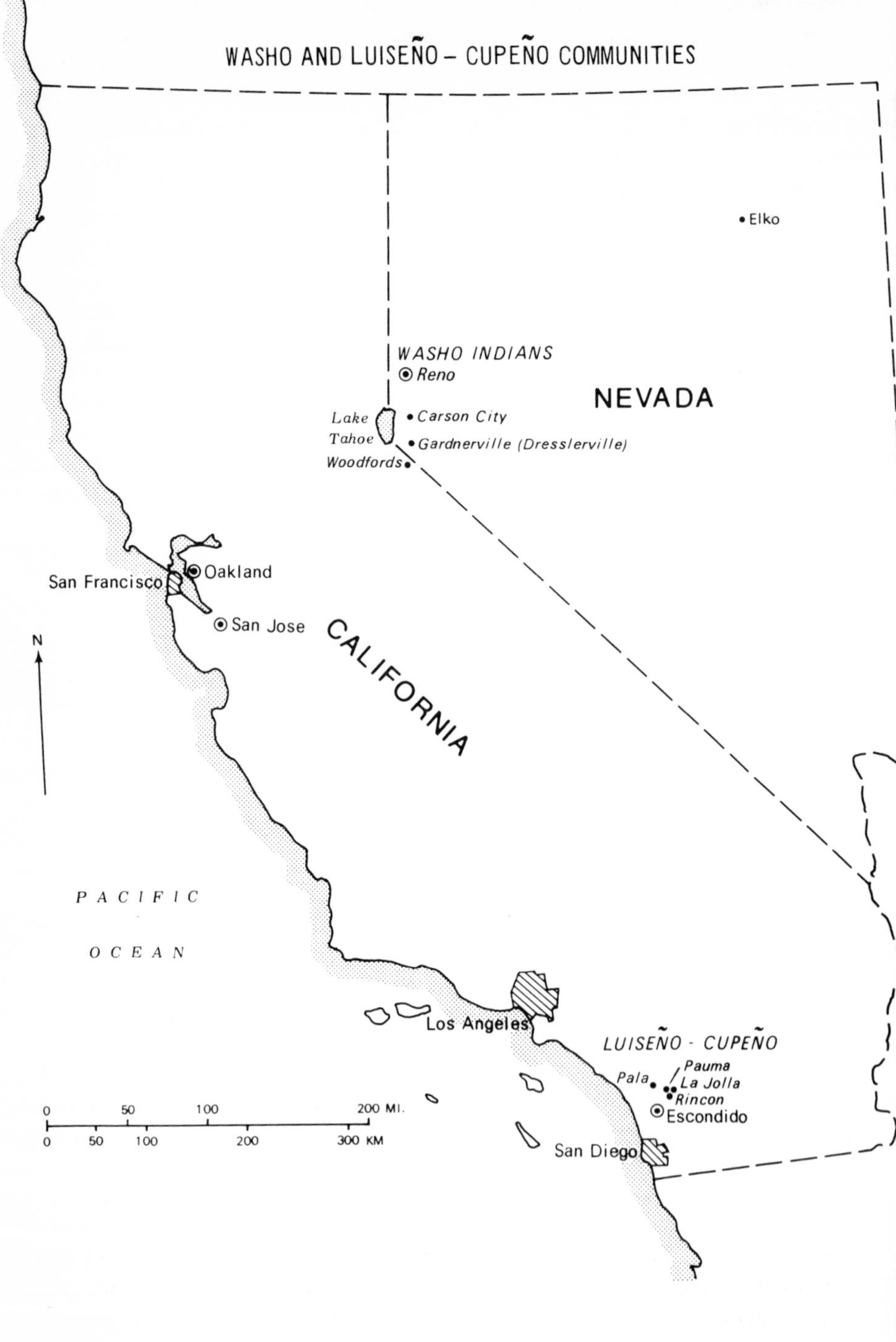
WASHO AND LUISEÑO – CUPEÑO COMMUNITIES
Elko
WASHO INDIANS
Reno
NEVADA
Lake
Tahoe
Carson City
Gardnerville (Dresslerville)
Woodfords
San Francisco
Oakland
San Jose
CALIFORNIA
N
PACIFIC
OCEAN
Los Angeles
LUISEÑO - CUPEÑO
Pauma
Pala
La Jolla
Rincon
Escondido
San Diego
0
50
100
200 MI.
0
50
100
200
300 KM

were given when the land was valuable only for grazing purposes. In 1891 this Act was amended to provide for an allotment of 80 acres of agricultural land and 160 acres of grazing land to each individual, regardless of age or marital status.

In 1917 the site of Dresslerville Colony was given, in trust with the government, to the Washo tribe by a rancher. In 1938 and 1940 three ranches (795 acres in all) were purchased adjacent to this colony for the Washo. In addition, the Carson City Colony of 160 acres was purchased for the Washo in 1940. These Indian colonies of Nevada were developed to eliminate Indian squatter camps at the town dumps and other urban fringe areas.

The Reno-Sparks Colony was formed in 1916 when the Washo and Northern Paiute living around Reno were given a 20-acre plot midway between Reno and the railroad town of Sparks. In the 1920s 8.8 acres were added to the Colony, in part for community buildings such as a school, a church, and a nurses' quarters. Only about a dozen families lived there in the beginning, but as Indians moved into the city from other parts of Nevada they often settled at the Colony because it provided free land on which to build a house. The Colony had 537 residents in our 1969 survey: 65% identifying themselves as Paiute, 28% as Washo, and 7% as having other ethnic backgrounds.

Jurisdictional disputes between federal and local agencies slowed the development of public services such as piped water, a sewer system, and pavement of the roads. Problems within the Colony were being worked out in such practical terms as acquiring federal support for a twenty-unit self-help housing program, negotiating for increased police protection, and campaigning for educational improvements. Complaints of employment discrimination, unfair treatment by school teachers, and inequalities by public officials were frequently handled in a vigorous way by the Reno Colony leaders. Construction work was the most common occupation in the Colony and it paid enough to give the Colony a fairly good economic base.

The more rural Washo reservations were also working to solve their problems, but they lacked the expertise of the Reno Colony in dealing with government agencies. Their economic base was poor and they were not organized to deal effectively with discrimination and segregation. For example, the city of Gardnerville expanded its suburbs so far that a new housing subdivision was built right up to the Dresslerville Colony. The Whites managed to plan the roads in such a way that there were no roads from the new subdivision into Dresslerville. The city of Elko, Nevada planned a similar kind of segregation by routing a new freeway between its Shoshoni Colony and the rest of the city.

LUISEÑO URBANIZATION

The Indian reservations of California tend to be smaller and more numerous than in other Western states. In aboriginal times the approximately 133,000 Indians of California were, with the exception of certain mountainous and desert portions, rather evenly distributed over the state. They were then in effect drawn to the coast by the Spanish missions and then assimilated or pushed back in a scattered way for many miles by the rush of the American settlement.

The eight Luiseño reservations are scattered in an area around Mount Palomar in northern San Diego County. In 1875 the U.S. President established such reservations as Pala, Rincon, and La Jolla by executive order, after public opinion had been aroused in favor of the Indians by two books by Helen Hunt Jackson, *Ramona* and *Century of Dishonor*. In 1902-1903 a band of Cupeño Indians were relocated in Pala. At the same time a small group of Diegueño were also brought in. Some permanent buildings were erected as living quarters for the new arrivals. A small school, a health clinic, an Indian Agency office, and roads were built. There was a small police force and a jail. This community around the old Mission was supervised by the Indian Agency officials who lived there. The B.I.A. discontinued most of its services to Pala over twenty years ago.

The San Felipe Diegueño merged in time with the Cupeño and many of the Luiseño left Pala, leaving the Cupeño as the dominant population. A few Luiseño and Cupeño can speak the old languages and there are modern efforts to formally teach the languages. Some of the religion has been retained, especially the clothes burning rites related to funerals. Hand games are played at festivals, with teams of Indians from other areas such as Cahuilla or Diegueño. Acorn biscuits are still made and a few women remember how to do basketry.

Some work on local farms, but most of the employed work at jobs in the towns and cities of San Diego County; about 70% live off the reservation. Older teenagers typically leave for work in the city. Over half of the household heads who live on the reservations are retired, on welfare, or just unemployed. The people who have stayed or returned to reside on the reservation have usually done so because reservation life is less expensive and has the social security of a personal community. Old people can afford to live on their pensions or welfare much better on the reservations. Several women in Pala moved with their children back to the reservation when their marriages broke up. Several men with chronic health or drinking problems find they can get along better living with relatives on the reservation than carrying on a lonely struggle in the city.

A Pala man said, "We do not pay rent or taxes . . . . With the children I have if I were to live in the big city I would never be able to make it." A Pala woman said, "We do what we want here. We cannot do that in cities. People pass you by as though you are a thing. Here we know each other and if we want to make a noise we can make it." A young woman left to attend school in Los Angeles and then returned to Pala. "When we go off to the big cities we rarely know anybody there. Everything is new and strange and we get lonesome and afraid. We come from a small town and a small school. Soon we get into difficulty . . . . So, we end up coming home to our people. Here we know everybody, there is no need to be afraid."

People spend very little on housing. Furniture is rarely ever thrown away. After many years of use in the house it is often moved out in the yard and used there in the summers. Most households have a refrigerator, radio, and electric iron; about three-fourths have a television receiver, a sewing machine, a washing machine, and an automobile; one-half have a telephone; and one-fourth have a freezer. Around the reservation people spend little on clothing. Men usually wear denim work clothes and women typically wear cotton dresses. Children's clothes and maternity dresses are handed from one relative to the next.

A number of people living at Pala are not on the reservation roll, because they are enrolled at other reservations or they are Whites who married Indians. Major factions then politically divide the enrolled in terms of young and old, living on or off the reservation, and Cupeño or Luiseño. The young want to spend tribal money to make civic improvements, such as a community hall where children could participate in evening activities. The old want the money to be given directly to those enrolled. Community problems described for Pala were (1) the drinking and fighting of the men, (2) lack of recreational facilities for children, (3) lack of police protection, (4) lack of water and sewage systems, (5) lack of cooperation within Pala, (6) poor housing, and (7) "the broken promises of the government."

WASHO AND LUISEÑO COMPARED

Of the major Washo communities, Woodfords is physically the farthest away from major towns and cities. Although it is composed of individually owned homestead lots, it did not break up. It is considered to be the most traditional Washo community because a large number of people still speak Washo, a few women still make baskets, and people still process acorns for food on special occasions. Peyotism, an early twentieth-century pan-Indian religious movement, still exists at Woodfords. The Luiseño community of La Jolla is comparable to Woodfords, being the farthest away from major towns or cities of the main Luiseño reservations, and the most traditional because only old people live there. An early twentieth-century pan-Indian political movement of the region, the Mission Indian Federation, survives more fully at La Jolla than at any other reservation.

The intermediate reservations, Dresslerville and Rincon, also contain many traditional features in language use and ceremonies. The Washo girl's puberty ceremony survives more fully at Dresslerville and the Luiseño funeral rituals are still in practice in Rincon. The economic base of each has been agricultural wage work for Whites.

Reno-Sparks is within a metropolitan area and Pala is eighteen miles from the city of Escondido. Reno-Sparks and Pala are the most urban communities of their tribes. Both have large, compact villages. Both are more impersonal and have less of a sense of community than the more rural reservations. Both are ethnically mixed, Reno-Sparks with Paiute and Washo, and Pala with Diegueño, Cupeño, and Luiseño. This ethnic mixture became a basis of factionalism in Pala but it did not in Reno-Sparks. The economic base of each is such urban employment as construction.

Proximity to cities, in spite of the barriers created by the social segregation of avoidance and ethnic antagonisms and the physical segregation of the reservation itself, has had a major impact on these reservations. Those reservations far from cities have usually been abandoned as families migrated to cities to work. More families stayed on those reservations within a reasonable distance for commuting to work. Finally, the more urban reservations tend to increase in population as commuters and people on welfare settle down in a community where the cost of living is low and where many of their relatives and friends live. Generally, the more rural reservations are the most traditional in terms of tribal culture and the more urban reservations are the most politically sophisticated in dealing with modern bureaucratic governments.

Reservations were created for such functions as (1) a facility for the removal of Indians from lands desired by Whites, (2) military containment and protection, (3) a concentration area to facilitate the administration of programs of cultural indoctrination, and (4) as a land base for their own subsistence. These functions have generally disappeared and been replaced by new functions. Reservations are increasingly used as a place of residence for the retired, for those on welfare, for the visiting of friends and relatives, and for those who can commute to off-reservation jobs. They are often used as summer vacation places for urban dwelling Indians. The differential effects of urban proximity are somewhat extreme for the Washo and Luiseño, but the processes described here are increasingly important as the integration of reservations and cities proceeds in the U.S. and Canada.

Chapter 10

Migration and Adaptation to Los Angeles

The city of Los Angeles has the largest population of Indians in the U.S. or Canada. In this city the Indians are actively creating a pan-Indian sub-culture which accommodates their aboriginal history and reservation culture to the newer world of urban living. Athletic leagues, Christian churches, and other institutions have an exclusive Indian membership. The development of these institutions is part of the process of adaptation to city life.

The *adaptation* of the migrants is outlined here in terms of *assimilation* (the incorporation of a minority into the social relations network of the greater society), *acculturation* (the change of cultural characteristics of the minority in response to those of the surrounding majority), and *adjustment* (social and psychological health). Variations of urban adaptation according to tribal background are also shown to be important.

At the time of our study in 1966, Los Angeles had about 25,000 Indians, double the figure of only six years earlier. Estimates in 1977 ranged around 50,000. The majority of the Indians are migrants from other states. The first wave of migrants came largely from non-reservation areas outside of California. Many came in the 1930s from Oklahoma, and then from widely scattered areas during the 1940s and early 1950s. Los Angeles County had a population of 6,000 Indians in 1955, composed mainly of Cherokee, Choctaw, and Seminole who had come from Oklahoma.

The second, more massive migration began around 1955, the majority coming from reservation areas. They came particularly from Arizona (15% in Los Angeles versus 15% of the Indians in the U.S. live in Arizona), New Mexico (8% vs. 10%), South Dakota (9% vs. 5%), North Dakota (6%vs. 2%), and Montana (7% vs. 4%). Including those born in California (6% vs. 7%), some 76% of the Indians in Los Angeles came from these seven states. These Los Angeles proportions roughly reflect the national distribution of Indians. A similar correlation is found for tribal representation. Indians are invariably precise about their tribal identity, often specifying a tiny tribelet or reservation. The original 101 "tribes" listed by our respondents were condensed into the 76 categories in the following table.

TABLE 3
TRIBAL MEMBERSHIP OF 2,945 INDIANS IN LOS ANGELES

Navajo (14.1%)	417	Arapaho	25	Eskimo	4		
Sioux (12.0%)	354	Omaha	23	Mohican	4		
Cherokee (6.3%)	185	Crow	19	Athabascan	3		
Creek (6.0%)	183	Ponca	19	Klamath	3		
Pueblo (5.1%)	151	Shoshone	19	Kutenai	3		
Choctaw (4.5%)	134	Assiniboin	18	Pomo	3		
Seminole (3.7%)	108	Osage	18	Aleut	2		
Cheyenne (3.3%)	97	Yakima	18	Caddo	2		
Chippewa (3.1%)	92	Chickasaw	14	Chickahominy	2		
Apache (3.1%)	92	Colville	14	Coeur d'Alene	2		
Kiowa	85	Ute	13	Powhatan	2		
Papago	74	Mohave	10	Quapaw	2		
Gros Ventre	65	Nanticoke	10	Quechua	2		
Kickapoo	64	Shawnee	9	Chumash	1		
Comanche	59	Yavapai	9	Haida	1		
Pima	55	Mandan	8	Huron	1		
Blackfoot	47	Pawnee	8	Lillooet	1		
Mexican Indians	45	Tlingit	8	Maricopa	1		
Iroquois	42	Flathead	7	Ottawa	1		
Winnebago	42	Oto	7	Peoria	1		
Mission	38	Potawatomi	7	Salish	1		
Arikara	35	Cree	6	Shasta	1		
Yuma	34	Sac-Fox	6	Spokane	1		
Paiute	33	Wea	6	Umatilla	1		
Delaware	31	Cocopa	4	Umpqua	1		
Nez Perce	31			Washo	1		

A key to the great size of the post-1955 migration was the Employment Assistance ("Relocation") Program of the B.I.A. In 1952, the B.I.A. began to place Indians from reservation areas in jobs in western industrial centers. In 1958 it added the Adult Vocational Program to coincide with the relocation. These programs became a massive stimulant to the growth of the Los Angeles Indian community.

Snyder (1976) compared the use of "gatekeepers" among low-income Whites, Arabs, Blacks, Chicanos, and American Indians. Gatekeepers are like social brokers or mediators, who provide information links between a local group and the wider society for such things as information about jobs, housing, health advice, and legal aid. Snyder found the high proportion of 87% of the Indians had a personal network at arrival, the average size of their personal networks was large (at eight persons), they had the highest use of public services, at 81%, but a low use of gatekeepers, at only 10%—the same level as Whites. In reservation life they learn to depend on the federal government agencies for a wide variety of services and in their urban adaptation they tend to transfer that dependency to public services in the city. Personal networks are important in Indian migration generally and they are particularly elaborate in a city with a mature Indian ethnic community such as Los Angeles.

The incentive for migration was primarily economic: to find jobs, higher wages, and improved physical living conditions. Indians tend to dislike the smog, urban density, transportation problems, and high cost of living in the city, and they look with fondness at the social contacts and activities they had on the reservation. As the years go by in the city, they increasingly withdraw from previous reservation contacts (fewer returns to the reservation, fewer letters, etc.) while at the same time they increasingly tend to idealize the physical and cultural aspects of reservation life. Many older urban Indians talk of retiring to their reservations, where they own property or where, as members of the tribe, they have a right to reside.

ASSIMILATION

Our findings tended to validate the statement of Lurie (1967) that "the option to assimilate is far more open for Indians than for almost any other minority." There are few external, discriminatory barriers to assimilation. The movement from a reservation, where Indians are virtually the total society, to a city where they are a tiny minority is a major step toward assimilation into White society. But the Indian also has the option to continue to relate to other Indians in the city. The city contains a variety of Indian social groups (kinship, tribal, pan-Indian clubs or centers, etc.) with which Indians affiliate in varying degrees. Our study explored three aspects of assimilation: marriage, formal associations, and informal associations.

We found a significant decline with successive generations in the rate of marriage within the race and tribe. Sixty-four per cent of marriages in the generation of the respondent's parents were within the tribe; only 39% of marriages in the respondent's generation were within the tribe. About one-third of the married respondents had married Whites.

Although formal Indian associations (athletic leagues, churches, clubs, and centers) have extensive mailing lists of nominal members, only about 20% of Los Angeles Indians are active in such associations. Nine fundamentalist Protestant churches and one Latter Day Saints church in Los Angeles had predominantly Indian memberships.

Some 29% of our total survey sample reported their usual association as being only with Indians, 67% with Indians and Whites, and 4% with Whites exclusively. With residence considered as an aspect of informal association, 5% preferred an all-Indian neighborhood, 45% preferred a mixed neighborhood, and 8% preferred an all-White neighborhood (42% had no preference or did not reply).

Three patterns of residence were discernible: a primary concentration (46%) in the low-rental district of central Los Angeles City; a secondary concentration in a lower-class suburban southeastern extension of the City (28%); and a wide distribution throughout the remaining cities and suburbs of greater Los Angeles (26%). Indians are much more widely scattered than Negroes or Mexican-Americans in Los Angeles. There is a tendency for recent arrivals (particularly for the first two years) to reside in the central city; longer-term residents move outward to the suburbs. This outward movement is considered indicative of a shift toward assimilation, although some who are major Indian leaders live in the farthest suburbs.

ACCULTURATION

Urban acculturation for the Indian involves replacing or modifying his reservation culture, as well as acquiring new traits. It is not simply the learning of financial budgeting, industrial skills, or driving on the freeways, but the changing of a whole range of behaviors and attitudes. The Los Angeles Indians on the average spend a relatively small portion of their income on clothes and housing, while relatively large amounts go toward travel and entertainment. Although most of the surveyed households have a television set, Indians probably watch television less than Whites. When asked, "What do you usually do for recreation?" 46% said sports; 16% mentioned TV, movies or plays; 9% said powwows (Indian dances); 7% said they go to bars.

Other indices of acculturation are level of formal education, occupation, and the loss of ability to use an Indian language. We found a high median of 11.2 years of education; 5% were in professional occupations, with 31% in skilled occupations. The educational level comes close to that of Los Angeles Whites, although the occupational level is still very low. Some 54% speak one or more Indian languages, but in only 22% of the multiple-person households was an Indian language regularly used.

ADJUSTMENT

Adjustment—as the dimension of psychological and social health—can be measured by such maladjustive factors as rates of suicide, internment in mental hospitals, crime rates, and unemployment rates. Drunkenness was perceived by 32% of our respondents as their major problem. The high unemployment rate is another indication of maladjustment.

An incident in Los Angeles highlights the problem of adjustment. A newly-arrived Navajo who spoke no English became quite ill, and on the street approached a woman wearing a white uniform, in the belief that she was a nurse. The woman, a beautician, thought she was being attacked and had the Indian arrested. Unable to communicate with the man, the police placed him in a hospital where he was classified as an insane Mexican-American.

Acculturation and adjustment are not always correlated positively. Military service, for example, sometimes has a negative effect on Indian adjustment to White society, but a positive effect on acculturation to White culture. Martin (1964) found the Navajo better adjusted to urban life, in terms of fuller employment and lower arrest rates, than Sioux or Choctaw. This kind of passive adjustment to urban life can take place with minimal acculturation. Martin indicates that Navajo men are less *adjusted* than Navajo women, while our data shows Navajo men to be more *acculturated* than Navajo women.

We studied the emotional concerns of 24 adults (13 men and 11 women). The questions were framed as "What are the principal sources of ________ for the Indians in the city?" for the states of happiness, sadness, fear, anger, shame, love, and hate. Informants tended to respond in terms of their personal experiences. The following is a synthesis of their responses, showing a tendency for the women to be concerned more with kinfolk, family, and marriage and the men to be concerned more with employment and material matters.

TABLE 4
EMOTIONAL CONCERNS

	Men	Women	Total	%
1. Kinfolk, family, marriage	43	59	102	20.9
2. Employment, money, material	64	27	91	18.6
3. Law breaking, arrest	31	13	44	9.0
4. Personal achievement, failure	17	13	30	6.1
5. Religious, mysterious	12	14	26	5.3
6. Health, illness	13	11	24	4.9
7. Ethics	11	11	22	4.5

	Men	Women	Total	%
8. Friends	10	12	22	4.5
9. Drinking	11	9	20	4.1
10. City rewards, problems	10	9	19	3.9
11. Social success, failure	15	4	19	3.9
12. Sex	5	13	18	3.7
13. Recreation or lack of it	7	10	17	3.5
14. Politics	8	4	12	2.5
15. Fighting	10	2	12	2.5
16. Prejudice, discrimination	2	8	10	2.1
Totals	269	219	488	100.0%

TRIBAL DIFFERENCES IN URBAN ADAPTATION

For the analysis of tribal differences in adaptation, the survey forms were initially divided into six groups according to tribal location in the U.S. Individuals from tribes located in the northeastern part of the country were found to be closest to the expected pattern of direct adaptation to urban life: high on educational level, but low on use of an Indian language, intratribal marriage, and use of the relocation program.

A comparison of individual tribal groups indicated that the three major tribal groups in the city of Navajo, Sioux, and Five Civilized Tribes represent three degrees of adaptation to the city—from the weak adaptation of the Navajo to the relatively full adaptation of the Five Civilized Tribes. Our study indicated that Indians fresh from strongly rural or reservation backgrounds tend, like the Navajo, to shift over time to patterns of life exemplified by the Five Civilized Tribes. Also, as the Indian community in Los Angeles matures, we may expect tribal groups such as the Navajo to shift toward tribal groups like the Five Civilized Tribes. The latter in turn is culturally close to the general population of Los Angeles, except for the particular ethnic identity.

Compared to the total sample, the Navajo are more involved in reservation life and should continue to be so for a long time. More voted on the reservation, more plan to live on the reservation some day, and more visit the reservation frequently. A very high percentage of the Navajo speak their Native language. The Navajo turn more often to television, sight-seeing, or "nothing" for recreation; tend not to join clubs; and associate predominantly with other Indians, especially with other Navajo.

TABLE 5
MOVEMENT IN URBAN ADAPTATION

	WEAK··········>STRONG		
	Navajo	Sioux	Five Civil.
	Survey		
Speak an Indian language	89%	46%	40%
Intratribal marriage	46%	25%	14%
Came on B.I.A. relocation	49%	53%	32%
Reside in city center	55%	34%	30%
	Detailed Interviews		
Sports for recreation	18%	38%	49%
Belong to clubs	4%	36%	49%
Lived on a reservation	88%	82%	23%
Are on a tribal roll	80%	91%	43%
Plan to live on a reservation	52%	50%	11%
Write or phone reservation	68%	55%	20%
Associate entirely or mostly with Indians	64%	33%	26%

The Five Civilized Tribes are essentially represented in Los Angeles by Cherokee, Creek, Choctaw, and Seminole—primarily from Oklahoma. Fewer of these Indians have lived on reservations or are on tribal rolls. They have resided in Los Angeles longer than most Indians. Only about one-third have come on the B.I.A. relocation program. People of the Five Civilized Tribes are more involved with sports for recreation, particularly with the local Indian athletic leagues. These Indians tend to take their heritage lightly: it is only one of the several components of their identity.

CONCLUSIONS

Urban adaptation involves changes that enhance the survival and expansion of a minority population in the city. These changes are reflected in training in new and appropriate occupations, and in learning to function according to as well as alongside of the impersonal, legalistic standards of the city. As a factor in such adaption, one-fifth of the Indians in Los Angeles have found a security against the impersonality of the city in social enclaves, and a new and wider identity in pan-Indian associations.

There are several conditions in the city which support the pan-Indian enclave rather than tribalism. Common and exclusive occupation of a reservation gives a tribe a unity and stability which cannot be maintained as its members scatter across a city. Lack of discrimination in housing for Indians in Los Angeles leads them to scatter widely from each other and to live close to their work. Thus individuals, even members of tribes with over one thousand members in Los Angeles, rarely see other tribal members except their own kinfolk and a few friends.

Conditions in the city lead the Indian away from tribal patterns. The reservation offers a very narrow range of occupational, religious, political, and recreational alternatives. The range of possible choices is vastly increased in the city. This, together with a new relative social anonymity, and the high-pressure selling of the city, lead the Indian into making choices unnecessary on the reservation.

The physical appearance of the Indian invariably conditions many of the choices he makes. The majority of Indians "look Indian" and are defined and treated by the majority population of Los Angeles as Indians (or Mexicans). However, an Indian can "pass" as a White more easily than a White can "pass" as an Indian. One outcome of this is that those Indians who, although reared on a reservation, do not physically reflect their Native background have difficulty operating in pan-Indian associations.

As an ethnic group, Indians do have a common history and a shared heritage. But many individual Indians are not really aware of this until they leave their reservation with its narrow concerns and in the city meet Indians from other parts of the country. An awakened pan-Indianism then often becomes an additional dimension to, and sometimes a substitute for, their tribal affiliations. Although only one-fifth of our respondents were socially active in pan-Indian associations, the great majority of Indians in the city clearly are ideologically and emotionally affiliated with pan-Indianism. Pan-Indianism thus seems to emerge as a stabilizing element—and perhaps a permanent part—of the adaptation of the Indian migrant to the metropolitan areas, a significant facet of the ethnic diversity of the U.S. and Canadian cities.

Chapter 11

Urban Ethnic Institutions

The traditional culture of most Indians in the U.S. and Canada today is not aboriginal life but reservation life, an ethnic minority dominated by White governments, religions, economic systems, and social practices. The great aboriginal diversity has essentially been destroyed, but specific tribal and reservation cultures are still viable. Now urban life and institutions seem to be opening up a third general phase of Indian cultural development: aboriginal, reservation, and now urban.

This is a description of the urban-centered institutions that have been developed by U.S. and Canadian Indians. An important transition has occurred in terms of an increasing control and design of new urban-centered institutions by members of this emerging pan-tribal ethnic culture. In the reservation context the control and design of modern tribal institutions were largely patterned by federal government policies, but within the city Indians have sought pan-tribal commonalities and developed ethnic institutions according to those commonalities. Indian institutions have then helped to pattern subsequent urban migrations and adaptations and force the liberation of reservation institutions, wresting their control away from Whites.

Once beyond a skid-row phase, Indians who make a permanent adaptation to city life tend to settle down to semi-skilled and skilled jobs, to move outside the city center to mixed surburban areas, and to support the middle-class Indian ethnic institutions. Cities as a whole can also be seen as evolving in terms of the progressively comprehensive set of institutions that are oriented to and staffed by Indians. The first Indian ethnic institutions in the city are usually Indian bars, as well as perhaps certain government and religious service agencies for Indians. These are initially designed and staffed by non-Indians for lower-class Indians with little urban experience. Indian social cliques flourish in the urban bar culture and become the basis of the first urban Indian cultures, but individuals usually acculturate out of this somewhat dysfunctional and temporary setting. In time, the urban-adapted Indians become middle class and develop their own ethnic institutions, such as social centers, churches, powwow clubs, athletic leagues, political associations, and periodicals.

INDIAN URBANIZATION PATTERNS

A slightly smaller proportion of the Canadian Natives live in urban settings away from their "reserves" or other rural communities than in the U.S.: about 215,000 or 36% in Canada (26% of "status" Indians) versus about 350,000 or 41% in the U.S. However, the greater proportion of Natives in the total population of Canada has meant that the impact of this urban migration is much greater on Canadian cities than it is on U.S. cities. The Canadian Natives also are somewhat more traditional so that, for example, functionally monolingual Native speakers occasionally do live in cities with their bilingual relatives; this situation is extremely rare in U.S. cities. Only about one-third of the Indians in the U.S. have a Native first language, as compared to about two-thirds in Canada. In relation to total population, Native people are about six times more numerous in Canada than in the U.S. so that effectively Indian urbanization is on a much larger scale in Canada.

Los Angeles County today has the most Indians of any urban area in the U.S. or Canada, around 50,000. The San Francisco-Oakland area has an estimated 25,000; Tulsa, Oklahoma City, Minneapolis-St. Paul, Chicago, Vancouver, Winnipeg, and Toronto now all seem to be in the 15-20,000 range, Phoenix, Albuquerque, Denver, Seattle, Edmonton, Regina, Montreal, and New York City seem to be in the 10-15,000 range; and many other cities are in the 5-10,000 range, such as Saskatoon, Calgary, Gallup, Rapid City, Sioux City, Milwaukee, Tacoma, Spokane, Portland, Sacramento, Fresno, San Diego, Duluth, Detroit, Great Falls, Buffalo, and Boston. These estimates give a rough idea of urban Indian populations today and the scale of the migration that has occurred, primarily within the last two decades. Most of the approximately 565,000 Natives who reside in urban areas in the U.S. and Canada have steady jobs, maintain stable family lives, and have made a fairly satisfying adaptation to urban living. This satisfaction is often qualified by a continuing value for rural life and some political and poetic rhetoric about the negative aspects of urban life.

Some Southwest U.S. Pueblos were aboriginally large enough in size and diverse enough in functions to provide something of the context of urban life. The same could be said for some Indian villages in the U.S. Southeast and the North Pacific coast. Pueblo town life has evolved with more continuity than most archaic "urban" Indian cultures, thus pre-adapting Pueblo people for modern urban life to a degree. For example, Pueblos have tended to be more self-governing than other reservations. Thus, ancient Zuni continues as a gradually modernizing town of about 5,000 population. The 6,000+ Hopi are noted for their sophisticated and relatively trouble-free acculturation, although their internal disputes related to acculturation pressures are well documented. The populations in some of the other large ancient Pueblos are about 3,000 at Laguna, 2,000 at Acoma, Isleta, and Santo Domingo, 1,400 at San Felipe and Jemez, and 1,200 at Taos (Wax 1971: 218).

By close urban proximity many reservations have historically provided a context of rural, communal, and tribal residence alongside the possibility of urban jobs, education, medical facilities, and so forth. A few examples of this are the Salish reserves in the City of Vancouver; the Iroquois Six Nations Reserve near Brantford, Ontario; the Iroquois Caughnawaga Reserve across the river from Montreal; the Huron settlement in Loretteville outside of Quebec City; Taos outside of Taos, New Mexico; Sandia and Isleta outside of Albuquerque; Zuni a few miles from Gallup, New Mexico; the Yaqui village in the city of Tucson; and the Washo-Northern Paiute colony in Reno-Sparks, Nevada.

In a few cases fairly large urban settlements have developed on reservations in recent years. For example, on the Navajo Reservation large towns have developed in the east at the industrial site of Shiprock, in the center at the tribal capital of Window Rock, and in the west at Tuba City-Moenkopi. The latter two have evolved from Indian agency towns, a common development in Indian areas after the reservation development programs that have come in since the middle 1950s.

Agency towns in the U.S. are characterized by a predominance of civil service jobs; non-Indian entrepreneurs in such things as a retail store, a gas station, perhaps a restaurant, and an automatic laundry; more ethnic and religious diversity than is general for the reserve; and the heavy hand of federal and tribal government in community life (Nagata 1971). The community is largely governed by agencies with decision-making centers outside of the community itself. Housing, for example, in agency towns tends to be somewhat poor in quality for a variety of bureaucratic reasons. First of all, Indians have trouble acquiring building loans because they cannot mortgage reserve land. Thus, their homes tend to be more cheaply made than homes of non-Indians of the same income levels. Reserve Indians cannot acquire fee simple ownership over reserve land they build a house on; this moderates the incentive to build an expensive house because, for one thing, they could only sell it to another Indian of the same band. Under Canadian law a daughter who marries outside her band cannot reside in a reserve house she may inherit from her parents, because she loses her natal band membership upon marriage. Non-Indians living and working in an agency town on the reserve cannot own the Indian land so they tend to rent houses or use a mobile home they can pull away or sell easily when they leave. The great advantage to living on reserve land is that land taxes are not paid, although tribal governments could start this practice, particularly where White-operated industries are locating on reserve land to avoid land taxes.

There is a general process by which even reservations that are away from cities are becoming "urbanized." That is, at the same time that the nation becomes urbanized and an increasingly higher proportion of the population lives in towns and cities, the networks of transportation, communication, public services, recreational activities, and so forth are spread out to increasingly integrate the nation into basically an urban style of life. Native people are the most rural and most widely scattered large racial or cultural minority in the U.S. and Canada, but they are still influenced by these urbanization processes. Reservation life is in some ways becoming "urbanized" as paved roads and supermarkets are built, television reception becomes available everywhere, etc.

There are signs that an urbanization network has become specialized and international for Indians in that it covers both the U.S. and Canada in such things as the essentially simultaneous appearance of specific new ethnic fashions and ideas. Over two hundred Indian periodicals have begun publication in the last decade. Most of them are based in cities but have a significant rural and reservation readership. Collectively these periodicals form an information network because the various editors read and report news from each other's papers.

Across this U.S. and Canadian Indian network it is possible to follow the waves of one idea and action program after another. In politics there were the ideas that Natives have a continuing unique and "special status" in relation to the government; that Natives have some "aboriginal rights" in land, in hunting, and in fishing; that the early treaties should be reinterpreted in terms of modern culture. In radical action there was the "occupation" of famous and self-contained places: Alcatraz Island in San Francisco, Ellis Island in New York, Fort Lawton in Seattle, Mount Rushmore and Wounded Knee in South Dakota and, with the spread of militance to Canada, at Anicinabe Park in Kenora, Ontario and the "Indian Embassy" on Victoria Island in the Ottawa River. In education there was the idea that Indian children who are monolingual in an Indian language should be able to start school in that language, making it necessary to train Native teachers who speak the Native languages. When the ecology movement became strong the idea spread that Indians aboriginally had a compatible ecological relationship with the plants and animals in their environments.

RESERVATION INSTITUTIONS

Institutions, as used here, means an established social facility that provides some service to people. Government agencies, schools, churches, markets, transportation and communication systems are obvious institutions, but we should also include kinship-friendship networks, clubs, and other less formally established social facilities. Analytically at least, institutions always have both a personnel staff and clients, although the roles in informal institutions are usually very fluid.

Indian institutions are unusual in the extent to which they have been designed and staffed by non-Native people. This developed out of the unusual arrangements related to the conquest, dominance, and tutelage of Native peoples in an internal colonialism in the U.S. and Canada. Native societies did maintain some ancient tribal institutions and they developed many new ones to meet the changing circumstances of their lives. However, these tended to be narrowly confined to small social units, although there are a few exámples of historical pan-tribal movements. Still more significant is that their designs were heavily influenced by and surbordinate to non-Native contexts of culture, such as the federal reservation system and Indian laws. Thus, in nearly a century of neo-colonial reservation life the dominant institutions have been designed and staffed by people from a different race, religion, and government.

Local band or tribal councils usually operate according to models set down by federal government agencies. Band membership and land ownership are legalistically defined. Kinship, marriage, and divorce must conform to Whiteman's law. Plant gathering, hunting, trapping, fishing, and farming are restricted in terms of legal areas, legal times, and legal means. People outside the reservation community plan and carry out the education and medical care of the community. Christian missionary programs provide religious services to the community and displace Native religious practices. The individual is forced into the role of a consumer of services that emanate from outside the community. It is only through the experience of some self-determination that the community becomes motivated and integrated. In lieu of that possibility, in recent years some of the most important developments in Indian ethnic institutions have been centered in urban areas and are beginning to force the liberation of reservation institutions.

EARLY URBAN INDIAN INSTITUTIONS

The first and most prevalent Indian ethnic institutions in cities have been bars that develop a significantly Indian clientele. In hundreds of towns and cities Indians have tended to drink in particular places. This is usually in a setting of subtle discrimination and segregation today, but it has an historical basis; it was illegal for Indians to drink in most places in the U.S. and Canada until recent years. Indians are used to this segregation and find in the local Indian bar a climate of tolerance and ethnic camaraderie. There tends to be more social animation and interaction in Indian bars. People are louder, freer, more accepting of newcomers, and more mobile as they move from table to table and bar to bar. Gangs form easily for such petty crimes as rolling drunks and prostitution. Jail is a common, shared experience without much stigma for virtually every Indian who has been on skid row for a few months.

The social cliques that are formed at bars have usually been the first urban ethnic institutions that Indians themselves design and staff. There is pride among skid row Indian men in heavy drinking, fighting ability, the ability to "con" outsiders, generosity with insiders, and attractiveness to women. In comfortable situations Indians are vivacious. They may use silence as a shield against outside intrusions, but the defenses come down when they are together.

These cliques and the socializing at bars become very important to Indians because in this context they are known and respected, and through them they can enjoy life in the city. However, these cliques often acquire a counter-culture orientation that becomes dysfunctional as a long-term adaptation of individuals to city. life. The individual who has become a part of skid row society usually leaves it within a year or two and either returns to reservation life or acculturates into a different and more functional urban niche. In practice, this is usually the highly mobile time of life for young adults, typically involving short-term employment and frequent movement between the reservation and the city.

Social service agencies in the dominant society perceive the skid row culture in negative terms and are sympathetic with the troubles of Indian migrants to the city and the local "Indian problem." The typical pattern is for service-oriented religious organizations to be the first to set up an Indian center. In Los Angeles, for example, the Society of Friends of the Quaker Church established the first center. This was later supported by local civic clubs and churches. The initial orientation of the Center was social welfare, with such things as job and family counseling and distributions of donated food and clothing. In time, however, Indians who had already achieved an urban adaptation acquired control over the Center and directed the orientation away from social welfare. They set up a small, separate distribution center for welfare contributions, but the program shifted toward athletics, powwows, an actors' workshop to train people for the movie industry, and Indian politics. A second Indian center was established by another Christian church organization to fill the welfare needs of new migrants.

Federal government programs in both the U.S. and Canada have been traditionally oriented toward rural and reservation Indians, so in both countries there has been a period of lag between the urban migration of Indians and the development of government services to urban Indians. Other institutions, such as churches and civic organizations, have usually worked in that vacuum of government services. However, to some degree the federal government has been drawn into providing urban services to Indians. In both countries the primary Indian agency, the Bureau of Indian Affairs in the U.S. and the Indian Affairs Branch in Canada, did not fund urban Indian centers. In the U.S. this was carried out primarily through the Office of Economic Opportunity and in Canada by the Citizenship Branch of the Secretary of State.

LATER STAGE INSTITUTIONS

The initial stage, when the bar culture is the predominant setting of Indian institutions, still pertains to many small towns and cities, but the cities listed earlier with large Indian populations are into at least the second stage, with Indian centers and elaborated kinship-friendship networks. There appears to be some lag in the development of centers and other formal ethnic institutions when the Indians come from reservations in the immediate region. When this occurs there is more "commuting" back to reserves on weekends and for vacations, less tribal diversity in the city, and a greater ramification of viable kinship-friendship networks in the city that new migrants can depend on. These networks become institutions that carry many of the same functions as a bar culture or an Indian center, and thus serve as an alternate means of entry into urban life. These networks are second-stage institutions that promote and facilitate the chain-migration of Indians to cities. They operate without the social dysfunctions of bar culture and without the debilitating paternalism of non-Indian government and church agencies.

Kinship-friendship networks often operate within a tribal framework. Thus the large, tribalistic, or exclusive Indian societies may form important ethnic institutions in the city. In terms of occupational networks we know that many of the Caughnawaga Iroquois in New York City went into high steel work and many of the Navajo in Albuquerque went into manufacturing silver jewelry. The Iroquois in Brooklyn, New York and Navajo in Norwalk-Whittier, Los Angeles both formed early geographical enclaves in large cities, an uncommon development among U.S. and Canadian Indians.

In addition to tribal networks, there are other personal ethnic networks based on such things as powwow dancing, Indian political activism, and Indian athletic leagues and sporting events. The significance of these networks is that they promote rural-urban interactions, friendships, and migrations.

There is a decrease in the number of predominantly Indian bars during the second stage of ethnic institutionalization because, (1) other institutions take over the social and educational functions for most new migrants, (2) centers and networks take on the function of receiving newcomers, (3) people move away from the transient skid row area to more stable homes, and (4) people more often drink in their homes and at private parties.

The third stage of urban ethnic institutionalization comes when the ethnic institutions cover a broad range of common interest associations, such as Indian athletic leagues, Indian Christian churches, powwow clubs, and political organizations. In the first stage of urban institutionalization, the Indians are in some ways strangers to the city and to urban life, using institutions that are entirely designed and staffed by others. They also elaborate social cliques in the bar culture but these tend to be very temporary. In the second stage they participate in the design and staffing of institutions such as Indian centers and they develop relatively stable kinship-friendship networks. In the third stage the Indians develop their own unique ethnic institutions, typically related to positive ethnic identity and expressions, rather than to solving the "Indian problem" as perceived in such negative terms by the majority society. Institutions are then dominated by Indian staffs, who effectively put down much of the earlier social work style of paternalism.

In a few cities (Toronto, Vancouver, Chicago, San Francisco, Los Angeles, etc.) there seems to be emerging a fourth stage in which Indians become involved in creating academic, entrepreneurial, and professional institutions. One characteristic of these fourth-stage institutions is that they provide services to the general society as well as the ethnic community. Native studies programs are fourth-stage institutions. One example of a fourth-stage institution is an ethnic restaurant. Canada's first restaurant to serve only Native foods is Muck-a-Muck House, established in Vancouver in 1972. It has an all-Indian staff and specializes in Indian cooking in the style of the Haida Indians of the Queen Charlotte Islands.

ETHNIC DESIGN AND STAFFING

The question of who determines policy and who staffs the institutions is crucial to the ethnic group. Even though they may have genuine goodwill and concern about helping Native people, non-Native people have typically been misguided about what the Native wants and needs. Also, there are the matters of greater pride and identity when the institution is staffed by the ethnic group that uses it and the utility of acquiring the leadership experience in the process of running the institution. Native political leaders have in turn pushed this issue of Native control very hard in recent years, occasionally to such extremes as anti-White racism and the questioning of the racial and cultural credentials of other Indian leaders. Demonstrations at Wounded Knee, South Dakota and Saskatoon, Saskatchewan were both held by Natives who opposed the conservativeness of the local elected Indian leaders.

Liberal Whites involved in ethnic institutions have generally recognized their inability to set policy as well as Native people and have yielded leadership to them fairly readily. There has been, for example, extensive recruitment of Native people in recent years into institutions of the church and government. There are still many struggles, however, *among* Native people over the racial and cultural composition of this participation in ethnic institutions.

The first Native people to be recruited into or to develop Native institutions are usually the most acculturated Natives. They, in turn, develop policies that are relatively pro-White and assimilationist. For example, The Mission Indian Federation was formed in Southern California in 1919 as a pro-assimilationist, anti-government organization fighting for aboriginal land and water rights. Relatively acculturated Indians were originally the leaders, but they lost their land claim cases while young Indians were reversing their policies. The Federation finally died out in 1963, a time when most young Indian leaders had become nationalistic, opposed to assimilation, and pro-government in certain ways. They saw that the government agencies could be used to their ends while the termination of special government relations would weaken the separate viability of Indians.

There were several urban clubs of Whites and acculturated Indians in the 1920s: Chicago's Grand Council Fire of the American Indians; Seattle's National Society of Indian Women; and four clubs in Los Angeles: American

Indian Progressive Association, an Indian women's club, the Wigwam Club for Native dancing, and the War Paint Club for Indians in the movie industry.

In another early case, the Alaska Native Brotherhood was formed in 1912 by ten relatively acculturated Indians in Sitka, Alaska with the avowed goal of acculturation. It was patterned on a White fraternal society called the Arctic Brotherhood and fought for citizenship rights for Natives, educational facilities, and the abolition of aboriginal customs. Native political orientations today have almost reversed themselves from this early stand and fight for a "citizens plus" status, Native control of Native education facilities, and the restoration of as many of the aboriginal customs as possible, including language and religion.

The British Columbia Native Brotherhood was formed somewhat on the model of the Alaskan organization and, in part as an Indian fisherman's union, spread down the British Columbia coast. It became a model, in turn, for the development of Indian Brotherhoods in other Canadian provinces. The Allied Tribes of British Columbia is another early group, and it fought for the 1912 "Nishga Petititon" requests for land allotments and remunerations on the basis of "aboriginal rights." The Mission Indian Federation and the Allied Tribes of British Columbia both lost their land claim cases and then collapsed as effective political organizations, but they served as models for later, more nationalistic and anti-assimilationist organizations.

The central point of this discussion is that *progressive ethnicization* is a common process that occurs both within particular institutions and across the network of Indian ethnic institutions. Ethnicization involves a reinterpretation of every apsect of life in terms of the ethnic culture. Thus, there is a new way of looking at history, at politics, at religion, and so forth. A related point is that there is an important interplay in this progressive ethnicization between acculturated and unacculturated people. The ethnic institution may be started by Whites and then acculturated Indians are recruited into it, or it may be started directly by acculturated Indians. The clientele, however, are usually the less acculturated people and as they get involved they try to redirect the institution to their ends, rather than to the ends of the Whites or acculturated Indians. Most Indian institutions, however, are at least partially controlled by acculturated Indians because unacculturated Indians lack the administrative skills to successfully operate the institution. A similar arrangement in band and tribal politics often promotes the division of the reservation community into relatively acculturated and unacculturated factions. Thus a few people with extensive experience in the wider society come back to the reservation and are given political office and power because "they know how to work with Whites," but at the same time they have a significant extension of their social networks outside the traditional community and they may be disliked for their non-Indian ways.

The size of a city influences the visibility of Indian institutions, the awareness and personal concern of non-Native people for Natives, and the ease of communications among Indians. Towns and small cities generally are more discriminating against Indians than medium and large cities, particularly if they receive a large number of transient Indians from surrounding reservations. However, the Indians are extremely visible and seen as presenting a set of difficult social problems for small cities that receive a large number of relatively *unacculturated* Indians, such as Kenora, Ontario; The Pas, Manitoba; and Prince Rupert, British Columbia. Small cities with large populations of *acculturated* Indians do not have significant social problems with Indians. In Ontario this is the case in such cities as Brantford, Sarnia, and Sault Ste. Marie, where nearby reserves have become integrated into prosperous urban economies. In Toronto and Montreal, both with over two million population, the thousands of Indians in each city still constitute an "invisible" less than 1% of the total population.

The Indian data on Winnipeg and Los Angeles are compared here because each has a large number of Indians and relatively full institutional completeness (Price and McCaskill 1974). Winnipeg has the usual centers, common interest associations, and newsletters, although its institutional structure is less mature than that of Toronto because the Toronto Indians tend to be more acculturated. Thus, for example, Indian bars are still a prominent part of the Winnipeg skid row scene, indicating that the city is still in an early stage of Indian institutionalization.

We found these similarities in interviews with household heads between the Indian communites of Winnipeg and Los Angeles: (1) young average age (25 in Winnipeg and 29 in L.A.), (2) few average number of years in the city (4.5 and 5 years), (3) a high proportion of residence in the city center (48% and 46%), and (4) moderate average annual family incomes ($4,000 and $5,000). We also found these differences: (1) a *provincial* migration into Winnipeg (90% born in Manitoba) versus a *national* migration into L.A. (19% born in California), (2) lower average years of education in Winnipeg (8-9) than in L.A. (11.-2), (3) more could speak an Indian language in Winnipeg (70%) than in L.A. (46%), (4) less people belonged to an urban Indian association in Winnipeg (23%) than in L.A. (76%), and the Winnipeg Indians tended to turn more to sedentary recreations (television, movies, drinking in bars, and bingo) than the L.A. Indians (who turned more to sports and dancing).

TORONTO

In 1951 the North American Indian Club of Toronto was formed, primarily as an organization of Whites and relatively acculturated Indians who held common interests in the history, arts, crafts, dances, and so forth of traditional Native cultures. The organization, with over 500 active members, is still going strong in the 1970s. The Indians in Toronto at the time of the Club's founding were mostly mixed-bloods and acculturated Indians from the Iroquois Six Nations Reserve, and Ojibwa from relatively assimilated Indian populations in southern Ontario. Many of the men had served in the military during World War II and preferred to take a job in an urban area rather than return to reserve life. Then in the 1950s the less acculturated Indians from the more northerly reserves began to come into Toronto and other Canadian cities.

The presence of Natives in towns and cities created a higher visibility and awareness than earlier of the differences and conflicts between the dominant White culture and the Native cultures. For example, Indians had learned different patterns of drinking and drunken comportment than urban Whites: public rather than private drinking, expressing aggression in more physical than verbal ways while drinking, and more often drinking in the northern frontier style of periodic binges to complete drunkenness. White laws were used to suppress and control these frontier modes of drunken comportment, leading to extremely high arrest and incarceration rates of Native people. In another sphere the White-designed and operated school system failed to relate to Native cultures, thus failing to retain most Native students beyond the age of puberty. These and other Indian-White cultural conflicts constituted what Whites usually called "the Indian problem."

In 1958 a number of people who recognized "the plight of Canadian Indians" persuaded the Canadian Association of Adult Education to set up a National Commission on Indian Canadians. The objective of this commission was to collect information and make recommendations about national Indian policies. Following an Indian-Métis Conference, the Winnipeg Indian-Métis Friendship Center was established in 1959, primarily as a counseling and referral service for urban Native migrants. This became a model for later urban Indian centers in Canada. By 1960 it was obvious that Eskimos faced many of the same kinds of problems as Indians and that Native peoples would have to play a leading role in policy decisions if the decisions were to be effective. Thus, in 1960 the Indian-Eskimo Association of Canada was formed, with a head office and library in Toronto, and eventually other major offices in Winnipeg and Ottawa.

In 1961 the North American Indian Club of Toronto influenced a number of non-Indian individuals and organizations into forming a Special Committee on Indian Services within the Social Planning Council of Metropolitan Toronto. This committee evaluated the existing services of the Central Neighborhood House and the Anglican Information Centre; set up a mechanism to coordinate services to Indians; and in 1963 endorsed the Indian Centre of Toronto. About half of the people on the Centre's board of directors were Indians. The objectives they set were a counseling and referral service and the provision of opportunities for participation in ethnically relevant social, recreational, educational, and other activities at the Centre and in other locations.

In the early 1960s the Indian-Eskimo Association did research on many problems of Native people and acted as a political lobby for Native interests. In the later 1960s it helped stimulate the development of urban Indian centers and the formation of Native political organizations, usually province-wide in Canada. Organizational problems were very great because there are issues or traditions that split and politically factionalize Indians, Métis, and Eskimos; the various treaty groups; status and non-status Indians; the more acculturated but still nationalist tribes, such as Iroquois and Blackfoot, from other Indians;

etc. However, by 1970 even the Eskimos had formed Inuit Tapirisat of Canada and there was a working alliance of Native associations, particularly through the National Indian Brotherhood for status Indians and the Native Council of Canada for non-status Indians and Métis. The Native associations requested that the Indian-Eskimo Association change its name because it appeared to denote an official Native organization. In 1972 the name was changed to Canadian Association in Support of the Native Peoples and the head office was moved from Toronto to Ottawa to more effectively pursue a political lobby function.

In 1967 the Toronto Indian Centre became a member of the Community Folk Art Council, thus establishing itself in another way as a recognized ethnic organization of the city. Each year since 1969 the Centre or Anduhyan House has participated in Caravan, an ethnic festival in Toronto that emphasizes foods of the world. For this eight-day event they usually put up a tipi in front of the Centre, play recorded Indian music, and decorate the Centre with beaver mats, corn husk carpets, a canoe, baskets, and quilt work. They serve roast beaver, venison stew, hominy soup, wild rice, bannock, blueberry dumplings, and raspberry tea.

Seventy-one urban Indian centers had been formed in Canada by 1977, in large part because of a $26.1 million federal government granting program: Labrador 1, Nova Scotia 1, Quebec 4, Ontario 17, Manitoba 10, Saskatchewan 8, Alberta 8, B.C. 15, Yukon 1, and N.W.T. 5. Twenty of them, as well as the Ontario and B.C. associations of friendship centers, publish newsletters.

Many centers sponsor classes on Indian history, handicraft workshops, and powwow dance clubs. Daily activities at Toronto's center include such things as Weight Watchers, Ojibwa lessons, Native cooking, television and film viewing, and dinners. The sports director arranges with community schools and clubs for physical activities such as swimming, volleyball, hockey, and skating. On Sundays an Indian chapter of Alcoholics Anonymous has its meeting there. The center helps to support a summer camp and the regional round of powwow dances and festivals. It provides legal advice and a court worker and has an annual Christmas party.

Other associations based in Toronto are as follows:

1. Algonquians, arts and crafts store.
2. Anduhyan, a residence for newly arrived girls.
3. Association for Native Development in the Performing and Visual Arts.
4. Canadian Indian Ladies' Auxiliary.
5. Donner Native Scholarship Program.
6. Indian Craft Foundation.
7. Iroquois and Allied Tribes.
8. Manitou Arts Foundation.
9. Métis and Non-Status Indian Association of Ontario.
10. Native Big Brothers and Sisters.
11. Li'l Beavers, the children's program.
12. Nishnawbe Institute, administrator of the Indian Ecumenical Conference.

13. North American Indian Club.
14. Ontario Federation of Indian Friendship Centres.
15. Ontario Natives Development Fund.
16. Ontario Native League for Youth.
17. Pedabun Lodge, an alcoholic rehabilitation center.
18. Union of Ontario Indians.
19. Wenjack, a chapter of the American Indian Movement.
20. Wigwamen, a housing association.

OTHER CITIES

Almost all Canadian cities and most cities in the western U.S. have some significant matrix of Indian ethnic institutions. Most of them have a predominantly Indian bar, Indian center, a few tribal clubs, and perhaps things like an Indian Christian church and an Indian athletic league. Dosman (1972) described the situation in Saskatoon, Brody (1971) in the skid row of Edmonton, McCaskill (1970) in Winnipeg, and Nagler (1970) in Toronto. Seattle and Vancouver (Stanbury and Siegel 1975) have long had effective organizations of Indian women. The National Society of Indian Women was organized in Seattle in the 1920s. The American Indian Women's Service League in Seattle has long produced a high quality Native newsletter, *Indian Center News.* Then in Vancouver we find that the best newsletter, *The Indian Voice*, is produced by the Indian Homemaker's Association. This activism of Indian women has been primarily a West Coast phenomenon, extending down through California.

Data on Seattle by Chadwick and Strauss (1975) indicate an urban ethnicity that is related to a high level of urban acculturation, such as the high average of 11.3 years of education of adults and 24% married to non-Indians. Denver has an Indian center run by a Christian church, a pan-Indian organization called the White Buffalo Council (mostly Sioux), and a Navajo Club. Minneapolis-St. Paul, Minnesota draws migrants primarily from the north central states and thus has a relatively homogeneous population with about 60% Chippewa and some 10% each of Sioux, Winnebago, and Menomini.

In 1966-67 Los Angeles had the greatest Indian institutional completeness of any city with (1) three bars, (2) ten Christian churches, (3) two Indian centers, (4) two athletic league associations, (5) thirteen dance clubs (four main powwow groups and several tribal dance clubs), (6) nine Indian publications, and (7) the Los Angeles Indian Fair, a three-day event that brought together all the associations, with a pageant, dancing, sports, and booths selling foods and crafts. Wayne Bramstedt (El Camino College) found some 90 Indian voluntary associations and 21 publications had developed in Los Angeles since the 1920s.

Activities in the Indian communities of San Francisco, Oakland, and San José are coordinated by the United Bay Area Council on Indian Affairs and The Bay Area Indian Athletic Association so that there are no conflicts in scheduling major events. Powwows and athletic tournaments in softball, bowling, and basketball (14 teams) are very important. There are several publications, including the nationally prominent ones of the American Indian Historical Society: *Wassaja* (a monthly newspaper), *The Weewish Tree* (children's literature), and *The Indian Historian* (an academic journal).

Ablon (1964) found that individual migrants in San Francisco would typically go through an initial seeking-out period, usually including an approach to an Indian center, and then more diverse social interactions with friendships made in related jobs, places of residence, and church groups. Family life took up more time as the size of an individual's family grew and most families attended only the major Indian events, such as a Christmas party, an annual picnic, a dance or powwow. The formal institutions were used more by new migrants who needed security in a new situation and the opportunity to socially interact with others in a similar situation. The most important contexts of significant social contacts and interactions were, in order of importance, (1) kinship-friendship networks; (2) Indian centers and related clubs; (3) neighborhoods, housing projects, stores, and public places, and (4) places of employment. The social interactions increased over time in all four of these contexts. Interactions in church groups, government sponsored events or programs, and bars were unimportant and either remained about the same or declined over time.

Snyder (1971) gives somewhat comparable data on the Navajo in Denver. The locations of most of their informal social interaction patterns were, in order of importance, (1) in own home, (2) downtown, and (3) at homes of friends or relatives. The remaining 27% of the social interaction patterns recorded in his survey took place in such situations as church, White Buffalo Council or Indian Center, parties, dances, wrestling matches, bars, bowling, and playing pool. Paredes (1971) studied the scale of city involvement of a small sample of Chippewa in a northern Minnesota city and found what can be interpreted as a sequence of progressive involvement in the urban institutions: no significant involvement; then medical, church, school, and city politics; and finally the voluntary associations.

CONCLUSIONS

Indians are acculturating not only to a dominant White culture and to urban life, but to a new urban-based ethnic culture as well. We see that most of the cities in the western U.S. and Canada have flourishing systems of Indian ethnic institutions. In the larger cities there has been a development toward a relatively complete set of institutions to fulfill, if one chooses, the majority of one's services in social contexts where Indians are dominant.

Complete social and cultural autonomy is impossible for ethnic groups in cities, but some, like Jews or Chinese in North America, approach this and are perhaps the two *most urban* ethnic groups in North America. For example, there are almost no Jews or Chinese in North America who work on farms, fish, or work as lumberjacks. Indians are at the other extreme; they are *the most rural large ethnic group in North America*. Thus, it is not surprising that their urban ethnic institutions are just now forming and that they generally lack professionals or entrepreneurs, who are abundant among Jews and Chinese.

There seems to be a snowball effect of chain migration and increasing institutional completeness that attracts further migration. Thus, Los Angeles has the largest number of Indians, the greatest institutional completeness, and continues to be a favorite destination for new migrants. We can expect a similar development in cities such as Toronto and Winnipeg. The city is more accessible when kinfolk and friends live there. And it is a more desirable, more satisfying place to live when you have access to institutions of your own ethnicity. They carry some of the personal character of reservation communities into the urban life.

Indian ethnic institutions also draw from a broader legitimization and popularity of ethnic and sub-cultural diversity in the U.S. and Canada. An *ethnic ethic* now permeates society so that at least the facades of cultural difference are promoted in ethnic foods, dress, arts, music, dance, and so forth. This has promoted a situation in some cities, such as Los Angeles, in which young people today consider Indianness to be one of the best possible ethnic heritages to have. It is seen as much more exciting to be something like a Mohawk or a Hopi Indian than a Britisher or a plain Canadian or American.

In review, the following seems to be the general sequence in the development of urban Indian institutions in a city.

1. Predominately Indian clientele bars and government, church, and other welfare services.
2. Kinship and friendship networks proliferate in the city. Formal welfare-oriented "centers" and ethnic newsletters begin.
3. Middle class Indian clubs and centers, powwow dance groups, churches, athletic leagues, political action groups. Indian bars decline in number.
4. Native people offer professional, academic, and entrepreneurial services. Native studies is such a service. These fourth-stage institutions serve the general society as well as the specific ethnic society.

Chapter 12

Voluntary Associations

Voluntary associations are small, innovative, cultural systems that are built up as additions to the central culture and depend upon a vital sense of individual involvement for their continuance. The more "instrumental" voluntary associations solve the need for ideological involvement better than the "expressive" associations, but they have the perennial problems of followership: insufficient recruitment and attendance if ideological commitment is low and poor conformity and factionalism if ideological commitment is high. Among U.S. and Canadian ethnic groups where ideological commitment is currently high, such as the Chinese, Greeks, and Jews, as well as the U.S. and Canadian Indians, there is extreme proliferation of voluntary association factions.

A voluntary association is a social group with a distinct ideology and recruitment through the relatively free action of affiliation of individuals. By contrast, the non-voluntary or core associations are those social groups which individuals participate in by virtue of their *primary* (birth) ascriptive conditions, such as sex, age, kinship, and race, or *secondary* ascriptive conditions that are directly derived from one's childhood enculturation, usually including residence, religion, and occupation. U.S. and Canadian Indian voluntary associations seem to be more closely linked to their ascriptive associations than the voluntary associations of the majority society. Thus, for example, Indian adults more often bring their children along to association meetings and other activities. They are often urban-centered, but rural-oriented to where the majority of Indians still live.

Voluntary associations flourish in settings where there are competing ideologies for the commitment of adults and where the general cultural ideology is amorphous, where religious, political, aesthetic, or other ideologies do not instill enough meaning in the lives of individuals. Humans need motivated membership, affirmation through communication of their learned and elaborated symbols. Voluntary associations are inventions we create to solve our needs for secure, validated involvements that are enclaved and exclusive, symbolic and social. The culturally defined ends of the association are secondary to these neurological needs, because voluntariness means that individuals can easily drop out if their personal needs are not being met. The perennial complaint of leaders of voluntary associations is that their followers are not sufficiently committed.

There are many possible secondary, social functions, generally called "latent" because they are postulates of social process used by social scientists: socialization, preservation of the social order, initiation of useful social action, and so forth. Finally, there are the tertiary, "expressed," social functions that are often obvious in the title if the association is named: All Indian Rodeo Association (Cardston, Alberta); United Indian War Veterans (El Cajon, California); and the Winnipeg Indian and Métis Tenant's Association.

The voluntary association can be viewed as an intermediate stage through which social functions, both latent and expressed, may pass in the process of their institutionalization. That is, some foci of informal concerns of friends, relatives, or neighbors may become the objects of instrumental action in voluntary associations and finally the activity of publicly oriented institutions. Religions, businesses, unions, political parties, and so forth have often passed through a voluntary association stage in the process of their institutionalization.

On the Indian reservation the social institutions that an individual can adequately relate to are fairly well defined by limited tribal groups, common residence, and kinship-friendship networks. In the city approximately the same human range of associations are separated from an infinitely more complex total field of behaviors through an involvement in a limited set of institutions. This isolating institutionalization of behavior is probably the only structural way that cultures could have become increasingly more complex while individuals remained intellectually the same. That is, the general design of intimate integration of people through personal ties in primary communities was replaced in more evolved settings with functionally specialized institutions, at least some of which retained personal intimacy. Indian voluntary associations, regardless of their explicit functions, such as politics or welfare, typically are small and intimate enough to provide a social environment that is psychologically comfortable.

In practice, the city's great diversity is not open to the new Indian migrant because of his poor knowledge of city life and his learned dependence on government and church agencies and on a limited kinship-friendship network. Racial discrimination was once a limitation as well on freedom of choice, but has been largely eliminated for Indians in the major cities. New migrants make poor members, either as leaders or followers, in urban voluntary associations. By the time that Indian migrants are sufficiently adjusted to urban life to enthusiastically participate in formal ethnic voluntary associations they are retreating from an excess of choice, narrowing down the conception of their personal identity. The most active voluntary association members are acculturated, middle-class people who find more personal meaning in the Indian social enclaves, typically relating both to romantic and heroic symbols from the "noble savage" tradition and to the historic and ongoing political struggle of Natives against the White establishment.

Ethnic voluntary associations are social inventions of state societies that help create a community for individuals with enough familiarity of common custom and tradition, with enough intimate contacts with the same people; and with enough exclusiveness, discrimination, and boundary maintenance to be satisfying. Ethnic affiliations, along with some combination of social relations in a neighborhood, an occupation, social class, and so forth, may be used by individuals living in a complex urban environment to define a social sphere that is complex enough to be satisfying and simple enough to be workable and not lead to excess mental stress.

ABORIGINAL ASSOCIATIONS

Voluntary associations did not exist in band level societies. Some did contain *sodalities*, and thus had the rudiments of associational organization. A sodality is any organized social group not primarily patterned by kinship or common residence. Where these did occur in band societies, however, they were neither exclusive nor voluntary but society-wide sex and age groupings, usually involving participation after a puberty ritual. There were, for example, such things as the Kuksu cults of central California with their dramatized impersonations of supernatural beings and the Chunichnish cults of southern California with their vision quest initiation for boys and the use of the hallucinogen *Datura*.

There was considerable development of lineal kinship groups and sodalities in tribal societies as mechanisms of societal integration. A psychologically comfortable social sphere was created in the design of the sodality by members' extension to each other of their belief in a common ideology, mutual social acceptance, cooperation in sodality activities, and perhaps some sharing of material goods. We think here of the Kiva societies with their Kachina cults among the Pueblos, the warrior societies of the Plains, and the medicine societies of the Northeast, such as the False Face Society of the Iroquois. The Plains warrior societies particularly could be called "voluntary associations" in that voluntariness was genuinely present, instead of the determination of membership simply in terms of such ascriptive criteria as common age, sex, residence, kinship, or completion of the puberty ceremony.

The rich fishing chiefdoms of the Northwest elaborated secret and restricted sodalities, although membership was sometimes limited to people who had been cured by a medicine society or to persons of high rank who had inherited the right to play certain roles in the dramas of the sodality (Driver 1969). These dramas re-enacted an ancestor's encounter with a spirit who kidnapped him, took him to the woods where he was given supernatural powers, and then returned to his village where he demonstrated his new powers. The Kwakiutl, for example, had three mutually exclusive secret sodalities with elaborate public performances that included costumed dancers and visual and auditory illusions.

At the still more advanced level of the state we find a progressively greater elaboration of sodalities. Among the state societies of central and southern Mexico, such as the Aztecs, there was an elaborate system of schools, priestly orders, military orders, religious cults, and guilds. There is a general, worldwide correlation between urbanism and the proliferation of voluntary associations, and this seems to have been as true for the Native North American cities as it was for those of other continents.

Diversity is also a problem that has to be controlled by state societies. An official state culture is thus fostered by the agencies of the state. There is standardization of language, religion, law, and political procedure among the ruling class in order to maintain some central integration within the society. These forces of central integration may crush elements of diversity that are perceived as potentially threatening to the state while other harmless cultural differences are allowed to continue. Thus the ethnicities that diverge from the official state culture are typically thin in content, not much more than harmless aesthetic traditions of music, dance, costuming and literature.

One of the most radical actions a sub-culture can take in a state society is to behave as a separate and different kind of society that refuses to be integrated into the state cultural system. When U.S. and Canadian Indian societies did this they were physically enclaved on reservations. The relative isolation of reservations then contributed to the continuity and original elaboration of a culture that is separate from that of the dominant sub-culture within the nation state. We now have a great wave of new Indian voluntary associations that are designed by Indians as integrative mechanisms between Indians and the dominant culture institutions. These associations have an explicit ideology of Indian cultural pride, values, and separatism, but by their very structure and operation they provide an acculturating experience for the Indians who participate in them.

ASSOCIATIONS OF THE HISTORICAL AND MODERN PERIODS

The tribal level societies had a few voluntary associations aboriginally and they did play a moderate role in the early formation of modern voluntary associations. However, one of the most important features of the history of tribal societies was their militant reaction against White dominance, an experience of resistance that was often traumatic if not genocidal to the society. Those tribal societies that survived into the reservation period typically became centers of reactive and revitalistic movements. The chiefdoms of the Southeast also had relatively traumatic relations with White society, most of those left from the genocidal impact of war and disease being forcefully relocated to Oklahoma. The Indians of Oklahoma, and tribal societies in the Plains generally, developed such major pan-Indian movements as the Ghost Dance (adopted from a beginning in a Great Basin band society), Sun Dance, and Peyotism historically and the militant American Indian Movement currently.

The chiefdoms of the Northwest Coast had the most elaborated voluntary associations aboriginally in the area that became Canada, and they were the first and foremost to develop them in twentieth century Canada. The Northwest, by contrast with the Plains and Eastern agricultural Indians, had a relatively peaceful period of contact with Whites and thus did not develop reactive associations. Instead, they developed fishermen's unions and "brotherhoods" for men and "homemaker's" associations for women. Rather than reacting to Whites through military or religious associations as the tribes did, they related to Whites through political, legal, and unionized associations, and created the models for the most successful modern Indian associations.

Modern Indian voluntary associations usually retain enough of the traditional cultural influences to operate in a different way than those of White society. The typical comment of Whites is that the associations are inefficient. Meetings or social events so rarely start on time that the idea of a slower "Indian time" is a standing joke among Indians. In meetings people are allowed to make long, rambling, and personal statements that have little bearing on the issues at hand. Final decisions are often not taken by quick formal votes, but just talked out until some general consensus of action is agreed upon.

Men have more often learned the traditional styles of relaxed leadership and consensus politics while women have not and tend to use modern, "efficient" styles. In speech-making men will more often be self-deprecatory; say things such as "I'm speaking only for myself"; use a rather personal, joking, and story-telling style to make his points; and end with something formal, such as "And that's all I have to say." Indian women deal more directly with the issues at hand because they were usually not involved in traditional Indian politics and acculturated directly to the White style.

Guillemin (1975:264-5) described the political style of the Micmacs of Boston as egalitarian, unhurried, and very community-oriented. "Indians who take up too much floor time in expressing their opinions have to end their speeches by shouting above the noise of the smaller groups into which the disinterested audience has broken down. Indians who claim to speak for the group as a whole will quickly be contested by ten or fifteen other Indians voicing dissent . . . about the right of anyone to speak for the others. Individuals who suggest plans for action are apt to get themselves in trouble if there is any hint of coercion or manipulation in their presentation or if they show themselves impatient with prolonged debate." This slow, extremely democratic style is common to most Indian associations, from the Micmacs in the Canadian Maritimes to the Luiseño in Southern California.

In some cases a White association is completely reworked into a form that is compatible with a Native society. For example, Indian chapters of Alcoholics Anonymous are very common in the cities, usually meeting in a church or an urban Indian center. The methods of anonymity, confession of drinking as bad, through testimonials, and the buddy system to keep each other from drinking work better for the more acculturated Indians. Reservation Indians tend to be more tolerant of aggressive drunken comportment, but when they do use coercion they bring down social pressure through community and kinship mechanisms, not anonymous or individualistic mechanisms.

Formal clan associations have not developed among urban U.S. and Canadian Indians, as in the migration of tribals to cities in Africa, for overseas Chinese, and for the Bataks in Indonesia. Kinship networks are still very important to Indians but they are loose and informal systems. The Indian pow-wow clubs seem to be similar in some ways to the "dancing companies" of Sierra Leone in that both are voluntary associations that perform traditional music and dances and both occasionally raise money by their performances.

Allegiances to a specific village, tribe, or region are much more often expressed through voluntary associations in Africa and appear today in the U.S. and Canada only in the moderate tribal nationalism of the large tribes and tribal confederations. Thus Indians do not have formal village-of-origin or region-of-origin mutual aid societies in the cities. The need for organizing mutual aid societies is also diminished by the existence of extensive government programs for Indians.

CLASSIFICATIONS OF MODERN ASSOCIATIONS

A few political associations came on the scene early in this century, but like the other types, they have vastly increased in numbers in the last few years. These are "political" in that they see as their central purpose the changing of government policies, the development of new programs for Indians, and the administration of some programs by the political Indian association itself. In practice, the successful ones become large and multi-functional associations, eventually spinning off other specialized associations as their programs develop. Thus associations such as the All-Pueblo Council or The Manitoba Indian Brotherhood have stimulated the development of recreation associations, education associations, welfare associations, and so forth.

The provincial level of "brotherhoods" and other political associations is particularly important in Canada because (1) Indian land "reserves" are very small and numerous (about 2,281 vs. 270 reservations in the U.S.), (2) Indian "bands," the official units of government administration, are small and numerous (576), (3) an intermediate level of Indian organizations was needed between the bands and the Indian Affairs Branch in the national capital at Ottawa but was never created by the federal government, and (4) the provincial voluntary associations evolved to fill that important intermediate gap. Political power in the U.S. is diffusely spread across a wide variety of associations, but much more of it is retained by formally constituted Indian tribes than by the bands of Canada.

Table 6 gives a tabulation of Native voluntary associations in Canada by area according to the data of the National Indian Brotherhood (Whiteside 1973). The table shows a progressive increase in the rate of formation of voluntary political associations, particularly with a general burst of activities in the 1960s and then a phenomenal rate in the first three years of the 1970s. Most of these have lasted no more than a few years, although the same people often participate in one association after another.

TABLE 6
NATIVE ASSOCIATIONS IN CANADA BY AREA

Political Associations by Date of Formation

	Pre-1900	1900-19	1920-39	1940-59	1960-69	1970-73	Others	Total
National		1	2	2	2	6	14	27
Regional	4	1	5	1	1	1		13
Maritimes				1	4	7	3	15
Quebec	1	1	2	1	3	5	5	18
Ontario	1	1	2	3	6	7	41	61
Manitoba				2	2	7	39	50
Saskatchewan			2	7	1	4	28	42
Alberta			3	2	4	2	42	53
B.C.	1	3	3	5	8	2	48	70
N.W.T.			1		2	4	5	12
Yukon					2	3	5	10
Totals	7	7	20	24	35	48	230	371

Areal analysis shows the markedly greater activity of British Columbia, presumably because of such factors as the aboriginal sophistication of the coastal cultures and their relatively large populations. The Prairie provinces and Ontario are, as expected by these same factors, in the middle range. Quebec, which does have a large Native population, has had a different acculturation experience than English Canada, one that has not greatly stimulated associational activities. The exceptions in Quebec tend to be among English-speaking Natives, such as the Iroquois, and the recent active resistance to the James Bay Hydroelectric Dam Project. The Maritimes have had few associations because the Indians there were aboriginally of the band level and they now have small Native populations. Acculturation and communication have been generally slower to develop in the northern territories and the Natives were band level aboriginally so we see little associational activity there.

I have classified 839 Indian voluntary associations in Canada (426) and the U.S. (413) according to their predominant functions and their effective geographical spheres of activity. This classification is given in Table 7. The "social" category includes recreation, sports, and dance groups; most of the youth clubs; and organizations concerned with such things as the Native Princess Pageant in Canada and the Big Sky Handgame Tournament in Browning, Montana. Urban centers are now numerous in both the U.S. and Canada but are more financially secure in Canada because of a large scale federal-funding program for such centers. Canada also has one national and at least four provincial associations of Indian centers. The "economic, welfare" category includes economic cooperatives, development associations, housing associations, job training and placement groups, health and medical aid groups, and so forth. The Northwest Ontario Native Fisherman's Association is an example of this category. "Education, school clubs" includes Indian associations for the improvement of education and the correction of bias in texts, youth clubs established at schools, and various types of communication associations, a few of which now have regularly scheduled local radio or television programs. The B.C. Native Teachers Association and the American Indian Press Association are examples of this category.

The "Métis, non-status" split from the "status" Indians who are recognized as lawful recipients of the services of the Indian Affairs Branch is unique in its importance in Canada. The same split between those who are and those who are not eligible for federal Indian services exists in the U.S., but it has not become an important factor in voluntary associations in the U.S. Most of the Métis or non-status associations included here are multi-functional with a prominent political orientation and thus could have been included in the general political category, except that they are fairly distinct organizations in Canada. Other specialized Métis groups have been included in the special functional categories. Thus, for example, in Vancouver a Métis Women's Craft Society was included in the category of "arts, crafts."

Women's associations are also more important in Canada than in the U.S. because of extensive conflicts among the Native people of Canada over women's rights. "Arts, crafts" groups include local women's and youth clubs focused on Native arts and crafts. This category includes such groups as the Salish Weavers Association and crafts organizations that help to sell products. The "religious" category is mostly Indian Christian and formally organized traditional Indian churches. The hundreds of local chapters of the Native

TABLE 7
NATIVE VOLUNTARY ASSOCIATIONS BY PRIMARY FUNCTION

Canada

	Local	Provincial-Regional	National	Total
Political	50	40	6	96
Social	85	6	2	93
Urban Centers	51	4	1	56
Economic, Welfare	32	15	1	48
Education, School clubs	32	5	4	41
Métis, Non-Status	12	12	1	25
Women's Associations	8	15	2	25
Arts, Crafts	16	4	–	20
Religious	7	1	2	10
Prison, Parole	6	–	–	6
Legal	1	5	–	6
Total	300	107	19	426

U.S.A.

	Local	State-Regional	National	Total
Political	62	34	8	104
Social	62	4	5	71
Urban Centers	49	–	–	49
Economic, Welfare	23	3	3	29
Education, School Clubs	47	16	6	69
Women's Associations	7	–	–	7
Arts, Crafts	9	4	4	17
Religious	31	6	6	43
Prison, Parole	9	–	–	9
Legal	4	6	5	15
Total	303	73	37	413
Canada and U.S. Totals	603	180	56	839

American Church are not counted. Indian clubs within prisons have suddenly become popular and we can expect to see large increases in this category in the next few years. The "legal" category includes mostly Native courtworker associations at the local level and legal aid or legal research societies at the regional and national levels.

SUMMARY

Voluntary associations became increasingly important with the evolution of culture because the more complex that cultures became the greater the need there was to create neurologically simple social enclaves, such as voluntary associations. Band societies tended not to develop voluntary associations on reservations of the historic period and have only now begun to participate in them as they move into an urbanizing world. Some tribal level cultures had a few voluntary associations aboriginally, and if they survived their generally devastating early relationships with Whites, tended to develop reactive voluntary associations in historic times. Chiefdoms had a still greater elaboration of voluntary associations and these people tended to be involved as founders in the earliest modern pan-Indian voluntary associations. There have been shifts toward anti-assimilation, control and design of associations by less acculturated Indians, and toward more involvement by women without the traditional styles of political behavior.

Chapter 13

Native Periodicals

Periodicals that are aimed for a Native readership have become an important part of contemporary Indian life in Canada and the United States. Most of these are written in English by Natives for a particular formal association such as a tribe, an inter-tribal council, or an urban Indian center. Most are less than ten years old. While once extremely diverse in languages and tribal cultures, Natives are unifying in pan-Indian political, social, and ideological ways, and these periodicals are now central to that unification process.

Books by Natives, such as *Custer Died for Your Sins* and *The Unjust Society*, synthesized the political concerns of many contemporary Native intellectuals. However, these concerns had previously been discussed in the periodicals, and sometimes much more fully. Moreover the day-to-day concerns of Indians are more accurately expressed in the pages of these periodicals than in the books, many reporting births, marriages, deaths, who won athletic events or scholarships, and so forth.

There is also a large ephemeral literature of notices, conference reports, etc., that Natives participate in producing. This comes from government agencies; nation, state or province, and local Native associations; and from organizations such as church groups that have Native-oriented programs. However, the periodical literature has a more completely Native authorship and it is more widely read by Indians than this other material. To some degree, the periodicals have collectively become a body of literature in terms of both historical documentation and aesthetic expression.

ORIGINS AND TENUOUS LIFE

There are several Cherokee periodicals that would be well worth historical study. One of these is probably the first Indian periodical, dating back to a newspaper that used Sequoya's syllabary and began publishing in Cherokee in 1828. The Cherokee produced periodicals after they went to Oklahoma (*The Cherokee Times*) and now there are several urban-based Cherokee periodicals (*Cherokee Examiner, Cherokee Speaker, Keetowah Speaker*).

There were several Indian periodicals in Canada and the northern U.S. in the nineteenth century. They were part of educational and missionary programs, but they usually included writings in the local Native language. They followed the usual pattern of lasting only a few years. They were published in Ontario in Sarnia, Sault Ste. Marie, and in Hagersville; in Harbor Springs, Michigan; in Snohomish, Washington, and in British Columbia in Kamloops, Stuart Lake, and Nass River.

The American Indian Magazine of the Society of American Indians was founded in 1916 and it should be analysed. An early magazine was *The Indian: The Voice of the Mission Indian Federation* initiated around 1931. In 1934 it was very patriotic to the U.S. and "our flag," and opposed to the "communistic experiments" that the Indian Reorganization Act would impose on Indians.

The most common purpose for Indian periodicals has been the development of political awareness, cohesion, and action. Typically, the publication was originally conceived as a means to a political solution of practical problems in a democratic society. The original conception of the urban-based periodicals is usually either intertribal and directed at a specific regional collection of tribes, or it is a grand scale pan-Indianism, attempting to communicate to people of all tribes. The titles often reflect this common vision of organizing all Indians: *Aborigine, Americans Before Columbus, American Indian Horizon*, and *American Indian Tradition*. One newsletter with a wide distribution in the U.S. was *Indian Voices*, published in Tahlequah, Oklahoma for several years until 1969. It was replaced by newer national publications, particularly *Akwesasne Notes* and *Wassaja*. There are now three significant national Indian publications in Canada: *The Indian News, The Native Perspective*, and *C.A.S.N.P. Bulletin* (Canadian Association in Support of the Native Peoples). The first is published by D.I.A.N.D. in Ottawa and the second by the National Association of Friendship Centres.

There are no genuinely international Indian periodicals with a significant number of readers in more than one country. However, the national periodicals, such as *Akwesasne Notes, Wassaja*, and *The Indian News*, do a fair job of covering important events in the other's country. Perhaps more important than these national periodicals, both for national and international communication, is that local and state-province periodicals repeat each other's material. Thus an informal press association has developed through the network of periodicals, in addition to the formal Indian Press Association. Extracts of a particularly interesting or well-written article may appear in dozens of other periodicals in North America within a month or so of its original publication.

A series of summer workshops on the operation of Indian reservation newsletters was an important stimulus and influence on rural publications in the United States. Two were held at the University of Utah and one at the University of South Dakota. The *Leech Lake Newsletter, Ute Newsletter, War Cry*, and several more were developed by people who attended these workshops.

The *Toronto Native Times* is typical of a big city Indian center publication in its creative and sophisticated style. One valuable feature from the social science perspective has been its series of Indian folk legends in Odawa and English. It also serves as a bulletin for the large number of events in Toronto.

The Navajo Times is the best tribal periodical in terms of technical journalistic criteria. It is a weekly newspaper published by the tribe since 1960 at Window Rock, Arizona. It is usually about 30 pages, with balanced news coverage, an editorial page, professional and classified advertisements, and comic strips. The Bureau of Indian Affairs began much earlier (1943) to publish a monthly news magazine called *Adahooniligii* ("Events") in the Navajo language, with English summaries.

One of the best state or province periodicals is the Alaskan *Tundra Times*, which started publication in 1964. It is a bi-monthly newspaper, put out by the Eskimo-Indian-Aleut Publishing Company of Fairbanks. It has the format of a quality newspaper, clearly separating factual articles from editorials. It pursues stories vigorously, sending out its own reporters rather than just waiting for letters from readers or interpreting the articles of other Indian periodicals.

The Indian Historian is a professional journal that is published by the American Indian Historical Society. As a Native periodical it is in a class with the *Journal of American Indian Education* and *American Indian Law Review*.

Indian periodicals often carry poetry, short stories, ethnographic notes, and historical sketches. In fact protests are very often put into poetic form in the politically oriented periodicals. Dodge and McCullough (1974) compiled an excellent collection of contemporary U.S. Indian poetry.

COMPARATIVE CONTENT ANALYSES

There are regular differences in the content of these periodicals, related to the purposes of the associations backing them. Even those that are produced by religious organizations have quite different content. *The Blue Cloud Quarterly* is concerned with Catholic Indian missionary work and is based in rural South Dakota. *The Cross and the Calumet* is produced by the Episcopal Diocese of Chicago. *Indian Echoes* comes from a Bible Institute in Great Valley, New York.

Indian Liahona is a twelve-page quarterly magazine on Indian activities in the Mormon Church. *Indian Times* is ten mimeographed pages, without an Indian focus at all, that is produced by the First Indian Baptist Church of South Gate, California. *Indian Record* is a Canadian magazine, running more than 35 years, that mixes Indian political, historical, and ethnographic interests with Catholic missionary activities. Then there are several mission school publications: *A'atomone, Bells of St. Ann*, and *The Halne.*

Both pan-Indian associations and inter-tribal councils tend to be urban-based while the band or tribal council is, of course, generally rural. It is the large-scope urban-based periodicals of these associations that can shift from being monthly mimeographed newsletters to newspapers or magazines. The rural newsletters tend to have shorter articles and more articles per issue than the urban newsletters. They often have a lot of local gossip and notices of events and sports, in addition to lead stories, usually about major economic and political developments in the area. Urban newsletters are more often printed by offset press or are typeset so that the print can be smaller and photographs can be used more easily. In terms of order of content frequency, both rural and urban periodicals tend to concentrate on local news, on general national Indian news, on Indian agency activities, and on other events, in that order. In terms of their treatment of local news, however, the rural periodicals tend to concentrate more on schools, festivals, and other strictly local events while urban periodicals discuss the local aspects of national issues.

A comparison was made of three of the most widely read regional newsletters in Canada: *The Drum*, published in the "new town" of Inuvik for the Natives of the Northwest Territories; *The Native People*, printed in Edmonton for the Alberta Native Communications Society; and *The Calumet*, published in Toronto for the Indians of Ontario. All three are sent to a broad range of Native communities, but are still not national or pan-Indian in orientation. Their orientations are intertribal firstly, and then provincial. All are published in an urban center, although the Inuvik-Toronto contrast shows the extreme diversity of what can be the urban center for a broad rural region.

The NWT *The Drum* is the most assimilationist, favoring extensive cooperation with White society and acceptance of acculturation to most of White culture. The general orientation is to work within White institutions, rather than perpetuating Native institutions. Typically, articles describe how groups, and to a lesser extent individuals, are successful working within White institutions. This assimilationist orientation of the northern frontier is in sharp contrast to the settled provinces, whose Native news media emphasize the other extreme, of liberation from White control or even influence. At the most, the southern Natives talk of "integration" without further acculturative destruction of their life ways.

Within the above liberationist context, *The Calumet* of Ontario is moderate and *The Native People* of Northern Alberta is somewhat extreme. That is, the articles of the northern Alberta paper emphasize Indian self-sufficiency, Indian separatism, and events within Indian communities; *The Native People* is inclined to see Indians as apart from other Canadians and is intent on bringing Indians closer together, rather than closer to White society. It is heavily oriented toward active Indian politics, verbally attacking government agencies.

Articles in *The Calumet* of Ontario, much more often than in *The Native People*, describe the activities of Indian groups and communities in White-oriented institutions and in White society. Thus, for example, in *The Calumet* one often reads of the representatives of Indian reserves participating in conferences organized by Whites.

These orientations, of course, reflect the prevailing orientations of the regions. There are many indications that the Natives of the Northwest Territories, although they prefer living in their home country, are relatively *assimilationist* in value orientations. The northern Alberta Indians in turn tend to be more *liberationist*, while the Ontario Indians tend to be *integrationist*, to seek for a compromise with both freedom and effective cooperation with Whites. The Native cultures in Ontario, the most urban province, and NWT, the most isolated frontier, are similar in that Native-White relations are relatively peaceful and cooperative compared to the intermediately urban prairie provinces of Alberta, Saskatchewan, and Manitoba. There is an interesting contrast within Alberta itself, however, between the liberationist politics of the northern Cree as reflected in *The Native People* and the integrationist style of the Blackfoot in southern Alberta, as seen in the *Kainai News*.

Several themes appear repeatedly in the newsletters. The "Indian problem" is really a "White problem" if the history of Indian-White relations is considered. Whites, even the so-called experts, understand very little about life on the reservations, so that, even when they are well-intentioned, they make basic mistakes. Many traditional Indian values or techniques prove to be superior to those of the Whites. Indians must handle their own affairs, learn to work with government agencies, and develop the resources of their reservations. Indian culture should be maintained, restored when possible, and authentically presented to Whites and to Indian children. Indian crafts and books about Indians must be done by Indians to be authentic. "Blood" or biological heritage is crucial to being a real Indian. The land claims, allotments, leases, and sales must be settled. This and unemployment are the major reservation problems.

A retreat from the platform of political rhetoric has occurred in the Native movement and is reflected in changes in the Native press. Individuals are often first drawn out of apathy into leadership and into anger, militancy, and stereotyping of government officials and Indian-White relations. This general anger is usually replaced over the years with more practical action within the leader's sphere of jurisdiction. The Native press seems to be going through a similar kind of shift. There are now fewer general harangues about historical injustices. The orientations are more toward present and future practical concerns. There is less grand talk now about "organizing all the Indians," probably because many inter-tribal and pan-Indian organizations have already achieved an efficient level of organization.

Canadian Natives still generally use more angry rhetoric than U.S. Indians.

The Native problems are more severe in Canada than in the U.S. Further, recent attempts to appraise and reform Native policy have stirred up many old issues, especially the insufficient follow-through by the Canadian government on the old treaties. The later 1960s witnessed a sudden expansion of academic and government interest in contemporary Native life in both Canada and the U.S., as part of a larger search for racial and ethnic civil liberties. The Native protest movement in Canada lagged a few years behind its U.S. counterpart, but now seems to be stronger than in the U.S.

This scene of protest, however, is complicated by several structural differences that have accelerated the active protest process in Canada. Indians, Métis, and Eskimos form a much larger proportion of the Canadian population and this gives them a much better chance to be heard than in the U.S. There is also more protest within Canada in areas where Indians constitute a somewhat higher and more visible proportion of the population, the western provinces and northern territories. There is a greater Native-White cultural contrast in Canada because the Canadian Natives are more traditional and more often live on or near their reserves or traditional lands.

PERIODICALS BY AREA

Table 8 gives the area of origin of 255 periodicals that are directed toward Indian, Métis, or Eskimo readership in Canada (67) or in the U.S. (188). The list of active periodicals constantly changes with new additions, the cessation of publication by others, and changes in titles and addresses. Of the Canadian publications eight were published in Vancouver, seven in Ottawa, six in Winnipeg, five in Regina, and four in Toronto. In the United States ten periodicals came from both greater Los Angeles and Washington, D.C., seven from the San Francisco Bay area, six from New York City, and five from Chicago. Slightly more of the Canadian periodicals (57%) were published in cities than in the U.S. (50%). Also, specific tribal ethnicity was more important in the U.S. list than in the Canadian list. The Canadian Indian organizations tend to divide by province and community or status *vs.* non-status and not so much into specific tribal groups. The Canadian exceptions were predominantly in the separatism of the Blackfoot and related tribes in southern Alberta and the Iroquoian tribes of southern Ontario and Quebec. Thus Canada does not have the urban proliferation of specific tribal associations, such as the clubs formed by the Navajo and Cherokee.

TABLE 8
NATIVE PERIODICALS BY AREA

Canada

	Number	Proportions		
		Periodicals	Status Indians	Associations
Number		67	260,000	407
Maritimes	2	3%	4%	5%
Quebec	4	6%	11%	5%
Ontario	19	28%	22%	18%
Manitoba	8	12%	14%	15%
Saskatchewan	10	15%	14%	13%
Alberta	4	6%	12%	16%
B.C.	9	13%	19%	21%
Territories	11	17%	4%	7%
Totals	67	100%	100%	100%

U.S.A.

New England	5	2.7%	
New York	9	4.8%	14.9% East
Other East Coast	14	7.4%	
Illinois	7	3.7%	
North Dakota	8	4.3%	
South Dakota	14	7.4%	28.7% Central
Oklahoma	10	5.3%	
Other Central	15	8.0%	
Montana	7	3.7%	
Wyoming	1	.5%	
Idaho	1	.5%	10.0% Mountain
Colorado	3	1.6%	
Utah	3	1.6%	
Nevada	4	2.1%	
New Mexico	14	7.4%	
Arizona	16	8.5%	35.6% Southwest
California	37	19.7%	
Oregon	3	1.6%	
Washington	12	6.4%	10.7% Pacific
Alaska	5	2.7%	
Totals	188	99.9%	

My list of Native periodicals more than doubled from the 112 compiled in 1971 (Price 1972). The increases in the list were marked for those coming from new organizations in the national capitals of Ottawa and Washington, D.C., from the Canadian north and from Inuit, from Indian women's groups, from prisons, and from boarding schools, high schools, and colleges. The periodicals of Ottawa and Washington were both those of government agencies and the political lobbies of ethnic associations. Newsletters specifically related to legislation and legal services were added in Washington, D.C. (2), Albuquerque, and Berkeley. New York City, like Ottawa and Washington, D.C., has only a small population of Natives but publishes several social welfare-oriented periodicals concerned with Native life.

The proliferation of periodicals in a single city is usually a product of the proliferation of ethnic institutions. In the past three years this has been particularly noticeable in Vancouver, which now has one general protest newsletter, a private national newspaper, and then periodicals by the federal government, a provincial education agency, an Indian women's organization, the Native Brotherhood of B.C., the Union of B.C. Indian Chiefs, and the B.C. Association of Non-Status Indians.

Table 8 shows the lower levels of activity in the Maritimes and Quebec, the increase in Ontario, and the generally high level of activity across the rest of Canada. A low figure occurs in Alberta in part because of the dominance of two strong and widely distributed periodicals, *Kainai News* among the Plains peoples who speak the Blackfoot-Piegan-Blood language in the South and *The Native People* among the more Sub-arctic peoples who speak Cree and the Sekani-Beaver-Sarsi language in the north. The U.S. distribution shows some intensity of activity in the populous urban states of New York and Illinois, and the central Indian states of the Dakotas and Oklahoma, but very high levels of activity in the west. The table also shows the correlation between population, associations, and periodicals.

Chapter 14
Drinking Problems

This is the first of seven chapters on social problems and their solutions. Indian drinking is a particularly sensitive issue because it is also a major theme in anti-Indian prejudice and stereotyping. However, alcoholism and its effects are too important to be ignored, whether they involve Whites or Indians.

Drinking problems have become serious with the breakdown of traditional cultural controls in a context of racial discrimination, frustrations related to low economic success, peer group pressures to drink socially, and the spread of patterns of drinking to complete drunkenness. Simple legal solutions, such as the external imposition of prohibitions and arrest for public drunkenness, have been ineffective as well as unjust, but there is evidence of the kinds of practical things that can be done to improve the situation. There is especially a need to enhance existing social controls within Indian societies on self-destructive drunken comportment.

Public drunkenness, drunk driving, and liquor law violations are the most common crimes generally in the U.S. and Canada, constituting the basis for about one-third of all arrests, but these crimes are far more common among Indians and constitute the basis for about three-fourths of all Indian arrests.

The most serious problems in their use of alcohol are related to active personal behavior under the influence of alcohol, such as suicide and accidental death and injury, and the problems of personal inaction, such as unemployment and apathy toward the maintenance of a healthy community.

Given the disruption of acculturation situations, individuals or communities with a satisfactory access to newly acquired goals tend to have far fewer problems than those without it, particularly where social controls were traditionally weak or were destroyed in the acculturation process. For example, Graves (1967) found that favorable economic access led to low drinking rates among acculturated Southern Utes and neighboring Spanish-Americans while acculturated people of both groups with low economic access had high drinking rates. Degree of economic access did not significantly affect the drinking rates of unacculturated people of either group, but the presence or absence of traditional controls did affect their drinking rates. Strong social controls by the institutions of the family and the church operated among unacculturated Spanish-Americans to control excessive drinking, but these controls were not strong among unacculturated Indians so they had high drinking rates. Graves relates this lack of traditional controls among the Indians to their heritage of semi-nomadic hunting and gathering economy which gave "rise to independence of thought and action and to a reluctance to intervene in the lives of others."

Ferguson (1968) found that unacculturated Navajos responded better than acculturated Navajos to an alcoholism treatment program operated by the Navajo Tribe. Her explanation was that the acculturated were under greater stress and tended to become "anxiety drinkers," while the unacculturated were simply "recreation drinkers" in a peer group setting without social sanctions against excessive drinkers. The applied implications from these studies for reducing alcohol-related problems are such things as providing greater economic access, encouraging realistic goals, and maintaining local social controls on drinking behavior.

This chapter explores what can be done to promote the development of internal social controls by Indian societies on the excessive use of alcohol. This development should be designed to shift simultaneously some of the positive functions of drinking to other means while it reduces some of the negative functions. If Indians continue to drink at the same rate, they can still alleviate many of their problems by changing certain patterns of their drinking, particularly binge drinking. The topics discussed will be (1) aboriginal controls, (2) positive functions, (3) negative functions, (4)controls that are *external* to Indian societies, (5) controls that are *internal* to Indian societies, and (6) recommendations to shift some of the positive functions of drinking to other means and to enhance internal controls.

ABORIGINAL CONTROLS

The aboriginal use of alcoholic beverages was concentrated in areas of intensive agriculture in Mexico and Central and South America. Alcoholic drinks were most commonly made by fermenting maize or tapioca, but in northern Mexico and parts of the Southwest U.S., wines were also made from agave, dasylirion, sahuaro and pitahaya cacti, and mesquite or screwbean. At least forty distinct alcoholic beverages were made in Mexico alone, using such substances as honey, palm sap, wild plums, and pineapple (Driver 1969).

One of the common explanations for dysfunctional patterns of drinking among Indians is that Whites introduced alcoholic beverages to many of the tribes only in recent historic times so that they have not had time to develop effective internal controls (Stewart 1964; Wax 1971). Mexico had the time to elaborate controls and did so, but it also has one of the world's highest rates of alcohol consumption per capita. It appears that in Mexico the aboriginal controls on drunken comportment and the traditionally high rates of alcohol consumption continue into the present. Even the beverages are basically the same there, with some addition of European beers and distillation techniques. The use of pulque from the agave still exceeds all other alcoholic beverages in the nation and is distilled into tequila and mescal.

In some societies half of the men remained sober to keep order while the rest got drunk. There was also moderate secular drinking in some Mexican societies, comparable to the regular and controlled use of light wines and beers in the European tradition. Among the Zapotec only the upper classes and the priests were allowed to drink. Among the more severe Aztecs drunkenness was considered to be the root of most evils, and public drunkenness by students, nobles, and priests was punishable by death.

There are societies where social inhibitions remain largely intact even during periods of extreme intoxication because of the maintenance of traditional controls. The Mixtec of Oaxaca are discriminated against by the local townspeople, they are economically very poor, and they drink heavily of the traditional pulque. They seem to have every reason for aggressive behavior while drunk, but in fact are very peaceful and even have a stereotype that the non-Indian townspeople go crazy with aggression when they drink (MacAndrew and Edgerton 1969: 35).

The Mohave of southern California and Arizona do not appreciably change their behavior when drinking and the "overwhelming majority of intoxicated Mohave behave in a quiet and reasonable manner." (Devereux 1948: 228.) In the Mohave case there was an historic introduction of alcoholic beverages and apparently a transfer of some traditional controls into the new sphere of drunken comportment. This transfer of controls was probably easier for the Mohave than for many other U.S. and Canadian Indian societies because the Mohave were (1) settled agriculturalists, and thus had more extensive controls on the behavior of individuals than gathering or hunting peoples; (2) were relatively isolated from acculturation pressures in a desert region until modern times; and (3) continued to live in at least certain parts of their aboriginal lands, thus avoiding the deculturation of displacement suffered by most tribes.

The Pima and Papago live just east of the Mohave in southern Arizona and make a case for contrast because they have had a similar acculturation experience, but unlike the Mohave, they made and used alcoholic beverages aboriginally. The Pima and Papago made a cactus wine once a year, in association with a rainmaking ceremony held on their New Year's Day (Driver 1969). The controls here were (1) temporal—it was done only once a year; (2) religious, in that it centered around a socially sanctioned religious purpose; and (3) quantitive, in that each family contributed only one jar of cactus fruit syrup to the communal fermentation jar. The Papago today have two kinds of drunken comportment, depending on the social context. In the traditional wine ceremony people sing and are peaceful but in the secular drinking of White man's whiskey the behavior is aggressive.

The Washo Indians have modes of drunken comportment that depend on the social context. There is fairly consistent drinking and good-natured singing and dancing all night long at a girl's puberty ceremony. The ceremony ends at dawn, the more traditional participants go home, the dance shifts to a Northern Paiute social round dance, and a few fights invariably break out among the young men. Thus, in some societies drunken comportment is always peaceful; others have changed historically; and in others the social circumstances determine the appropriate behavior.

THE POSITIVE FUNCTIONS OF DRINKING

There is evidence that drinking has positive social functions for various Indian societies. Heath (1964) found that alcohol contributed to social integration among the Navajo. Among the Tarahumara of northern Mexico, the community that drinks together is crucial in terms of religion, economy, entertainment, dispute settlement, and marriage arrangements. Drinking markedly increases thelr social animation while at the same time excusing excessive behavior in a "time out" situation, as long as this behavior is within culturally prescribed limits (MacAndrew and Edgerton 1969).

Daily (1968) wrote that the early Hurons drank because of the novel physical sensation, the release from inhibitions, the opportunity to allow and excuse acts of otherwise suppressed violence, its communal integrating function, and the easy attainment of a dream-like state. The experience of intoxication may have acquired a supernatural meaning similar to the important dream experience. The transcendence of the physical to obtain a spiritual experience was valued and became identified with drinking. This kind of interpretation of the experience of drunkenness has been suggested generally for those Indian societies which valued the vision quest, dreams, trances, and related experiences.

For Canada's western Arctic, Ferguson (1971) claims that drinking became a substitute to shamanism and an outlet for individualistic behavior in otherwise conforming small Arctic communities. Whalers taught the Eskimos how to make home brew and it became accepted that a drunk person was not fully responsible for his actions. However, the best hunters, who are inclined to be more individualistic and less concerned about public opinion anyway, are also the heaviest drinkers. Thus, good hunting appears to be an important legimatizing factor, along with drunkenness, for deviance; there would be little tolerance for obnoxious behavior from a bad hunter even when he is drunk.

Among the Vunta Kutchin Indians of Old Crow, Yukon, Balikci (1968) found that people usually drink fast and become very drunk: joking, perhaps turns to quarreling and fighting, or to depression or heightened sexuality. In the Kutchin brew party "conversation almost invariably concerns aspects of interpersonal relations such as marital tensions." Balikci felt that drunkenness has some usefulness in overcoming reserve in interpersonal relations, deep hostilities, and suspicions, by breaking down the emotional isolation between people. People know each other extremely well in the community and are even "obsessed with what his fellows are doing," but still develop ambivalences and hostilities that can be worked out in brew parties.

R.P. and E.C. Rohner (1970: 48) maintain that drinking has a positive function among the Kwakiutl of British Columbia in relaxing "normally constricted interpersonal communication, thus allowing dissatisfactions to be freely and openly expressed in ways they would not be if the person were entirely sober." It lowers sexual inhibitions and allows latent hostilities to be expressed, often in physical fighting, and later forgiven in sober periods. Lemert (1958) found similar patterns among the Salish of British Columbia, with drinking to get drunk and to excuse otherwise socially unacceptable aggression. He was also impressed with the exaggeration of symptoms of drunkenness, like a parody or act of it; there were quick transitions from drunk to sober and back again, depending upon the situation, and intoxication on small quantities of alcohol.

A study of Indians in a city in the Canadian Prairies (Brody 1971: 71) discussed the advantages of skid row. Indians who migrate from the surrounding reservations find that skid row is an enclave of acceptance in the usually hostile milieu of the city, with its dominance by middle-class non-Indians. The 1969 Task Force on Alcoholism of the U.S. Indian Health Service concluded that (1) most Indians have tried alcohol by fifteen and some are drinking regularly by that age, (2) heavily drinking males outnumber females by about three to one, (3) Indian drinking reaches its peak of greatest frequency between ages 25 to 44, (4) there is a marked decline in drinking after the age of forty, and (5) many Indians of all ages are abstainers.

NEGATIVE FUNCTIONS

The negative functions of drinking can be classified as primary (alcoholism), secondary (suicide, murder, accidental death and injury, assault, theft, etc.), and tertiary (social discord, unemployment, divorce, etc.). The primary function is what the drinker does to himself in the process of drinking; that is, acquires an addiction. In comparisons of U.S. death rates in 1967 by causes of death that are somewhat related to drinking patterns, the Indian rates were the following number of times greater than those of the general population for these causes of death: stomach ulcers and intestinal problems ("gastritis") 3.8, accidents 3.2, homicide 2.9, cirrhosis of the liver 2.8, and suicide 1.6 (Wax 1971: 225). Cirrhosis of the liver seems to be partially due to dietary deficiencies, but they are deficiencies that commonly occur among people who regularly drink relatively large quantities of alcohol. The 1967 U.S. rate of death per 100,000 by cirrhosis of the liver was 14.1 for the general population and 38.9 for Indians and Alaska Natives in 24 reservation states. The fact that Indians died 2.8 times more frequently of cirrhosis of the liver stresses the urgent need for alcohol control programs among Indians.

Medocino State Hospital in Talmage, California has a residential treatment program for Indian alcoholics (Kline and Roberts 1973). They found that their patients became alcoholics when about five years younger than White alcoholics: average first drink 13 years of age, first drunk 14.5 years, first "blackouts" 25.1, first "shakes" 29.1 years. Most drinking occurred in a car or outdoors, over 80% reported that most of their drinking was with friends, and about half reported binge rather than steady drinking.

Drinking patterns and alcohol-related death patterns are very different between the Hopi and the Navajo, Native societies that live next to each other in northern Arizona. It appears that the Navajo drink more, have a more active and visible public drunken comportment, and have a higher rate of violent deaths, including accidents, than the Hopi. However, "liver cirrhosis death rates among the Hopi Indians are over four times higher, but among the Navajo the age-adjusted is only slightly less than the U.S. population." (Kunitz, *et al.* 1971: 706). Levy and Kunitz (1974:25) develop the thesis that "highly visible group drinking is socially acceptable in loosely organized rather than tightly integrated tribes" with data from the loosely organized White Mountain Apache, moderate Navajo, and integrated Hopi. Few Hopi drink, but they are intensive secret drinkers who more often end up dying from cirrhosis of the liver.

Secondary functions are what the drinker actively does to himself and others. The U.S. B.I.A. claimed that the 1971 Indian suicide rate was 21.8 per 100,000, almost twice the non-Indian rate. Resnick and Dizmang (1971) see alcoholism as a major contributing factor in Indian suicides. The Shore, *et al.* (1972: 77) study of seventeen completed suicides on a reservation of Plateau Indians near Portland, Oregon showed a pattern of young (60% under 25), males (82%), with an arrest record (88%), by hanging (66%), and in association with alcohol abuse and/or inhalant sniffing (94%). High rates of suicide have been associated with drinking in studies on Navajo, Cheyenne, Shoshone, and British Columbia Indians. The general pattern is violence against oneself during an episode of depression that is heightened by drinking.

An Indian Affairs Branch survey in 1968 indicated that status Indian suicide rates were very low in Quebec (3.8/100,000) and the following *number of times greater* than the general provincial rate in the three most western provinces: Saskatchewan 2.8, Alberta 1.8, and British Columbia 2.7 (D.I.A.N.D. 1969). The epidemic pattern of suicides occurred among seven young (17 to 31 years of age) Indians in 1975 on the Wikwemikong Reserve, Manitoulin Island, Ontario. All were in the same section of the reserve, all had low self-esteem, all came from large families, all were single, four were male and three were female, and six died by shooting themselves and one by hanging. The first in the series occurred a week after the victim saw *The New Centurions* on television, a movie that ends when the hero shoots himself. These suicides seem to have been supported by local ideas about suicide as a heroic way out of problems; it is also believed that some people commit suicide when they are cursed by a bear spirit, a type of Windigo psychosis.

A study of sudden deaths in British Columbia in 1969 showed that an unusually high proportion of them were of Indians who had been drinking (Cutler and Morrison 1971: 35, 56). "The Indian death rate for suicide was almost three times greater, the accidental death rate was almost four times greater; and the death rate due to homicide was over 30 times greater for Indians than for non-Indians . . . . While about 34% of the non-Indian sample were at least 'slightly' under the influence of alcohol when they died . . . 66% of the Indians who died by accident, 83% of those who died by suicide and all of the homicide cases had been drinking beforehand." The average level of alcohol in the blood was also higher among Indians who had been drinking than among non-Indians who had been drinking.

For drinking-related offenses, such as public drunkenness and driving while intoxicated, U.S. Indians had an arrest rate in 1968 that was 21.7 times greater than that of Whites and 9.0 times greater than Negroes. Of all reported arrests of Indians in 1968, 75% of them were for drinking-related offenses.

Excessive drinking is only one contributing factor in social discord, unemployment, and divorce, but these are important tertiary negative functions of drinking. We know, for example, that reservations are often split into drinking and non-drinking factions and that Indians refer to these kinds of problems when they talk about the disruptions of excessive drinking. Levy and Kunitz (1972) found that fewer Navajo adults drink (42%) than do U.S. adults generally (71%), in part because a relatively high proportion of Navajos had quit drinking.

EXTERNAL CONTROLS

Laws, police, and courts enforce formal external controls and non-Indian missionaries, social workers, employers, etc. enforce informal external controls on excessive drinking. The dominant society requires that the negative functions of excessive drinking influencing it be kept in check. Thus, for example, high arrest rates are the experience of negative functions as external controls are applied.

Treaties and laws applying to both Canadian and U.S. Indians often made reference to the prohibition of alcoholic beverages. In the U.S. the first federal regulation of intoxicants to Indians was in 1802, and further restrictions were made in the Indian Trade and Intercourse Act of 1834, and then repealed in 1953, with a reservation option of continued prohibition. In Canada it was excluded prior to 1951, permitted only in certain public places off the reserve until 1958, and then opened up to band option in 1963. These restrictions created an unnecessary class of legal offenses, stimulated conflicts between Indians and law enforcement agencies, led to financial exploitation of Indians, reinforced binge drinking patterns, and prevented Indians from developing internal social controls on drinking.

In 1960 a court decision gave most Canadian Eskimos the same drinking privileges as Whites. During the next two years at Frobisher Bay there was a marked increase in public drunkenness, which contributed to fighting and other offenses (Honigmann and Honigmann 1971). Town controls through fines and jail sentences, the distribution of anti-drinking literature, and radio broadcasts on the violence and social problems that come out of heavy drinking were not very effective in controlling excessive drinking. However, the administrative measures were effective: beer sold in taverns could no longer be taken off the premises and liquor store customers had to wait three weeks before they could pick up their orders.

The Indians and the Law Survey of the Canadian Corrections Association (1967) found that the number of liquor infractions and alcohol-related crimes in every region of Canada except French-speaking Quebec were so great that they almost excluded all other kinds of Indian crimes. In 1961 the per capita arrest rate for Indians was 5.4 times greater than for the general population. This ratio varied by area from a low of 1.2 in Quebec, about 3.0 in the Maritimes and northern territories, 4.3-4.9 in most southern provinces, to 11.7 in Saskatchewan. The 1967 Indian:White felony conviction ratios ranged from a low of 0.7 in Quebec to highs of 6.0 in Saskatchewan and 7.7 in Alberta for a national ratio of 4.6 (Judicial Statistics 1968). The following percentages of the inmates were Indians in the federal penitentiaries in 1967: Quebec .3%, Ontario 3.5%, New Brunswick 4.1%, Nova Scotia 6.0%, B.C. 13.1%, Alberta 19.7%, Manitoba 24.8%, and Saskatchewan 25.3% (Heumann 1973). In brief, the Prairie provinces are extremely hard on Indians.

A 1965 study of the Uintah-Ouray Utes of northeastern Utah found that the quantity of alcohol consumed by the Indians was not significantly more than that of the Whites in the area, but that the arrest rate of Indians for alcohol-related offenses was almost one arrest for every two tribal members. "One-third of the adults and older teenagers were arrested one or more times during the year because of drinking too much." (Slater and Albrecht 1972: 361). In Barrow, Alaska the Whites actually consume far more alcohol than the Eskimo, perhaps as much as fifteen times more (Wax 1971, citing A. Hippler). Still, it is the Eskimos who are considered to have the serious drinking problem, because the Whites drink privately at cocktail parties while the Eskimos drink in public and on binges.

In "social drinking" there is an ideal of conviviality and self-disciplined comportment while in 'binge drinking" the condition of feeling drunk is valued and inhibitions are more fully released. The age range of social drinking is wider, including more middle-aged and older people, and the times and places of drinking are more routinized and socially regulated. The distinction is important because the incidence of binge drinking is much higher among Indians than among Whites. It is also associated in urban skid row areas with small informal gangs of young men and these gangs frequently break the law while on a binge. Their drinking is thus controlled by force through the external controls of the larger society.

INTERNAL CONTROLS

The initial reaction of those Indians who had no previous experience with alcohol was generally a quiet and restrained drunken comportment (MacAndrew and Edgerton 1969). Some later abstained, some drank only out of respect for White guests, and some drank regularly in moderation. The explorers Lewis and Clark found in crossing the Plains in 1804 from the Mandan to the Yellowstone that all the tribes knew of liquor but only the Assiniboin would drink and then only in moderation. White explorers, traders, trappers, soldiers, whalers, and other frontiersmen then provided a model to the Indians for drunken comportment. Indians learned from these Whites that drunkenness excused excessive and irresponsible behavior, especially when binge drinking to complete drunkenness. At first liquor was given as a gift, then it became a drinking occasion along with trade, and finally it became an object of trade.

The early French Jesuits described some of the social controls that were developed by Indians (Daily 1968). They might tie an intoxicated person down or at least take his weapons. Indian chiefs began to plead with the French not to sell any more liquor to Indians. One Abenaki chief complained to the English in Boston. Some Indian bands set penalties for inebriation such as exclusion.

Among the Choctaw, prior to 1830 and the forced federal government removal to Oklahoma, the use of liquor was quite well controlled by the traditional tribal government. In the removal process the tribal government was abolished, thus permitting Whites to peddle alcoholic beverages and to use alcohol to facilitate the land swindles of that time. It was common in the eighteenth and nineteenth centuries for traditional Indian leaders to speak out against the use of liquor by Indians. Chief Pontiac of the Ottawa called it "the poison firewater, which makes you fools." Red Jacket, a Seneca chief, complained that in relations with Whites, "We gave them corn and meat. They gave us poison (liquor) in return."

A central feature of the religious movement among the Iroquois after 1799, founded by the Seneca leader Handsome Lake, was the prohibition of the use of alcoholic beverages. The Native American Church also forbids the use of alcoholic beverages. The Hopi is one Native society in which drinking never did flourish, apparently because of the society's great continuity in religion and social structure. There are Hopi who drink today, but they have adopted the White patterns of more private drinking.

Steinbring (1971) described the extensive participation in Alcoholics Anonymous among the relatively unacculturated bands of Ojibwa around Lake Winnipeg, Manitoba in the late 1950s and early 1960s. AA participation spread along with a new road system, especially among Salteaux-speaking Ojibwa. Alcoholism was not a problem there and some of the AA members had never even been drinkers. In this case the AA system was reworked as a nativistic revival movement in which the use of alcohol became a symbol of the deterioration of traditional culture. Meetings were usually held in the Native language. The traditional male orientation, decentralized and autonomous communities, public recitation and oratory, and shamanistic confessions were compatible with the AA social structure and testimonial style of meetings. Instead of emphasizing the usual anonymous character of AA membership, the various chapters held popular public dances and people proudly talked about the members, who included most of the adult males as well as many of the women in the Al-Anon women's auxiliary.

The development of internal controls such as AA has become increasingly frequent, but they have focussed on prohibition, rather than on teaching positively functional drinking patterns. By 1966, 215 of Canada's 529 provincial bands had held a referendum on liquor prohibition, but only 7% of the total bands had voted to prohibit liquor on their reserves. Generally the abolition of liquor on the reserves was favored more by those who wrongly believed that allowing liquor would invalidate treaties; by band chiefs and councillors, in part because of the policing problems connected with drinking; by older people; and by those living on the reserves, rather than the voting members of bands who lived off their reserves.

In the years since 1966 there has been a remarkable swing by bands against liquor on reserves. According to a 1971 survey (D.I.A.N.D. 1973), only 231 of the 560 bands had liquor privileges on their reserves, leaving 59% dry. The Quebec bands are the most restrictive with 85% dry; those in the Prairie provinces are intermediate; and the bands of Ontario, B.C., and the Maritimes are the least restrictive. In the U.S. lower 48 states, 68% (180 of 266 units in 1974) of the reservations, pueblos, etc. are dry.

RECOMMENDATIONS

For a short period of time I was once a consultant to the U.S. Bureau of Indian Affairs on their operation of a residential training school for Indian adults and their families in California. The school had been converted from a small abandoned military airbase, but the White staff was so afraid of the Indians that they kept up the chain-link and barbed-wire fence, kept uniformed guards posted at the entrance gate, and lived in a nearby town while requiring all of the Indians to live on the base. Alcoholic beverages were outlawed on the base, but the Indians would still walk into town and get drunk. My advice included such things as removing the fences, discontinuing the use of guards, having the staff live on the base, and starting a club on the base with a positive program of teaching Indians how to drink in moderation. They did not want that kind of advice and discontinued my services.

The cultural analysis of behavior associated with drinking alcoholic beverages supports the position that there is a universal tendency toward relaxation and lack of social inhibition. Within this context of inebriated behavior, however, there are culturally patterned variations. People learn most of their drinking patterns and how to behave when drunk. Dysfunctional and self-destructive drinking behavior, once established, seem to be perpetuated in the society because of a variety of simultaneous positive functions. However, it is possible for people to develop new patterns of more positive functional drinking behavior and to diminish the negative functions through the development of social controls.

Indians are being drawn into various kinds of existing alcoholism programs, but these programs are generally designed for physiologically addicted alcoholics. Alcoholics Anonymous works through non-Indian cultural patterns on physiologically addicted individuals, making it effective usually only with acculturated Indians, unless it is radically reworked as among the Lake Winnipeg Ojibwa. The use of disulfiram (Antabuse) seems to work for Indians in part because it validates a person as a non-drinker and thus offsets peer group pressures to drink.

Indian societies need programs that work through Indian cultural patterns, that work in large part on existing social groups rather than just on individuals, and that work on changing just the destructive drinking habits of non-addicted people. Litman's (1970: 1784) study of Indian alcoholism in Chicago concluded that "we must free ourselves from thinking in terms of abstinence as the exclusive criterion for improvement." He recommended opening up a cooperative bar and grill run by and for Indians where food is also served, violence is controlled, and Indians can learn to drink in moderation. There is a need for Indian drinking counselors to work with individuals, bands, and associations in liaison with court workers, parole officers, and other agents of social control.

The system of arrest, trial, incarceration, and parole of Indians for alcohol-related crimes has not worked as an effective social institution for Indians. It imposes a dominant cultural model of drinking and drunken comportment on Indian societies through police and legal systems, with apparently little thought as to the extremely adverse effects on those societies.

The patterns of moderation that are already emphasized in Indian religions, such as the Native American Church and the Iroquois Longhouse Society, and in the Indian participation in Christian religions should be supported and enhanced. The facts of cultural destruction through alcohol-related arrest, suicide, murder, and other means should be publicized within the Indian communities through films and Indian periodicals and in the positive framework of a serious problem that can be alleviated by implementing local controls and changing drinking habits. This means the transmittal of messages such as drunken comportment is learned, limits to behavioral extremes can be applied to people who are drunk, and moderate social drinking is much more functional than heavy binge drinking. More recreation services are needed for urban Indians to transfer this positive function of recreation out of the skid row bars.

In the U.S. there is now an American Indian Commission of Alcoholism and Drug Abuse, with several Indians on the staff, that helps people set up local programs. In Canada in 1975 D.I.A.N.D. developed a three-year, $13 million National Native Alcohol Abuse Program. This program's emphasis is very local: (1) home counseling, (2) community workshops, (3) liaison with police and magistrates to ensure fair treatment in every Indian case, (4) youth programs, and (5) centers for detoxification, rehabilitation, and family help.

Chapter 15

Stereotyping in Motion Pictures

During the silent film era (1908-1929), Indians were portrayed as horse-riding tribal warriors of the Plains, harassing the White settlers through the late 1880s. This negative stereotype worsened, especially in serials, from 1930 to 1947. Forty years of this formation have given way to thirty years of dispelling the stereotypes. There has been a turn toward a more sympathetic understanding of Indians, a greater use of Indian actors, and an increase in the production of documentary movies.

The American motion picture industry has elaborated a body of ethnic stereotypes about North American Indians. They were usually characterized as riding horses, hunting buffalos with bows and arrows or guns, and wearing tailored leather clothing and feathers in their hair or headdresses. They were seen as having been consistently cheated by Whites and therefore as consistently against Whites. They were portrayed as continually involved with warfare, fighting as tribal units under a chief, and taking the scalps of their enemies as war trophies. In more racist terms they were stereotyped as sexually desiring White women and therefore abducting them, being more adversely affected by alcohol than Whites; and being humorless, taciturn, and speaking in simple languages.

Some of these characterizations, such as the use of elaborate feather headdresses, were correct for about ten Plains tribes in the late 1800s, but they are usually false for the remaining over 500 other Native societies in North America. As a predominant feature in their way of life, most Indians did not regularly ride horses, hunt large game, wear tailored hide clothing, or wear feathers in their hair. By population, more Indians lived in more civilized agricultural chiefdoms and states than in the simple hunting tribes of the movie stereotypes. Instead they were fishermen and farmers. They wore robes of woven bark in the populous North Pacific Coast and of cotton in the agricultural Southeast, Southwest, and in southern Mexico. This other rich and diverse North American cultural heritage should not be displaced or demeaned through such biased and narrow portrayals.

We cannot dismiss the stereotypes as unimportant film portrayals because hundreds of millions of people the world over have acquired their beliefs about North American Indians through motion pictures. They were created as entertainment, but they cumulatively built a separate reality about Native cultures. They are, for example, difficult stereotypes to correct in university courses on American Indians. Even modern American Indians draw heavily from these films in constructing their *own* views of their cultural heritage.

Many of the basic film stereotypes of Indians were formed in the period of silent movies. The movie story was told by White American producers and directors to a White North American audience, assuming and building the plot from anti-Indian attitudes and prejudices. Indian life was seen as savage and at an earlier stage of development, and therefore rightly vanishing as Indians were exterminated or assimilated into White society. The central figures were usually Whites while Indians were used as villains, for local color, and to provide action sequences. Cawetti (1971: 38) writes "The Western formula seems to prescribe that the Indian be a part of the setting to a greater extent than he is ever a character in his own right." This sharpens the moral issues and dramatic conflicts for the White principals. Also, "if the Indian represented a significant way of life rather than a declining savagery, it would be far more difficult to resolve the story with a reaffirmation of the values of modern society."

Visual stereotypes that emphasized the Plains Indians were spread very early through the paintings of George Catlin, Karl Bodmer, Alfred Miller, Paul Kane (although Kane also showed the diversity across Canada), Frederick Remington, and Charles Russell, as well as early still photography. These pictures tended to be posed, of adult males, and in formal dress or in set action pieces such as horse riding, fighting, or buffalo hunting.

As western movies became a part of the culture, writers and directors built their stories with symbols that had been established in earlier motion pictures. The genre became gradually removed from real history, becoming a kind of allegorical history. The western became a milieu of fictional history with symbols for such frontier concepts as freedom, pragmatism, equality, agrarianism, and brutalization. These ideas were commonly expressed in the popular wild west literature, in traveling "Indian medicine" shows, and in stage plays of the nineteenth century; they were then expressed cinematographically in the early twentieth century. A romantic parallel literature was created in German by Karl May (1842-1912) who wrote 70 fiction books. Because the film stereotypes were still forming during the silent era, there was some breadth of diversity in kinds of Indian societies portrayed and the roles of Indians in the stories. The costuming was often more authentic than in later years and there were occasional pro-Indian movies in the earliest silents.

The wild west shows of Buffalo Bill Cody, Annie Oakley, and others, with their Indian actors, were included in the variety show acts that were filmed by the earliest kinescope motion pictures of 1894. These usually included Indian attacks on a settler's cabin or a stage coach. Chief Joseph, Geronimo, and Sitting Bull actually participated in some of these shows, the latter even selling autographed photos of himself for $1 each (Friar).

D.W. Griffith's second picture was an Indian melodrama called *The Red Man and the Child*, although this was not an important film because, like others at the time, it was so rapidly and poorly made. He shot the film on the Passaic River in New Jersey in 1908, taking about one week to make it (Fulton 1960). Griffith made thirty Indian films, about 7% of his total production. The year 1908 also saw the beginning of the Broncho Billy character who played in several Indian movies over the next several years, as an eternal friend of noble Indians. In the early films Indians "were forever shading their eyes to illustrate their acute vision . . . They were forever folding their arms, a gesture which film makers must have thought represented a particular brand of stoicism . . . " (Friar and Friar 1972:86).

There were several early semi-documentaries and historical reconstructions, especially of military actions such as Custer's Last Stand and the Battle at Wounded Knee. One huge effort for the time (1913) was *The Indian Wars*, shot on the Pine Ridge Reservation with Buffalo Bill, the U.S. 12th Cavalry, and some Sioux Indians. The Sioux, of course, have a very different view of the historical events than that portrayed in the movie.

Indians were leading figures on the side of right in such 1911 films as *An Indian Wife's Devotion, A Squaw's Love*, and *Red Wing's Gratitude*. In *The Pioneer's Mistake* (1911) the Indians go on the warpath because an Indian was shot by a pioneer, who mistook him for a bird because of his feathers. In 1913 there was the moderately pro-Indian movie *Heart of an Indian*. The setting of these pro-Indian movies was usually among the eastern agricultural tribes, rather than the Plains buffalo hunters or the mounted Apachi and Yaqui of the Southwest, where the stereotypes of warlike Indians were still historically close and flourished in writings of the time. *Ramona*, a strongly pro-Indian story set among the Mission Indians of Southern California, was filmed at least four times. Later silents shifted toward a more villainous Indian image, as in *In the Days of Buffalo Bill* (1921), *The Vanishing American* (1925), and *Redskin* (1928). *The Vanishing American* had some interesting authenticity, such as a battle between Puebloan cliff-dwellers and the Navajo.

D.W. Griffith filmed *Ramona* in 1910 when he moved to Southern California to take advantage of the sunny weather for shooting outdoor movies. But even Griffith was ethnocentric about Indians. In *The Battle of Elderbush Gulch* (1913) Griffith showed the Indians' preparations before they attacked the settlers. The preparations included an emotional war dance and the eating of dogs, obviously uncivilized practices to a White audience. An early story of the problems of Indian-White miscegenation in old Wyoming was *The Squaw Man* (1913) by Cecil B. DeMille. This story of a White man who loved an Indian girl was so popular that DeMille remade the film twice, in 1918 and 1931.

DeMille's *Call of the North* (1914) had Indians wearing a realistic mix of Native and White clothing. William S. Hart, who lived among the Sioux, is noted for his struggle for realism, even playing a half-breed Indian chief who tried to bring White education to his people in *The Dawn Maker* (1916). Colonel Tim McCoy, as an Indian agent to the Wind River Shoshone, was an advisor to James Cruz on his use of the tribe in the first epic western, *The Covered Wagon* (1923). McCoy later became a prominent actor in 75 westerns, who influenced film-making with his knowledge of Indian history and customs. Hart and McCoy made mistakes, but they were at least advocates of authenticity. If their early tradition had continued, there could have been a florescence of great films of lasting value on the ethnography and history of the American Indian.

The classic western movie with frontiersmen and pioneers struggling against the difficulties of the elements of nature, lawlessness, and the Indians was developed in the silent era. It was in turn derived from the popular Wild West literature of the nineteenth century. This form was particularly emphasized in the serials, along with melodrama and slapstick comedies. The serials used a technique of steadily building suspense to climaxes through speed, action, and "cross-cutting" from one scene of action to the next. It was in these that a band of horse-riding Indians was used to attack the settlers in order to introduce the elements of threat and action to the routine story. Extensive dialogue was unnecessary; the threat and action were obvious from the pictures, so the story captions remained extremely simple. The serials were easy to make because there was little writing or dramatic entanglement. Movements could virtually replace acting, the story pattern was easy, stock footage from past films could be incorporated, and sets were inexpensive. All shots involving a given set or a key actor were filmed at the same time, although this often confused the actors because the scenes were out of sequence and they might not know to which circumstances they were supposed to be reacting.

Indians were usually portrayed as villainous, but in the silent days they were often individualistic, intelligent, and culturally diverse adversaries. "Under the influence of a mystical Indian drug, beautiful Ann Little is prepared to do as she is told by Indians, but rescue by *Lightning Bryce* (1919) is imminent." At least they were assumed to have the intellectual ability to use devious methods like drugs when abducting beautiful White women. *The Moonriders* (1920) used Pueblo Indian Ruins for one setting rather than the usual Plains tipi set-

STEREOTYPING OF INDIANS IN MOTION PICTURES

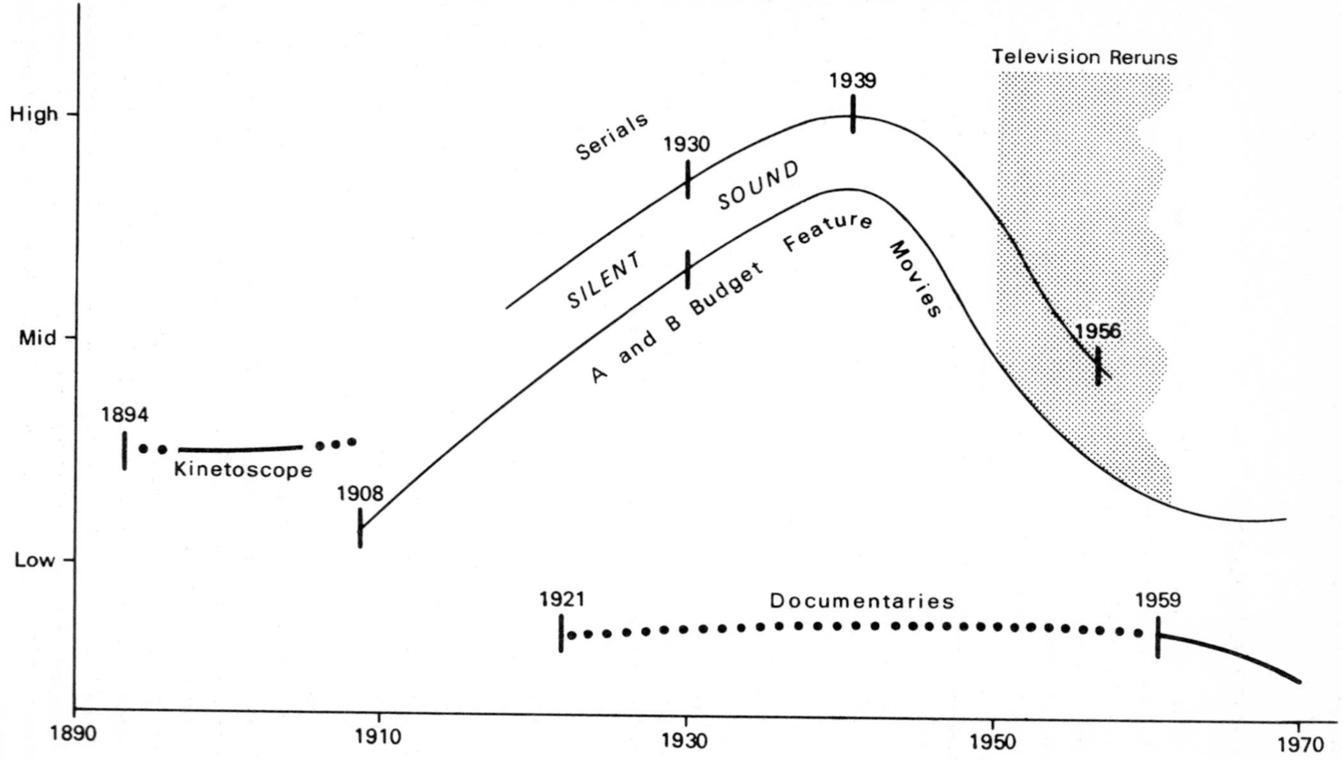

ting. Frank Lackteen played individualistic Indian villains in *White Eagle* (1922) and *Leather Stocking* (1924). By *Hawk of the Hills* (1927), it was Plains tipis and costumes as the Indians catch the beautiful White girl.

THE SOUND SERIALS

The serials continued to be popular even after sound movies were developed, so that the major American studios shot 235 serials between 1930 and 1956, all with from ten to fifteen episodes. Some 40 of these, or 17% of the total, can be classified as westerns. These often used two or even three directors, each specializing on different elements of the same film: one on drama and dialogues, one on action scenes such as fights, and a third on second-unit locations, such as car chases and Indian-cavalry encounters. Thus the dialogue man did not worry about Indian dialogue. If the Indians spoke at all that was handled by the Indian-cavalry specialist, who was more interested in the photographic depiction of action.

Tim McCoy fought Indians in a film that was made in both silent and sound versions, *The Indians are Coming* (1930). That was the first talking serial of any kind. It had poor pacing and synchronization and no musical score. Gradually these sound features were improved as three or four major studios began to produce about one western serial every year or two, reaching peak production in 1938 and 1939. The western serials and B-western movies tended to use the same writers, directors, and leading characters. They were inexpensive to produce, the interior sets were cheap to make, and appropriate exterior scenes were readily available in Southern California. Some of the important Indian western sound serials between 1930 and 1956 were *Battling With Buffalo Bill* (1930), *The Last of the Mohicans* (1931), *Custer's Last Stand* (1936), *The Lone Ranger* (1938), *Black Arrow* (1944), *Blackhawk* (1952) and *Son of Geronimo* (1952).

The serials had emerged from pulp fiction, although a few of the later movie serials, such as *Red Ryder* (1940) and *King of the Mounties* (1942), were originally comic strips. In the early 1940s there was a total of 44 different western pulp magazines, none of them Indian-oriented. The B-western Zorro series is considered to be an ancestral form of the Lone Ranger, an Americanized version of the Spanish California Zorro. Paralleling these movie series were the B-westerns, an occasional big budget or A-western, and the radio adventure series, so there was an interchange among the different forms of mass media. The Lone Ranger was on radio, in two film serials and three B-westerns, and then in a television series and in comic books.

This material was rapidly developed for television when it initially flourished in the 1950s. Thus the serials died out in motion pictures and radio, but thrived for about fifteen years on television with 51 different western serials, including such titles as *Hopalong Cassidy* (1947), *The Lone Ranger* (1948), *Gunsmoke* (1955), and *Bonanza* (1959). Again, none were particularly Indian-oriented.

THE 1930S AND 1940S

When sound came in Indians were rarely ever given speaking lines, not even in mock-Indian language, such as Tonto's use of *kim-o-sabe* with the Lone Ranger. In one serial of the mid-1930s (*Scouts to the Rescue*) the Indians were given a language by running their normal English dialogue backwards. By keeping them relatively motionless when they spoke, the picture could be printed in reverse and a perfect lip-sync maintained.

Another feature of sound is that the character of individual heroes and villains could be more subtly developed and were less expensive to employ than massed warring Indians. This led to some decrease in the use of Indians. The stereotype had developed that Indians always fought as a tribe and that individually they were disinterested in White concerns. Therefore the western villain became a crooked White gambler, mayor, banker, or rancher and his gang.

The Plainsman (1937) was one of the first movies to use an Indian Chief by name as the tribal leader, Yellow Hand in this case. The standard use of Indians-for-excitement occurred in *Union Pacific* (1939) and *Stagecoach* (1939) when they attacked the train or stagecoach, as usual without historical accuracy or even sufficient fictional explanation. Indians were simply presented as hostile to Whites. *The North West Mounted Police* (1940) was an important full-color fictional account of the Riel Rebellion of the Canadian Métis. *Unconquered* (1947), set in the American Colonies, includes Indians torturing a White woman, the illegal sale of firearms to Indians, an Indian massacre of colonists, and an attack on a fort. This was about the last fully anti-Indian movie; ironically it was by DeMille, who was also one of the first to make Indian movies, beginning in 1913. In WORLD WAR II the Nazi, Fascists, and Japanese were the major villains, but still *Geronimo* (1940) was one of the first Indian chief biographies, portrayed unsympathetically as a naturally violent man. *They Died With Their Boots On* (1942) portrayed the Battle of the Little Big Horn with some historical accuracy, but was sympathetic to General George Custer and unsympathetic to Chief Crazy Horse.

THE SHIFT TOWARD PRO-INDIAN MOVIES

John Ford directed the important trilogy on cavalry life in the 1880s—*Fort Apache* (1948), *She Wore A Yellow Ribbon* (1949), and *Rio Grande* (1950). These films viewed Indians through the eyes of a sympathetic White, such as the lead actor John Wayne in *Fort Apache*. The constant striving for mutual understanding between the Indians and at least certain Whites is a constant theme in the three films. The true villain now tends to be a White: a martinet colonel, a trader who sells liquor and guns to the Indians, etc. The names of Indian chiefs, bands, and tribes and the Apachean dress are accurate. There are glimpses of the Indian women, as well as the standard masses of male warriors. John Ford directed over two hundred feature films, mostly outdoor pictures, and his Indian westerns have been more authentic portrayals than those of other directors at the time, but he never portrayed a Native culture from the inside until *Cheyenne Autumn* (1964). The intellectual shallowness and visual orientation of Ford is illustrated in his comments: " . . . on *She Wore a Yellow Ribbon* I tried to make it as Remington as possible . . . On another picture I might try to make it as if it were seen by Charlie Russell." (Friar and Friar 1972: 39).

Kitses (1969: 13) discussed the history of Ford's westerns in terms of changes in Ford's personal philosophy. "The peak comes in the forties where Ford's works are bright monuments to his vision of the trek of the faithful to the Promised Land, the populist hope of an ideal community . . . But as the years slip by the darker side of Ford's romanticism comes to the foreground . . . we find a regret for the past, a bitterness at the larger role of Washington . . . The Indians of *Drums Along the Mohawk* and *Stagecoach*, devilish marauders that threaten the hardy pioneers, suffer a sea-change as Ford's hopes wane, until with *Cheyenne Autumn*, they are a civilized, tragic people at the mercy of a savage community." Another explanation could be that Ford finally acquired a more sophisticated understanding of Indian-White relations.

These Ford films and other later ones usually attempted rationalizations of Indian behavior, although as people they often came across as simple, childlike creatures, who spoke in short, ungrammatical sentences. *Broken Arrow* (1950) carried this theme of understanding the Indians further by trying to depict Indians as people with a legitimate culture, and to portray cases of stupidity and bigotry on both sides in cultural conflict, and the difficulties of achieving peace between the Apaches under an honorable Cochise and the Whites. Delmer Daves, a writer and director who had lived among Hopi and Navajo as a youth, adapted the story from the historical novel *Blood Brother*. This film brought more realism, as well as nostalgia and sophisticated satire, to the big budget western. Jeff Chandler had his first important success as Cochise in the film, taking a White man as a blood brother and trying to make peace with the army. Audiences were now receptive to the idea of a more noble redman who had been victimized and forced into impossible situations. Indian heroes were often friends to the White heroes and there were both Indian and White villains. Indians were victims of circumstances created by Whites and only renegade Indians caused trouble.

The wave of pro-Indian movies that immediately followed *Broken Arrow* attempted to shoot the story more from the Indian point of view but were often poorly done, such as *Taza, Son of Cochise* (1954). Two Indian western serials were rushed out in 1952, *Blackhawk* and *Son of Geronimo*. Other rather pro-Indian films that came out within four years of *Broken Arrow* were *Devil's Doorway, Across the Wide Missouri, The Savage, Arrowhead, The Big Sky, Chief Crazy Horse, Sitting Bull, White Feather, Navajo, Hiawatha*, and *Jim Thorpe: All American*, an Indian athlete's biography. There was even a television series based on an Indian policeman in New York, *Hawk*. These pro-Indian films of the 1950s often dealt with the difficulties of assimilation into White society because of White prejudices, as in *Devil's Doorway* (1950), *Reprisal* (1958), and *The Unforgiven* (1960). *The Half-Breed* (1952), *Broken Lance* (1954), *The Last Wagon* (1956), and *Flaming Star* (1960) included half-breeds who had to work out the dilemmas of their dual ancestry. Negative stereotypes were then formed about the Indian-hating, treaty-breaking cavalry officers, merchants, and Indian agents, who usually ignored the enlightened hero.

The Unforgiven (1960) had a young Indian girl brought up as a White by Whites until a stranger revealed her past, which caused conflicts among her adopted brothers and the local people. In *Flaming Star* Elvis Presley portrayed a half-breed who had to choose between his two ancestries, and was an Indian hero again in *Stay Away Joe* (1966). In *McLintock* (1963) a group of Indian chiefs were released from prison only to find trouble from land-hungry Whites and a stupid government agent. In *How the West Was Won* (1963), the obsessed railway man was determined to get his tracks laid across the Indian land as fast as possible, ignoring Indian burial grounds and having treaties rewritten for his own good. The Indians retaliated by stampeding a herd of buffalo into the railroad camp. *Cheyenne Autumn* (1964) was based on historical accounts of 286 Cheyenne who left their sterile reservation and tried to return to a traditional hunting range over 1,500 miles away, only to be pursued by a cavalry unit which had been ordered to return them to their reservation.

In the late 1960s intimate Indian-White relations became even more important. *Hombre* (1967) had a White hero who had been raised by Indians and *The Stalking Moon* (1968) had a White woman with an Indian baby. In *The Intruders* (1967) a half-breed is hassled when he gets out of jail and tries to return to his home town. A sign at the edge of town says "No deadbeats or Indians allowed." He is refused a drink in the local saloon. Indians could not be buried in the town graveyard.

THE RECENT BREAKING DOWN OF STEREOTYPES

A few recent films have been particularly authentic and sympathetic, breaking down the traditional filmic stereotypes of Indians. There has been a drastic decline in the number of Indian movies produced. There are no more Indian western serials, B-budget films, or television series being made. Even the old Indian westerns are rarely rerun on television. However, the quality has improved for those that are made, and Native people are now active in movie criticism and review. *The Boy and the Eagle* (1968) was an excellent depiction of a Hopi myth. *Tell Them Willie Boy is Here* (1969) told of bigoted White justice related to conflicts in assimilation, the superior ability of a Paiute to survive in the desert, and the eventual destruction of the Indian hero by a posse. The story is based on a 1909 historical incident in Southern California.

Little Big Man (1970) and *A Man Called Horse* (1971) again dealt with violence in the northern Plains and repeated many cinematic cliches, but the assimilation of Whites into Indian cultures was treated in a sympathetic and realistic way. Friar and Friar (1972) point out some mistakes that were made in *A Man Called Horse*; the film draws on Catlin paintings of the Mandan to portray a Sioux culture. The AIM chapter in Minneapolis picketed the movie theatre when *A Man Called Horse* opened in that city, complaining about its cruelty, its desecration of Indian religion, its use of non-Indian actors, and technical errors. A Sioux reviewer pointed out that the traditional Sioux mounted their horses on the *right*, did not desert the elderly, and were not routinely cruel, contradicting the film's representation. Nevertheless, while *The Savage* (1952), *Pawnee* (1957), and *Hombre* (1967) had earlier dramatized White men brought up by Indians, it is the two more recent films that are more realistic. They both give many ethnographic details on the day-to-day life in northern Plains Indian cultures by following the events in the life of a White captive. The films were still told from a White point of view, but the White heroes learned to respect many Indian customs. *Little Big Man* reversed the usual situation so that the Whites became stereotypes while the Indians were interesting, individualistic, and unpredictable. General Custer, for example, was played strictly for laughs.

Billy Jack (1971) is a half-breed, Western Pueblo, ex-Green Beret, counter-culture super-hero who protects wild horses and the children of a racially mixed school on a reservation from harassment by the local White bigots. As in *Little Big Man* it is the Whites who are stereotyped. The hatred of Indians is greatly overstressed, particularly for the Santa Fe area where the film was shot. Another problem with the film was that completely false Indian rituals were contrived for the film, while dozens of beautiful Indian ceremonies occur each year in the local Rio Grande Basin that could have been incorporated into the movie. *Billy Jack* was so successful that a sequel was made, *The Trial of Billy Jack* (1975). Another recent sequel was *The Return of the Man Called Horse* (1976).

I Heard the Owl Call My Name (1975) is one of the finest Indian films ever made. It is about contemporary life in a Northwest Coast fishing village and the experiences of a White priest who moved there. *Cold Journey* (1976) was made by the National Film Board of Canada specifically to break the old film stereotypes, but in the process of telling the story of the identity struggle of a 15-year-old Cree boy it relies heavily on modern Indian stereotypes. It stars Buckley Petawabano and Dan George with narration by Johnny Yesno and music by Willie Dunn. It was shot in Indian communities in Manitoba (The Pas) and Saskatchewan (Piapot Reserve and Pelican Narrows).

INTER-RACIAL SEX RELATIONS

Cecil B. Demille handled the problem of miscegenation during the silent era in *The Squaw Man*. In this adaptation of a play the Indian wife committed suicide and the White man took their son to England. *Duel in the Sun* (1948), *Broken Arrow* (1950), and *Across the Wide Missouri* (1951) all showed love affairs between a White man and an Indian woman. The Indian woman always dies to provide the tragic but "inevitable" ending for a racist audience. The reciprocal form of miscegenation, Indian man and White woman, has been totally unacceptable to White audiences because of the combination of the double standard for the sexes and racism. Even that code was broken in the late 1960s; White women finally wanted Indian men in *Dual at Diablo* (1966), *The Stalking Moon* (1968), *Little Big Man* (1970); *Billy Jack* (1971), and *Climb an Angry Mountain* (1972). However, something tragic almost invariably happens to these miscegenous matches so that the audience is not left with a happy mixed marriage at the end. The Indian husband is usually the one who dies, reversing the earlier formula.

COMPARISONS WITH HISTORY TEXTS AND CARTOONS

Motion pictures and history books both concentrate on White concerns—accordingly, Indians are described in both in relation to Whites, especially in Indian-White conflicts. Just as there is extremely little filmic portrayal of Native cultures in their own terms, there is extremely little written history of Indian societies in their own terms. However, at least history texts have far more stereotypes than films: meeting Puritans; selling Manhattan Island; engaging in fur trade, fighting *with* the French, British or Americans as well as against them; etc. Films concentrate on the mid-to-late 1800s, on the Plains area, and on Indian-White wars.

The proportion of material on Indian and Black events in recent U.S. history textbooks is very low, averaging about one per cent each, or 4½ pages at the high school level (Bowker 1972). There is some tendency to mention Indians slightly more in grade school textbooks than in junior high or high school texts. There is also a tendency for a progressive decrease in the material on Indians through historical time: more on pre-1777, moderate on the middle periods, and extremely little on post-WW II. Also, periods of Indian and Black history are never reviewed when Whites have historically acted poorly, according to current moral standards. In magazine cartoons the predominant stereotypes are (1) wearing feathers in the hair, (2) using a bow and arrow, and (3) using pottery, tipis, or smoke signals (Houts and Bahr 1972). These stereotypes remind me of the dedication that introduces the book *Stories California Indians Told*—"To all boys and girls who like Indians and animals."

An analysis of patterns of prejudice in 73 social studies textbooks used in Ontario schools (McDiarmid and Pratt 1971) revealed that the only favorable evaluations of Indians were found in primary grade texts. The history textbooks all evaluated Indians negatively. In pictorial portrayals Indians were the least favored of all groups: primitive, unskilled, aggressive, hostile, almost always (95%) shown in tribal dress or partly clothed, shown (86%) wearing feathers, shown in their past culture rather than their present culture, and never shown in skilled or professional occupations. The extinction of the Beothuk Indians of Newfoundland at the hands of Whites was ignored in all but two, one giving a passing reference to the fact that they were there and "have now disappeared completely" and the other a single but rather adequate page. None of the texts made a serious attempt to discuss the present status of the Canadian Indian. Some examples of textual materials are as follows:

> *"Champlain spent the winter with the Hurons, living in a longhouse swarming with Indians, mice, fleas, and lice."*
> *"Everyone put on their Sunday best for the ceremony. Even the Indians, tomahawk in hand and scalps at the belt, joined as spectators."*
> *"Often the Indians had to be treated as naughty children, punished when necessary and rewarded with a pound of tobacco when the punishment was over."*
> *"Then the white man decided to give the Indians separate pieces of land to live on, and money to buy the things they needed."*

THE NEED FOR INDIAN ACTORS

One of the problems in Indian westerns has been the use of non-Indians in acting roles as Indians. Indian actors were rarely ever given lead roles, although they were used occasionally as tribal members. A few of the MGM silent westerns that starred the Indian specialist Tim McCoy, such as the *Covered Wagon* and *The Vanishing American*, were made on Indian reservations with Indian extras. There was even an association of Indians in silent motion pictures in the 1920s called The War Paint Club, and an Indian Actors' Association after 1936. The silent era saw such Indian actors as Charles Stevens, a grandson of Geronimo, and the husband-wife teams of Dark Cloud and Dove Eye, Young Deer and Red Wing, and Art Ortega and Mona Darkfeather. John Big Tree made the silent-sound transition in Ford's films. John Ford has usually used Navajos as extras since his *Stagecoach* (1939). Several of the recent films have used real Indian tribes: *Cheyenne Autumn* (Navajo), *Little Big Man* (Crow), and *A Man Called Horse* (Sioux).

Part of the problem is that real Indians do not behave according to the film stereotypes that have been developed about Indian behavior, so they must learn to "act Indian." Indians, of course, are not automatically good actors, even as Indians, but Whites know so little about Indian culture and behavior that even good White actors usually do a poor job imitating Indians. An Indian Actors Guild was formed in Los Angeles in 1966 to promote the use of Native people in Native roles, to promote the training of Indians in trick riding and other horseman skills, and to promote the teaching of dramatic skills to Indians. Jay Silverheels was behind this movement and helped to form an Indian Actors' Workshop at the Los Angeles Indian Center with the help of other Indians such as Buffy Sainte-Marie, Iron Eyes Cody, and Rodd Redwing.

Chief Thundercloud was in *Wild Bill Hickok* (1938) and then played Tonto in the first serial version of the radio show *The Lone Ranger* (1938), which was an Americanized version of the Zorro stories. Tonto, the Lone Ranger's assistant, like Zorro's assistant, was originally considered so insignificant that the hero could be literally called the ranger who works alone. In fact, the word "tonto" means "fool" in Spanish and this pair, whether as the Zorro or the Lone Ranger team, worked in the Southwest where Spanish is spoken. Also there is some lore about occasional "crazy" Indians who left their tribes and associated with Whites. However, as developed by Chief Thundercloud and the show's writers, Tonto began to emerge as a major figure in the movie series.

Tonto became the first major fictional Indian film hero, particularly after Jay Silverheels played Tonto in *The Lone Ranger* (1956), television's *Lone Ranger* (1948) series, and then in *The Lone Ranger and the Lost City of Gold* (1958). Jay Silverheels is a tall, handsome, and intelligent Iroquois who played Indian roles in over 29 motion pictures, including *The Prairie* (1947), *Fury at Furnace Creek* (1948), *Broken Arrow* (1950), *War Arrow* (1953), and *Indian Paint* (1967). While many politically active Indians have since criticized Silverheels for playing a role that was clearly subservient to a White man, he actually developed Tonto into one of the most intelligent and individualistic Indians to be portrayed on serial television.

Silverheels (1968: 9) discussed the problem of recent Indian criticisms of Indian actors in comic television commercials. In one spoof selling house insurance, six Indians attacked a peaceful surburban house. "Suddenly painted Indian riders attack the dwelling, yelling and shooting fake arrows, and throwing tomahawks at the buildings. One Indian slips on a roller skate and takes a fall. The Indians ride out of the scene, they have left a man tied. The narration accompanying this scene concerns insurance, never at any time is ridicule implied toward the Indians." Indians in Minnesota protested that the commercial degraded the Indian image, it was withdrawn from further showing on television, and the Indian actors lost out on some of the royalties they would have received if it had been shown. The commercial, of course, capitalized on film stereotypes about Indians, but by showing them in a ridiculous light they helped to dispel them. In another one Silverheels is shown stuffing pizza rolls in his pocket. Again he was criticized. His reply was that this kind of criticism "promotes and strengthens the image that projects the Indians as being stoic, undemonstrative, incapable of showing emotion and entirely lacking a sense of humor." Young militant Indians today appear to be insensitive to the contexts of the Indian liberation movement in the 1940s and 1950s and to the problems of Indian leaders like Jay Silverheels. They look for inspiration instead to the nineteenth-century military leaders, particularly from the Plains where the movies have told them the significant heroics were carried out.

Jim Thorpe made several films between 1932 and 1944. Iron Eyes Cody, a Cherokee, has portrayed Indians in over 35 motion pictures. Rodd Redwing (a Chickasaw known for his trick gun handling), John War Eagle, and Chief Yowlachie have made many appearances. Chief Dan George came to prominence in *Little Big Man* demonstrating the potential of Indians to surpass Whites in Indian roles.

THE NEED TO PORTRAY SOCIETIES OTHER THAN HORSEMEN OF THE PLAINS AND SOUTHWEST

Over 2,300 feature-length western films and serials had been produced by 1967 (Eyles 1967). About 400 or 17% of these included significant Indian portrayals. A few *thousand* Indian motion pictures have been made, but most of these were very short films of the silent era. After 1910 the industry began producing more than 100 per year. The shift toward a greater use of Indians as a violent threat is indicated in the frequent portrayal in the silents of (1) the more peaceful Indian groups as well as the agriculturalists of the East and Southwest and (2) themes such as Indian love affairs, occasionally even between Indians, rather than the usual preoccupation with Indian-White relationships. The silent era had both violent and non-violent portrayals while the sound era shifted almost exclusively to violent portrayals. The sound era lost the regular production of such non-violent, silent films as *Indian Day School* (1898), *Moki Snake Dance by Wolpi Indians* (1901), and *The Indian Runner's Romance* (1904).

The frequency of designated tribes in feature-length sound motion pictures shows the predominance of the horsemen of the Plains and Southwest in these Indian movies: Apache—93, Sioux—45, Comanche—25, Iroquois—15, Cheyenne—10, Navajo—8, Kiowa—7, Seminole—7, Shoshoni—6, Blackfoot—5, Arapahoe—4, Paiute—4, Pawnee—4, Shawnee—4, Cree—3, Modoc—3, Hopi—2, and at least one each of the following: Creek, Crow, Delaware, Huron, Ottawa, Métis, Mission (Southern California), Mohican, Osage, Powhatan, Ute, and Yaqui. About 83% of the specific tribal portrayals in sound motion pictures are of Plains-Southwest horsemen societies. One also sees the predominance of Native societies with an historical reputation for violence, particularly the Apache, Sioux, and Comanche. Societies with a more passive, non-violent reputation are almost never represented, such as the Hopi in the Southwest, the Washo or any other Great Basin society, and any Sub-arctic society.

Following the success of *Broken Arrow*, which apparently popularized the Apaches, 43 Apache films were produced in the 1950s and 33 in the 1960s. Geronimo, an Apache, has in turn been the most frequently portrayed Indian chief, most sympathetically in *Geronimo* (1962). There are at least fourteen feature-length sound motion pictures on Geronimo, six on Sitting Bull, four on Crazy Horse, seven on Cochise, and four on Red Cloud. Hundreds of historically important, but non-military, Indian leaders have been ignored by the motion pictures.

The selection of the Plains-Southwest horsemen as the source for the majority of stereotypes about Indians is understandable in the context of the vitality of those Indian cultures in recent historical times. The Indian military resistance to the occupation of Indian territory by White society force was significant and the memory still vivid in the Plains and Southwest. Cultural adjustments related to this traumatic period reverberated in both Indian and White societies for decades after. The White conquest and occupation probably had to be justified and rationalized to White society through literature, the Wild West Shows, and finally motion pictures. Perhaps the extreme stereotyping soothed the guilty conscience of the nation, as time and again it was shown how White European Christian manifest destiny must conquer the forces of paganism and barbarism. The Plains and Southwest Indian cultures themselves rebounded after the military period to become the major source of Native cultural revitalization, coinciding with the development of extremely negative stereotyping for White audiences. This rejuvenation was particularly in the form of the social and religious pan-Indian movements, such as the Ghost Dance, Sun Dance, Peyotism, and powwow dancing.

In the context of long-range history this particular selection of societies is ironic; the Plains Indian cultures were not fully aboriginal, did not evolve until after Whites introduced the horse, and were not similar to most other American Indians. No American Indians rode horses before Columbus and most still did not hunt from horseback in the middle 1800s. Most American Indians did not depend upon large game as their primary source of food, but were in fact agriculturalists. Most American Indians lived in permanent houses, not in temporary hide tents. Most American Indians did not wear tailored hide clothing, but woven robes.

Motion pictures have ignored most of the spectacularly rich cultural diversity of some 560 different languages and societies in North America. Instead, they have repeatedly presented the same dozen or so Plains and Southwest tribes that acquired enough military prowess to give the Whites a brief resistance. Motion pictures have virtually ignored the state societies of Mexico and Central America, the agricultural chiefdoms of the Southeast, the marine chiefdoms of the Northwest Coast, and the agricultural Pueblos of the Southwest to focus instead on elaborately fictionalized accounts of Indian military harassment of the struggling pioneers.

In fact, the whole horse-riding, buffalo-hunting complex was a brief cultural florescence that was created indirectly by Whites. The horse was introduced into the New World by the Spaniards and it diffused northwards, initially from the settlements around Santa Fe in the 1600s. This diffusion process went on through the 1700s, gradually providing more and more of the Indians of the Southwest and Plains with the great economic and military advantages of the use of horses. Societies that had gathered plants and did some hunting on foot, such as the Blackfoot and Comanche, had much greater success on horseback. The Ute decreased their plant-gathering orientation and increased hunting. Some societies, such as the Arapaho, even abandoned horticulture to take up the rich complex of buffalo hunting on horseback. People could be more mobile, could carry more things, and could build bigger tipis. They could locate herds, keep up with the herds, chase down buffalo on horseback for the kill, and carry large quantities of food and skins back to camp.

This new wealth and new way of life brought on many changes in Plains Indian life. Peripheral societies were attracted into the Plains, rapid population growth followed, warfare and other competition between tribes increased, and the buffalo population was gradually reduced. The Whites then entered the Plains, encountered some brief military resistance from Indians, and added their contribution to bringing the buffalo close to extinction. The story material is as good in dozens of other areas. If the fixation on Indian-White conflicts is necessary for a sufficiently violent tale, there is much substance in Spanish-Indian or French-Indian conflicts in other areas. The real needs, however, are to describe Native cultures in their own terms, in time periods other than the late 1800s, and in areas outside the Plains and Southwest.

INUIT AND THE DOCUMENTARY MOVIE

Indian movies have been generally successful as popular entertainment and as financial productions, but despite their quantity they have done little to advance the art or science of films. For example, they have not won Academy Awards, unless we count *How the West Was Won* (1963). Discussions about artistic creativity or the development of new techniques never seem to mention Indian films, although there have been occasional comments about their content as depictions of historical events or of frontier life. The historical judgment on the cinematographic creativity in over 2,300 feature length westerns is that it was a mass medium within which the industry learned to use the American natural landscape, learned to use apparent visual movement to build excitement, and learned to synchronize the sounds of outdoor action, such as horses' hoofbeats and gun shots.

Inuit cultures have largely escaped the stereotyped portrayal of Indian cultures; academy awards have been won for *Eskimo* (1934) and *The Alaskan Eskimo* (1953). Films on the Inuit are particularly noted for their creativity in the field of documentary ethno-cinematography, a tradition that is very careful about the use of stereotypes. There seem to be several reasons for this. The Inuit retained much of their traditional culture into the modern era, so that it was available for direct photography. Because of the extremely different environmental setting of the Arctic, there has been much interest in the Native solutions to the problems of cultural adaptation, even in the modern period. By contrast, the life of nearly one million Indians who live on or near reservations in the U.S. and Canada has rarely ever been portrayed in popular feature films. Inuit were never a threat to Whites.

Another reason for the relatively realistic portrayal of Inuit is the precedent set by Robert Flaherty's *Nanook of the North* (1922). This was one of the most important movies ever made, setting standards that are still difficult to meet today. Flaherty was raised in northern Michigan and northern Ontario and knew many Ojibwa Indians as a youth, even learning some of the Ojibwa language (Calder-Marshall 1963).

He built continuity and integration into his film by focussing on the annual round of activities of the head of a family, Nanook from Port Harrison in northeastern Hudson Bay. He came into the community, became well acquainted with the Natives, worked without a script, and allowed the incidents that happened in the course of his filming to determine the content of his film. He let the story develop out of the lives of the people in their daily struggle for survival in a harsh environment: walrus hunt, harpooning a seal, visit to trading post, etc. He not only avoided building negative stereotypes by honest cinematic reporting, but through intimate portrayal he showed the humanity of the Inuit. The word "documentary" was first written in English by a film critic in relation to *Nanook of the North.*

CONCLUSION

A review of the history of the portrayal of Indians in motion pictures shows (1) the initial development of the filmic stereotypes of Indians in silent films, (2) the extreme emphasis on these stereotypes in the serial and B-grade westerns of the 1930s and 1940s and (3) the gradual elimination of the stereotypes in big budget movies of the 1940s and 1950s. The decline of Indian stereotyping seems to have begun during WORLD WAR II, the Germans, Italians, and Japanese replacing the Indians as the major villains. After WORLD WAR II John Ford's more realistic westerns, *Broken Arrow*, and a host of imitators handled Indians in more sympathetic, although still fictional, ways. A few films of the 1960s and 1970s have even approached the documentary quality of Flaherty's *Nanook of the North: Cheyenne Autumn, The Boy and the Eagle, Tell Them Willie Boy is Here, Little Big Man*, and *A Man Called Horse*. This same period has seen a florescence in the production of true documentaries. Part of the solution to the problems surrounding the production of motion pictures free from film stereotypes is to promote the commercial success of quality documentaries.

Chapter 16

Stereotyping by Indians

Native studies needs to include some analysis of what Native people themselves say, about each other and about non-Native people. This helps us explore the Native ideologies, their design, development, and social uses. Just as distorted stereotypes about Indians developed within the motion picture industry, there are comparable stereotypes about Whites within Indian society. The knowledge of Indians about Whites seems to be somewhat better than that of the Whites about them, but there are still important gaps in this reciprocal knowledge. Perhaps more important today is that Indian social cohesiveness is being actively bolstered by the use of stereotypes of Whites. Thus in speeches, Native periodicals, and simply day-to-day conversation, White culture, its perception of history, and its institutions have become the butt of jokes that circulate through Indian society.

The word "stereotype" was originally a printing term to refer to "a type plate cast from a mold." That is, rather than being the movable letters of type it is the fixed plate that is molded and used in the printing. The word has since been generalized to mean any narrow and fixed idea about someone or something that distorts reality. A stereotype is a preconceived and routinized belief, the cognitive part of a prejudice. The essence of stereotyping is that a characteristic that is somewhat true is overemphasized, thus yielding a distortion. For example, everyone would agree that the horse-riding tribal Indians of the Plains and the Southwest were a threat for a number of years to White expansion into the West. That itself is not a distortion. It became a stereotype in the movies by endless repetition and ignoring other kinds of Indian societies, other kinds of Indian-White relationships, Indian societies in their own terms, and the role of women in Indian societies. Stereotyping ignores the broad range of normal behavior in a society and the similarities between the stereotyper's society and the society that is being stereotyped. Stereotyping presents as normal that which is rare and different.

Indian stereotyping comes partially from a high degree of selection in what Indians say about White society, based of course on their own perceptions and interests. In comes from a high degree of repetition of those limited things. It comes from some general and reciprocal lack of knowledge of Whites and Indians about each other. And finally it comes from just that social and political use possible in creating ideological cohesiveness within a group by castigating those people and ideas that are different. Politicians can use stereotypes to build political commitment and focus political attacks.

Scientific analysis also creates many generalizations about people and things, but science attempts to avoid the distortions of stereotyping by such means as adequate sampling, holding descriptions as tentative and susceptible to further testing, and remaining sensitive to the statistical character of social generalizations. Thus, for example, we do not expect individuals in fact to behave fully in the way that their social group has been characterized, for we believe that individuals are unique.

The White majority's self-stereotypes are generally the perceived traits of national character: efficient, honest, hard-working, etc. The White stereotypes of Native people today are to some degree a reversal of White self-stereotypes. That is, they are held as usually inefficient, dishonest, lazy, and so forth. They judge the Indians in terms of White values and characterize them as inadequate to the degree that they have not assimilated into White society.

The ideological defenses of a minority group operate in a somewhat different way than those of majority society. Minorities use both their specific cultural values and those of the contextual majority society to define themselves and to stereotype the majority. The general culture is permeated with majority values, in the law, in business, in government administration, in the churches, and so forth. Thus, *the Indians make most of their claims to moral superiority in the terms of the majority.* They are holding a mirror to White society to show up its flaws, and thus by implication are saying "We are better than that." They claim that the majority is guilty of racism, historical injustices, legal injustices, environmental pollution, and so forth. They claim an ancestry without these vices, which of course is true because their ancestry is that of bands, tribes, and chiefdoms, not industrial states. Racism, historical injustices, etc. were not moral issues in the band, tribe, and chiefdom societies. If we must make racially stereotyped comparisons, at the least, abstract comparisons should be made using Native states, such as the Incas, Aztecs, and Mayas. Were they guilty of racism, historical injustices, and legal injustices to the people they conquered and colonized? Of course they were. The distortions in racial stereotypes become clear when we hold them up to genuine cross-cultural comparisons.

In poetry, speeches, and writing the symbols of modern White culture to Indians have become urban, industrial, and legal dimensions of modern cultures, such as money, pollution, clocks, and jails. The symbols of Indian culture have become simple and natural practices—wearing hair long, making crafts and living in the country to canoe, fish, and hunt. These symbols have a parallel importance to "counter-cultural" Whites so the two often find themselves occupying quite similar ideological ground, although each group is generally ignorant of the other's traditional culture.

There are also expressions that come from direct conflict between the essential values of Indian cultures and those of the conquering state, but these have circulated mostly within local reservation cultures, occasionally spreading beyond in some pan-Indian expression. One reason for this shattered expression of value conflicts is that there were hundreds of different Native societies, each with a different set of values, each with a different history of conflicts with Whites. Thus, it is only when they came down to that broad level of common experience that pan-Indian stereotypes were constructed about Whites. Then those stereotypes that had the most utility in the contextual White value system became emphasized. The final products are such basic sayings as "We were here first," "Our lands were taken from us by unfair means," "We do not want to be culturally White," and "We do not like the way the White government interferes with our lives." These problems are all important to Whites. Indians rarely complain that White conquest took customs such as plural marriage, intertribal warfare, and magic as a medical practice away from them. Whites do not respect these customs, but they do respect the fact that Indians were here first, that everything should be done legally, and that within the law people should have a wide latitude to live their own way of life. Thus, while Indians undoubtedly have had changing stereotyped views of Whites since the days of initial contacts, there has been some recent convergence and consolidation of these views with the creation of an Indian ethnic culture.

EARLY FRENCH AND INDIAN STEREOTYPES

A case that is useful for exploring historically early patterns of stereotyping is that of seventeenth-century French Canada. The Natives at the time were leading a relatively aboriginal life in their own homelands with mostly indirect influences from Whites through diseases, trade, and an intensification of intertribal warfare brought on by the new use of guns and competitions to control fur trapping and trade. The Whites were in the minority and were often dependent upon the Natives for their survival. The Indians were generally more successful at assimilating young French men into their societies, as trappers and *coureurs-de-bois*, than the French were at assimilating Indians into French society.

The French thought of the Natives as uncivilized, lacking religion, writing, laws, science, metallurgy, and so forth. They were the "children of nature," close to life in the Garden of Eden, "noble savages." They admired the elements of freedom, equality, and the absence of theft and extortions in Native life. They were impressed by the Algonquian ideology of living in harmony with nature, their belief that hunting was guided by spiritual rules, and that the animal allowed itself to be taken. Some French criticized the nomadism of the hunters, calling them idlers and vagabonds.

Of the agriculturalists they said the men played at hunting while the women worked at growing corn. They were shocked by the use of torture to demonstrate bravery in warfare. They were also repulsed by the taking of body parts as war trophies and by ritual cannibalism.

The French tended to think of the Indians as physically superior to themselves in strength, agility, speed, and even beauty. One visitor in the 1630s said "they are as handsome young men and beautiful young women as may be seen in France. They are great runners and swimmers . . . . They are usually more slim and nimbler than we and one finds none who are paunchy, hunchbacked, deformed, niggardly, gouty or stony among them . . . . They have a good memory for material matters, such as having seen you, the qualities of a place where they have been, or what one did in their presence some twenty or thirty years ago." (Jaenen 1976:25)

Indians generally considered the French to be ugly, especially in their hairiness. In reply to a French request for young Indian wives, a chief from Tadoussac replied that only after the young Frenchmen had joined with the Montagnais warriors in war would they find Native girls willing to marry them. Indians knew that new diseases were spreading after French contacts. They did not know why, but they often assumed that the introductions of diseases were being done deliberately by the French. The French were seen as having some filthy habits. "A Savage one day saw a Frenchman fold up his handkerchief after wiping his nose, he said to him laughingly, 'If thou likest the filth, give me thy handkerchief and I will soon fill it.' " (Jaenen 1976:105).

Native women could not understand why French women would have their children raised by nursemaids or send their children away to school. Native women thought the French women were callous toward their children, like "porcupines." The Indians called the Frenchmen "women" for their emotionality and their tendency to "speak all together and interrupt one another."

Indians thought that the celibacy of priests was abnormal, comparable to homosexuality. They were not as impressed by the priests' vows of poverty or self-denial as the priests themselves seem to have been. They could not understand calendar-oriented fasting. They were, however, impressed by the ritual of the mass, the practice of drinking the blood and eating the body of Christ, and the use of crosses and rosaries, as well as such apparently powerful objects as weather vanes and clocks. The Indians who traveled to France were shocked to find such inequality, begging, poverty, and theft there.

The French admired Indian freedom, egalitarianism, and physical fitness but could not see the connection between those traits and many traits they disliked, such as permissive child rearing, nomadism, and the extreme emphasis on bravery in warfare. Indians seem not to have admired much about French society since the Frenchmen's presence brought only misfortunes, such as disease and French attempts to manipulate them toward Christianity or in war alliances.

A relatively pro-Indian bias has persisted in French Canada right up until the present time. Thus, for example, in a national attitude survey reported in 1976, Reginald Bibby tested how many would agree with the anti-Indian biased statement "It's too bad, but in general Canadian Indians have inferior intelligence compared to whites." The level of agreement with this negative statement ranged from a high of 24% in the Prairie provinces; through about 20% in B.C., Ontario, and the Atlantic provinces; to a national low of 11% in Quebec. In the national sample, 25% did not approve of marriages between Whites and Indians and 10% felt that they would feel uneasy in the presence of Indians.

DEEPLY AND MODERATELY INTEGRATED EXAMPLES

Because stereotypes have a social utility there is always a question about how deeply they are believed. Thus, for example, movie characterizations are to a large degree perceived by the general population as systematically removed from reality. One might say that movie life is not *real* life, it is a fictional adventure in which we participate in a projected way, an escape from real life. Still, even with that knowledge of their fictive character, we do acquire knowledge and attitudes from movies, and other mass media.

The following cases of what I would judge to be stereotypes illustrate a level of complete and unquestioned belief of the stereotype. A story that recently came from the Northwest Territories illustrates that the Indian fear of Whites can be extreme and can become incorporated into the supernatural system of an Indian society. This appears to be a case of the personification and projection of a fear of Whites (*The Indian News*, July 1972). "A wild bushman, reported to be blonde, white and over six feet tall has been terrorizing the Slavey village of Trout Lake. The Slavey people call him 'Nahkah', a native term for bushman who sneaks and spies from cover . . . The people have known of the man's presence for the past five years because of such occurrences as dogs barking frantically, unexpected footprints in the snow, glimpses of a pale face through cabin windows and gunshots echoing through the forest . . . Fish nets have been robbed of their catches, dried moose and caribou meat taken from drying racks and more recently, a cabin across the creek from the village was looted . . . we are worried for our kids, he might do something to them. He might grab a child or a young girl."

If the fish and meat have been stolen or a cabin looted, why assume that it was done by a White male? Is it because this fits the Indian stereotype of White behavior? Why is it that this strange White man is never seen close up? These people are great trackers in hunting, why do they not follow his tracks? Of course a White may have done one or more of these acts, but the systematic attribution of unexplained and frightening phenomena to a White shows a deeply integrated pattern of stereotyping.

Among Ojibwa, the Devil (*Jimnido*) today is often seen as a White man who wears formal black clothes. He silently watches people from the shadows and he likes to play cards at your house while everyone is sleeping, but he will stay away if you leave a Bible on the table.

The Cree value of sharing is compared with White greediness in their view of history and social relations (Braroe 1975:153).

> *The Queen's men came and brought us rum . . . they called all of the chiefs together, and after they gave them lots of rum, they read them this paper and asked if Whites could come and live here with us. The chiefs, they did not know what that meant, so they said yes and signed the paper . . . And then Whites took everything, and they killed all our buffalo. They left us nothing but this little Indian land. And now they treat us bad. We have to beg from the agent for anything we need.*

A more moderate integration of stereotypes exists when there is some awareness that the stereotype is a distortion, but is believed to be based on the truth. In this area poets, politicians, and story tellers will stretch the truth to fit the ends of the art of poetry, political goals, and entertainment. It is a dramatization of a belief, often with a humorous twist.

Joseph Brant, the Mohawk leader, was made Sachem of the Iroquois Long House Society in 1807. Shortly before his death the same year he presented contrasts between Iroquois and White society to a reporter. "Among us we have no prisons, we have no pompous parade of courts, we have no written laws, and yet judges are as highly revered among us as they are among you, and their decisions are as highly regarded. Property, to say the least, is well-guarded, and crimes are as impartially punished. We have among us no splendid villains above the control of our laws. Daring wickedness is never suffered to triumph over helpless innocence. The estates of widows and orphans are never devoured by enterprising sharpers. In a word, we have no robbery under color of the law." These practices are generally true of all tribal societies.

Through a Métis interpreter, Blackstone, an Indian chief, told the Bishop of Algoma in Canada in 1877 that "We Indians are good. The Great Spirit loves us. He has prepared happy hunting grounds for us after death, but you White people are only half of you good. The Great Spirit has made two places for you to go to, a good place and a bad place."

Chief Harry Chonkalay of Hay Lake, Alberta used some colorful speech in "telling off" some Indian Affairs Branch people, after the disastrous misuse of their band funds. He spoke in Cree, but this is some of what came out in the English translation. "We keep dogs for our trapping in the winter. We just keep them and feed them, that is all. That is the way you treat us . . . We are being treated like children that you can give candy to, then cheat."

INDIAN ETHNIC JOKES

The least integrated or believed stereotypes are those in which the stereotyped symbols are played with largely for the sake of their humor. In fact, one of the most common forms of humor is to carry a stereotype about a believed truth to a ridiculous extreme.

(Q) "What is the biggest joke you ever heard?"

(A) "This treaty will last for as long as the sun shines and the river flows."

(A) "The biggest joke I ever heard was the B.I.A. It's phasing out Indians and will now provide services only to its own employees."

(A) "The biggest joke I ever heard was having someone converse with an Indian in English and then ask him if he speaks a foreign language."

Highly repeated symbols are important to ethnic jokes. Indians use the standard White symbols about Indians, such as tipis, smoke signals, and bows and arrows as rather unreal symbols, but still something that is good for a joke.

In the midst of sending smoke signals in Yucca Flats, Nevada, an atomic bomb was detonated. The smoke signal reply was "You don't have to shout!"

Commenting on Indian teenagers doing the new dances. "Now *that* should bring rain."

The Lone Ranger saw a wave of hostile Indians and shouted to his trusted Indian guide Tonto, "We're being surrounded!" Tonto said, "What do you mean '*we*', Whiteman? You never did understand what *kimosabe* means."

Much more important than the White ethnic symbols of Indians to Indian humor are their own ethnic symbols of Whites. Certain themes have developed into a genre quite comparable to the anti-Indian jokes of the serial movies: Columbus and the discovery of the New World, General Custer's defeat, negative things they associate with Whites such as pollution and war, and by far the most important of all—government programs for Indians.

Will Rogers started a classic tradition when he talked about his Indian heritage by saying, "My folks didn't come over on the Mayflower, but they were there to meet the boat."

On the landing of Columbus: "There goes the neighborhood."

On the sale of Manhattan Island for $24: "Ever since the Whites moved in, our property values have been shot to hell."

On the landing of a U.F.O. on Indian land: "Oh no, not again!"

"How did Indians get into the New World?" "We had *reservations*."

"What do you think of the increasing concentration of the population in the cities?" "We'll have the country back soon."

General Custer was well dressed for his "last stand." He had on an Arrow Shirt. Custer boasted that he could ride right through the Sioux nation. Well, he was half right. He got half-way through. The defectors from Custer's cavalry said "Better Red than dead" (Deloria 1969: 150-151)

Wilf Pelletier, an Odawa Ojibwa living in Toronto, does monologues on Indian philosophy. I have selected a few lines from his routine about the "Dumb Indian" (Pelletier 1972:5-12).

> *The discovery of America came as a surprise to my people. They weren't expecting anyone to discover America right then . . .*
>
> *. . . All we knew how to read was smoke, and animal footprints, and clouds . . . One of the results of having no schools . . . was that no one had any degree . . . We had no way of knowing who was smart and who was dumb . . . Everyone was automatically . . . equal . . . we didn't have any word for that. We just had equality . . . We just didn't have any poor people. We still experience equality, of course, even today. But this is equality, White style. We get just as much strontium 90 in our milk as anybody—and just as much smog in our air.*

There is a minor genre of joke that reverses concepts such as "Indian problem," "Bureau of Indian Affairs," and "Indian policy." When a jury acquitted a White rancher for shooting an unarmed Indian, the following was included in a letter to the *Rosebud Sioux Herald* (Oct. 20, 1969): " . . . the world has a 'white problem.' Since two-thirds of the world is peopled by our dark brothers and sisters, we know that we will eventually solve it . . . we'll invite you for turkey on Thanksgiving after we've fulfilled our 'manifest destiny.' "

The "Alcatraz proclamation" of Richard Oakes and Grace Thorpe in 1969 included the following. "We will purchase said Alcatraz Island for twenty-four dollars (24) in glass beads and red cloth . . . We will give to the inhabitants of this island a portion of the land for their own to be held in trust . . . by the Bureau of Caucasian Affairs . . . Alcatraz Island is more than suitable for an Indian reservation . . . It is isolated . . . has no fresh running water . . . has inadequate sanitation facilities . . . no industry . . . soil is rocky and non-productive, and the land does not support game . . . . The population has always been held as prisoners and kept dependent upon others."

A "White Policy" was proposed in *The Indian News* in 1971 (February). "It is hereby suggested that we create a Department of White Affairs for a trial period of 100 years. This department will be run strictly by Indians selected on the basis of their political affiliations and their incompetence in the business world. White people will be looked on as White savages unless they adopt the Indian religion and the Indian way of life . . . They may keep the cities."

This woman's comments are from the *Native Press* of the Brotherhood of the Northwest Territories: "Indian is discovering that mothers of the little white girls who bring you home after school for a snack wash your dishes a second time. Indian is having a white woman tell you over and over and over that you are equal. Indian is having a white man approach you to tell you how much he likes Indian girls. Indian is having your teacher give you an assignment about 'being Indian' and wondering what she would write if you asked her to tell about 'being white.' "

Concerned about the Black use of Indians to further Black causes, Sam Kolb, an Indian leader in Los Angeles, said "Maybe they should create a NAACPAIL, National Association for the Advancement of Colored Peoples *and Indians Later*!" A cartoon in the *Bulletin* of the Indian-Eskimo Association of

Canada (1971, Vol. 12, No. 1) shows a Black riding at the back of the bus and an Indian still further back, outside riding on the back fender.

A Black man asked why there are so few Indians. "There wouldn't be many of your kind either if you had decided to play 'cowboys and Blacks.' They used to shoot us just to get the feathers."

"Indians go home!"

"What did the bleeding militant say?" "My Red Power is leaking out."

"The B.I.A. is having trouble with the Navajo's tribal computer because it prefers to think in Indian."

Williard Ahenakew, a Sandy Lake Cree cartoonist: Indian hunter shoots down Santa's reindeer, Indian Affairs hires *East* Indians, Indian wife chops the wood *before* attending her women's liberation meeting. In one of Duke Redbird's cartoons he had Charlie Squash see the sale of Japanese-made Indian souvenirs and then Charlie started selling Indian-made Japanese souvenirs.

CONCLUSIONS

There are indications that people from small-scale social settings, such as most reservations, do not stereotype as much as people from large-scale social settings. Instead, they tend to have concrete knowledge about people and make their differential value judgements about people in those terms. For example, a study on racial relations in an Alaskan fishing village (Jones 1973) indicated that the Whites grossly stereotyped the Natives while the Native Aleuts related to and discussed the Whites in concrete terms and as individually different people. When Natives enter large-scale society, however, they seem to stereotype Whites as much as they themselves are stereotyped.

Deloria (1970: 44) criticized minority groups for their stereotyping. "They must not fall into the same trap by simply reversing the process that has stereotyped them. Minority groups must thrust through the rhetorical blockade by creating within themselves a sense of 'peoplehood'." We need to understand and be somewhat tolerant of the fact that both majorities and minorities create stereotypes to work out their ideological problems. In the realm of stereotyped ethnic joking the extreme statement of beliefs can be played with to express deep feelings in a socially acceptable way.

Chapter 17

Militance Within the Native Movement

Militance is the regular social use of physical force or the threat of such force, not just individual acts of violence or nonviolent but enthusiastic activism. Militance in state societies is legally limited to authorized state agencies of internal policing and external warfare, but it is also illegally used in certain conditions of social protest, in organized crime, and in guerilla movements designed to disrupt or overthrow the existing state government. Militance is also expressed in gang warfare. One important problem of political militants is how to keep the public presentation of their acts defined as a morally valid social protest, rather than as immoral crime or warfare.

The popular level of explanation of the Indian political use of force is usually in the terms of the legal, moral, and value system of the dominant state society. The deprivation and frustration they feel may be very different than that of Whites living in their circumstances, but they must frame their complaints in White terms to win concessions from a White-dominated society. Thus, even though legalism, democracy, and materialism are not central values to traditional Indian cultures, they must validate their protests within these White values.

Social scientists who come from White middle-class cultural backgrounds find these rationalizations very reasonable. Therefore, the basic theories of militance revolve around relative deprivation and frustration of legal, democratic, and material values. The idea that the material poverty of the Indians is the basic cause of their protests is widely used by both Indian leaders and social scientists. Thus governments regularly mount programs for such things as Indian employment and housing, but the protests continue. What *do* Indians want? A lot of what they *really* want flows from their traditional values and cannot be created by laws or bought: retention of their heritage, pride and self-determination.

Indians do not assassinate, that is, kill public figures for political reasons. In fact, very few people have actually been killed in the twentieth century as a result of Indian political violence. Indians do not kidnap. They do not sabotage or wantonly destroy property. They did not bomb public places until 1975, when a B.I.A. office in Alameda, California was bombed. They are not generally "terroristic," do not commit impersonal, politically symbolic, violent acts against the general population. They are personal and they specifically target their violence. They rarely ever use economic protests, such as boycotts or strikes. Although they constitute a major segment or even a majority of the population of many prisons, they do not organize prison riots. In fact they tend to be such passive prisoners that, as one recent British Columbia study indicated, they do not push for their rights, and thus are rarely moved on to minimum security prisons where life is much better.

Indians do try to create mass media dramas, such as the occupation of Plymouth Rock and the Mayflower replica on Thanksgiving Day in 1970. There is a *long* history of these demonstrations. For example, in 1882 Piapot had his band camp on the right-of-way of the Canadian Pacific Railway in order to stop construction and further loss of Indian territory. They enjoy developing deeply symbolic "demonstrations," "occupations," "marches," and "confrontations," but of course these actions have somewhat different meanings to Whites than they do to the participants.

Crossing the U.S.-Canada border by force violates the values of both laws and nationalism of Americans and Canadians, but their claim of a right to do this is one of the few things which sets Native people apart from all others. To Natives it is a symbolic act which validates their identity, as well as being a social event and an annual holiday ritual for Indians in the border area. Indians are in the process of creating a new proud ideology and social cohesiveness, rather than arguing substantive issues with the dominant society; this process necessarily involves propagandizing both their own people and the dominant society. The activists are highly moralistic. They bring in religious issues and cultural heritage issues, and they take a moralistic stand on drinking, sex, and family life. They oppose individual heroics and favor collective action, although it is a basic pattern to say "We are ready to go to jail or even die for our cause."

An occupation is a cultural event of great significance to Indians, the stuff of which legends are made. While it has an aura of danger, it is a socially secure, institutionalized protest. The leaders paint a black picture about government oppression, the horrors of poverty, and the racism of White vigilantes, to satisfy the press and the social scientists. Meanwhile, the Indian followers in the background are basically having a good time for a good cause. They learn to drum and sing traditional chants. There is the camaraderie for young people in a crowd action, feeling powerful in a group.

One end product of a militant protest is that it can become an institutionalized symbol of a common history. Thus the U.S. celebrates its common symbol of militant protest, the Revolutionary War. The U.S. South celebrates the Civil War. The Iroquois border crossing protest became, in time, a mild, middle-class institution. Problems are minimized by crossing *into* the U.S., which agrees with the Jay Treaty provision on the free crossing of Indians (unlike Canada).

On July 17, 1976, the Ladies Auxiliary of the Native Canadian Centre of Toronto chartered a bus to Niagara Falls, Ontario for the *49th* Annual Border Crossing Parade. There they neatly lined up with other Indians from Tuscarora, Six Nations, the Indian Defense League of America, and the surrounding towns. The Oneida Drum and Brass Band, wearing large Plains-style feather war bonnets, led the parade. They were followed by The Indian Majorettes, the Tuscarora Indian Princess of 1976, and then the regular marchers—mostly women and children.

After the crossing, a celebration was held in a park on the U.S. side. Booths were set up to sell Indian crafts, corn soup, and bannock. There were speeches. The Mayor of Niagara Falls, New York and the guest speakers were made honorary members of the border crossing organization. A new Miss Indian Defense Association of America was chosen. Prizes were given for "traditionally" dressed babies, such as those wearing feather war bonnets. A baseball game and ballroom dancing followed in the evening.

WOUNDED KNEE II

The occupation lasted for 71 days, February 27 to May 8, 1973 in Wounded Knee, South Dakota. About three hundred Indians eventually became part of the armed force within the village and three hundred U.S. federal marshalls, Federal Bureau of Investigation servicemen, and policemen surrounded and blockaded the village. Two Indians were killed and two were wounded in the village and one federal agent was wounded. After several battles, ceasefires, and negotiations, the final agreement to abandon the occupation called for the Indians to, among other things, surrender their weapons and provide a list of persons who occupied the village in exchange for a meeting with the federal administration on certain requested issues. Before the occupation was ended more than one hundred Indians were in jail and a federal grand jury handed down more than thirty indictments, mostly for major felonies, as a consequence of the occupation. While most Indian periodicals disagreed with their methods, a wave of Native support came from all across the U.S. and Canada.

The news coverage by the White press was poor, reflecting once again that Native and White are two quite separate worlds. A large number of reporters went and they published many very shallow reports; they seem to have been satisfied with a few sensational events, quotable sayings, dramatic photographs, and historical analogies with the nineteenth-century massacre. As the press got tired of the story over the weeks of occupation they turned to cynicism. Thus, *Harper's* published an article in June titled "Bamboozle Me Not At Wounded Knee" with the central theme that "most of the press was fooled most of the time" by the sophisticated urban Indian leaders, who stage-managed a media event. At first they said that if the police would go away there would be no event and finally that if the news media would go away there would be no event. The Indians did a terrible job of public relations because the media repeatedly said that the basic violent protest was intended to remove a lawfully elected tribal president. To the militants the official had become a symbol of White assimilation and "selling out" to the government.

Russel Means was the major ideologist of Wounded Knee and, along with Dennis Banks, one of its organizers. I have abstracted an interview that Means gave to *The Indian Voice* in April 1973, in Wounded Knee.

"The American Indian Movement was founded by Dennis Banks, George Mitchell, and Clyde Belcourt in July 1968. It was primarily formed because there were 22 Indian organizations in the City of Minneapolis . . . that weren't reaching the people even though they were receiving funds, sizable funds . . . . The first issue they attacked was law and order . . . . They were primarily responsible for the creation of a legal rights center where poor people could attain private lawyers who donate their time . . . . They branched out into attacking and challenging the churches . . . . I joined after these two accomplishments . . . at an urban Indian conference in San Francisco . . . in October of 1969. At that time, a Crow by the name of . . . and myself had created our own organization . . . the Cleveland American Indian Center . . . "

(*Note*: On Thanksgiving 1970 Means led the group that "captured" the ship Mayflower II. In June 1971 they briefly "occupied" Mount Rushmore and in September 1971 attempted to seize the B.I.A. central office. A.I.M. was involved in several important protests in 1972 and in early 1973 before Wounded Knee: investigations of the murder of Raymond Yellow Thunder in Gordon, Nebraska; a demonstration for the fishing rights of the people of Cass Lake, Minnesota; the Trail of Broken Treaties in Washington, D.C.; a protest in Custer, South Dakota over the beating of some Indian people and a complaint that the murderer of an Indian was getting his charge lowered from first degree murder to second degree manslaughter; and a protest in Lincoln, Nebraska where an Indian was given ten years for "attempted rape.")

"After the Custer incident, we were in Rapid City . . . there was an internal political struggle happening on this reservation. And I, because I live on this reservation in Porcupine, South Dakota, but as an A.I.M. official I was prevented from coming home because if I did it had adverse effects on what the Oglala people wanted done internally and politically on this reservation. So I stayed in Rapid City . . . And finally, when we got official invitation from three organizations which represented about 85% or more of the Oglala people on this reservation . . . So we came down, and met two days with the chiefs and Holy men of Oglala, and got their complete support and direction in the maneuver, in the decision to take the Wounded Knee. We decided on Wounded Knee because primarily they had turned Pine Ridge Village, where the Bureau of Indian Affairs has its office, into a fort.

"I would say that 90% of the people here at Wounded Knee are Oglala and from this reservation. Now, that's the reason we decided by 7:30 Tuesday night, February 27th that we would go into Wounded Knee, rather than Pine Ridge, because it was fortified, you know, and we had no chance of a confrontation there. And also because of the historic value here where they massacred Indians . . . also the issue here was this trader who rips off Indian people continuously and violates federal law every day . . .

"Violations by the trader were the Truth and Lending Act, the Usury Laws, Postal violations. The fact that he hasn't had a license to operate on this reservation for 15 years . . . extortion and coercion of Indian people . . . . Threats, assaults, you know, both verbal and physical have happened to Indian people here by the proprietors of this trading post.

"We demanded . . . our treaty rights. And then, we want separation of landowners on reservations . . . Indian landowners out from underneath B.I.A. and tribal authority so that they can deal directly with the Secretary of Interior . . . . We want to find out about easement rights of way, taxes that the federal government through the Department of Interior is supposed to be collecting at least for this tribe since 1936. They are supposed to collect $5 per ten foot of easement per year from the rural electrical companies and telephone companies . . . . White people who are using Indian land on this reservation leased out by the B.I.A. . . . the ranchers, the farmers, the traders, the White businessmen . . . gross, out of Indian land, twelve million dollars a year, on this reservation . . . . We also want an investigation into the B.I.A. educational system on this reservation which spends two and a half times the national average per pupil per school year . . . . And we still have a 63% dropout rate? . . .

"The Whiteman has always dealt in violence and that's the only thing he understands. As far as Indian people go the only time you can get the Whiteman to open up his eyes and his ears is when there is a physical threat. Now the strategy of the American Indian Movement is to present that physical threat . . . .

"There's only two kinds of Indians in my mind. There's the Indian people and there's the sellouts. And there's no shades of grey. There might be ignorance. But, in my mind, in the Indian world, you are either an Indian or you're a sellout. But if you're an Indian and you use a different tactic in a total war, you know, I can respect that."

Violence was part of the culture of Pine Ridge before and after the occupation at Wounded Knee. The occupation greatly intensified a general pattern of violence. It accelerated personal revenge and retaliations through shooting sprees on individuals and rifle and fire attacks on each other's cars and houses. In 1974 alone there were 23 unsolved murders on the Pine Ridge Reservation, as well as a large number of beatings and property damage actions. In 1975 the carnage continued, picking up press attention when two F.B.I. agents and an Indian were killed and hundreds of federal police officers occupied the reservation in July.

At Means' trial in Sioux Falls, South Dakota in May 1974, Indians in the courtroom refused to stand for the judge, the judge asked the police to clear the courtroom, and a battle took place in the courtroom that led to the hospitalization of six police officers and four Indians. Two Indians were killed when their car was struck by a police cruiser speeding to the courthouse fight. Means and Dennis Banks eventually won their case because of illegal activities of the government and their attorneys: illegal wiretaps, paid witnesses, F.B.I. informers, the submission of altered evidence, lies under oath, and the unauthorized use of military people in civilian disguise.

On June 7, 1975 Means tried to stop a fight in North Dakota and was shot in the back by a police officer's son. The son was not charged. Means was charged for resisting and interfering with a federal officer. Later Means was charged with assaulting a man in a bar which Means denied even entering. Means was shot at about 4:00 p.m. The first hospital he was taken to refused to treat him because, they said, if Means should die here "They'll burn this place down." They finally found a hospital that accepted him for treatment at 10:30 p.m.

Means said "Since Wounded Knee I've been arrested twelve times, an average of once every two months. I'm facing seven trials now. It's kind of ironic that I moved to North Dakota to get away from South Dakota and confrontations and danger. And right away, I'm arrested twice, shot in the back, and forced into a confrontation situation . . . any person with a bloody nose can go in and sign a complaint against me. It is like the old days when militants were called renegades and a chief would be blamed for five different raids in five different states within five days on horseback."

On June 23 charges of assault were laid against Means for an assault on June 6 in McLaughlin, *South* Dakota at a time when Means was actually the guest of honor at a powwow at Fort Berthold, *North* Dakota. Investigation later proved that the policeman who brought the charges had accidentally shot himself.

On July 9, en route by air from New York to North Dakota to attend his trial in the case in which he was shot, Means was arrested at the Minneapolis, Minnesota airport, on an old charge related to being in a car that was displaying improper car license plates. He was arrested and booked at the county jail. The Minneapolis police are hypersensitive to A.I.M. activities because the organization began in their city in 1968.

In the three years between the end of the occupation in May 1973 and May 1976, over two hundred Indians died of violence in South Dakota. In one 1976 case the autopsy report claimed that a Canadian Indian woman died of exposure, but the woman's mother did not believe it. She had her daughter's body exhumed and a new autopsy done. The first autopsy had been done so rapidly that it missed the obvious fact that she had been shot to death and the bullet was still in her head.

Red Power demonstrations have some integration and similarity by drawing from the new international Native movement everywhere, but they also vary locally in systematic ways according to the nature of contemporary local cultures. The Alcatraz occupation was significantly different from the Wounded Knee occupation, from the point of view of both Indian action and White reaction. Broadly characterized, the Alcatraz Indians were more culturally diverse, academic, idealistic, and acculturated. They were more from West Coast Indian cultures, although one of the organizers, Richard Oakes, was a Mohawk and many eastern militants dropped in, such as the Sioux Lehman Brightman and the Iroquois Mad Bear Anderson.

The San Francisco Bay location of Alcatraz meant that this racial and ethnic protest was relatively well received by the local White culture. San Francisco is extremely tolerant of racial and ethnic diversity while South Dakota is comparatively intolerant of it. Alcatraz was fun for all, but Wounded Knee was a more serious, even deadly game as Indians began to be killed. This kind of dangerous game of military confrontation, however, brought the local covert racism to the surface and into the light of national news media as U.S. armored vehicles and federal police surrounded the town.

Rosalie Wax (1972) wrote about the patterns of physical expression, individual heroics, and peer-group ranking and loyalty among young Oglala Sioux men, patterns I felt were expressed at Wounded Knee II.

> *Sioux boys are reared to be physically reckless and impetuous. One that does not perform an occasional brave act may be accepted as "quiet" or "bashful," but he is not considered to be a desirable son, brother, or sweetheart. Sioux boys are reared to be proud and feisty and are expected to resent public censure. They have some obligations to relatives; but the major social controls after infancy are exerted by their fellows—their "peer group . . . ."*

Wounded Knee II in retrospect is more comprehensible when we add to Sioux male enculturation that some had military experience in Viet Nam. These men then returned to a state with a highly visible percentage of Indians in the total population and a long history of Indian-White conflicts. Some were involved with incidents and militant protests of the A.I.M. in 1972 and early 1973. At the Pine Ridge Reservation, as at so many reserves, those "quiet" men with the skills and temperament to work in White bureaucracies are usually elected or appointed but they are still opposed by the "reckless" men as too easily co-opted and conned by White society. The protest at Pine Ridge in the Winter of 1973 had a complex setting in terms of the memory of an historic massacre, local White prejudice, patterns of the enculturation of Sioux boys, military experiences, A.I.M. protests, and conflicts in reservation politics.

ANICINABE PARK AND THE BATTLE OF PARLIAMENT HILL

Public Indian protests in Canada picked up significant momentum and militance in the late summer and fall of 1974. The general public was made aware of (1) the blockade by Indians of the highway through their reserve near Cache Creek, B.C.; (2) the occupation by the Ojibway Warriors' Society of Anicinabe Park in Kenora, Ontario from July 22 to August 28; and (3) the journey of a Native People's Caravan, which left Vancouver on September 14, crossed the country giving speeches at rallies along the way, had a violent confrontation with the RCMP on Parliament Hill in Ottawa at the fall opening of Parliament, and then occupied the abandoned Carbide Warehouse on Victoria Island in the Ottawa River, declaring it to be the Native People's Embassy.

There is no ethnography of Kenora, but there is one of Sioux Lookout, 144 miles to the east. (Stymeist 1975). Indians in the town are largely transient and outcasts, although Indian shopping and government services to Indians support major industries in the town. The patterns of racial prejudice, legal discrimination, and employment discrimination are among the most severe in Canada. This is where the urban-White versus bush-Indian cultural frontiers meet in the mid-corridor area of Canada; thus this is where Indian-White conflicts are the most severe. The situation is much better for Natives in the urban world, which is primarily in southern Canada, or in the true bush, such as the hunting and trapping areas and the Arctic. To live with Whites in the city, Indians must learn to ignore insults and to clown, joke, and shuffle like southern U.S. Blacks have traditionally done. A small Indian boy died in the hospital and they shipped his body back to his parents, notifying them only that he was coming back. The family gathered at the train stop to greet their son; only a coffin was unloaded.

In reaction to the idea that the Indian and White hospitals in the city would be amalgamated, "A typical argument ran as follows . . . If you were going in to have a baby how would you feel if you found one of those long, black Indian hairs in the linen? Even if you wash the sheets several times you can't be sure to get it all out." (p. 75) An Indian man and wife were arrested for arguing outside a pub. The judge said "What were you people doing in town anyway? Did you have a job here? . . . Well, if you would stay out of places that you don't belong none of this would happen to you. Fifty dollars or thirty days." (p. 79)

Kenora is a small city with 11,000 population on the north shore of Lake of the Woods, 150 miles east of Winnipeg. It is the urban center for 7,000 Indians who live in surrounding reserves. There are 23 reserves in Treaty No. 3 Grand Council from Thunder Bay to the Manitoba border and from the Minnesota border to Red Lake. Three of the reserves are adjacent to the Kenora city limits. The Indians in the area continue to do some hunting, fishing, and gathering, but have become increasingly dependent upon welfare. The major Western-oriented industries in the area are tourism and forestry. Tourism and fishing have declined somewhat in recent years because the pulp and paper mills have been contaminating certain major streams with mercury. In 1973 there was a further decline in Kenora's economic situation when its railroad repair shops were relocated out of the city. However, economic growth in this area has always been slow, with a chronically high and seasonal unemployment problem.

In 1965 the Indians of Kenora, under the leadership of Peter Kelly, made a protest march on the City Council and complained about discrimination, policing problems, lack of jobs and lack of treatment for alcoholics. In response the Alcohol and Drug Research Centre opened a branch office and a detoxification service in 1968, but this apparently had little effect on the growing Indian alcoholism and alcohol-related arrest rates. In 1973 there were about 6,900 arrests for public drunkenness in Kenora, predominantly of Indians. Kenora created a housing authority that provided some inexpensive housing in the city, but one survey showed that almost all of the families living in them were White. A housing survey in June 1973 found that 85 Indians and Métis in the city had *no* homes.

A report on sudden Indian deaths in Kenora released by the Concerned Citizens Committee of Kenora described a "deadly cycle of liquor, welfare, and violence." In the report Peter Kelly complained that the Indians living on the islands of Big Island, Big Grassy, Gabaskong, and Northwest Angle were relocated to their present mainland sites without their consent. Kelly believes that this move disrupted the early social stability, in part by disrupting the clan system. The report is credited as one element in the creation of the Ojibway Warriors' Society, although the leader Louis Cameron considers his society to be one branch of the American Indian Movement. The Warriors oppose the use of alcoholic beverages, observe the traditional Midewiwin religion, and believe that Christianity has degraded their culture.

In November 1973 the Kenora Indian Affairs office was occupied by the Ojibway Warriors' Society for one day to protest a nearby sawmill's mercury poisoning of fish on the Grassy Narrows Reserve, police brutality, racial discrimination, the possession of Ojibway Medicine Society sacred scrolls by museums, and the relocation of Indians in the James Bay Hydroelectric Project. Louis Cameron, the co-chairman of the Warriors at the time, said "We want basic freedom of government, complete with economic co-jurisdiction over our communities. We are going back and learning from our elders, and learning the old ways . . . . Many people feel that when we leave the building this morning it will be over. Well, it won't be. This is just the beginning."

In July 1974 the Warriors sponsored an Ojibwa National Conference in Anicinabe Park that drew three hundred participants, including Dennis Banks, the A.I.M. leader, as a speaker. The Warriors asked the Kenora City Council to close down all the bars in the city during the Conference, but the Council refused and added to its police staff instead. They did, however, grant permission for the park to be used for the Conference. At the end of the Conference on July 22 the Warriors barricaded the roads into the park and announced that they were seizing it as "liberated Indian territory." Cameron said that those in the park "are willing to die before giving the park back to the Whiteman." The Warriors said that it was Indian land anyway, really a part of the Rat Portage Reserve purchased with Indian Affairs money in 1929 and sold illegally and without Indian consent to the town in 1959.

Indians today usually "occupy" places that are of particular symbolic importance in Indian-White relations and are vulnerable to public sentiment because they are owned by government—or occasionally by churches or big businesses. Land squatters the world over quickly learn who the vulnerable land owners are, and generally it is government owned land, whether in Latin America, Africa, or North America. It appears that the fourteen acres of land had become a symbol of the Indian-White conflict in Kenora. Before the sale of the land the Indians from surrounding reserves would pitch their tents there while visiting Kenora. Whites, concerned about the appearance of drunken Indians on the main street and the growth of a shack town on the outskirts, and hopeful regarding the possibility of added income and services in tourism, pressured the federal government into selling the Indian land to the city to establish a campground.

This is some of what Louis Cameron said to a *Toronto Star* reporter in August in Anicinabe during a ceasefire period. At the time there were about eighty Indians in the park, including some fifty women and children. "I'm from Whitedog. We cannot fish any more because the fish is dangerous to eat with mercury pollution . . . . If life is to continue for Indian people, life must depend on free land. And our people must take guns and free that land. By law and by administration of government we cannot go to Ottawa because they wouldn't even listen to us . . . . They are constantly giving Indian organizations hundreds of thousands of dollars, millions of dollars to Indian organizations across the country . . . the tribal nations never benefit from any of that millions of dollars . . . the Indian organizations, just like the government, don't know what they are doing . . . Ninety-five percent of the 7,000 Indian people in Northwestern Ontario have no jobs . . . There is no base of economy on any of those (23) reserves. Some of them have semi-economic outfits like sawmills and tanning factories, sewing factories—things very preliminary . . . We seek to abolish the Indian Affairs department. We seek to abolish the Indian Act. We demand that the brothers from Wounded Knee who face criminal charges have their charges dropped. We demand that police brutality in this area stop. We demand that court judges get fired, that the racist employees of Indian Affairs in this area get fired and taken away. We are demanding that we get representation in the municipal council because hundreds of our people come to town.

"This is the first part of the Ojibway nation that has been liberated in a long time . . . . We believe that we're standing on the same ground as Louis Riel, the same ground that Crowfoot was standing on, and Chief Red Sky of Lake of the Woods. And what they are fighting for is what we are fighting for, the same thing, a human right."

The final agreement on August 29 under which the Indians agreed to leave the park included the declaration that the park would remain "free land" until further settlement is reached. However, four Indians had been arrested and warrants were issued for 23 others considered to be "ringleaders."

Cameron said he was impressed with a tiny band of Quakers who camped in the park during the occupation in order to put their bodies between the two sides if shooting started. "We accepted them, not because they were Quakers but because they were people prepared to act."

This is some of what Cameron said in an interview published n the September issue of *The Indian Voice*, after the occupation had ended. "The Department of Indian Affairs is prone to give cultural grants, when what we need is bread and butter. In reality, the Department of Indian Affairs are keeping our people in regional concentration camps, in wretched and dangerous conditions. In an effort to solve some of these problems we had the Ojibway Nation Conference. We invited experts in the medical, economic, and social welfare to consult with our people.

"The town council of Kenora ordered 150 extra armed police to come to Kenora during our conference. We considered this was an outrageous insult to the Ojibway Nation . . . . Before the Conference was over there were 300 armed police brought in from as far as Sault Ste. Marie. We were completely surrounded, everywhere police were lurking around us.

"The park was a historical site of our people. The Department of Indian Affairs stole the property from us and sold it illegally to the town of Kenora. When we went into the park to liberate our land we took guns, not to attack the community but to protect our women and children from outside belligerence . . . . Our medicine men told us that guns were a serious tool of survival . . . . Our women cautioned us to be aware of the responsibility of using guns.

"Our women cooked constantly . . . . We had coffee and sandwiches all night long. The women brought food to our Warriors at their security posts. We were under fire from vigilantes shooting into our camp. We returned fire to make them back off.

"During the first truce we pulled back our front line . . . . We negotiated for two or three days and then the negotiating broke down. The second truce was broken by the Justice Department of Ontario. That is when they cut off our food, communications, and completely surrounded us. We were engulfed by police on the water, in the air, and on the land. Police cars cruising back and forth every 15 seconds, sirens screaming, and blow horns telling us to surrender. With high-powered telescopic rifles aimed at us we were under 24-hour surveillance. All through the crisis there were phone calls . . . messages from families . . . watch out!, be careful, we are worried!

"It was during the third truce that we asked all Indian leaders across Canada to come and talk with us . . . . The Indian leaders said we support your objective, but not your methods. And we accepted that because we did not want to split the Indian community. We respect our Indian leaders and feel a deep urge to embrace our people, each one, every man, woman, and child. But if our people are to condemn us for taking up arms, then they must condemn Louis Riel, Crowfoot, and Almighty Voice because our problems have not improved since their time, but have grown worse . . . . We're not radicals or militants. We are just Indian people taking a stand against the tragic plight of our people."

On September 14 a Native People's Caravan left Vancouver to go to Ottawa for the fall opening of Parliament. Speeches were given at several Indian rallies along the way. Rumors circulated through the mass communications media that some young Warriors were prepared to die for their cause and planned to storm into Parliament as human bombs with explosives strapped to their bodies.

The Toronto Rally of the Caravan on September 28 said "The Caravan is going to Ottawa on September 30th to make these demands at the opening of Parliament.

1. Recognition and respect for the treaty rights and aboriginal rights of Native people.
2. An end to the Indian Act.
3. A full investigation of the Department of Indian Affairs *by Native people* for the purpose of dissolving it.
4. A just settlement of Indian land claims.
5. Decent housing for Native people.
6. Economic development of the reserves.
7. Adequate health care and education for Native peoples."

On September 30 about three hundred Indians charged the barricades set up in anticipation of their attack in front of Parliament, scuffled with the RCMP, pushed toward the central doorway, and shouted for the Prime Minister and the Indian Affairs Minister. Meanwhile, some Indians threw rocks, some drummed and chanted, and others burned a Canadian flag. Then about two hundred RCMP formed a three-deep human wall by the shattered barricades in front of Parliament. The Indians surged forward again, pressing against the line of police, smashing street lights, and setting fire to a clump of pine trees. Nine officers were reported as injured by flying objects. A special RCMP riot squad arrived armed with long batons, plexiglass shields, and tear-gas guns, driving back the advancing Indians.

Some Indian spokesmen said that the RCMP riot squad launched a premeditated assault on the Indians. The Indian Affairs Minister deflected blame from both the police and the Indians by emphasizing that White Communist agitators were involved in the demonstrations. "The Maoists were out in fairly substantial numbers and I don't think the Indians were happy to have them."

After "the Battle of Parliament Hill" about seventy Indians moved into the Carbide Warehouse on Victoria Island. Cameron, who emerged as one of the leaders of the Caravan when it reached Ontario, said "For now, we claim this building, wrecked as it is, as the Embassy of the Native People. We have always recognized ourselves as an independent nation in this formal democracy."

The next day Peter Kelly, also a leader of the Caravan and head of the

Treaty No. 3 Grand Council based in Kenora, asked the federal and provincial governments to (1) pay for food and essentials for members of the Caravan who were occupying the deserted federal building in Ottawa, (2) pay the return fare for the Ottawa demonstrators, (3) drop all criminal charges laid against Indians the previous day (about fifteen arrests had been made), and (4) investigate the provoking attack made by the RCMP squad on the Indians.

MILITANCE IN CANADA

Indians lean toward what we could classify as "warriors," those who would use violence for both social control and social change. That is, they would not be classified as "pacifists" (who avoid violence), "anarchists" (who use violence for change), or "vigilantes" (who use violence for control). Large numbers of Indians volunteered and fought in the U.S. and Canadian armies during times of war. They are also noted for their excellence in police work. On the other side they are noted for their use of violence to induce social changes. Studies by two sociologists in southern Alberta help us to understand some of the complexities involved in the Canadian Indian uses of violence.

Frideres (1975) did a content analysis of newspaper reports of collective actions by Indians in Canada. He sampled nine major newspapers in three-year sequences from 1950 to 1974 for (1) number of incidents, (2) whether the incidents were "facilitative" (conferences, legal, civil libertarian, etc.) or "obstructive" (occupations, blockades, marches, etc.), and (3) whether the incidents were provincial or national in focus. His data indicate an increase over time of over 400% in 24 years of the number of collective actions reported. There are also generally correlated increases in the proportion of these actions which are "obstructive" (from 10% to 40%) and of "national focus" (from 10% to 47%).

His data include the usual patterns of regional differences in recent Indian-White relationships: the most peaceful in Quebec, moderate conflict in Ontario and British Columbia, and high conflict in the Prairies. There is also a suggestion in his data of distinct histories of Indian obstructive militance, perhaps correlated with the phases of urban ethnic institutionalization: little ever in Montreal, a variable and moderate level in Vancouver, a single strong wave in Toronto in the 1950s, a strong wave in Winnipeg from 1959 on, and finally late waves in Regina and Calgary in the 1970s.

In 1970 Boldt (1973) surveyed the attitudes of 69 Canadian Indian leaders. Thirty-nine, or 56%, of the leaders said they would approve and participate in extra-legal activities for Indian causes. I have ranked some of the data from this survey. The percentage figure in each case is the proportion of this category of the survey sample who would *approve and participate in extra-legal activities.*

1. Age is more than 60 years (100%) or less than 30 (83%) (Ages 30-59 - 33%-47%).
2. Dark in skin color (83%) (medium 47%, light 17%).
3. Reside off their reserve (80%) (on reserve 50%).

4. Attended a Catholic school (74%) (integrated 30%, Protestant 25%, government 13%).
5. Have a low income (68%) (high income 23%).
6. Have an elementary education (68%) (secondary 54%, university 42%).
7. Male (62%) (female 33%).

The 1970 Canadian Indian leaders who in an interview context were particularly oriented to extra-legal actions tended to be old or young, but not middle-aged; believe that Indians need independence or autonomy; are strongly Indian in cultural orientation; are dark in skin color; are pessimistic; and reside off their reserves.

Beyond this personal context we need to understand why the Kenora Ojibwa turned to militance. The popular theories seem to be a "drinking theory" and some combination of a "White injustice theory," and "unemployment theory," and a "poverty theory." While I think these are important factors in the relative social status of Indians, there are other underlying conditions that may be even more significant, in part as determinants of drinking, injustice, unemployment, and poverty.

The primary problem of the Ojibwa has been their cultural destruction; their current political activism is a healthy sign that they are reestablishing their society in a modern form to deal more adequately with their underlying problems. They are trying to unify their society once again and militance seems to be one effective channel.

It is only now, in the later twentieth century, that the Ojibwa are developing tribal nationalism. The Ojibwa of southern Ontario have been in closer and more harmonious contact with White culture and thus are more acculturated to it. This can be shown by comparing their situations, structurally similar in certain ways, with those Ojibwa who come into Kenora. Ojibwa live on the Garden River Reserve just outside of the city of Sault Ste. Marie, on the Sarnia Reserve just outside of Sarnia, and on the Walpole Island Reserve just outside of Wallaceburg. Each of these cities has a large number of Ojibwa Indians who regularly visit there, shop there, drink there, and so forth, and yet in each case Indian-White relations seem to be fairly harmonious. It may be that the north is somewhat more of an intolerant, rough, frontier context for interaction.

In the southern Ontario cities there has been a fairly strong demand for permanent, rather than just seasonal, labor. Indians have been able to get jobs in the cities. Their reserve land itself is so valuable that parts of it may be leased to Whites for cottage, industrial, or farm use. Urban Indian ethnic institutions have been built up in Sault Ste. Marie, Sarnia, and Wallaceburg in the form of kinship-friendship networks and voluntary associations. These institutions provide the contexts for satisfying social interaction beyond the somewhat dysfunctional first-order institutions, such as bar cliques and White-dominated agencies that are designed to solve "Indian problems." Kenora's Ojibway Warriors' Society is best understood as a relatively advanced, third-order ethnic institution that is competing for a social commitment by Ojibwa people with the dysfunctional first-order ethnic institutions such as the ones mentioned above.

Chapter 18

Politics and Economics

THE POLITICAL LEFT

A recent conference of The Toronto Alliance Against Racism and Political Oppression illustrated some of the problems that Natives have in alliances with the White political left. The Native speakers came late and left early. They talked in an anecdotal and emotional way about their personal experiences. The Natives had no specific plans or schedules, no political tracts to hand out, no rallies to attend. One Indian speaker was booed when he said he was leaving his telephone number with the conference officials, "just in case some of you girls want to call me." In the Indian context this is a joke, but to the urban political left it is a sexist slur.

Natives talk about the sacredness of the treaties, the need to expand the reserves and to respect the traditional religious leaders, the "special status" and "citizen's plus" character of the Native position in society, and the importance of tribalistic and nationalistic movements. In opposition to this, the political left favors total equality and opposes Indian treaties, reserves, religious leaders, special status, and nationalism. The far left would like Natives to join the oppressed proletariat: women who are being discriminated against, the racial minorities, and the industrial laborers. They want Indians to abandon their middle-class multi-cultural aims; admit that they are integrated in the bottom of a class-structured society; and ally themselves with the proletarian revolutionary movement. Native problems are very attractive as a political bandwagon for the left, but the Native people insist on solving their problems in their own way.

The traditional politics of tribal societies was extremely egalitarian, tolerant of individual opinions and differences, and consensual when collective action was called for. There was, in brief, very little politics at all, with only limited powers allocated to political representatives. Chiefdoms were more political. They did have social ranking, some general development of social classes, more entrepreneurial elements, and more centralization of political power.

In historic times the White bureaucracy pressed all of the diverse Native societies into using elections and political centralization. Economic dependency in government programs as communal groups on communal land was a politically left kind of pressure in history. On the right there have been such facts as the volunteering of many Indians for military service in WORLD WAR I and WORLD WAR II and their activity in war veterans' associations. There was a right-left dilemma in the U.S. in the 1930s, when Indians were divided over the enhancement of traditional tribal communalism by the Indian Reorganization Act or a continuation of the individual and free enterprise elements of the Indian heritage. While the contextual societies were capitalistic, the bureaucratic administration of Indians has tended to be socialistic. There has been very little government effort to promote the capitalistic abilities of Indians: individual enterprise, savings investment, and business management.

Recent books by three social scientists in the Canadian prairies show a shift toward politically left interpretations of Indian problems: James Frideres, a sociologist in Alberta; Howard Adams, a Métis professor of education in Saskatchewan; and Peter Elias, an anthropologist in Manitoba.

Frideres (1974) wrote that the reserves are exploited hinterlands from which the natural resources were taken, that industries are not developed on the reserves, that Natives are purposely kept as a cheap labor pool, and that the profits from the raw material production from reserves goes to Whites. "Corporations don't want natives to get federal finance. They have so far been successful because of the close relationship in the past between the political and economic elite. If natives were able to get finance for economic development . . . (i) they would remove a source of income from these companies . . . and (ii) they would drain off the labor surplus and increase prices . . . the white structure wants to convince the native that individual entrepreneurship is the answer but the result will be continued subordination." (P. 172.) Frideres claimed that the practice of keeping Indians in a state of colonial subordination has been economically advantageous to Whites, with "profits" of $60 billion accruing to Whites over the past 100 years. His solution is community-run enterprises.

In fact, the 2,281 Indian reserves in Canada are small, scattered, and usually poor in natural resources. Most of the productive land was taken from Indians by military, legal, or administrative means long ago. Whether it is owned by

Indians or Whites, very little of this kind of rural land is industrially developed in Canada. On the question of net economic flows, it is true that total per capita government expenditures are greater for services to Whites than for Indians, but Whites per capita pay far more taxes and make a greater economic contribution. The net balance of payments to and from Indians, including the relatively minimal natural resources taken from their reserves, has probably not been on the positive side for Whites, since Canadian society seriously began to provide reserve Indians with social services about twenty years ago. The question of social justice, however, is a different matter and Canadian society should expect to support the services and economic development of Native communities for the sake of justice, as well as a return to the aboriginal rights of Natives.

Adams (1975) maintains that Indians in Canada were maintained as a special class of workers so that they could continue to be easily exploited as trappers in the imperialistic fur-trading industry. This dominant-subordinate relationship was maintained through racism. "White supremacy, which had been propagated since the beginning of European imperialism, became woven into Canadian institutions such as the church, the schools, and the courts, and it has remained the working ideology of these institutions. In addition, native people cannot avoid seeing the cultural images and symbols of white supremacy, because they are everywhere in society . . . " (p. 8).

Adams writes that native society was prevented from developing along with the nation's advancing technology and economy. Emphasis was placed on the archaic features of native societies so that they ossified. "Indians and Métis collaborate with their white oppressors by portraying archaic culture through such public spectacles as the Calgary Stampede. They present themselves as aboriginal people with a primitive culture . . . Teepees are exhibited, tomahawks and primitive tools displayed . . . They dress in traditional Indian garmets, sit around and smoke the peace pipe . . . Whites insist upon seeing Indians in this primitive way because it corresponds to their stereotypes."

Adams presents the Riel Rebellion as a legal struggle for Western rights that was converted by the Eastern establishment into an Indian uprising, enabling the Canadian government to acquire greater control over the Western territories. Adams is critical of the National Indian Brotherhood and the Native Council of Canada as "typical middle-class bureaucracies that are not at all representative of the native masses." He believes that the current cultural nationalism of Natives is reactionary and "part of the ideology of imperialism . . . it involves the revival of indigenous native traditions and tribalism." He favors a "radical nationalism" with "civil-rights methods such as picketing, demonstrations, boycotts, sit-ins, as well as confrontations and guerilla activities." (P. 202.)

Adams opposes integration, capitalism, most government self-help programs, most educational and cultural programs, and most Native organizations. He favors decentralized, local organizations that are based on local grievances. He supports democratic, politicized, spontaneous, revolutionary activities that can rupture the system by confrontations, such as seizing control of a school.

I appreciate the need for mass action, but Adams presents a very narrow view of the development of Native society. Natives also have many other productive avenues open to them to increase their self-determination, such as voting in a democratic society and entrepreneurship in a capitalist society.

Elias (1975) is an anthropologist who disagrees with deculturation theories and denies the value and reality of multiculturalism. He prefers a class-struggle analysis. He claims that the Natives are integrated into an industrial, class-ranked, capitalistic society as a rural proletariat dominated by a metropolitan-based, powerful elite who maintain a conspiracy of economic and political control over the rural hinterland. He writes that in the colonial period Indians were resource laborers; they could trap, but only the Europeans could trade or hold skilled jobs. The trading empires were carefully managed monopolies, keeping the trapper tied to a single post by debts and restriction of the trapping territories. In time, the colonial situation gave way to the incorporation of more and more Natives into the jobs at the bottom of the class system. Natives were absorbed into a wage economy to transport goods, clear land, and build houses and churches.

Elias did a study of Churchill, Manitoba. It began in 1927 as a rail terminus to ship grain from the prairies through Hudson Bay. It later became a stopping point for American aircraft in WORLD WAR II and then a center for rocketry research. Elias found extreme job discrimination: (1) 65% of the adult Whites, but only 29% of the adult Natives are employed; (2) the private sector keeps costs low by employing White women and Natives and paying them the minimum wage; (3) only 4% of all Whites work part-time, but 40% of all working Natives work part-time; and (4) Whites receive the high-paying jobs through nepotism, friendships, and hiring in southern Canada.

Natives are counted as taxpayers in applications for local government grants to maintain services, but are not given those services: garbage collection, fire protection, snow removal, street lighting, etc. This is locally rationalized by saying that the Chipewyan are treaty Indians so the federal government is responsible for them; the Cree live on crown land so the provincial government should look out for them. It is also said by Whites that most of the Cree are unemployed and are not pulling their weight anyway.

Natives are counted as full citizens when allotments are made for education in the community and 52% of the students are Natives. However, these funds are diverted to satisfy White, upper-class education needs: library, swimming pool, skating rink, community hall, and administrative offices. There are no plans to provide the Native communities with water, sewer, or electrical services. Two native communities, the Flats and Dene Village, are not even on the architect's maps. What can the Natives do about these local level politics? Whites are clearly in control. In view of the overlapping directorships and extra-group powers of Whites, and the extreme fragmentation of Native political powers, there are no indications that the local Natives are capable of making any significant changes in the racism and discrimination in Churchill.

Apparently, it will take the help of outside organizations, such as the Manitoba Indian Brotherhood and the National Indian Brotherhood, to politically organize the Churchill Native community. This is the kind of situation where the revolutionary confrontations that Howard Adams speaks of should have been generated out of local grievances. The leftist theory is that problems lead to their own solution through mass action. This ignores the evolutionary and historical differences between societies, since mass action comes easier to societies with a tribal and chiefdom heritage than to the rather apolitical band heritage societies, such as the Chipewyan, Cree, and Inuit of Churchill.

WENJACK: THE TORONTO CHAPTER OF A.I.M.

In 1971 a few young Indian men, mostly recently arrived Ojibwas, were stimulated by the idea of using militance within the general Indian movement. They patterned their methods after the American Indian Movement, founded in 1968 in Minneapolis: (1) patrolling the downtown streets to prevent police harassment of Indians; (2) travelling around to settle reservation and rural problems by the encouragement of legal cases or political pressure, and, when all else fails, physical force; (3) appealing to funds and other support from Church groups, university students, and others in the White liberal establishment; and (4) pressuring the established, government-financed Indian organizations to move faster and more militantly for Indian ideals.

These informal militant cliques began to coalesce in Toronto in 1974 when they participated in the occupation of Anicinabe Park and the Native People's Caravan. In 1975 they had an office and a formal organization in Toronto called Wenjack. They also had loose alliances with other "warriors" societies which collectively claimed to have 45,000 members in the U.S. and Canada. Wenjack is a political association, a third-order ethnic institution, that evolved in the city directly out of dysfunctional first-order ethnic institutions, the bar cliques. The third-order quality of this institution is illustrated in the opposition it has with the first and second order institutions. The following is an abstract of a presentation Wenjack made at York University in 1975.

"We named ourselves Wenjack after Willie Dunn's song about Charlie Wenjack, a young boy who ran away from residential school in the winter, and tried to walk the 640 miles back to his home. We feel there is more than a little of Charlie in all of us, escaping the smothering prisons of an alien culture, the white man's world, to attempt the long walk home, and perhaps—like Charlie—to die trying.

"We were all beat up pretty bad at first, but we kept coming back night after night, until they knew they couldn't stop us from protecting our people. It was like a rebirth to many of us, standing up and saying 'NO' to the conditions that kept us down for so long . . . We were proud to be Indian, but many of us knew very little of our language and culture. Our parents and their parents had been beaten in residential schools for speaking Indian, isolated from their elders and imposed in a regimental system that taught them to be ashamed of anything Indian, taught them to become second-class white men . . .

"The main problem in Toronto with Indian people is drinking in the bars. We have all tried to stop the pain with the oblivion of alcohol, many of us have seen that we don't have a need to drink as much or as often since we've been engaged in positive action. Any persons who participate in our peace-keeping patrols are not allowed to drink on duty . . . Our patrols are established in the Silver Dollar at the owner's request. We've successfully negotiated for Native people to be hired by the management as bouncers, for more considerate treatment of our people and to defuse racial tensions. Our patrols are recognized as legitimate with the support of the Police on that beat . . .

"Larry Johnson taught us the ways of the drum: to respect it and learn the songs. We now have several groups in Ontario who have started their own drums. The drum is the power of the earth and we are communicating our return to the ancient heritage of our people . . . We are invited to powwows many times a year where we drum and communicate our position by our actions . . . We always listen to our older people who advise us on our lives and goals and who instruct us on the legends and ways of our people. We've established and supported wilderness camps where this instruction takes place. Our Spiritual Advisor is Art Solomon, an older man in his fifties who has taught us how to make our lives in harmony with our mother the earth . . .

"Many times we've been involved in negotiations with different groups, as in Kenora . . . Last year, we took a trip that covered over 2,500 miles of visiting different reserves to ally our people into a realization of their rights under the Jay Treaty, a treaty between Britain and the United States in 1794, that gave Indian people free access to both sides of the border. We see the border as an arbitrary line put here by the White man that cuts Indian lands in half . . .

"We are aware of the 'social' problems that face Indian people today: racism, alcoholism, suicide, high infant mortality, low life expectancy, malnutrition and high rate of incarceration in prisons are only *symptoms* of one problem: the lack of spiritual, psychological, and physical sovereignty . . . desperate Indian people all over North America have taken their own destinies into their hands by supporting moves to land they have title to . . .

"All of us have worked 'within the system' at one time or another for the various government-funded organizations . . . we only saw programs that were designed to put people off, to appease them rather than get to the root of the problem. We saw that Ontario had over twenty different Indian organizations all fighting for the same piece of government pie. We saw conscientious, principled men who wanted to go directly to the heart of the problem but were restricted by an imposed structure which is inherent with the money and its source. We decided that we were going to form a group of people without any restrictions or strings attached. We would not subscribe to a structured hierarchy, people would find their level by their actions and not only their words. We became a movement, and we later realized that we instinctively adopted the traditional form of government that our forefathers used.

"Indian Affairs' main objective is to assimilate Native people into the mainstream urban dependent culture—in other words, so we can be completely destroyed as an independent sovereign people and disappear from sight. Witness the move afoot to turn reservations into municipalities. When this happens the land is no longer owned by the tribe. It is owned by individuals and is subject to the taxes and land deals of all other land.

"We hope our straightforward approach to the rebirth of Indian way can hopefully influence the members of the Native community to not be swayed by the government divide and conquer policies and cooptating grants . . . We could not exist without strong grass roots support nor would we want to . . . all our project funding has been from daily personal sources . . . So far we have Woods Cree, Plains Cree, Delaware, Seneca, Algonquin, Sioux, Mohawk, and Ojibway members."

NATIVES AND THE LAW

Most of the specialized legal courses on Natives and the law are concerned with the grand and sweeping questions of treaties and the unique legal positions of Native people—that is, where Natives legally seem to soar above the masses. These issues also tend to preoccupy Native politicians who prefer to dwell on what makes Native people exceptional. At the other end of the law, however, you find the tough and dirty legal work where White criminal law and family law systematically crush the differences out of the Native cultures; where racism and bias permeate the laws, the policing, the courts, and the prisons. Here the lawyer has to deal, not with prosperous politicians, but with Indians who are usually having a difficult time just coping with daily life. Some hopeful changes are being made at this "common person" end of the law. See the U.S. Commission on Civil Rights (1972) for a practical guide to Indian Civil Rights.

The U.S. set up tribally run courts and police forces many years ago, with a wide variety of arrangements for employment and jurisdictions depending on whether or not state laws apply on the reservation. The Indian courts tend to be family courts concerned with juvenile problems, misdemeanors, and family problems. For a single offense, they cannot impose a penalty "greater than imprisonment for a term of six months or a fine of $500, or both." Unlike federal and state trials, a free lawyer is not guaranteed in tribal courts. Tribal courts must guarantee the right to a trial by a jury of six or more persons for offenses that are punishable by imprisonment, but the jury need only come to a majority verdict, rather than a unanimous verdict.

U.S. courts have usually held that the Constitution does not have jurisdiction between members of the same tribe when they live in a tribal context on reservations. This necessitated a restating of the Constitutional guarantees of individual rights in a special Indian Bill of Rights in 1968. However, there are still certain subtle legal differences between Indians and non-Indians in the U.S.

1. Tribes are not required to select their leaders by elections, and thus may use traditional kinship and religious criteria.
2. The Indian Bill of Rights does not include the separation of church and state in tribal governments, but tribes may not interfere with the individual rights of members to hold religious practices different from those of the majority.
3. The right to express a culture or taste in dress and appearance is protected so Indians may wear long hair and traditional clothing. Court cases have verified this for schools, on the job, and even in prisons.
4. The old state laws that discriminated against Indians have been repealed or overruled: separate schools, limiting voting, limiting marriage, preventing jury duty, and preventing the purchase of liquor or firearms.
5. All federal agencies must provide equal employment opportunities, except the B.I.A. and the Indian Health Service, which are required by law to give employment *preference* to Indian applicants at all pay levels. "Indian" is defined here as one-fourth or more biological heritage, a racial definition, and must be proven. B.I.A. labor contracts usually contain a pro-Indian racial discrimination clause for hiring. Indian tribes may legally discriminate against non-Indians and hire Indians for tribal jobs. Even White businesses on or near reservations may offer preferential employment to Indians.
6. States may not discriminate against Indians in the provision of services, such as schools, on the basis of their race, their economic status, or *the tax-exempt status of their land.* The last fact has been widely used in the past as a rationalization by states and counties for the exclusion and non-provision of services to Indians but the federal government has declared this illegal.
7. Indians may vote for school boards and in school bond elections even though they do not "own property within the school district." Literacy tests and election taxes are prohibited.

Today there are about 900 law enforcement personnel on reservations not under state jurisdiction, about half employed directly by the tribes and the rest employed by the B.I.A.. Indian police forces in Canada have been much slower to develop because the Canadian reserves tend to be much smaller, more scattered, and more numerous than the U.S. reservations. Generally, it would have been cumbersome to create police forces in Canada with jurisdictions just on Indian land. However, some of the more progressive reserves, such as the Walpole Island Ojibwa, began to create their own police forces in the early 1970s. The federal government then developed a program to split the funding of Indian police forces with the provinces, with the Indian police trained and officially affiliated either with a provincial force or the RCMP. In fiscal 1977 there were some 171 special Indian police and the projection is to be at a full strength of 500 within a few years. Another problem is in the Canadian courts, especially the lack of Native judges and the distance people must travel to the courts.

The Canadian Parliament enacted a Migratory Birds Convention Act to fulfill its obligations under international treaties to protect migrating birds from hunters. However, this Act contradicted hunting rights specifically granted in earlier Indian treaties.

In 1960 the Canadian Parliament enacted a Bill of Rights that, among other things, guaranteed equality before the law in terms of race, national origin, color, religion, and sex. This forced the granting of full citizenship and the voting enfranchisement to status Indians, thereby making the Indian Act meaningless in its position that status Indians are not "enfranchised." Discriminatory laws against Indian drinking were reversed in 1967 under the Bill of Rights, using the case of Joseph Drybones, a Dogrib Indian in Yellowknife, N.W.T.

ADMINISTRATION

The major questions today about Indian administration revolve around the problem of transferring decision-making to Native people without having them lose their special rights and privileges, but retaining an accountability to the country at large. The federal governments in both the U.S. and Canada have been 'trying to get out of the Indian business' for decades now, but a maze of legal, political, economic, and moral factors prevent them from doing so. In the 1950s B.I.A. personnel told me that success to them would come with the gradual phasing out of the B.I.A. They talked about "purposely doing ourselves out of our jobs." Instead the B.I.A. has continually expanded.

The governments have been boxed into an apparent dilemma by their histories in which they are constantly criticized by the Natives, calling for more money and less control, and by the taxpayers, calling for fewer taxes. They are criticized by Indians if they try to get into the Native communities and actively change them toward integration with the national culture because that is being paternalistic, manipulative, and destructive of traditional ways. They are also criticized by Indians if they try to terminate or withdraw the federal services, which flow from the Native's rights by treaty and traditional Indian-White relationships.

Termination was the major strategy of the 1950s and 1960s. It was the official policy put forth in the U.S. in 1953 and a strong element in the Canadian White Paper in 1969. At the same time there were minor strategies to Indianize the government agencies by employing Indians and to transfer decision-making out of the hands of the federal government to provinces or states, bands or tribes. By 1974 some 62% of the B.I.A.'s employees had Indian ancestry. It is this second minor strategy, transferring power directly to the bands and tribes, that has become, however, the predominant one of the 1970s. This has a tendency to force the federal agencies to continue to function like a provincial or state government, in many ways, with direct relations with hundreds of local tribal and band councils for such intimate services as education, medicine, and welfare. Every one of the local councils wants to have a direct reciprocal relationship with the federal government. Federal Indian Affairs agencies would like to divest themselves of these functions and become simply a funding agency for Indian associations and councils and a legal trustee of Indian land and special rights. They are trying to get the Indian associations and councils to act as municipalities and to employ their own people or to make direct contracts with provinces, states, or counties for these services.

Progress so far in the transfer of power has been possible because of great increases in the federal Indian Affairs' budgets. In the last decade or so Native people have been able to draw upon a great well of public good will because there has been public support for massive increases in federal budgets for Native programs of all kinds. Federal expenditures have consistently increased faster than the high rate of population increase of the Natives (almost double that of the general rate) and faster than the inflation rate. In fiscal 1975 the budget was $635 million for the B.I.A. in the U.S. and $389 million for the Indian Affairs Branch (not including the Inuit of the Territories) of D.I.A.N.D. in Canada. Then in both countries many more millions were spent on Native people by other federal and provincial-state government agencies. For example, in the U.S. in 1974 the various non-B.I.A. federal agencies spent more than $463 million on Indian programs, about half of that on the Indian Health Service. These federal expenditures in the U.S. work out to be about $1.1 billion for 880,000 people, or $1,250 per capita.

Since 1965 D.I.A.N.D. has recognized the band councils as the primary local government ideally, responsible to their electorates for implementing and delivering local services. Indian politicians agree, but the actual transfer of this control of local affairs to the band councils has been gradual, only at the request of the individual councils, with the explicit assurance that this transfer of power will not jeopardize the reserve system, Indian status, or the level of funding.

Over $100 million of D.I.A.N.D. funds were managed directly by band councils in 1975. There was about $10 million in core funding for such things as office staff, equipment, and maintenance. About half of the bands administered their own housing programs. Some 190 bands administered their own social assistance programs and 197 bands participated in 314 "work opportunity" programs. Many bands now operate their own foster homes for children, day care centers, and senior citizen's homes. In 1972 the National Indian Brotherhood presented a policy paper on education to the government calling for more parental responsibility, local control, and Indianization of the curricula. D.I.A.N.D. adopted this policy and has been encouraging the development of local school committees, has employed 1,200 local para-professionals to work in the schools, and has been trying to deemphasize the federal Indian school system and have the bands make direct contracts with their provinces for their school services.

Canadian Indian Affairs expenditures in fiscal 1975 (in millions) were $163 on community affairs (a variety of services, particularly financial assistance to the unemployed, "work opportunity" programs, and welfare assistance); $165 on education; $31 on administration; $4 on research and liaison; and $27 on economic development. Medical services are delivered by a separate agency, as in the U.S.

ENTREPRENEURSHIP

Natives generally have had very little entrepreneurial orientation or ability. The historical exceptions were mostly those with a chiefdom heritage and only then in traditional farming, fishing, or crafts. Extremely few Indians owned and managed even the stores, gas stations, and motels in their own communities; Indians who were considered to be economically successful generally worked in government bureaucracies, as teachers, nurses, and administrators, and the few rich Indians came by their wealth through the sale of oil or other resources from their land. Now, that condition is changing, with the investment by the government and private enterprises of hundreds of millions of dollars into reserve industries, and the education of Native people in business practices.

In 1970 D.I.A.N.D. created the Indian Economic Development Fund to make direct loans, loan guarantees, and grants to the Indian business community. In fiscal 1975 the Fund made $32.5 million available, offering loans to 916 applicants: agriculture 491, transportation 158, fishing and trapping 84, manufacturing 70, forestry 60, and construction 53. D.I.A.N.D. also funds feasibility studies, planning services, initial managerial services, and the establishment of accounting systems. D.I.A.N.D. has brought in a volunteer organization, Canadian Executive Service Overseas, of 1,500 senior executives and technical specialists to help Indians get businesses started. Also, with D.I.A.N.D. funds, the University of Western Ontario makes available the services of graduate students in business to help Indian enterprises anywhere in Canada.

Canadian Indians today operate more than sixty independent tourist outfitting camps all across Canada, ranging from salmon fishing camps on both coasts to big game hunting in the north. These operations often involve complex entrepreneurial abilities to arrange diverse forms of transportation (such as flying the hunters to a lake or river and then transporting them around by canoe), hunting equipment, food supplies, accommodations, and guides.

At the $1.3 million Abenaki Motor Inn in Truro, Nova Scotia the cuisine has a Native touch with smoked fish, rabbit stew, and bannock bread. There is also oyster farming in Nova Scotia at Eskasoni. In Quebec a fiber glass canoe manufacturer near Trois-Rivières makes 2,000 canoes per year. There is a lacrosse stick factory at St. Regis, a fish-packing plant at Mingan, and a $9 million shopping center run by the Montagnais of Sept-Isles. In Ontario there is a shoe factory on the Tyendinaga Reserve, an industrial park on the Sarnia Reserve, a mink coat factory at Whitefish Bay, and a ski resort at Thunder Bay.

Indians in northern Manitoba now operate nine hunting camps and there is a new $6.5 million general shopping mall at The Pas. The Roseau River Reserve in Manitoba successfully started the commercial production of honey in 1973. Many Saskatchewan and Alberta Indians have been going into cattle ranching. There is logging at Saddle Lake and other reserves in Alberta, the Sarcee golf course outside of Calgary, and a summer cottage development by the Blackfoot. The Bloods at Standoff have been manufacturing prefabricated homes since 1971, and there is a new motor hotel at Sawridge, Alberta. British Columbia operates a fish processing plant at Port Simpson, a cattle ranch at Kamloops, vineyards at Osoyoos, logging at Ehattesaht, and suburban housing rental at Musqueam. Five bands around Merritt, B.C. joined to create an Indian Services Association and, as an outgrowth of putting up their own office building, now sell commercial office space to a variety of government agencies.

Four Carrier bands in B.C. formed the Burns Lake Native Development Corporation. This led to the establishment of companies involved in logging, trucking, construction, and fishing. It also bought stock in Babine Forest Products, the local sawmill. Through participation in the ownership of the sawmill, the Indians have been able to increase Indian employment and direct business to the Indian-owned companies. Thus about half of the workers at the sawmill are now Indians. The Native logging company cuts timber for the mill and the Native trucking company hauls timber for the mill. Darkhawk Mines is an Indian company in copper exploration in B.C. Another successful Indian company in B.C. manufactures furniture with Indian designs, *within Mountain Prison*.

When oil development began in the Canadian Arctic several years ago, the workers were almost all Whites. However, Natives have gradually been drawn into this high-paying work. There are only 45,000 people in the Northwest Territories and the effective labor force is only a fraction of that when you subtract the unemployable people whose ages prohibit employment. Add to this the fact that it is difficult to keep Whites from southern Canada interested in working in the north, particularly in the wintertime, while northern Natives prefer to live and work in the north. Thus the oil boom continued to expand until it became economical, as well as politically wise, to train and hire northern Natives. Gulf Oil began flying Inuit workers in for its Mackenzie Delta oil exploration work in 1972. For example, Native workers were flown in from Coppermine, 800 miles to the east, on a rotating basis: two weeks on, one week off.

In the U.S. there are over 245 industries and 16 lodges and motels on reservations. There are industrial parks on most of the large U.S. reservations, from Cattataugus, New York to Warm Springs, Oregon; from Turtle Mountain, North Dakota to San Xavier Papago, Arizona.

Stoffle (1975) described the development of an electronics factory on the Zuni Reservation after 1967. The Zuni had the advantage of their pre-industrial skills in silversmithing, but it took a few years to work out cultural accommodations on such issues as (1) the special demands for time off for religious ceremonials, (2) developing acceptable means of competition, (3) allowing Native languages to be used at the place of work, (4) allowing a diverse ethnic mixture of employees, and (5) turning the management over to Native people. The Zuni factory also had the unusual problem of excessive time being spent on the visual appearance of their product (p. 223). "The workers were producing electrical components as though they were producing jewelry. In some cases, workers did not realize that 'messy soldering' made no difference when the unit would be installed later in a cabinet." This was solved by placing functionally excellent, but visually messy completed units as models on display near the plant entrance.

I am somewhat optimistic about the economic future of Native people, because the rate of their economic improvement is strong. In the 1971 Canadian census, family incomes of status Indians averaged $4,417; with provincial averages that ranged from a low of $3,271 in Saskatchewan to a high of $5,924 in Quebec. The value of locally gathered food is undervalued in this income data, but it still indicates a relative poverty, since it was only 44% of the national average family income in 1971 of $10,112. In 1975 a survey of reserve facilities showed that 81% of the houses had electricity, 34% had running water, 31% had sewer or septic services, and 33% had telephones.

Chapter 19

Land Problems

TREATIES

After Champlain's colonies were established in the St. Lawrence Valley in the early 1600s, Indian-White relationships tended to be close and symbiotic, particularly through the fur trade. France did not form an explicit theory of aboriginal title and did not arrange for the surrender of rights in the land. A few Indian colonies were established by missionaries, but more often they went out to work with the tribes in their homelands. The Spanish, like the French, did not make treaties. The British, however, tended to treat inter-societal relationships collectively, as if all societies they met had an effective representative government, and legalistically, as if all societies could relate to each other in terms of the laws of a nation state. It seems now that treaties were originally made in part to salve the consciences of the British, the legal ritual making their acts moral, ostensibly. The British applied models of inter-societal relationships they had used with state societies in Europe, Asia, and Africa to the band, tribal, and chiefdom societies they met in North America.

Despite the conflicts that are inherent in relationships between societies of different evolutionary levels, the treaties were regarded seriously by the Native people. Native societies were earnest in trying to negotiate some peace and perhaps subsistence provisions, while the British were systematically buying up a continent. For example, in reference to the eastern agricultural tribes, Jacobs (1972:34) comments that "Europeans were continually surprised by the ability of Indian Chiefs to remember the terms of ancient treaties. During conferences the chiefs also exhibited their amazing memory by replying point by point to lengthy proposals made by the white Indian commissioners." Edmond Atkin, who became the British southern superintendent of Indian Affairs in 1755, wrote that "in their publick Treaties no people on earth are more open, explicit, and direct. Nor are they excelled by any in the observance of them." There was also some support for treaties in the pre-European practices of non-aggressive alliances.

The U.S. negotiated treaties from its inception for almost one hundred years (1777 to 1871) and then turned to other means to alienate Indians from their lands, such as the permitting of Whites to homestead on Indian land and the outright sale of "surplus" Indian lands. The treaties were often ignored soon after they were made as White squatters repeatedly moved on to Indian land. Indian-White conflicts ensued and a new treaty was made, further diminishing Indian land or even removing the Indians to small reservations. As we would predict from evolutionary theory, the more advanced a society was, the more attention was paid to these legal niceties. Thus the treaty-making process was intensive with the Southeast chiefdoms and Eastern and Plains tribes, but was dropped for the western bands who could give no significant resistance. Another major process was that of treaty making as an historical wave that began in the east and swept westward when White settlers wanted Indian land. Finally the more militarily resistant societies, such as the Sioux and the Utes, were given a greater number of treaties. At least 32 existed with the various Sioux bands from 1815 to 1868.

One of the first North American treaties was made by two Dutch traders with the Iroquois in 1613 near present day Albany, New York. Although it was disregarded by the various White groups that came to power in the area, the Iroquois tended to treat it as a permanent agreement between all Whites and them for some 160 years.

The first official U.S. treaty was with the Delaware in 1778; some 370 were made in total with a few almost every year, and the last to be officially called a treaty was with the Nez Perce in 1868. In fact a land cession treaty was made in 1889 in South Dakota and even the 1970s Alaskan Native agreement is essentially a land cession treaty. Most of the large Native societies signed a long series of land cession treaties in which the land was gradually taken away. Thus, for example, the Creek had several major treaties from 1785 to 1832. Further land was taken by force and administration without treaty in the 1830s. Some of the Creek escaped the forced removal and became the Seminole, but even some of these Seminole signed a treaty in 1832.

British practices were applied in Canada after the Royal Proclamation of 1763: protection of Indian lands from settlers, explicit surrender of lands to the Crown, treaties, the designation of lands reserved for Indians, and the establishment of permanent reciprocities in exchange for Native lands. At first, in southern Ontario, the treaties offered only cash, reserve land, and the right to hunt and fish on unoccupied Crown land. Later, with the westward move, health, education, and economic provisions were added. Treaties eventually were made with about half of the registered Natives.

Several treaties were made by the British in southern Ontario after the American Revolutionary War, between 1781 and 1857, with the Ojibwa, Algonkin, Ottawa, Potawatomi, Iroquois, and Huron. In 1850 the Robinson treaties were made with the Ojibwa along the north shore of Lake Huron and Lake Superior. In 1850-4 the Douglas treaties were made between The Hudson Bay Company and a few villages on Vancouver's Island. After that the treaties were numbered and involved the cession of vast tracts of land.

1.–2. 1871 Essentially southern Manitoba
3. 1873 Northwest Ontario
4. 1874 Southern Saskatchewan
5. 1875 Northern Manitoba
6. 1876 Central Saskatchewan and Alberta
7. 1877 Southern Alberta
8. 1899 Northern Alberta
9. 1905 Northern Ontario
10. 1906 Northern Saskatchewan
11. 1921 Western Northwest Territories

A final, unnumbered one was the Williams Treaty of 1923 involving Ojibwa in southern and central Ontario. That still left about half of Canada without formal land cessions: Maritimes, Quebec, eastern Northwest Territories, Yukon, and British Columbia.

British Columbia is a special case in terms of evolutionary theory, having chiefdoms but almost no treaties. The Douglas Treaties of 1850-4 were made on Vancouver's Island with the single villages of Songhee, Saanich, Nanaimo, and Sooke. The coastal Indians were too effective at economic and political bargaining to be easily displaced. They were capable of militarily defending themselves, but they were not particularly hostile to Whites slowly settling in. The British government just could not sweep aside the Native populations from large areas of coastal British Columbia through legalistic means and there was no pressing military need to do so. Most important to this relationship was that they were primarily oriented toward marine resources, since (1) they occupied relatively little land compared to the farming Native societies of the East; (2) British law was concerned with *land* ownership, not the Indian's fishing and marine rights, which were validated and transmitted through the potlatch system; and (3) the British could steal the Native marine resources by non-recognition of Native laws of marine ownership and by gradually imposing their own quotas, fishing seasons, and areal restrictions. These factors made treaty making in British Columbia difficult, because the Indians were too sophisticated and politically organized to be easily cheated, and unnecessary, because they could be displaced through slower processes. As early as the late

1800s the West Coast Indians began to use political pressure and legal means to have their lands returned to them. At the turn of the century two delegations were sent to England to appeal directly to the Crown. In 1912 the 'Nishga Petition" for lands was first made to Ottawa. The Nishga case stimulated improvements in the administrative handling and distributions of lands to Indians; set the precedent of "aboriginal rights"; and is still being actively pursued by the Nishga.

The Canadian Maritimes, Quebec, and the Northern Territories lack treaties because of such factors as occupation by the French, who did not usually make treaties at all, and the simple evolutionary level of the Native societies. One major exception is Treaty #11 with the Slave, Dogrib, Loucheaux, and Hare in 1921. This was made because oil had just been discovered in their territory and Canada was concerned that the Natives might make a claim to the oil resources, as of course many Oklahoman Indians had, becoming wealthy as a result. Similarly, the federal government and the courts forced the French-Canadians into the James Bay agreement of 1975, in effect a new treaty, when the Quebec government began developing hydroelectric power projects in Arctic Quebec.

THE ALASKA SETTLEMENT

In 1968 oil was discovered in the Prudhoe Bay area on Alaska's North Slope. Plans to pipe the oil south through Indian lands of the Yukon River Valley were legally resisted by the Natives. In 1970 a District of Columbia judge ruled that aboriginal title still existed for Alaska's Native people. The U.S. Congress then, at the end of 1971, extinguished their aboriginal title and made a settlement. Some 80,000 persons who are biologically one-fourth or more Alaskan Native may share in the settlement.

A single Native corporation run by the Alaska Federation of Natives was created from the 220 villages in twelve tribal regions. The Natives are individual shareholders in their particularly regional corporation, in a design that is a synthesis of communalistic and capitalistic relationships. The regional corporations were allowed to select 60,000 square miles for full ownership, including subsurface rights. Ownership of the remaining 286,000 square miles was essentially divided between the state and federal governments. Large total cash payments and royalties, over $1 billion, are involved, but they are largely used up in investments and capital improvements of the regional corporations and villages. Thus in 1974 the per capita payment to individuals was only $181.

Natives do not seem to have special rights to hunt and fish, as they do in the James Bay Agreement, and the settlement itself terminates in 1991, twenty years after its formation. At that time there will be no special status, laws, or rights for Alaskan Natives and the B.I.A. will be in a legal position to terminate its programs. Its services will be assumed by the state government and Native individuals and corporations will be subject to state taxes. Also, the Native corporations will be free to sell their land to non-Native people. Although it is much more liberal than the treaties of the historical period in terms of both money and land guarantees, it is also meant to terminate special obligations of the government toward Native people.

CLAIMS IN THE NORTHERN TERRITORIES

Several kinds of concerns are now being considered: the rights of non-status Indians, the rights of non-treaty status Indians and Inuit, the non-fulfillment of treaty clauses, the non-fulfillment of verbal promises during the treaty period that never became part of the treaties, and various kinds of illegal losses of lands or other rights. The most pressing issues, however, are the aboriginal claims where treaties were not made—in British Columbia, Yukon, Northwest Territories, Quebec, and the Maritimes.

Lloyd Barber was appointed Indian Claims Commissioner in December 1969 to make recommendations on the processes for the settlement of land claims. At the end of 1974, 49 claims had been submitted. Of these 16 were found to have "no basis for negotiation," 17 were "under review," 13 were "being negotiated," and 3 "specific" claims were settled. For example, in one settled claim $275,000 was agreed upon for an ammunition claim and legal expenses to Treaty 7 bands.

In 1975-6 Justice Thomas Berger of the B.C. Supreme Court, a former lawyer for the Nishga Indians, conducted an inquiry into the social, economic, and environmental aspects of the proposed pipeline intended to carry natural gas from the Mackenzie Delta in the Arctic to southern markets. The potential for general land claims settlements and other possible positive aspects, as well as potential disadvantages, stimulated a great amount of political organization and activity around the Berger Commission. The Commission heard over 700 witnesses in the north and received about 500 submissions in a swing across southern cities. A great many people have voiced opinions about the proposed pipeline: Native leaders, pipeline companies, environmental groups, chambers of commerce, engineers, geologists, anthropologists, economists, and so forth.

At Ft. McPherson a Loucheux Indian social worker, Philip Blake, said that if the pipeline is imposed against our will "we will have no choice but to react with violence." At Ft. Good Hope Chief Frank T'Seleie said "All these people have told you one thing, Mr. Berger. They have told you that they do not want a pipeline . . . There will be no pipeline because we have our own plans for our land. There will be no pipeline because we no longer intend to allow our land and our future to be taken away from us so that we are destroyed to make someone else rich. There will be no pipeline because we the Dene people will force your own nation to realize that you would lose too much if you even allowed these plans to proceed . . . We love our land and our future enough to blow up the pipeline. We, the last free Indian nation, are willing to fight so that we may survive as a free nation . . . (to the President of Alberta Gas Trunk Line). You are plotting to take over from me the very centre of my existence. You are stealing my soul. By scheming to torture my land, you are torturing me."

The owner of a lodge in Norman Wells said, "the feelings in the North have drastically deterioriated until finally one feels on the defensive because one is in business and one is White." He complained that Natives receive free education, room and board, transportation, clothes, and books, and yet Native parents lack an interest in their children's education, there is high absenteeism, and social and moral problems. "The fault of their almost 100% failure to complete their education lies on the very doorstep of the Native people." A former nun and currently a settlement manager at Norman Wells said, "How many people in the North really want to live in the past and live off the land? Those who really want to are already doing it. Those who think they want to live off the land, nothing but themselves is stopping them." In 1976 the N.W.T. Speaker of the House, David Searle, urged the Northerners to throw out the southern socialists, such as Justice Berger and the left wing "biologists, anthropologists, economists, sociologists, and political scientists . . . cultivating their sluggish sickness among our innocent and idealistic Native people."

At the second annual general assembly of the Indian Brotherhood and Métis Association of the Northwest Territories in 1975 a declaration was made that "We, the Dene nation of the N.W.T. insist on the right to be regarded by ourselves and the world as a nation." The meetings declared that citizenship in the new nation would be open to people who can trace their ancestry to one of five N.W.T. language groups: Loucheux, Slavey, Dogrib, Chipewyan, or Cree. All of these are Dene languages, except Cree which is Algonquian. The consensus was that a person would qualify with one-quarter or more ancestry in any combination of these "tribes." By this definition about 30,000 of the total population of 42,000 in the N.W.T. are Natives. In order to insure control over the government while the land claims are being settled, the assembly resolved that only those who had lived in the North for ten years will be allowed to vote in municipal, territorial, and "perhaps" federal elections.

The Canadian Council of Roman Catholic Bishops made a declaration on northern Native land claims in their 1975 Labour Day message, with the endorsement of the leaders of the Anglican and United Churches and the Canadian Council of Churches. "What we see emerging in the Canadian North are forms of exploitation which we often assume happen only in Third World countries: A serious abuse of both the native peoples and the energy sources of the North . . . We are especially concerned that the future of the North not be determined by colonial patterns of development wherein a powerful few end up controlling both the people and the resources." The document criticized secret planning of such projects as the James Bay hydroelectric project and called for just land settlements; fishing, hunting, and trapping rights; and fair royalties.

In the Mackenzie Valley the Natives still claim control and rights for a land claim settlement before development of the $6 billion Arctic gas pipeline and road, and possibly an oil pipeline. In the Yukon the 5,000 Natives are asking for a large share in the development of the territory, including land, cash settlements, and a royalty on petroleum and mineral production. Indians in the Mackenzie area did sign a treaty in 1921 waiving land rights up to the Arctic

Ocean, but a N.W.T. Supreme Court judgement declared that Indians still have a caveat or legal interest in the Mackenzie region. The proportion of Natives (including all persons of mixed ancestry) in the total population is much higher in the Mackenzie region (ca. 60%) than in Yukon Territory (ca. 20%) because a large number of Whites moved into the Yukon, first because of the gold rush there and then because of development related to the accessibility through the Alaskan Highway passing through the Yukon. The Yukon Natives are also more assimilated than the N.W.T. Natives, for these same developmental reasons. These are the factors which explain why the Yukon Natives are asking for a relatively pro-assimilationist land claim settlement. The Mackenzie "Dene," however, are demanding what approaches sovereignty, with some threatening to blow up the pipeline when it is built if their demands are not met.

The Inuit are in an even better position for self-rule than the Indians because in their territory they constitute more than 90% of the population. There are about 18,500 Inuit in Canada. Few Whites will go and live year-round in the high Arctic. Inuit Tapirisat of Canada has very competent leadership, making them capable of self-government. I.T.C. prepared a $2 million land use study showing what lands have been occupied, hunted, trapped, and fished by Inuit as part of their land ownership claim. In 1976 they claimed 250,000 square miles and hunting, fishing, and trapping rights over the remaining 500,000 square miles of land and 800,000 square miles of ocean. The Inuit plan calls for a 3% royalty on non-renewable resources; some control to protect the environment and wildlife of the north; and the creation of a new province to be called Nunavut, "Our Land" in Inuktitut, the Inuit language, to cover the one-third of Canada that lies in the eastern Arctic and the Arctic Islands. This is most of the land north of the tree line.

THE JAMES BAY AGREEMENT

The James Bay Agreement of November 11, 1975 is the first "comprehensive" Indian land claim to be settled in Canada. "Comprehensive" here means something like a modern form of treaty. The "federal recognition of comprehensive claims is based . . . on the loss of traditional use and occupancy of lands in areas where the native interest has never been extinguished by treaty or superseded by law." (*Indian News* 7:7:1) These are being negotiated primarily in British Columbia, the northern territories, and northern Quebec. The settlements include land and money, but because the loss of the traditional way of life is involved, they are also dealing with "cultural, social, and economic problems" in a continuing way.

The federal government gave grants of $320,000 to the Natives of Quebec to conduct the research and legal defense for their lands threatened by the $12 billion James Bay Development projects. The roads, towns, dams, and power lines desired by the Quebec government will be built, but the Natives will be compensated for the land. The Agreement itself is a 900-page document by which the Natives, through the Grand Council of the Crees and the Northern Quebec Inuit Association, renounce their claims to collective land title in return for guarantees of exclusive hunting, fishing, and trapping rights in certain lands; a considerable degree of self-government; and $225 million over twenty years. The developers agreed to move the site of a major dam, La Grand River Basin Dam #1, back 33 miles to decrease the effects on Native communities. They also agreed to substantially clear the Reservoir basins of timber before flooding and the Cree will have first refusal rights on clearing contracts.

The lands are divided by categories. Category I lands cover 5,408 square miles in and around existing Native communities that will be controlled solely by Native people. Category II lands are where Natives have exclusive hunting, fishing, and trapping rights: 25,130 square miles for Indians south of the 55th parallel and 35,000 square miles for Inuit north of the 55th parallel. If any of the lands are taken away for development, the Native people will be entitled to replacement lands or to compensation. Category III lands constitute the bulk of the territory, where all people will have equal access under ordinary provincial laws and regulations. The exception here will be that the Native people will be entitled to hunt, fish, and trap these lands all year, without regard to game season restrictions, and 22 important species will be reserved for their use. Native game wardens will be trained and paid by government agencies. Also, Natives will be free to cut wood for their own needs on these lands without payment of cutting fees.

The total population of Actic Quebec is about 20,000 people and about half of these are Natives: 6,000 Cree and 4,000 Inuit. Thus payments made to Natives over twenty years in excess of $225 million would work out on an annual per capita basis at over $1,000 per person per year. Since there are investment plans and continuing royalties there will be further income beyond the twenty years. Most of this will go to community development and operating costs, rather than as direct payments to families, but it will work through the Native economies and be a sizable supplement to the usual subsistence gained from hunting, fishing, and trapping and income from government sources such as family allowance payments.

The Agreement includes a guaranteed minimum family income plan for those involved in traditional wildlife harvesting: $1,000 each for head-of-house and spouse; $400 for each family and for each unattached individual not living with his parents, grandparents, or children; and $400 for each dependent child under 18. Since people often mix harvesting with other activities, the new plan allows part-time work at a guarantee of $10 per adult per day, up to a maximum of $2,400 per adult per year. This plan includes a pension fund for the hunters on retirement.

Other articles in the Agreement cover such elements as administration, job training and placement, government funding of key local services such as sanitation and fire protection, and the establishment of businesses by individuals or cooperatively by groups. These are some of the features:

1. Regional government in the south will be handled jointly by the Cree and

the James Bay Municipality, each to name three delegates to a James Bay Zone Council.

2. North of the 55th parallel the Kativik Regional Government will have representatives from each community, and will in effect be a region governed largely by Inuit people alone.

3. French, English, and the local Native language will all be official languages of local administration.

4. The Cree and Inuit will each have regional school boards with the same powers as other school boards in the province. Education may be provided in the students' mother tongue.

5. Native units of the Quebec Police Force will be established.

6. Judicially the entire territory will constitute one district, under the name Abitibi, with a system of itinerant courts.

7. An Advisory Committee on the Environment will review all projected developments and monitor works in progress, such as reservoir water levels and erosion related to hydroelectric dam projects.

8. La Grand Complex Remedial Works Corporation will be funded with $30 million over eleven years to pinpoint and correct negative effects of hydroelectric development.

9. A James Bay Native Development Corporation will invest, make developments, and encourage commercial trapping, sports outfitting for tourists, and art and craft production.

10. Among the Inuit a government-funded support program will provide produce to Inuit who are aged, handicapped, or otherwise disadvantaged and cannot harvest for themselves. This program will hire 53 community support hunters at an annual salary of $9,000, the fee to be increased by indexing to the Quebec cost of living each year.

McCullum and McCullum (1975: 71-2) compared the Alaskan and James Bay agreements. This summation is largely drawn from their comparisons.

	ALASKA	JAMES BAY
Native population	80,000	10,000
Common features	Both Indians and Inuit involved Native development corporations Royalty income on resources Relatively autonomous muncipal governments	
Emphasis	Modern	Traditional
Administration	Complex	Simple
Status	Termination in 20 years	Continuing provincially
Land emphasis	Communities, development, and sale	Harvest wildlife
Payments over 20 years	$1 billion	$225 million, more per capita
Special features	Full ownership of 60,000 square miles	Guaranteed income for trappers Environmental controls

The Native leaders directly involved in the negotiations were rather proud of the agreement that they had helped to create over the previous years of negotiations. This was not just another White-imposed program, but one with fundamental Native input every step of the way. Charlie Watt, President of the Northern Quebec Inuit Association, said, "Although we did not get all the points that we hoped for, we are an adaptable people and we must make the change. We are satisfied with agreement. We are prepared to go back to the communities and defend it." The final Inuit vote on the agreement in March 1976 was 1,253 "yes," 45 "no," and 660 "abstain." Billy Diamond, Grand Chief of the Crees of Quebec, said, "We feel this agreement can serve a good purpose in that it will protect our way of life and will give our children a choice between the traditional way of life and the non-Native way of life."

Native leaders outside of Arctic Quebec criticized the agreement. The National Indian Brotherhood maintained that the fact that Quebec's assumption of responsibilities that were once those of federal Indian Affairs was proof that the government intended to proceed with its goals to extinguish aboriginal rights across the country. Inuit Tapirisat of Canada stated that the cash settlement "comes nowhere near being adequate compensation." The Indians of Quebec Association, based in southern Quebec, believed *all* Quebec Indians should participate in the benefits.

The Indians of Quebec Association stepped in early in a strong way. They made a request in 1972 for $5 *billion* for the lost hunting grounds. In 1973 they received a brief court injunction to stop the James Bay Development Corporation. By June of 1974, however, the means and ends of the northern and southern Natives in Quebec had diverged so much that the northerners eased the southerners out of all future involvement entirely.

Technically the Indians of Quebec Association was declared not to have any "standing in the court," meaning as the essential complainant. Then the Grand Council of the Cree was created in 1974 and the IQA was asked to stand by in an advisory role. However, the Cree were impatient with the IQA anyway. Billy Diamond said, "There were times we just couldn't see any results from the IQA negotiations with the government. It was just as if the IQA was standing by watching a fire burn and talking about 99 different ways to put it out—meanwhile the fire was still burning while they were talking, the project was still being built." The Grand Council of the Crees allied with the Northern Quebec Inuit Association to negotiate directly with the various governmental and corporate agencies involved. They finished after five months of negotiations.

Our sympathy with the Native struggles today would support an even better settlement, but this agreement is good enough to make it appear that Canada is beginning to accept Natives as citizens with full rights and special claims. There is no country in the world that is trying as hard as Canada to do what is right for the aboriginal people of that country. Beyond the appearance of a good settlement, of course, is the delivery on the promises that have been made. Natives have made treaties before that turned out to be worthless. The success of the James Bay Agreement will depend on both parties, the ability and diligence of Native politicians, and the honesty and humanity of the government in carrying out its side of the Agreement.

Chapter 20

An Ethnographic Approach to Education

We assume today that every normal child should complete high school. Thus when we see that 88% of all Canadian children but only 6% of Canadian Indian children compplete high school, we assume that there is a problem in Indian society which needs to be corrected. A more humanistic perspective would be to judge success individually and in the context of the culture that particular individuals live in. Dropping out of a high school which is irrelevant to one's life, perhaps alienating to one's home community, and destructive to one's home culture might be the healthiest thing an individual could do. The "problem" of Indian education lies more with the existing character of that education than with Indian society.

The essence of a humanistic educational policy is in the discovery and teaching of that which enhances individual well-being. This recognizes that individuals find their primary fulfillment within a narrow social context defined by such overlapping criteria as race, primary language, ethnicity, religion, occupation, and residence. The resolution of a satisfactory *enculturation* or incorporation into culture *per se* is particularly difficult if the ethnic subculture one lives in is moving simultaneously into an *acculturation* with the national culture. A common stress point in the meeting of these two processes comes where one's ethnic subculture has a low evaluation in the national culture, with the result that enculturating ethnic children form a self-evaluation by generalizing from the pervasive low evaluation of their subculture.

It is impossible to develop any specific curriculum that would be appropriate for all Indians. I am suggesting just the opposite kind of flow of information in the creation of curricula, to introduce some local, ethnically relevant curricula through ethnography by teachers and the community itself. That is, to balance the abundant, easy, and authorized flow of curricula materials from the national culture with an often unauthorized flow from the teachers and the community. The introduction of locally relevant curricular materials is often extra work, but it is the kind of satisfying work that encourages teachers to remain in "isolated" Indian reservations.

The bulk of this would not be very formally structured presentations, but guest speakers, field trips, local "show and tell" material. It might mean shifting the school calendar to coincide with the calendar of local events, perhaps ignoring Hallowe'en and Easter, but celebrating "ice breakup time" and "the return of the geese." It could be a set of lessons in the local Native language, or lessons on how to hunt, or trap, or fish, or collect wild rice by those skilled in these areas. It could be having an older Native woman go along on a trip to the woods to tell the children about the names and uses of wild plants in the Native tradition, or perhaps an historical or archaeological field trip; visits by a local storyteller or Native priest are another possibility. In this way the teacher could learn some of the content and explore the values of the local culture, as well as assimilate them into the curriculum. Thus local Indian life could have a proud place alongside that of Western civilization.

School systems have historically been used by White culture as a means to acculturate and assimilate Indians into White society. Schools have been an institutional arm of White society, along with Christian missionaries, the law, police, courts, and jails, social welfare agencies, and federal Indian agencies, working to force Indian cultures to change so that they would be compatible and contribute to White society. Sir John A. Macdonald, upon introducing the Indian Act of Canada in 1874, explained how Indian children had to be taken away from their parents so as to eliminate their barbarian influence and expose the children to the benefits of civilization. The teacher has been sent out as an educational missionary to induce cultural changes in Indian societies. (The exceptions to this rule show us that acculturation can be rather free from trauma. The Danish school systems in Greenland, for example, have fostered cultural continuity among the Eskimo there with the Eskimo language included with Danish in the curriculum.) These institutions have been rather effective in destroying the old cultures, but there also occurred a number of unforeseen and undesirable side effects in the process. For example, the usurpation of local authority by outside agents has been undermining the traditional cultural means of local social control for generations.

Perhaps more serious than adult politics is the undermining of the enculturation of children. There has been a loss of pride in their heritage. There has been a loss of respect for social role models within their own ethnic society. They have lost the health of continuity in cultural orientation and values with the imposition of White values. Now that we have begun to realize the value of ethnic diversity, we can work to rectify some of the unnecessary deculturation of Indians.

EDUCATION AND INDIAN CULTURAL DIVERSITY

In early historical times there were about 275 societies north of Mexico, all speaking different languages. These societies were changed in ways that depended upon their evolutionary level and their particular histories of contact with Whites. Those in the more isolated areas of the West and the far North have tended to be less affected by Whites. Within this diverse context of historical pressures for change, the higher the aboriginal evolutionary level of a society, the greater the capacity its people have had to acculturate or use White culture for their own ends. Thus aboriginal levels of cultural evolution still have some effect on the education of Indians today. Teachers among Inuit, Sioux, and Cherokee will have different problems due not only to the different historical relationships those Indian societies have had with Whites but also to the "band" heritage of Inuit, the "tribal" heritage of Sioux, and the "chiefdom" heritage of the Cherokee. Generalizations about "Indian culture" have to be tempered by the recognition that in fact, even after the destruction and extinction of over 200 Native societies north of Mexico, there are still about 165 different Indian societies scattered in over three thousand residential communities.

The few early White schools for Indians were operated by the religious organizations, occasionally with some minor government aid. In 1865 U.S. government relations shifted to a program of assimilation through schooling; Canada soon followed with its Indian Act (1876). Boarding schools were designed to aid assimilation into White society by replacing an Indian enculturation with a White enculturation environment. The reservation system created many enclaves, each with differing degrees of cultural continuity, while Indian administrative systems and schools became the common experience of these originally very different societies.

The National Study of American Indian Education (Fuchs and Havighurst 1972) brought out many of the differences in Indians across the U.S. For example, one of the things they measured was how favorable Indian students felt toward Indian culture. The rank order of attitudes, from least to most favorable, came from the following populations: (1) non-Indian control sample, (2) Oklahoma, (3) Southwest, (4) Plains, urban, and Minnesota-Wisconsin, and (5) Northwest and Eskimos. Urban Indians were found to have a stronger sense of difference between Indian and White cultures, and a preferential attitude toward Indian cultures. Urban Indian youths seem to be more alienated from White culture than reservation Indians. Most Indian students evaluate both Indian and White cultures positively, view themselves as belonging to both, and have a moderate level of self-esteem or self-acceptance. Those urban Indian youth who have a low rating of Indian cultures, however, tend to have a low level of self-esteem.

There can be a wide range in the attainment of formal education by Indians in different parts of the same province. This was illustrated in a 1971 sample survey of high school completions of adult Indians living off reserves in British Columbia (Stanbury 1973A). There was a positive correlation between high percentages of high school completion and urban proximity: Vancouver—32%, Lower Fraser—27%, south interior—18%, north coast—15%, Vancouver Island—11%, north interior—10%, Okanagan—5%, and prison sample—0%.

There is also some correlation between the aboriginal level of cultural evolution of a society and the current level of high school completion of people from that society. The Tsimshian and Haida (and Kwakiutl) were the most highly developed Indian societies on the North Pacific coast, by most criteria. Living in this area they have relatively little urban proximity, but they have a relatively high level of high school completion. The Carrier, the linguistic-cultural group at the lowest aboriginal level of cultural evolution, also with a low level of urban proximity, have one of the lowest levels of high school completion. The figures are Interior Salish—22%, Tsimshian-Haida—20%, Coast Salish—18%, Wakashan-Bella Coola—14%, Carrier—11%, and Others—11%. These correlations are at least suggestive of some of the factors behind the differences in high school completion among Indians.

The average of the total sample was 17%, much lower than the approximately 70% for the general B.C. rate of high school completion. Significant differences within the Indian survey sample also showed up by sex (males—20%, females—13%) and particularly for age (20-24 years—71%, 25-44 years—44%, and 45-64 years—10%). Youth's shift to education is true for both Whites and Indians but it is much more extreme for Indians.

The median number of grades completed in various surveys of Indian adults are as follows: 7.9 for B.C. Indians off-reserve (1971), 9.3 for B.C. non-status Indians (1971), 8.5 for Indians on five U.S. Southwest reservations (1968), and 9.6 for Indians in three Minnesota cities (1967) (Stanbury 1973B). In a 1971 survey of the Omaha, Margot Liberty found averages of 8.0 on the reservation and 10.6 in the city of Lincoln, Nebraska. Other urban surveys found median grades of 8-9 completed in Winnipeg (1965) (McCaskill 1970), 11.2 in Los Angeles (1966) (Price 1968), and 11.3 in Seattle (Chadwick and Strauss 1975). The average education level of Indians in Los Angeles and Seattle is similar to the general urban level.

TEACHING IN THE NORTH

Education is particularly difficult in the Northwest Territories because of the cultural diversity, and its vast size, severe climate, isolated settlements, and high teacher turnover. In 1971 the N.W.T. Department of Education had 506 teachers in an area of 1.3 million square miles. Teachers were working in 56 schools, more than ten per cent with only one teacher. The largest schools were at Inuvik (72 teachers), Frobisher Bay (58), Fort Smith (53), Hay River (40), and Yellowknife (33). Generally the teachers were young, with an average age of 33 and 85% under 40 years of age. Nearly all had a provincial teaching diploma and about one-half had a university degree as well. The most important reasons they gave for teaching in the North were by rank order: (1) interest in the region and its inhabitants, (2) desire to travel, (3) opportunity to contribute to northern development, (4) financial considerations (Westgate and Ross 1973). Those who went North for financial reasons tended to be disappointed, stayed a shorter time, and were less inclined to settle in the North. Half of the teachers stated they would consider living permanently in the North.

Several advantages were seen in teaching in the North: slower pace of life, less social pressure, time "to relax and think in relative peace and quiet," ability to get closer to people and to the land, the children—"a delight to teach," —unmarred landscapes, friendly people, community involvement, ease of walking to work and shopping. A sizable segment of the teachers thought of working in the North in relation to things like their personal maturation, enrichment, and satisfaction of living in a new and challenging milieu and assuming more responsibility in the affairs of a small school and a small community.

Complaints dealt primarily with the poor quality or lack of services and amenities, such as quality housing, medical facilities, water and power supply, radio and television reception, and libraries. Teachers particularly wanted to buy and improve a house, not just rent one from the government. The inability of teachers to buy land where they work in the North or on Indian reservations is almost a universal problem. It is extremely difficult to sell Indian reservation land to anyone because it is corporately owned by the whole Indian band or tribe, and ownership is held in trust by the federal governments.

At Bethel, Alaska on the Kuskokwim River the non-Indians speak of Bethel in terms of contracts, projects, missions, and tours of duty (Fuchs and Havighurst 1972). There is little cross-cultural sensitivity among the teachers, who tend to be in a low level of cultural shock for their year or two of contracts and who leave before they become genuinely familiar with the local Eskimo culture. Teachers usually end up leaving with some disgust, without much understanding of the experience they have been through. The village schools of Alaska have a southern curriculum with no accommodation for Native events, such as berry picking, muskrat hunting, beaver trapping, or salmon fishing. A successful Northern education is defined as one which leads the students to leave the North, although society then does an about-face and pays hardship condition wages to southern Whites to work in the North.

GENERAL PATTERNS

An *enculturative* education focusses on teaching the child to be like its parents and people in its natal community, while an *acculturative* education focusses on teaching the child to be like the teacher and people in the teacher's world. Teachers need to be sensitive to this conflict. Most sub-cultural systems already have their own integrity and validity, and constitute a healthy set of solutions to the human equation. Thus, the disruption of that equilibrium through acculturative education should be done with careful attention to what it does to individuals.

A 1965 U.S. Public Health Survey showed that young (15-24 years of age) Indian suicides were about four times more frequent than young non-Indian suicides. This suicide syndrome, which shows up in some boarding schools in epidemics, seems to occur in certain Indian societies and yet is entirely absent in others. However, the National Study found a rather positive picture of mental health among the Indian students. "Looking at the Indian boys and girls in thirty varied schools ranging from Alaska to North Carolina, we are impressed by their basic good mental health. The adolescents . . . have the same level of self-esteem as non-Indians, they enjoy life, they have an active and rewarding peer-group life" (Fuchs and Havighurst 1972: 155).

The Indians were found to be positive about their schools and their teachers, but negative toward academic achievement. School is where the action is, the sports, the peer-group activities, but grades are not important and are not seen as related to future opportunity or success. Less acculturated students tend to be more positive about.their schools than do the more acculturated students, particularly those in cities. The most acculturated have higher expectations of school and are more often in the minority at the schools they attend.

Indian parents differ little from White parents in their opinions of what should be taught in school, except that most want more on Indian history and culture. Still, there are conflicts between a White school system and an Indian community that do not appear in what the parents say they want for their children. A sign of this is that parents-and-teachers association meetings are very poorly attended by Indian parents. Indian parents are prone to say to the teacher, "You know best. You are educated. You teach my children what they need to know." This indicates the feelings of inferiority on the part of the ethnic subculture. The teacher, of course, could be quite naive about what is best for the child in these circumstances, but it can be worked out through an in-depth reciprocal involvement between the teachers and the community.

Indian parents usually know very little about what goes on in school, even to the point of not knowing what grades their children are in. The school system still has the connotation of a foreign institution in many Indian communities. Usually the teachers are Whites, they live outside of the Indian community, and they do not socialize with the Indians. White teachers tend to remain relatively ignorant of the daily lives of the parents of the children they teach. Indian community leaders are more critical of school than the parents. They look to school increasingly as a tool they can use to solve local problems, and as a means to improve the capacity of Indians to participate in both White and Indian cultures.

There are about 12,000 teachers with classes of predominantly Indian children in the U.S. and Canada. In the U.S. there are 1,800 teachers in B.I.A. boarding and day schools, 4,900 in public schools on or near reservations, and 300 in mission and private schools. About another 3,000 teachers in public schools have five to 15 Indian pupils in their classes, mostly in rural areas and towns. In 1971-72 there were 1,497 teachers and counselors in Canadian federal schools for Indians, 45% with a bachelor's degree, and 16% were of Indian status (Indian Affairs 1972). The approximate attendance by Indians in Canada in 1971-72 was 30,000 in federal elementary schools on reserves and 40,000 in provincial elementary schools. Most of Canada's approximately 10,000 Indians in high schools attend provincial high schools in the larger towns and cities, usually living in student residences, group homes, or boarding homes.

Almost all schools see themselves as teaching White culture, but are agreeable to the idea of introducing Indian content. On the other side, most Indians resist assimilation, but they still want the school to teach the skills necessary for effective participation in White culture. The basic problem with introducing Indian content into the curriculum is that the existing system developed within White culture. Teacher training, books, films, and methods of academic presentation are all from the White culture. How do you introduce a a local Indian method of teaching into the school system? Few teachers know much more about the Indian heritage than White stereotypes. The problem with even explaining Mayan mathematics (with a base of 20 instead of 10) is that mathematics teachers have studied European mathematics. Politics is the European heritage of politics. Despite the whole catalog of literature, history, religious studies, music, and so forth, the material on Native New World cultures has never been incorporated into the White school system.

In the National Study it was found that Indian student achievement in learning White culture is lower than White children, although their performance is high in the early grades and they tend to perform better on the Draw-A-Man Test but are below average in English verbal skills. Excellence in spacial abilities, as opposed to verbal abilities, has often been noted for traditional Indians. This has implications about the kind of teaching methods that might be more successful in some traditional Indian communities (Fuchs and Havighurst 1972: 121).

> *A number of people have noted what they consider to be an unusual ability on the part of native Americans to perceive and to remember aspects of space. Examples are the ability to track animals and men, the ability to find one's way in a trackless wilderness, and the ability to draw a map of an area one has walked over. Eskimo do very well on tasks that require one to draw figures which have been flashed on a screen for brief intervals, as well as on tests for comparing geometric figures hidden in a complex background . . . in the Tlingit Indian village of Angoon, children all crowd into the cinema, and they are proud of their ability to remember every detail of a movie. Teachers often comment that Indian children seem to learn especially well from films.*

Many aspects of Indian life become handicaps for school achievement. The material support of children is often poor so there may be a poor quality of health facilities, and no books or space at home to study. Indian culture generally is more of a physical than an intellectual or academic environment. Young men must often fit into a status system that is based on physical prowess: fighting, hunting, drinking, and womanizing. The academically oriented child in this environment is usually at the bottom of the status system. Another handicap is that the language of the home is often different than that of the school. There are also value conflicts. The students are coming from a tradition of close family solidarity and cooperation, mutual support of kinfolk, cooperation among age cohorts, and belief in the value of the past; they are thrust into an environment whose values emphasize autonomy, competition, materialism, future orientation, hard work, and punctuality.

Teachers in the National Study tended to agree with statements that (1) "In class, Indian children are shy and lack confidence," (2) "Indian children are well-behaved and obey the rules," and (3) "Indian parents want to help their children in school." Parents are frequently seen as indifferent toward the school and about one-half agreed that "The school's teaching conflicts with the Indian parent's teaching." Teachers do not see the teaching of Indian culture as their job. Indian teachers in the schools tend to have close association with the Indian community, greater knowledge of it, and more positive attitudes toward Indian students. However, they tend to be as much in favor of White assimilation for Indians as White teachers, sometimes more so. These are Indians who successfully received a White education, leaving their home community for high school and college work, and came back to an Indian community, usually encouraging other Indians to do as they did.

> *Few teachers of Indian children overtly express bigotry, and most have a favorable attitude toward their pupils. But observers of Indian schools were often impressed by a view prevalent among many—that they did not treat their Indian pupils differently than others, that they saw children, not Indians. While this appears as an expression of egalitarianism, it does reflect an absence of sensitivity to the actual differences among pupil populations and a denial of Indian identity* (Fuchs and Havighurst 1972: 199).

VALUE CONFLICTS AND THE ETHNOGRAPHIC TEACHER

White culture tends to be future-oriented while Indian culture tends to be oriented to the present and the past. Whites are inclined to tightly schedule things in time while Indians have more relaxed schedules. Whites encourage saving and investment while Indians encourage sharing. Whites tend to value work as a good in itself while Indians tend to work in relation to survival, comfort, and social obligations. These are broad stereotypes that may not apply to hundreds of Indian communities. At most they are very shallow generalizations. Underlying these generalizations, every local community has a specific and complex culture influencing how children from that community learn what their ideals are, and so forth. The "ethnographic teacher" has enough interest in the students, enough simple curiosity, and enough interest in adapting well locally to find out about the local culture.

One hears that Indians are not competitive, that teaching a Western style competitiveness through examinations and sports is destructive. However, there are marked differences between Indian societies in the degree and kind of competitiveness they instill, from the socially interfering "cooperative" Pueblos, to the "coup" competitions of the Plains and the sharp trading of Northwest coast chiefdoms, to the Eskimo, with individual competition for men in hunting and womanizing but a strong social cooperation in groups characterized by not insulting or emotionally upsetting people. Competition is not so much absent as it is socially organized in different ways and oriented by different values of what is worth competing for. All Indian societies had competition in gambling and games. Tribal and chiefdom societies had warfare competitions, although there the social units were cohesive and cooperative in their opposition to other social units. Perhaps the difference is that it is not the impersonal competition of Whites.

White culture places a high value on material wealth. Poverty is thus seen as bad and the cause of many problems in society. The segments of modern North American society that we define as being in poverty usually have more material wealth than most people have had in the entire history of mankind. Even fairly recently in the European tradition there have been some monastic, peasant, and other life styles with little wealth, but a high quality of life. Indians do need jobs and support for the economic development of their reservation areas, but they should also send missionaries to White society to keep it from destroying itself through excessive materialism.

Can a White teacher be made to understand that what White culture would call "nepotism" and label as bad can be a genuinely good thing in a society where the support of kinfolk is essential to harmonious operation of the society? Often when Indians acquire control of school boards, they spend much of their time deciding how to allocate jobs (janitors, teachers' aides, guest speakers, etc.) to other Indians according to the kinship-based factions within the Indian community. White teachers are often repelled by this obvious patronage, but they may forget that jobs are one of the most scarce resources in a reservation community. Impersonal, legalistic, bureaucratic methods of allocating jobs on the basis of ability alone might contribute to the destruction of the social fabric of the society.

Should a teacher oppose fixed sex roles, social group cooperation over individualistic liberation, and what they perceive as male chauvinism in Indian societies, even though these egalitarian concerns arise from cultural processes at work in the most modern segment of urban society? Should a teacher direct classes more to educating children for life in their home community than in the broader White-dominated world? Should a teacher propose that representative democracy is superior to kinship and consensus politics when the latter is how reservation politics operate? Whites usually insist that kinship politics is corrupt or at least an indication of a flaw in the character of the people. Should a teacher encourage students to aim for an occupational goal in the aboriginal sector or in the general sector of activities, and if the latter, as a skilled laborer or a professional? In looking over Luiseño and Diegueño schooling I found that even the brightest high school students were being encouraged to go to trade schools rather than to college.

The answers to these questions vary somewhat in relation to individual children as well as to tribal characteristics. However, an ethnographic knowledge of the local community would help greatly in working out humanistic answers for the teachers. It is much better if the teacher has enough cross-cultural sensitivity to explain the value conflicts that the child is involved in.

INDIANIZING INDIAN SCHOOLS

Indian teacher training programs have been developed by colleges and universities in areas where there is a large Native population. These all try to recruit Indians into the profession. In about 1951 Arizona State University began developing Indian education programs and eventually formalized programs in teacher training, Indian education research, and services to interested agencies, such as workshops which bring together tribal leaders and teachers. They have a master's degree in Indian education and have been publishing the *Journal of American Indian Education* since 1962. There are prominent Indian education programs at such schools as the Universities of New Mexico, South Dakota, and Alaska.

In Canada special teacher training and an Indian education research program began at the University of Saskatchewan in 1960. Saskatchewan was then the first school in Canada to offer a B.Ed. and M.Ed. in Indian and Northern Education. Eight universities now offer teacher training programs specifically for Indians. There are also 38 "Native cultural education centres" that help the schools develop curricular materials.

Integrated schools in Canada began in 1954 with the provision of per capita grants to regular public schools which included Indian children. Education services provided by the non-federal schools to Indians are arranged through joint agreements negotiated between the federal government and a provincial government or local school boards; over 500 of these agreements have been made. Indian band councils have recently been included as the second party to some of these agreements, with the federal government as the funding third party. However, the National Indian Brotherhood complained that the schools are usually in White residential areas, forcing the Indian children to commute. They want consolidated schools built on Indian reserves when the number of Indian children exceeds the number of White children.

After 1956 school committees began to be organized on Indian reserves. For several years these functioned in a social and advisory association. Since about

1971, after strong Indian political pressure, the Indian Affairs Branch has moved to give these committees some significant power. This is happening at the provincial level as well so that, in Ontario, for example, an Indian representative must be on a school board whenever the system has 10% or more Indians or more than 100 Indian students. The first steps are being taken to introduce Native languages and to use Native "paraprofessionals," teachers and counsellors with a limited education. In many cases the local people now have complete control over staffing and curriculum. For example, in 1973 the administration of Qu'Appelle Indian Residential School in Saskatchewan, with 240 students, was turned over to a 13-person Indian council representing the 24 Indian bands sending students to the school. Their first curriculum change was to introduce the teaching of Cree in grades one and two.

Historically, in the federal systems the curricula has been inflexibly prescribed in terms of both content and technique of presentation. This curriculum is identical to the standard subjects taught in non-Indian schools, except that there are more drills in the use of English. Several years ago in the U.S. locally elected school boards were called for by a presidential directive, but they have had very little power compared to the B.I.A. system and staff.

Indian schools have often encouraged Indians to work in traditional arts. Thus the thriving art traditions of the Southwest were brought into the Indian School at Santa Fe, New Mexico and many famous artists attended. When the movement to Indianize curricula came on the scene, this school was one of the first to try seriously. In 1963 it was changed into the Institute of American Indian Arts and in 1975 it added a two-year junior college program.

In 1966 the Rough Rock Demonstration School became a Navajo-run elementary boarding school deep on the reservation at northeastern Arizona. Instruction is given in Navajo history, language, and art as well as English, mathematics, and other subjects. Parents work as paid dormitory aides and attend adult education programs. Most of the staff is Indian, with a regular home visiting program for the teachers. Other attempts for local control were made on the Pine Ridge Reservation in South Dakota and by the Mesquaki Indians in Iowa. In 1971 Rocky Boy's Reservation in Montana shifted to an all-Indian school board to operate its elementary school system, and the Navajo Indian community in Ramah, New Mexico began running its own high school.

Most Indian schools have added at least some nominal Indian content in the past few years, but it has usually been a band-wagon swing without preparation or depth of commitment. Almost as if people were following fads in dress, we have seen peer-tutorials, remedial reading, Head Start, Follow Through, demonstration schools, community schools, values schools, and now survival schools. At the high school level we had Project Vision in Oklahoma; Project Awareness in Minnesota; Upward Bound, an Office of Economic Opportunity project in dozens of communities; and so forth. Under heavy political pressure, Indian Affairs in Canada quickly added Native language courses to over 200 Native schools in the 1970s.

Some solid programs exist. Haida language, crafts, and legends are taught at the Chief Matthews School in Haida Village, Queen Charlotte Islands. Rae-Edzo, the N.W.T. Dogrib community school, was deliberately designed after Rough Rock. Thus, for example, the first years are in Dogrib with English taught as a second language. Blue Quills at Saddle Lake, Alberta, after years of demonstrations and political struggles, became an Indian-controlled school. Quinalt language, culture, and history is taught in Taholah, Washington. The Sahaptin language is taught on the Yakima Reservation in Washington. Santo Domingo is noted among the Pueblos for its culturally relevant elementary school and its teacher training program.

Beyond these additions, however, there is a need for a fundamental reworking of the curricula. Every subject could start from a Native perspective. The Government course should include Indian government, the governmental structures of the bands, tribes, chiefdoms, and states of the New World. The history course should start from the New World, explore the long milennia of prehistoric development, examine the arrival and impact of the Europeans, and then delve into Old World history. Indian content means more than a few stereotyped crafts. In time we hope that the great works of literature, philosophy, history, and science of the aboriginal New World will be introduced into the curricula of Indian schools. These materials are largely outside of the European academic tradition in which White or Indian teachers were educated, so it will take a special effort for them to do the research necessary for them to bring it into the classroom.

Beyond curricula, there is a need for Indianization of Indian schools in terms of teaching techniques, integrating the school into the local community, and adjusting the annual calendar of events to that of the local community. Teachers need to help the community incorporate the school as an integral part of community life. Perhaps this means adult education classes. Perhaps it means an extra-curricular recreation program using the school facilities. It is the responsibility of the teachers to explore and participate in the community enough to help their students. Then as Indians enter modern society they can more effectively use their education as a means to individual and social liberation and advancement.

Chapter 21

Designs for the Future

This concluding chapter touches on themes that will be important for Native studies in the future: ethical guidelines, the design of local community projects, and the search for the best philosophical base of Native studies. I argue in the end for a humanism that is based on a worldwide sample of societies and the entire history of mankind, a scientific humanism.

Deloria's (1969) attack on "Anthropologists and Other Friends" expressed a frustration that various scholars have powers that should be tapped more by Native people. The Native movement is a power movement to a considerable degree and here are some so-called "Indian experts" who have the power to interpret, to explain, and to advise on Indian policy to the general society. Indians want more of that power. Deloria characterized anthropologists as working in a closed system of obscure, useless, intellectual concerns; of sloganeering and being faddish; of experimenting with and using people as objects; and of encouraging people to follow tradition.

Deloria was overestimating the power of anthropologists. When major independent policy research was done for D.I.A.N.D. a decade ago and reported in *A Survey of the Contemporary Indians of Canada* (1966-7), it was opposed by the government's own White Paper in 1969. Millions of dollars have been spent each year for the last several years on Indian and Inuit "research" in Canada, but almost none of it went to anthropologists. D.I.A.N.D. spent $4 million in fiscal 1974-5 on "research and liaison." This is mostly politically motivated, often secret, internal research by their own employees or by instant expert consultants who are willing to produce "research" that will validate the bureaucracy's existing policies; conferences and negotiations; and grants to Indian associations. Over $9 million went to Indian organizations for treaty and rights research from 1970-1975 in Canada.

How intrusive is anthropological research? We had a survey in 1973 of 120 professional anthropologists in Canada, which included data on their main forms of recent research methods (Price 1975). This indicated that non-disruptive methods were being used: (1) 52 used historical methods, (2) 30—census or demographic, (3) 25—applied, (4) 16—analysis of written records, and (5) 11 —others, such as surveys and participant observation.

In 1976 the Canadian Sociology and Anthropology Association agreed upon a Code of Professional Ethics. It calls for free inquiry without manipulating others. With research subjects it asks for consent; disclosure of funding; privacy and dignity; right to be anonymous; and to be advised on research aims, findings, and consequences. It also examines several disciplinary concerns, such as disclosing methods used, not jeopardizing further research, not overly saturating a research field, and not exploiting students. In recent years there has been the creation of standing ethics committees within the various professional associations. Thus complaints about the unethical research on any professional person can be submitted to the ethics committee of that person's association. The associations have few legal sanctions, but they can be very persuasive at a personal level.

SOCIAL RESEARCH ETHICS

Within the Native movement there are many strains of protest that affect researchers, as Whites in non-White research, as Westerners in non-Western research, and as academics in non-academic settings. Native people themselves should become involved in Native studies, of course. They need to use the tools of the social sciences, for example, to study neo-colonialism and White society as the dominant context within which Native societies are operating today. They need to explore how Natives may best contribute to tomorrow's world. The extensive involvement of Native people in Native studies, however, will not end the need for disciplinary ethics. Native people are nearly as critical of Native academics as they are of White academics. The ethical relations of the social sciences have been widely discussed by Natives and academics in the past decade. I simply bring forward some of these ideas as they have been applied to Native studies.

1. Every individual and social group has certain rights of privacy and consent in relation to social research on his behavior. These are already legally limited by government requirements for national census, taxation, and some

policing information. Schools, businesses, news media, and other modern institutions also ask for personal information. Thus further intrusions in the name of social research into private and community lives must be done with consent and great care.

2. Research should be carried out to develop scientific and applied reasons, not for antiquarianism, simple curiosity, or financial profit. The latter reasons are insufficient for the penetration and possible disruption of a community.

3. Once having penetrated a cultural system and used the time and resources of a community, the researcher is obligated to make the best analysis and most appropriate dissemination of the data possible. One should not enter research unless one intends to complete it and disseminate the results in teaching, publication, or policy determination.

4. Researchers should keep their work free from constraints on publication and avoid secret methods of data collection, such as electronic eavesdropping-devices. Specific material which would be damaging to the community of study should not be published, although abstract scientific understandings and applied policies can still be drawn from the data. The process of making research anonymous is often carried too far. That is, most people prefer to be mentioned by name in reports and, although the report may stir up a brief storm of discussion, in the long run factual inaccuracies and depersonalization are resented more than a researcher's criticisms.

5. Communities should be protected from being overstudied by the news media, government agencies, amateur ethnographers, and so forth. One resolving test of whether a new researcher should enter a field situation is whether a significant majority from a broad spectrum of representative numbers of the community would consent to the research work. You cannot expect unanimous consent.

6. The researcher should encourage the community to define its goals in a realistic manner, and then should apply his special information and good offices toward achieving those goals. If the researcher's values are extremely divergent from those of the community of study he should withdraw, rather than attempt to subvert his community of study.

ARCHAEOLOGY AND ANTIQUITIES

There have been many recent moves by Native groups that are important to archaeology and to museums. Native groups have restricted or stopped excavations in some cases and are pressuring for the return of Indian artifacts from museums to the Native societies they were taken from. Essentially, this seems to be a desire to acquire more control over the ideology of one's ancestry and the objects and sites that can be used as symbols of heritage. There is a great richness in the traditional Native cultures that can be used to instill pride in Native people and to validate contemporary Native movements. Thus the Native people need to have more control over the development and use of their antiquities for socially relevant ends.

Stopping the excavations of burial grounds is an acculturated type of protest for equality. "Whites don't allow their burial grounds to be excavated so why should we?" Now Natives maintain that all Indian burial grounds are sacred and are to be left alone. To do this they must become defined as cemeteries in legal terms.

At a workshop on "People, Resources and the Environment North of '60" at Carleton Universlty in 1972, Abe Okpik from Frobisher Bay complained about archaeologists. "When I would travel with my dad on trapping areas and we would come to a certain area, he would tell me that my great-grandfather and my grandfather from my mother's side whom I had never seen were buried there. This was their secret ground, and instead of setting traps there, we directed the traps somewhere else. We have never been allowed to go up and see the graves, to us it was a secret . . . The archaeologists who come here to dig up our graves and our implements have not consulted with us about our secret burial grounds." Taber Hill Memorial Park was created in Scarborough, Ontario in 1956 to rebury bones that had been recovered in a nearby excavation. After a period of protest certain wampum belts were returned to the Onondaga Iroquois by the University of the State of New York. At the National Museum of Man in Ottawa the Iroquois are allowed to come in to "feed" the false face masks in the ethnology collection in an annual religious ceremony. In 1972 negotiations between the Canadian National Museum and the Kwakiutl Tribal Council arranged for the return of a valuable collection of ceremonial regalia that had been confiscated by the courts in the 1920s. In 1973 the Museum of Anthropology at the University of Michigan yielded to pressure by a group of Indians and agreed to the reburial of skeletons that date back 2,000 years. In 1976 the Provincial Museum of British Columbia returned ten totem poles it had in storage to the Haida Indians. The Inuit Cultural Institute under Tagak Curley has been moving toward effective control over all archaeology in Nunavut, Inuit Quebec, and Labrador.

Antiquities laws and archaeological services should be carefully developed. This work must avoid the desecration of sacred Native sites and artifacts. Native communities should be helped to form museums enhancing the local knowledge of their heritage. The Malki Museum in Southern California and the Navajo Museum in Window Rock, Arizona are models of the Native operation of museums. The other major Indian-operated museums are at (1) the Wind River Reservation in Wyoming; (2) Fort Hall Reservation in Idaho; (3) Cherokee, North Carolina, (4) Pawhuska,Oklahoma (Osage); (5) Mohawk Institute, Brantford, Ontario; (6) 'Ksan, Hazelton, B.C.; and (7) Museum of the Abenakis, Odanak, Quebec.

Society must avoid the destruction of aboriginal Native sites without proper recording of the excavation, publication of the findings, and public ownership of the artifacts. Because excavation cannot help but destroy part of the heritage, we expect archaeology to be particularly sensitive in serving the humanistic needs of society and not be an avocation of the elite and the private museum builders that it has been in the past. Archaeology evolved from antiquarianism and an appreciation of pre-modern and non-Western art. In time it began to fill out the story of prehistory and historical archaeology. The "new archaeology" of today is moving away from these earlier humanistic trends toward scientific questions and "problem-oriented" excavations. However, Native people are still primarily interested in the humanistic side of archaeology and it is their heritage in particular that is being destroyed in excavations, so the discipline should not abandon humanistic archaeology. Currently the universities are pursuing the scientific side while the lower status humanistic archaeology is left to the amateur societies and the government agencies who do salvage, rescue, and conservation archaeology just preceding the bulldozers, building pipelines, highways, dams, and residential subdivisions.

It is necessary to control the commerce in Native antiquities so that public museums have the primary right to purchase antiquities. The existing high private demand and prices for Native antiquities lead to extensive private excavation and sale of antiquities for private collections.

The Museum of Navajo Ceremonial Art in Santa Fe, New Mexico has a particularly sensitive policy on acquisitions. No material will be accepted (1) without legal proof of how it was obtained, (2) if its possession by the museum is legitimately objectionable to the people whose culture it represents, (3) if it does not contribute to current or future research or display, (4) if the acceptance is inconsistent with the museum's goals or operations, and (5) if they require anything but a realistic appraisal based on current market value.

COMMUNITY DEVELOPMENT

There are hundreds of examples of successful economic development going on today in Indian communities. The Hurons of Loretteville, Quebec commercially manufacture snow shoes, hockey sticks, and moccasins. A $5 million shopping complex is owned and operated by the Pas Reserve in Manitoba. Kainai Industries manufactures prefabricated houses on the Blood Reserve in Alberta. Indians are producing honey and wild rice in Manitoba, commercially processing as well as catching fish in British Columbia, running a lumber industry on the Navajo Reservation, and operating tourist and vacation enterprises on dozens of reservations. Many reservations now have Indian-owned gas stations and motels.

The U.S. Department of Commerce sponsored a study of economic development programs on Indian reservations, with special reference to seven reservations: Passamaquoddy in Maine, Pine Ridge Sioux in South Dakota, Oklahoma Cherokee, Navajo and Papago in Arizona, Morongo in southern California, and Lummi in Washington. Only two of the projects were considered to be clearly successful: a Lummi fishing project and a Papago program to build fences around range land. Sam Stanley of the Smithsonian Institution summarized this study, which is an example of Native studies in the area of community development.

1. Personal relationships, particularly kinship, are important in Indian communities. Economic development schemes must take these into account.

2. Indian people are determined to maintain their own identity.

3. Government policies must be directed away from the destruction of the institutions that hold Native communities together.

4. Indians must be involved in the planning and execution of development projects. Indians should be encouraged to carry out the middleman and entrepreneurial economic functions, now usually done by Whites, as a factor in both pride and professional education.

5. There is a need for better coordination between the cyclical annual budgets of governments with their built-in boom and bust funding, and the long-term demands of most development projects. Projects also often fail because of a lack of sufficient operating capital.

6. Economic development should only be done with a thorough understanding of the specific local community. The various Indian societies are sufficiently unique that it is necessary to take into account such local things as work habits and social institutions.

7. Projects which were felt to be successful in the people's own terms had these qualities: a feeling of involvement by the people, a tendency for the programs to come from the people, the ability for the Indians to use outside expertise without being used by it, a sense of continuity with the past, and considerable freedom from the B.I.A. in the operation of the project.

8. Failing projects tended to be pre-packaged proposals, especially those made by promoters with profit motives rather than Indian interests in mind. Success in development was somewhat differently perceived by Whites and Indians, with Indians placing less stress on material, medical, and education indices and more on social cohesion and pride.

PATERNALISM AND ROMANTICISM

Most Whites who live and work within Native communities are not researchers, but often teachers, doctors, nurses, and government workers. The most common problem in situations where Whites are politically and economically dominant but numerically a tiny minority in a Native community is that the Whites form a small separate social enclave. The Whites treat each other as unique individuals with names and personalities while the Indians are rather faceless—"the Indians" or just "they." "Who came to the meeting?" Bill, the constable; Mary, the teacher; Bob, the trader, and several Indians." A few Indians are, of course, typically known to the Whites, but these tend to be just intermediaries and translators, the good Indians, and the troublemakers, the bad Indians. It seems to me that some Indian-White conflicts would dissolve if Whites would take the time to become involved enough in the Indian community to make a wider variety of Native friends, to learn the names of local Natives and use them, and to assess local Native people individually. One other problem of Whites in Indian communities is distortion through paternalism or romanticism. Paternalism grows out of a sense of superiority. "Here we are in the bush, the wilderness, to help these poor people and they don't really respect us enough for the tough job that we are doing for them." Some educators, medical people, social workers, and journalists decry the Indian way of life as a culture of poverty. Paternalists need to understand why Indians usually prefer their way of life. Paternalists need to understand their own psychology because they often deflect a socially unacceptable dislike for Indian culture into a socially acceptable plea to "improve it." Between societies, the concept of poverty may be a materialist's way of putting down a non-materialistic culture. Within the European cultural tradition, poverty is the word that a middle economic class uses to define and feel superior to a lower economic class, although today's lower class has more wealth than the middle class did a few decades ago.

Romanticism is the opposite kind of distortion, but even if it is more pro-Indian than paternalism, it too undermines useful communications. The extreme romantic searches for the noble savage and few Indians fill his idealistic requirements. A few Indians respond to the call and become noble savages. However, the romantic himself may become what he admires to some degree by wearing Native dress and finding more profound mystical insights in the Native culture than the Natives ever imagined were there. Grey Owl (George S. Belaney) is the classic case, an Englishman who became the perfect Indian, in the eyes of the English. He had a special kind of paranoia, a well-integrated delusion of being an Indian.

One Grey Owl of today is Carlos Castenada, who wrote *The Teachings of Don Juan: A Yaqui Way of Knowledge* (1968). Castenada asked me to read this manuscript when it was an M.A. thesis he was working on as a graduate student and I was teaching at the University of California, Los Angeles. Most students "went native" to some degree as a normal by-product of genuinely appreciating the cultures they were studying. Castenada was unusual in the extent that he found personal validation through his field work and through constantly reworking his data. Although in the book he reports his experiences in an experiental, autobiographical way, in fact the manuscript went through draft after draft of rewriting, expansion, and systematizations by Castenada; the book is really Castenada's extensions of his informant's ideas. It is not a traditional Indian Shamanistic philosophical system, although it contains some elements of such a system. No rigorous ethnoscience techniques were used in the collection or analysis of data. The informant appears to be at least partially a fictional creation for the purposes of narration. He is an old man without relatives or friends dropping in to see him. The ethics of informant anonymity were used in such a way that no one could go and interview his informant to recheck Castenada's work. Just as Grey Owl's romantic books dispelled some prejudice against Indians, there is value in Castenada's books, but as scientific ethnography Castenada's fantasies about a personal philosophy are only marginally better than Grey Owl's friendships with beavers.

It is important to study Indian philosophies, but it should be done with pride and openness. The Native American Church, for example, took an open stand against *The Teachings of Don Juan* because of its irreverence toward peyote and its lack of recognition of the social obligations of religion, such as the universal curing orientation in the Shamanistic tradition. Indian religions are socially oriented, but *The Teachings* are extremely self-centered and individualistic, a situation that is more characteristic of non-Indian than of Indian philosophies. Perhaps the best we can say for *The Teachings* is that this is how a young, unmarried, Western man without a community would reinterpret the religious and philosophical discussions of a Mexican *curandero*, but there is very little that is specifically characteristic of either Yaqui Indians or of Shamanism.

According to Alfonso Ortiz, a Pueblo anthropologist, *Book of the Hopi* by the novelist Frank Waters "has been repeatedly denounced as a fabrication by many traditional chiefs." Rupert Costo, a Cahuilla scholar, claims that the author of *Chief Red Fox* was exposed as a fraud. He also wrote that *Seven Arrows* by H. Storm falsifies and desecrates Northern Cheyenne religion and tradition. Indians are "in." There are many people today who would like to shift their identity to that of an Indian, particularly if they can demonstrate that they have some Indian heritage. Indians themselves are very skeptical of the "professional Indians" who acquire economic and political benefits by playing up their Indianness.

Those who see romanticism or mysticism in Indian life should be aware that Indians are also human beings with cultures that are fulfilling universal needs, albeit in a particular way. Both the paternalist and the romantic need to discover what the culture is in a holistic sense and to respect it in its own terms, not for the wrong reasons or for purposes of change.

There are academically sound philosophical discussions in the literature of biographies and quality recordings of oral literature. *Teachings From the American Earth* edited by Dennis and Barbara Tedlock (1975) is an excellent anthology. J.G. Neilhart's *Black Elk Speaks* and J.E. Brown's *The Sacred Pipe* present the philosophy of an historic Oglala Sioux. *The Zuni's Self Portrayals* was produced by the Pueblo of Zuni itself. A recent anthology of contemporary Native literature is *The Man to Send Rain Clouds* edited by K. Rosen (1975). Some of the bettern known biographies are W. Dyk, *Son of Old Man Hat*; S.W. Hopkins, *Life Among the Paiutes*; T. Kroeber, *Ishi*; N. Lurie, *Mountain Wolf Woman*; P. Nabokov, *Two Leggings*; M. Metayer, *I, Nuligak*; P. Radin, *Crashing Thunder*; H. Sekaquaptewa *Me and Mine*; L. Simmons, *Sun Chief*; and J. Spradley, *Guests Never Leave Hungry*. For a discussion of the special relationships between Native informants and anthropologists see Joseph Casagrande's *In the Company of Man*.

SCIENTIFIC HUMANISM AND NATIVE STUDIES

Humanism is a philosophy of social ethics that affirms the value of mankind, both collectively and as individuals, and maintains that it is possible through rational means to enhance life. It specifically denies that one particular culture has the best model of behavior for other cultures. Human enhancement takes the form of helping individuals and social groups to function in a positive way, to restore their impaired capacities, to provide them with resources, and to prevent social dysfunctioning. Scientific humanism is that branch of humanism that is based on a scientific understanding of mankind, both biologically and culturally. It recognizes the universal patterns in the material, social, and ideological spheres of culture. It also recognizes the validity and positive functioning of different kinds of societies, and that both universality and variation are healthy and normal. It recognizes legitimate variation in value systems, according to the differing needs of different societies. It recognizes that ideological systems with internal parts that can be labeled religious, political, aesthetic, and so forth, are normal and necessary for cultural commitment and the transcendant inspiration that goes beyond any simple form of rationality, yet is so enhancing to human nature.

The ethnic core of early NorthAmerican cultural anthropology was a culture of Jewish intellectuals, several of whom were escaping the anti-Semitism of Europe. Franz Boas, Alfred L. Kroeber, Edward Sapir, Melville J. Herskovits, Alexander Goldenweiser, and others attacked the myths of racism and supported the values of ethnic diversity and multiculturalism in modern society. They, in turn, understood the value of tribal societies and helped to protect them from destruction. In 1914-1915 Sapir fought against Canada's infamous Potlatch Law. Boas, Marius Barbeau, and James Teit also fought against the law in the 1920s.

Sapir (1924) expressed the values of the North American anthropology of his day when he wrote about destructive cultural situations, which he called "spurious" rather than "genuine." Genuine culture is inherently harmonized and self-satisfying, richly varied and yet with a consistent and holistic attitude toward life, a "culture in which nothing is spiritually meaningless."

> *The American Indian who solves the economic problem with salmon-spear and rabbit-snare operates on a relatively low level of civilization; but he represents an incomparably higher solution than our telephone girl of the questions that culture has to ask of economics.*
>
> *. . . The Indian's salmon-spearing is a culturally higher type of activity than that of the telephone girl or mill hand simply because there is normally no sense of spiritual frustration during its prosecution, no feeling of subservience to tyrannous yet largely inchoate demands, because it works in naturally with all the rest of the Indian's activities instead of standing out as a desert patch of merely economic effort in the whole of life.*

Robert Redfield (1953) saw humanistic values in rural cultures. He was in favor of the domination of life by a "moral order" that rose from shared convictions of what was believed to be inherently right, an absolute system of moral values. He saw this as characteristic of "folk" society, while urban society is dominated by a "technical order" of mutual usefulness, where people are bound by things. The new technical order banishes hunger and disease, but by using impersonal, legalistic, and universalistic mechanisms it fosters alienation and another range of problems.

Eric Wolf (1964: 24) emphasized that applied anthropology involved the spirit of flexible inquiry and a respect for other cultures that is tempered by cultural relativism. "Whether or not American Indians are to be allowed to use the narcotic peyote in the services of their Native American Church is in part a question of religious freedom in America, but in part also a theoretical question, involving consideration about integrative adjustments of people to conditions of cultural stress. Whether the Indian cultures of the United States are to be rooted out through forced acculturation or permitted to go their own way in cultural oases sheltered against encroachment by the law of the land is not only a question of justice, but also of feasibility, hence of anthropological theory."

There has been a shift in anthropology away from extreme cultural relativity, and even the structural values ("spiritual commitment," "shared convictions of morality") mentioned by Sapir and Redfield, toward some acknowledgement that the evolution of culture has generally been an increasing enhancement of mankind. For example, the increase in physical health and life span and in security of food supply are to me unquestionable advantages that came with the evolution of culture. There had to be some tradeoffs, some accompanying deleterious changes, for example a loss of personal quality of community life as populations, political systems, and economic systems expanded. The popular tendency, however, is to overvalue modern cultures and to incorrectly assume general superiority from one or two spheres, such as food production and medicine, as applying to all spheres. The scientist needs to admit to himself the advantages of modern life while showing the rest of society the values of other cultures and other times. Both traditional and modern cultures have their problems such that a dilemma of modernization is that the advantages of technical, rational order are usually gained at the loss of individual significance and commitment in the world.

More important for humanism than the grand design of worldwide cultural evolution is that different cultures of the same evolutionary level cover some range in the humanity of their designs. Thus at the band level of culture I would not want to be a grasping and selfish Siriono as described by Allan Holmberg in *The Nomads of the Long Bow*. At the tribal level the diversity of life styles is even greater, but in Reo Fortune's *The Sorcerers of Dobu* for example, the evidence is that some, like the Dobuans, are clearly less humanistic than others. The Ik of East Africa have been portrayed by Colin Turnbull as becoming inhumane through selfishness brought on by the destruction of their ecology.

Good intentions, a commitment that favors the social group one is working with, and simply a general knowledge of the culture are not enough in applied work any more. Too much damage has been done by well-intentioned but naive people. It is possible now to base social policies on a somewhat sophisticated knowledge of cultural systems and how they change. For example, it is important in the establishment of social policy to work holistically, to understand the system being changed with all its economic parts, political parts, religious parts, social parts, and so forth. Economists too often ignore non-economic parts, political scientists tend to ignore non-political parts, and so forth.

Anthropologists, who may have a holistic grasp of a cultural system, are often so awed by its complexities that they make poor administrators. They are intellectuals, not people of social action, and while realizing the potential damage of new policies and actions they are often ineffective. Anthropologists often see themselves as a genteel elite, observers of the working world. Thus it is not surprising to see that Native leaders enjoy pointing to the pretensions of anthropologists, to bring them down to earth. Ideally we need the combination of holistic understanding and the capacity for decisive action. Intellectual and academic elitism needs to be humbled by the social worker's and civil servant's question of "Will your ideas work?"

White culture today seems to stress the rationality of the left hemisphere of the brain: verbal abilities, "linear" logic, mathematics, science, and law while Native cultures stress right hemisphere rationality: non-verbal, "spatial" logic with particular value on abilities in things like art and religion. It may be more than just custom that traditional Indians typically have a more casual concern about the precise starting time for events than most Whites, that "Indian time" comes from a slower and more holistic regard for persons and events than the clockwork rationality of most Whites. This is not genetic or racial, but just that the specific cultural environment of any child can emphasize one side of the brain or the other. In Indian cultures, artistic homes, religious homes, etc., the abilities of the right side of the brain may become more used, more developed, and more dominant. If these considerations are true, then a humanistic philosophy should accept the validity of both "verbal" and "artistic" cultures.

The well-being of individuals is the ultimate test of a humanistic policy. Social institutions, buildings, art objects, religions and so forth are of no inherent value. They are valuable only in relation to enhancing human life. And in this understanding of individuality we need to be broader than our current medical-psychological orientation toward health and disease. We need to include the cultural dimension of mankind because humans have evolved for two million years in an increasingly cultural environment.

The Native movement is a reintegrating, culture-building, healthy process. The survivors of genocide and ethnocide are gradually building a new culture that protects itself from destruction. Beyond the initial contact period the societies that went through a period of traumatic deculturation, such as the relocated Oklahoma chiefdoms and the Plains tribes, developed religious revitalization movements that often spread rapidly from one society to the next. These have continued in a minor way into the present, with some new reintegration of Native religions now in the Indian Ecumenical Conference.

The early decades of this century are marked for Natives by a great sense of loss of a viable culture, by apathy, and by resignation to White domination. The Native protests in the first half of this century were largely framed in terms of the egalitarian values of North American society: abolish laws against inter-racial marriage, drinking, religious practices, give Indians citizenship and the right to vote; and stop discriminating against Natives in employment and housing practices. These were generally pro-assimilationist protest moves.

Since the 1950s there has been an anti-assimilationist shift, a retreat from apathy, and the rise of new means to Native goals: militant takeovers for demonstration purposes, forcing the courts to uphold Native legal rights, political organization and lobbying, and Native studies. There is some cautious optimism among Natives because of their successes. The tide of government termination policies has been slowed, stopped, and even reversed in some administrative areas. Thus, for example, we see the provision of urban Indian centers and legal services to some Indians who previously never received federal government support.

Methods are being developed to diffuse decision-making downward to Indian associations and tribal and band councils without threatening continued federal funding and the special status of Indians inherent in their treaties and land rights. In Canada this is seen in direct grants for various economic development projects and in contracts for the Indian operation of Indian schools. In the U.S. this is in the new official policy set down in U.S. Senate Bill 3157, The Indian Self-Determination Act of 1972. The methods of community control that were worked out in the "War on Poverty" of the Office of Economic Opportunity and the Indian Community Action Programs are being adopted by the older and more conservative B.I.A. The Rough Rock School, for example, began as an O.E.O. project in a B.I.A. school and then was turned over to the Navajo Tribe to operate on a contract basis. The large size of the Navajo population and its land area gives it an uncommon capacity for autonomy as a tribe, but cooperative associations of the bands and tribes of other societies might be able to achieve the same efficiency of size. If the policies of the Senate bill are actually carried out, Castile (1974) suggests that reservations may shift from being federally "administered communities" to become self-managed "sustained enclaves," comparable in time perhaps to such culturally different yet self-sufficient communities as those of the Hutterites, Mennonites, and Amish.

Working with the Fox Indians, Sol Tax and his students at the University of Chicago developed a style of scientific humanism usually called "action anthropology." It involves studying a group, encouraging them to formulate their goals, and then helping them in a variety of practical ways to achieve their goals. Nancy Lurie is one of Tax's practical students who has helped the Menomini (1972).

Lurie (1971) characterized the Native response today as essentially an "articulatory movement," not a "civil rights struggle" for acceptance as an equal ethnic group and not a "revitalization movement" that focuses on internal reforms. The articulatory movement lacks a clearly identifiable leadership, but has patterned action toward widely held goals. It seeks to avoid both the historic economic marginality of their communities and the destruction of their communities through individual assimilation in an individualistic search for prosperity. "The solution is seen as successful redefinition . . . with the larger socio-economic system . . . The larger system is recognized as inescapable and even necessary, but to be dealt with on a contractual basis. Ideas and experience are diffused among the different communities and the general Indian minority into the larger pattern. Such models assure a decent material foundation for existence, with Indian identity maintained and actively utilized as an essential component of satisfactory community life . . . what . . . justifies speaking of a movement is the development of a united Indian voice, even relating Indians in Canada and the United States, able to verbalize its goals, and stressing the sense of crisis for Indian people."

Native studies has become a positive means of adjustment in today's world. It is a means to help discover satisfactory ways of bringing the best of traditional and historical Indian cultures into societies of the future. In political terms Native studies legitimizes and validates an ethnic cultural protest through academic respectability. It is one channel of power in the Native movement for self-respect and self-determination.

BIBLIOGRAPHY

Ablon, Joan

1964 "Relocated American Indians in the San Francisco Bay Area: Social Interaction and Indian Identity." *Human Organization*, Vol. 23, No. 4.

Adams, Howard

1975 *Prison of Grass: Canada From the Native Point of View*. Toronto: New Press.

Adams, John W.

1973 *The Gitksan Potlatch*. Toronto: Holt, Rinehart & Winston.

Bailey, Alfred G.

1969 *The Conflict of European and Eastern Algonkian Cultures, 1504-1700*. Toronto: University of Toronto Press.

Balikci, Asen

1968 "Bad Friends." *Human Organization*, Vol. 27, No. 3.

Barber, Bernard

1972 "Acculturation and Messianic Movements." In *Reader in Comparative Religion: An Anthropological Approach*, W.A. Lessa and E.Z. Vogt, eds. Evanston, Illinois: Row, Peterson.

Barger, Kenneth and Daphne Earl

1971 "Differential Adaptation to Northern Town Life by the Eskimos and Indians of Great Whale River." *Human Organization*, Vol. 30, No. 1.

Black, Robert

1967 "Hopi Rabbit-Hunt Chants: A Ritualized Language." In *Essays on the Verbal and Visual Arts*, J. Helm. ed. Seattle: University of Washington Press.

Boas, Franz

1955 *Primitive Art*. N.Y.: Dover (First published in 1927).

Boldt, Menno

1973 "Indian Leaders in Canada: Attitudes Toward Equality, Identity, and Political Status." Ph.D. dissertation, Yale University.

Bowker, Lee H.

1972 "Red and Black in Contemporary American History Texts." In *Native Americans Today: Sociological Perspectives*. H.M. Bahr, et al., eds. New York: Harper & Row.

Braroe, Niels W.

1975 *Indian and White: Self-Image and Interaction in a Canadian Plains Community*. Stanford, California: Stanford University Press.

Brody, Hugh

1971 *Indians on Skid Row*. Ottawa: Information Canada.

1975 *The People's Land: Eskimos and Whites in the Eastern Arctic*. Markham, Ontario: Penguin Books Canada.

Bureau of Nutritional Sciences
1975 *Nutrition Canada: The Indian Survey Report.* Ottawa: Department of National Health and Welfare.

Burnette, Robert and John Koster
1974 *The Road to Wounded Knee.* New York: Bantam.

Calder-Marshall, A.
1963 *The Innocent Eye: The Life of Robert J. Flaherty.* London: W.H. Allen.

Canadian Corrections Association
1967 *Indians and the Law.* Ottawa.

Cardinal, Harold
1969 *The Unjust Society: The Tragedy of Canada's Indians.* Edmonton: M.G. Hurtig.

Carneiro, Robert L.
1968 "Ascertaining, Testing, and Interpreting Sequences of Cultural Development." *Southwestern Journal of Anthropology*, Vol. 24, No. 4.

Castenada, Carlos
1968 *The Teachings of Don Juan: A Yaqui Way of Knowledge.* Berkeley: University of California Press.

Castile, George P.
1974 "Federal Indian Policy and the Sustained Enclave: An Anthropological Perspective." *Human Organization*, Vol. 33, No. 3.

Cawetti, J.G.
1971 *The Six-Gun Mystique.* Bowling Green: Popular Press.

Chance, Norman A.
1966 *The Eskimo of North Alaska.* New York: Holt, Rinehart & Winston.

Chadwick, Bruce A. and Joseph H. Strauss
1975 "The Assimilation of American Indians into Urban Society: The Seattle Case." *Human Organization*, Vol. 34, No.4.

Clemmer, Richard O.
1974 "Truth, Duty, and the Revitalization of Anthropologists." In *Reinventing Anthropology*, Dell Hymes, ed. New York: Vintage Books.

Convocation of American Indian Scholars
1970 *Indian Voices.* San Francisco: The Indian Historian Press.

Corrigan, Samuel W.
1970 "The Plains Indian Powwow: Cultural Integration in Manitoba and Saskatchewan." *Anthropologica*, Vol. 12, No. 2.

Crowe, Keith J.
1974 *A History of the Original Peoples of Northern Canada.* Montreal: McGill-Queen's.

Cutler, R. and Morrison, N.
1971 *Sudden Death.* Vancouver: Alcoholism Foundation of British Columbia.

Dailey, R.C.

1968 "The Role of Alcohol Among North American Indians as Reported in the Jesuit Relations." *Anthropologica*, Vol. 10, No. 1.

Davis, Arthur K.

1965 "Edging Into Mainstream: Urban Indians in Saskatchewan." *A Northern Dilemma: Reference Papers*, Vol. 2, Calgary.

Deloria, Vine, Jr.

1969 *Custer Died For Your Sins: An Indian Manifesto*. New York: Macmillan.

1970 *We Talk, You Listen: New Tribes, New Turf*. New York. Macmillan.

Devereux, George

1948 "The Function of Alcohol in Mohave Society." *Quarterly Journal of Studies on Alcohol*, Vol. 9, No. 2.

Dewdney, Selwyn

1975 *The Sacred Scrolls of the Southern Ojibway*. Toronto: University of Toronto Press.

D.I.A.N.D.

1969 *Mortality by Suicide, Comparison of Indian to National Rates, 1968*. Reference No. 5075. Ottawa: Indian Affairs.

1973 *The Canadian Indian: Statistics*. Ottawa: Information Canada.

Dodge, Robert and McCullough, Joseph B., editors

1974 *Voices from Wah'Kon-Tah: Contemporary Poetry of Native Americans*. New York: International Publishers.

Dosman, Edgar J.

1972 *Indians: The Urban Dilemma*. Toronto: McClelland & Stewart.

Dozier, Edward P.

1970 *The Pueblo Indians of North America*. New York: Holt, Rinehart & Winston.

Driver, Harold E.

1969 *Indians of North America*. Second Edition. Chicago: University of Chicago Press.

Duff, Wilson

1975 *Images, Stone, B.C.: Thirty Centuries of Northwest Coast Indian Sculpture*. Toronto: Oxford University Press.

Dundas, Alan

1965 "Structural Typology in North American Indian Folktales." In *The Study of Folklore*, A. Dundas, ed. Englewood Cliffs, N.J.: Prentice-Hall.

Dunn, Dorothy

1968 *American Indian Painting of the Southwest and Plains Areas*, Albuquerque: University of New Mexico Press.

Eggan. Fred

1966 *The American Indian: Perspectives for the Study of Social Change*. Chicago: Aldine.

Elias, Peter D.

1975 *Metropolis and Hinterland in Northern Manitoba*. Winnipeg: Manitoba Museum of Man and Nature.

Evans, Bessie and May G. Evans

1975 *American Indian Dance Steps*. New York: Hacker Art Books. (First published in 1931).

Eyles, A.

1967 *The Western: An Illustrated Guide*. New York: A.S. Barnes.

Ferguson, Frances N.

1968 "Navaho Drinking." *Human Organization*, Vol. 27, No. 2.

Ferguson, Jack

1971 "Eskimos in a Satellite Society." In *Native Peoples*, J.L. Elliott, ed. Scarborough: Prentice-Hall.

Friar, Ralph

1970 "White Man Speaks With Split Tongue, Forked Tongue, Tongue of Snake." *Film Library Quarterly*, Vol. 3, No. 1.

Friar, Ralph E. and Natasha A. Friar

1972 *The Only Good Indian: The Hollywood Gospel*. New York: Drama Book.

Frideres, James S.

1974 *Canada's Indians: Contemporary Conflicts*. Scarborough: Prentice-Hall.

1975 "Indian Identity and Social Conflict." pp. 21 Ms.

Fuchs, Estelle and Havighurst, Robert J.

1972 *To Live on This Earth: American Indian Education*. Garden City, New York: Doubleday.

Garbarino, Merwyn S.

1971 "Life in the City: Chicago." In *The American Indian in Urban Society*, J.O. Waddell and O.M. Watson, eds. Boston: Little, Brown.

Graves, Theodore D.

1967 "Acculturation, Access, and Alcohol in a Tri-Ethnic Community." *American Anthropologist*, Vol. 69, No. 3.

1971 "Drinking and Drunkness Among Urban Indians." In *The American Indian in Urban Society*, J.O. Waddell and O.M. Watson, eds. Boston: Little, Brown.

Guillemin, Jeanne

1975 *Urban Renegades: The Cultural Strategy of American Indians*. New York: Columbia University Press.

Harrison, Gail G.

1975 "Primary Adult Lactase Deficiency: A Problem in Anthropological Genetics." *American Anthropologist*, Vol. 77, No. 4.

Hawthorn, Harry, B., Editor

1966 *A Survey of the Contemporary Indians of Canada*. Part I. Indian Affairs Branch, Department of Indian Affairs and Northern Development, Ottawa, Ontario.

Heard, J. Norman
1973 *White Into Red: A Study of the Assimilation of White Persons Captured by Indians*. Scarecrow: Metuchen, N.J.

Heath, Dwight B.
1964 "Prohibition and Post-Repeal Drinking Patterns Among the Navaho." *Quarterly Journal of Studies on Alcohol*, Vol. 25, No. 1.

Heidenreich, Conrad
1971 *Huronia: A History and Geography of the Huron Indians, 1600-1650*. Toronto: McClelland & Stewart.

Hertzberg, Hazel W.
1971 *The Search for An American Indian Identity: Modern Pan-Indian Movements*. Syracuse, N.Y.: Syracuse University Press.

Heumann, Hans, et al.
1973 *The Native Offender in Canada*. Law Reform Commission of Canada.

Honigmann, John and Honigmann, Irma
1971 "The Eskimo of Frobisher Bay." In *Native Peoples*, J.L. Elliott, ed. Scarborough: Prentice-Hall.

Houston, James
1971 *Eskimo Prints*. Toronto: Longman.

Houts, Kathleen C. and Bahr, Rosemary S.
1972 "Stereotyping of Indians and Blacks in Magazine Cartoons." In *Native Americans Today: Sociological Perspectives*, H.M. Bahr, et al., eds. New York: Harper & Row.

Indian Affairs
1972 *Indian Education Program*. Ottawa: Indian and Northern Affairs.

Jacobs, Wilbur R.
1972 *Dispossessing the American Indian: Indians and Whites on the Colonial Frontier*. New York: Charles Scribner's Sons.

Jaenen, Cornelius J.
1976 *Friend and Foe: Aspects of French-Amerindian Cultural Contact in the Sixteenth and Seventeenth Centuries*. Toronto: McClelland and Stewart.

Jilek, Wolfgang C.
1974 *Salish Indian Mental Health and Cultural Change: Psycho-hygienic and Therapeutic Aspects of the Guardian Spirit Ceremonial*. Toronto: Holt, Rinehart & Winston of Canada.

Jones, Dorothy M.
1973 "Race Relations in an Alaska Native Village." *Anthropologica*, Vol. 15, No. 2.

Jorgenson, Joseph G.
1972 *The Sun Dance Religion: Power for the Powerless*. Chicago: University of Chicago Press.

Judicial Statistics
1968 *Statistics of Criminal and Other Offences, 1967*. Ottawa: Statistics Canada.

King, Richard A.
1967 *The School at Mopass: A Problem of Identity*. Toronto: Holt, Rinehart & Winston.

Kitses, J.
1969 *Horizons West*. London: Thames & Hudson.

Kline, James A. and Roberts, Arthur C.
1973 "A Residential Alcoholism Treatment Program for American Indians." *Quarterly Journal of Studies on Alcohol*, Vol. 34, No. 3.

Kunitz, S.J., et al.
1971 "The Epidemiology of Alcoholic Cirrhosis in Two Southwestern Indian Tribes." *Quarterly Journal of Studies on Alcohol*, Vol. 32, No. 3.

LaViolette, F.E.
1973 *The Struggle for Survival: Indian Cultures and the Protestant Ethic in British Columbia*. Toronto: University of Toronto Press.

Landes, Ruth
1971 *The Ojibwa Woman*. New York: W.W. Norton & Co.

Leacock, Eleanor B. and Nancy O. Lurie, editors
1971 *North American Indians in Historical Perspective*. New York: Random House.

Lemert, Edwin M.
1958 "The Use of Alcohol in Three Salish Indian Tribes." *Quarterly Journal of Studies on Alcohol*, Vol. 19, No. 1.

Levitan, Sar A. and Hetrick, Barbara
1971 *Big Brothers Indian Business—With Reservations*. New York: McGraw-Hill.

Levy, Jerrold E. and Stephen J. Kunitz
1974 *Indian Drinking: Navajo Practices and Anglo-American Theories*. New York: Wiley.

Litman, Gerard
1970 "Alcoholism, Illness, and Social Pathology Among American Indians in Transition." *American Journal of Public Health*, Vol. 60, No. 9.

Lurie, Nancy O.
1967 "The Indian Moves to an Urban Setting." In *Resolving Conflicts: A Cross Cultural Approach*. University Extension, University of Manitoba.
1971 "The Contemporary American Scene." In *North American Indians in Historical Perspective*, E.B. Leacock and N.O. Lurie, eds. New York: Random House.
1972 "Menominee Termination: From Reservation to Colony." *Human Organization*, Vol. 31, No. 3.

MacAndrew, Craig and Edgerton, Robert B.
1969 *Drunken Comportment*. Chicago: Aldine.

Martin, Harry W.

1964 "Correlates of Adjustment Among American Indians in an Urban Environment." *Human Organization*, Vol. 23, No. 4.

Martin, Paul S. and H.E. Wright, editors

1967 *Pleistocene Extinctions: The Search for a Cause*. New Haven: Yale University Press.

McCaskill, Don N.

1970 "Migration, Adjustment, and Integration of the Indian into the Urban Environment." Ottawa: Carleton University M.A. Thesis.

McCracken, Robert D.

1971 "Lactase Deficiency: An Example of Dietary Evolution." *Current Anthropology*, Vol. 12, No. 4-5.

McCullum, Hugh and Karmel McCullum

1975 *This Land is Not For Sale*. Toronto: Anglican Book Centre.

McDiarmid, Garnett and Pratt, David

1971 *Teaching Prejudice*. Toronto: Ontario Institute for Studies in Education.

Miller, Frank C.

1971 "Involvement in an Urban University." In *The American Indian in Urban Society*, edited by J.O. Waddell and O.M. Watson, Boston: Little, Brown.

Nagata, Shuichi

1971 "The Reservation Community and the Urban Community: Hopi Indians of Moenkopi." In *The American Indian in Urban Society*, J.O. Waddell and O.M. Watson, eds. Boston: Little, Brown.

Nagler, Mark

1970 *Indians in the City*. Ottawa: Canadian Research Centre for Anthropology.

Nettl, Bruno

1967 "American Indian Music." In *The North American Indian: A Sourcebook*, R.C. Owen, et al., eds. New York: Macmillan.

Oswalt, Wendell H.

1966 *This Land Was Theirs*. New York: John Wiley & Sons.

Patterson, E. Palmer

1972 *The Canadian Indian: A History Since 1500*, Don Mills, Ontario: Collier-MacMillan.

Patterson, Nancy-Lou

1973 *Canadian Native Arts: Arts and Crafts of Canadian Indians and Eskimos*. Don Mills, Ontario: Collier-Macmillan.

Pelletier, Wilf

1972 "Dumb Indian." In *Who is Chairman of This Meeting?* Ralph Osborne, ed. Toronto: Neewin.

Price, John A.

1962 "Washo Economy." *Nevada State Museum Anthropological Papers*, No. 9.

1968 "The Migration and Adaptation of American Indians to Los Angeles." *Human Organization*, Vol. 27, No. 2.

1972 "U.S. and Canadian Indian Periodicals." *The Canadian Review of Sociology and Anthropology*. Vol. 9, No. 2.

1973A "The Superorganic Fringe: Protoculture, Idioculture, and Material Culture." *Ethos*, Vol. 1, No. 2.

1973B "The Stereotyping of Indians in Motion Pictures." *Ethnohistory*, Vol. 20, No. 2.

1974 "An Ethnographic Approach to U.S. and Canadian Indian Education." *Canadian and International Education*, Vol. 3, No. 2.

1975A "An Applied Analysis of North American Indian Drinking Patterns." *Human Organization*, Vol. 34, No. 1.

1975B "Sharing: The Integration of Intimate Economies." *Anthropologica*, Vol. 17, No. 1.

1975C "U.S. and Canadian Indian Urban Ethnic Institutions." *Urban Anthropology*, Vol. 4, No. 1.

1975D "Anthropologists in Canada: Results of the 1973 C.S.A.A. Survey." 11 pp. Offset.

1976 "North American Indian Families." In *Ethnic Families in America: Patterns and Variations*, C.H. Mindel and R.W. Haberstein, eds. New York: Harper & Row.

Price, John A. and McCaskill, Don N.

1974 "The Urban Integration of Canadian Native People." *The Western Canadian Journal of Anthropology*, Vol. 4, No. 2.

Reasons, Charles

1972 "Crime and the American Indian." In *Native Americans Today*, H.M. Bahr, et al., eds. New York: Harper & Row.

Redfield, Robert

1953 *The Primitive World and Its Transformations*. Ithica, N.Y.: Cornell University Press.

Resnick, H.L. and Dizmang, Larry H.

1971 "Observations on Suicidal Behaviour Among American Indians." *American Journal of Psychiatry*, Vol. 127.

Rohner, Ronald P. and Rohner, Evelyn C.

1970 *The Kwakiutl Indians of British Columbia*. New York: Holt, Rinehart & Winston.

Rosen, Kenneth, editor

1975 *The Man to Send Rain Clouds: Contemporary Stories by American Indians*. New York: Vintage

Rothenberg, Jerome, editor

1972 *Shaking the Pumpkin: Traditional Poetry of the Indian North Americas*. Garden City, N.Y.: Doubleday.

Sapir, Edward
1924 "Culture, Genuine and Spurious." *American Journal of Sociology*, Vol. 29.

Schwartz, Richard D. and Miller, James C.
1964 "Legal Evolution and Societal Complexity." *American Journal of Sociology*, Vol. 70, No. 2.

Scotch, Norman A. and Scotch, Freda L.
1963 "Social Factors in Hypertension Among the Washo." *University of Utah Anthropological Papers*, No. 67.

Shephard, Roy J. and S. Itoh, editors
1976 *Circumpolar Health.* Toronto: U. of Toronto Press.

Shore, James H., et al.
1972 "A Suicide Prevention Center on an Indian Reservation." *American Journal of Psychiatry*. Vol. 128.

Shore, James H. and Von-fumetti, Billie
1972 "Three Alcohol Programs for Americans." *American Journal of Psychiatry*, Vol. 128.

Silverheels, Jay
1968 "Lo! The Image of the Indian!" *Indians Illustrated.* Los Angeles.

Slater, Arthur D. and Albrecht, Stan L.
1972 "The Extent and Costs of Excessive Drinking Among The Uintah-Ouray Indians." In *Native Americans Today*, H.M. Bahr, et al., eds. New York: Harper & Row.

Snyder, Peter Z.
1971 "The Social Environment of the Urban Indian." In *The American Indian In Urban Society*, J.O. Waddell and O.M. Watson, eds. Boston: Little, Brown.
1976 "Neighborhood Gatekeepers in the Process of Urban Adaptation: Cross-Ethnic Commonalities." *Urban Anthropology*, Vol. 5, No. 1.

Spicer, Edward H.
1962 *Cycles of Conquest.* Tucson: Unviversity of Arizona Press.

Spindler, George and Spindler, Louise
1971 *Dreamers Without Power: The Menomini Indians.* New York: Holt, Rinehart & Winston.

Stanbury, W.T.
1973A "The Education Gap: Urban Indians in British Columbia." *B.C. Studies*, Fall.
1973B "Comparison of On-and-Off Reserve Educational Achievements." *Journal of American Indian Education*, Vol. 12, No. 3.

Stanbury, William T. and Siegel, Jay
1975 *Success and Failure: Indians in Urban Society.* Vancouver: University of British Columbia Press.

Steele, C. Hoy
1975 "Urban Indian Identity in Kansas: Some Implications for Research." In *The New Ethnicity: Perspectives From Ethnology*, J.W. Bennett, ed. St. Paul: West.

Steinbring, Jack
1971 "Acculturational Phenomena Among the Lake Winnipeg Ojibwa of Canada." *Proceedings of the International Congress of Americanists*. Vol. 3.

Stewart, Omer C.
1944 "Washo-Northern Paiute Peyotism: A Study in Acculturation." *University of California Publications in American Archaeology and Ethnology*, Vol. 4, No. 3.
1964 "Questions Regarding American Indian Criminality." *Human Organization*, Vol. 23, No. 1.

Stewart, T.D.
1973 *The People of America*. London: Weidenfeld and Nicolson.

Stoffle, Richard W.
1975 "Reservation Based Industry: A Case from Zuni, New Mexico." *Human Organization*, Vol. 34, No. 3.

Stymeist, David H.
1975 *Ethnics and Indians: Social Relations in a Northwestern Ontario Town*. Toronto: Peter Martin Associates.

Swadesh, Morris
1964 "Linguistic Overview." In *Prehistoric Man in the New World*, J.D. Jennings and E. Norbeck, eds. Houston: Rice University.

Tedlock, Dennis and Barbara Tedlock
1975 *Teachings From the American Earth: Indian Religion and Philosophy*. New York: Liveright.

Terrell, John U. and Donna M. Terrell
1974 *Indian Women of the Western Morning: Their Life in Early America*. Garden City, N.Y.: Anchor Press.

Tomkins, William
1969 *Indian Sign Language*. New York: Dover.

U.S. Commission on Civil Rights
1972 *American Indian Civil Rights Handbook*. Washington U.S. Government Printing Office.

VanStone, James W.
1962 *Point Hope: An Eskimo Village in Transition*. Seattle: University of Washington Press.

Voegelin, C.F. and Voegelin, F.M.
1966 *Map of North American Indian Languages*. Seattle: American Ethnological Society.

Vogel, Virgil J.
1975 *American Indian Medicine*. New York: Ballantine Books.

Vranas, George and Stephens, Margaret
1971 "The Eskimos of Churchill, Manitoba." In *Native Peoples*, J.L. Elliott, ed. Scarborough: Prentice-Hall.

Wallace, Anthony F.C.
1972 "New Religions Among the Delaware Indians, 1600-1900." *The Emergent Native Americans: A Reader in Culture Contact*. D.E. Walker, ed. Boston: Little, Brown.

Washburn, Wilcomb E.
1975 *The Indian in America*. New York: Harper & Row.

Wax, Rosalie
1972 "The Warrior Dropouts." *Native Americans Today: A Sociological Perspective*. H.M. Bahr, et al., editors. New York: Harper & Row.

Wax, Murray L.
1971 *Indian Americans*. Englewood Cliffs, N.J.: Prentice-Hall.

Westgate, Wendy and Ross, W. Gillies
1973 "Why Teachers Go North." *Education Canada*, Vol. 13, No. 2.

Whiteside, Don
1973 *Historical Development of Aboriginal Political Associations in Canada: Documentation*. Ottawa: National Indian Brotherhood.

Willey, Gordon R.
1966 *An Introduction to American Archaeology*. Vol. 1. Englewood Cliffs, N.J.: Prentice-Hall.

Witmer, Robert
1973 "Recent Changes in the Musical Culture of the Blood Indians of Alberta, Canada." *Yearbook*, Department of Music, Institute of Latin American Studies, University of Texas at Austin.

Witt, Shirley H. and Stan Steiner, editors
1972 *The Way: An Anthology of American Indian Literature*. New York: Knopf.

Wolf, Eric R.
1964 *Anthropology*. Englewood Cliffs, N.J.: Prenctice-Hall.

Wuttunee, William
1971 *Ruffled Feathers: Indians in Canadian Society*. Calgary: Bell Books.

Subject Index

Name Index